PRAISE FOR <u>OPEN LANDS</u>

"An extraordinary and beautifully written chronicle that combines the best of different genres: travel writing, journalism, and history . . . A modern classic tale of a foreigner's travels through Russia."

—KIRKUS REVIEWS

"Mark Taplin took the trips that we old-timers could only dream about. He saw a Russia that western travelers had not seen for most of the twentieth century. He took with him a marvelous eye and a sharp pen. This fascinating book brims with vivid scenes and intriguing details. And it's great fun to read."

—ROBERT G. KAISER, author of *Russia: The People and the Power*

"*Open Lands* is wise and gentle and, inevitably, crushingly sad. Through its accumulation of detail it conveys better than any other recent work the single most terrifying aspect of modern Russia: the condition of soul-destroying ugliness to which 75 years of centrally planned vandalism reduced the landscape and everything in it."

— THE ECONOMIST

"The old Russia that enchanted 19th-century travel writers — the Russia of frozen lakes, blasted tundra, desert landscapes, and old believers — is finally reemerging from the ashes. With *Open Lands*, Taplin begins the slow process of kindling it back to life."

— THE BOSTON PHOENIX LITERARY SUPPLEMENT

OPEN

TRAVELS THROUGH

RUSSIA'S ONCE

FORBIDDEN PLACES

LANDS

MARK TAPLIN

STEERFORTH PRESS
SOUTH ROYALTON, VERMONT

For information about permission to reproduce selections
from this book, write to: Steerforth Press L.C., P.O. Box 70,
South Royalton, Vermont 05068.

The views expressed are the author's own, and in no way reflect those
of his employer, the U.S. Information Agency.

In several instances, the names of individuals mentioned in
this book have been changed.

Library of Congress Cataloging–in–Publication Data

Taplin, Mark, 1957-
Open Lands : travels through Russia's once
forbidden places / Mark Taplin — 1st ed.
p. cm.
Includes bibliographical references and index.
ISBN 1-883642-01-9 (alk. paper)
1. Russia (Federation)—Description and travel.
2. Taplin, Mark, 1957- — Journeys — Russia (Federation) I. Title.
DK510.29.T37   1997
914.704'86˙dc21   97-26738
CIP

Manufactured in the United States of America

FIRST PAPERBACK EDITION

To my parents, Ellajean and Winn;

To Kathy and Benjamin, and our life together.

CONTENTS

DARK MATTER

AN INTRODUCTION

*Oh, what a glittering, wondrous infinity of space the
world knows nothing of! Russia!*
                                                    GOGOL

I FIRST CAME TO RUSSIA AT A BAD TIME. It was August 1984. The
summer had given way prematurely to wet, bone-chilling autumn. The
leaves were already a dull brown. Moscow had a sullen air; somehow,
the city knew it had been shortchanged of precious days of light and
warmth. One night, at the very end of the month, the thermometer
dipped down to the freezing mark. I remember because my apartment
had no hot water; my shower the following morning was more than
just bracing.

Chernenko, the last of the Brezhnev era's geriatric leaders to come
to power, remained propped up at the helm of the Soviet Communist
Party. It was a time of unalloyed gloom, of all-encompassing decay.

Everyone recognized that the country was like a frostbitten man. To leave him in the cold any longer would only cause more damage; to bring him inside was to face the rot that had set in, to condemn the body to the scalpel. Appropriately enough, Chernenko carried out his last public act of politics in a hospital; his room was disguised as a polling station so that he could be seen to take part in one of the Party's sham elections. His trembling hand, his wobbling body shepherded to the voting urn by orderlies: this was his most eloquent moment. A week later, he was dead. Even the party faithful could not wait to consign his ashes to the Kremlin wall. Such was the impatience to be done with him that the conventional three days of official mourning were summarily curtailed to two.

It was also an era of bitter assumptions in international relations, assumptions that were much more brittle than anyone at the time realized. It had been less than a year since the downing of the Korean airliner over Sakhalin — one act which confirmed all of the West's worst ideas about the Communist regime in Moscow. Reagan's characterization of the Soviet Union as an "evil empire" had an analogous effect on Russians. It seemed that history was trapped under a glacier; few could imagine anything different than the Cold War — unless it was Armageddon.

Soon, we may lose sight of the fact that for most of the twentieth century, Russia was a closed book to the outside world. True, one could tell something about it just by taking it down from the shelf, running a hand along its spine, pondering its weight, its density. For all of its solemnity, though, the book had a garish — and oddly involving — cover. The critics' notices, moreover, were almost too lurid to be believed. Browsing through this book had its charms, its numbing terrors. A few readers managed more, much more. But in the end, they, too, saw only a fraction of the whole. Some chapters were never read, never even imagined.

The map in my office at the U.S. Embassy was the same; it raised more questions than it answered. It showed the old Soviet Union, stretching from the Baltic to the Pacific, from the Arctic to Afghanistan. The place names were in Roman letters, spelled in precise transliteration from the Russian. A number of large cities were marked in green, including Moscow, Leningrad, and the capitals of the other

Soviet republics. These were places that foreigners, at least in principle, were allowed to travel. Here and there, the map showed green highways and green rail lines. If all your papers were in order, you could drive from Minsk to Moscow; you could ride a train from Riga to Leningrad. If everything was in order.

Even Moscow and Leningrad, however, were surrounded on the map by an unwelcoming margin of red. Virtually every spot outside the city limits was closed to foreigners. Elsewhere, whole regions were awash in official crimson: Gorky, Sverdlovsk, most of Kazakhstan, nearly all of the Baltic states. Dotted across the entire country, like measles, were red-colored cities, some famous, some not. There were red roads, red rail lines, red rivers. All along the country's vast borders, too, was a strip of red land, a scarlet *cordon sanitaire* against the outside world. It was a map of the late, great Cold War, a map of Russia's forbidden cities and spaces.

There was no great mystery about why the map existed. Everyone knew that out there were thousands upon thousands of prisons, labor camps, rocket silos, testing sites, closed research facilities, tank factories, air bases, and so on. There were also plenty of rumors of nuclear tests gone awry, killer chemical spills, ethnic riots.

I was a naif, not a spy. In my first months as a junior-level U.S. diplomat in Moscow, I barely knew how to ride the city's subway system, much less plumb the depths of Soviet secrecy. Yet what fascinated — and frustrated — me was the idea that there existed in Russia vast areas that no outsider had visited for half a century. The map represented a challenge. I spent hours poring over it, dreaming of reaching the places behind the veil.

Russia was never an easy country in which to travel. Unlike Italy or France, it had few attractions that could compensate a traveler for the rigors of the journey: no sun-washed villages by the sea, few distinguished wine cellars. Neither the classical legacies of Athens and Rome, nor the glory of the Renaissance, nor the marvels of the Industrial Age attracted anyone to a journey across Russia. Russia was indescribable roads, inhospitable taverns, inexpressible rudeness, and superstition.

There was another problem, too. For centuries, foreigners had been met in Russia more with suspicion than charity. In fairness, visitors from East and West had too often come with sword in hand; the Turks,

Teutonic Knights, and Tartars were far from innocent tourists. Moscow's tsars made sure that foreign merchants and envoys were kept under careful scrutiny wherever they went, flattered or cajoled as circumstances warranted. Even under Peter the Great, who radically altered Russia's whole approach to the West, foreigners resident in Moscow were made to live in the "German Quarter" — so labeled because all Europeans at that time were thought of as Germans. When the clash between Tsarist absolutism and Western political ideals broke out into the open in the nineteenth century, police surveillance of visitors became the norm.

Bolshevism only deepened this long-standing wariness of outsiders. It posited a death struggle between us and them, between heroic Soviet workers and fat-cat capitalists and fascists. It encouraged Russians to view outsiders — and ultimately even their own neighbors — with suspicion.

The vivacious open-door policy of the early years of the Revolution, when free spirits like Isadora Duncan merrily danced about the country, gave way soon enough to the old pattern. If you were judged sympathetic to the Bolshevik cause — a fellow traveler — you would be allowed out and about, albeit under proper supervision. Otherwise, foreigners traveled in small herds on carefully orchestrated tours of dams, factories, and hospitals, the ostensible fruits of the new utopia.

With collectivization and the purges, the Soviet Union gradually began to sink deeper into the shadows. Ironically, the wartime years let in some light. Yet the influx of Allied military men was small, and they did not stay for long.

The formal system of closed areas and cities was first introduced under Stalin in the late forties; perhaps at that time the whole tortured scheme made some sense. There were not so many people left in the West who were willing to apologize for the Gulag; the camps themselves were swollen with more prisoners than ever before. For Stalin and his entourage, this was probably reason enough to shut off vast tracts of the country. As for guarding military secrets, American reconnaisance flights might penetrate the margins of Soviet airspace, but they could not venture very far without running the real risk of being shot down. High-resolution satellite photography was still just a pipe dream. Espionage had to be carried out the old-fashioned way, by agents with tiny cameras and microfilm skulking around the perimeters of army bases. Forbidding foreigners from wandering about the country (including any would-be spies) was seen as a logical way of protecting the security of "the motherland of socialism."

However, if shutting off three-quarters of the Soviet Union to foreign interlopers appeared halfway rational at the beginning of the Cold War, it was glaringly anachronistic by the time I arrived in Moscow. The truth of the matter was that the closed area map represented far more than just a stack of rules and regulations. It was the cartographic projection of the entire Soviet cult of secrecy, a cult with Party manuals for sacred texts, secret policemen for priests, informers for altar boys. Whether the common man believed in this gospel or not, he knew enough not to tempt fate by sharing his true thoughts with a foreigner. Sinners did not need to wait for the next life to be judged. There was already a hell on earth known as the Gulag.

So pervasive were the travel restrictions that the number of functionaries involved in administering them was, quite literally, incalculable. A "special section" of the Ministry of Foreign Affairs did nothing but review travel requests from foreigners. By law, hotels had to report the arrival of any foreigners to the militia. Aeroflot clerks were barred from selling tickets to foreign visitors; they could only be purchased abroad, for hard currency. Intourist guides knew where to take tourists — and where not to. If something went wrong, if someone took a wrong turn, there were always the ever-vigilant forces of law and order: the Ministry of the Interior and the KGB.

In reality, even "open" cities could, in fact, be out of reach. For diplomats, journalists, and businessmen, all travel outside the Moscow city limits had to be requested at least seventy-two hours in advance. The travel plan had to include the city-by-city itinerary, including the conveyance: airplane, train, car, boat.

If your destination was a conventional one — Leningrad, Kiev, one of the historic towns of the "Golden Ring" — approval was virtually certain. Any place even slightly off the beaten track, however, could present problems. One might be denied permission to visit, say, Volgograd for "reasons of a temporary nature." In Embassy parlance, you had been "ROTNed." You might learn afterward, with a sigh of recognition, that the General Secretary had been there during the dates of your planned visit.

From time to time, you could make an educated guess. The wife of one Foreign Service officer had her request to visit Baku turned down repeatedly. She was a Parsee from Bombay; she wanted to see the "fire temple" built by the early Zoroastrians outside of Baku. Never mind that the temple was a regular fixture for Intourist groups; she might have intended to stir up religious feelings among the locals. (The last Zoroastrians in Azerbaijan died out centuries ago.)

More often than not, you would never know.

Another way of discouraging foreigners from traveling was by denying them space on airplanes and in hotels. This had the advantage of not being, technically, a rejection of a travel request. It was common to be informed a day or so before your planned departure that there was no room in a particular city's hotels or that all the flights for the next week were full.

No one ever said that he or she was sorry. "No" was the answer to most requests in the Soviet Union. Nor could you simply find another travel agent. The only office authorized to issue tickets or make hotel reservations for foreigners living in Russia was UpDK, another "special section" of the Ministry of Foreign Affairs. UpDK was also the only organization allowed to supply employees for foreign embassies, news bureaus, and businesses. So even the Soviet citizens working in your own office owed their allegiance to the "special section."

These travel restrictions had not been slapped together during a boozy night at the KGB. The rules were diabolically clever, the product of careful deliberation. Each time one examined the map, it revealed yet another perfect catch-22. Areas that were declared closed, pure and simple, did not dominate. Instead, vast expanses of Siberia and the Far East simply had no specific status. These regions, Soviet officials argued, were "open." The plain reality, however, was that it was impossible to get to most cities in the Urals and beyond because the gateways to reach them were closed. For instance, there was no way to visit Kyzyl, the capital of the Tuva Republic, without changing planes in either Krasnoyarsk or Abakan. Both of these cities were closed. Hence, Tuva was off limits also.

As with so many other matters in the life of the two superpowers, action brought forth tit-for-tat reaction. Within a few years, the U.S. government unveiled its own set of travel restrictions for citizens of the

Soviet Union and its Eastern European allies. The map of the United States was carved up into green and red. Washington and New York were "open" cities, as was San Francisco, where a Soviet consulate was located. Los Angeles and St. Louis, on the other hand, were not. To add insult to injury, a vindictive U.S. State Department declared both Disneyland and Disneyworld closed. Each side was allowed one "dacha" and one "beach house" on the basis of strict reciprocity. There was at least one important difference, however; the Russian beach was on Chesapeake Bay, the American on the muddy banks of the Moscow River.

Back then, we were allowed to travel only in pairs. A few nasty incidents over the years — druggings, beatings, a diplomatic courier who mysteriously fell off a train in a tunnel — had put an end to solo voyages across the countries of the Iron Curtain.

My first trip outside of Moscow was all too typical of the problems we faced. My colleague Stephen and I arrived in Murmansk in mid-January. Above the Arctic Circle, beyond the tree line, it was still the polar night; for weeks at this latitude the sun does not even break the horizon. We landed in a snow squall, the plane's approach lights revealing an unnerving galaxy of flying ice.

I remember now that Stephen was something of a tightwad. Instead of taking the one taxi waiting in front of the airport terminal, we hauled our bags onto a city bus. As we climbed aboard, we saw several men jump out of a black sedan and run in our direction. Gasping for breath, they hopped aboard just as the bus began to pull away. The bus was unlit and unheated. Only a blowtorch could have melted through the months of frost accumulated on the inside of its windows. Even the press of our fellow passengers' bodies did nothing to warm us. My gloved hand felt as if it had been planted on a block of ice; it began to stiffen preternaturally around the handrail.

We drove on for mile after mile. Soon I was shivering uncontrollably. Only when the bus began to make stops did we know that we had reached the city; I could just manage to peek out of the doors by peering between our fellow passengers. We were not sure where the hotel was located. Just as we were debating whether to ask someone for help, one of the men who had sprinted over to the bus squeezed his way over to us and stated matter-of-factly, "Your hotel is at the next stop." He was right. In the same helpful spirit, he and his colleagues got off the bus behind us and pointed us in the proper direction.

Since no one would agree to meet with two American Embassy officials — especially in the home port of the Soviet Northern Fleet — we had to content ourselves with strolling about the frigid streets of the city. In a bookstore, I found a curious "tourist" map of Murmansk. It showed several of the city's central avenues, including the street where our hotel was located. But it appeared that the rest of the city had evaporated. The side streets branching east, west, and north inexplicably led away into nothingness. There was no sea inlet, no port, no hill looming over the city. We knew the explanation: since the twenties, Soviet maps had been purposefully made incomplete or inaccurate in order to throw off snooping foreigners like ourselves.

We saw the few sights Murmansk offered. The highlight was the crusty International Mariners' Club, which sold Polish beer for hard currency. We decided to seek out dinner at the Northern Lights restaurant (the only one that was open, according to the hotel clerk).

The restaurant overlooked the city from a high bluff. We could see it from down below, a blob of greenish light on the side of the mountain. For lack of anything better to do, we decided to walk there.

Like hardened explorers, we shuffled determinedly up the hill despite the intense cold. After a while, we reached a set of wooden stairs tacked onto the hillside. The bluff was steep; I felt disoriented under its hallucinatory facade of white. We headed up, heavily gulping in the frigid black air. Several times, we stopped to catch our breath; Murmansk spun dizzily below.

We were nearing the top, just a few flights short of the overlook. Suddenly, a young drunk appeared at the top and came stumbling down the stairs. He was slaloming comically, theatrically toward us. He was both hatless and gloveless — killing oversights in this climate. We stopped, mesmerized by his performance. Miraculously, he managed to reach us, each step in itself a high-risk circus act. He mumbled something as he passed, went a dozen steps or so further, and then, with astounding artistry, fell over the handrail eight feet into the snow below.

Involuntarily, we laughed. Then we paused, waiting for an encore. Yet, after a minute or so, there was still no sign of life.

"Maybe we should see how he is," Stephen said.

We walked back down to where the drunk had begun his spectacular aerial. Leaning over the wooden handrail, we saw him sprawled on
his stomach in the snow. He looked up at us, and managed to rise onto
his hands and feet. Somehow, his face had become covered in blood. We
addressed him first in Russian, then English, then, most improbably, in
Stephen's German. In reply, he grunted back something unintelligible
and collapsed back into the snow.

Stephen pondered the situation aloud. "We've got to get down
there, help him out," he urged. For some reason, I hesitated. A warning
light flashed in the recesses of my brain.

We argued for a minute or two while the drunk flailed about in the
snow, yelping like an injured seal. His hands were raw and blue, inar-
ticulately reaching, perhaps, for a chair or a wall. Meanwhile, Stephen
had cast me in the role of the heavy, the vile Hun. "If we don't do something, he'll freeze," he insisted. Yet something told me not to leap down
into the snow to grapple with a blood-stained inebriate; the good
Samaritan gesture might go completely awry.

A young couple hurried past us on the way down to the city. They
looked at us, then at the figure sprawled in the snow. They said not a
word; they were by us like a cloud in the night.

I suggested that we report the drunk's whereabouts to the militia. It
was not much of a suggestion, and it too was fraught with potential
complications. But I convinced Stephen to start walking back down the
stairs while we debated how to proceed.

After a minute or so, we looked again toward where we had left the
drunk in the snow. Incredibly, he had managed to climb up onto the
wooden staircase and was working his way down the steps behind us.
When he saw us, he spun back around and began to climb back up.
After a moment's hesitation, he remembered to stagger. Now we began
to understand.

We walked down farther, then wheeled around to see where he had
gone. The man, who a few moments before had apparently been unable
to rise to his feet, was now bounding confidently down the slope to our
right, despite the heavy snow cover. We stood there in silence, and
watched him cross the road below and run into an apartment complex.

What would it have meant to help the "drunk?" Who knows? But
in those days, the Soviet media regularly supped at the table of the KGB,

which fed it scare and scandal stories about Western diplomats black-mailing, kidnapping, and, yes, even beating up innocent Soviet citizens. How could we have explained away the blood, after all? The couple that passed by on the steps would have served nicely as witnesses to our crimes. We barely comprehended what these moments were all about, but a Russian would have described it without a moment's hesitation with a word that one heard not so rarely: a provocation.

Here is where the deepest chill of the Cold War resided. To this day, I cannot get over the pure cynicism of the trap that was laid for us that night in Murmansk. Our normal, human impulse to help someone in trouble was to have triggered the whole unsavory business. It seemed an idea hatched in another world, another universe. It was moments like this that led foreigners to conclude: they are different, they are not like us.

The Red Terror, the Great Purges, the Katyn Massacre, the Berlin Wall, the Korean airliner — could we possibly belong to the same solar system? The best measurements and calculations of Western observers about the Soviet Union always seemed unnervingly incomplete. It was as if some other force, beyond our sight, beyond all of our senses, infused the entire country with a different type of energy, another source of gravity and mass. Back then, we despaired of ever understanding this dark matter. With a mixture of awe and fear, we waited for we knew not what.

Then, as unexpectedly as any cosmic event in deep space, the Soviet Union collapsed, a weary star falling apart in full view of the world's telescopes.

I returned to Russia in 1992. For all of the West's optimism about the country's future, Russia's antipodes were the same as always: the boundless fusion of history and geography, the explosive fission of space and soul. Instinctively, I knew I had to go beyond Moscow and St. Petersburg, sly old deceivers of travelers past. Was there a truer expression of Russia's past — and its future — in those forbidden places of the Soviet era?

That same year, Russia and the United States signed an accord allowing free travel throughout both countries. It was called the "Open Lands" agreement.

It was time to take a new set of measurements.

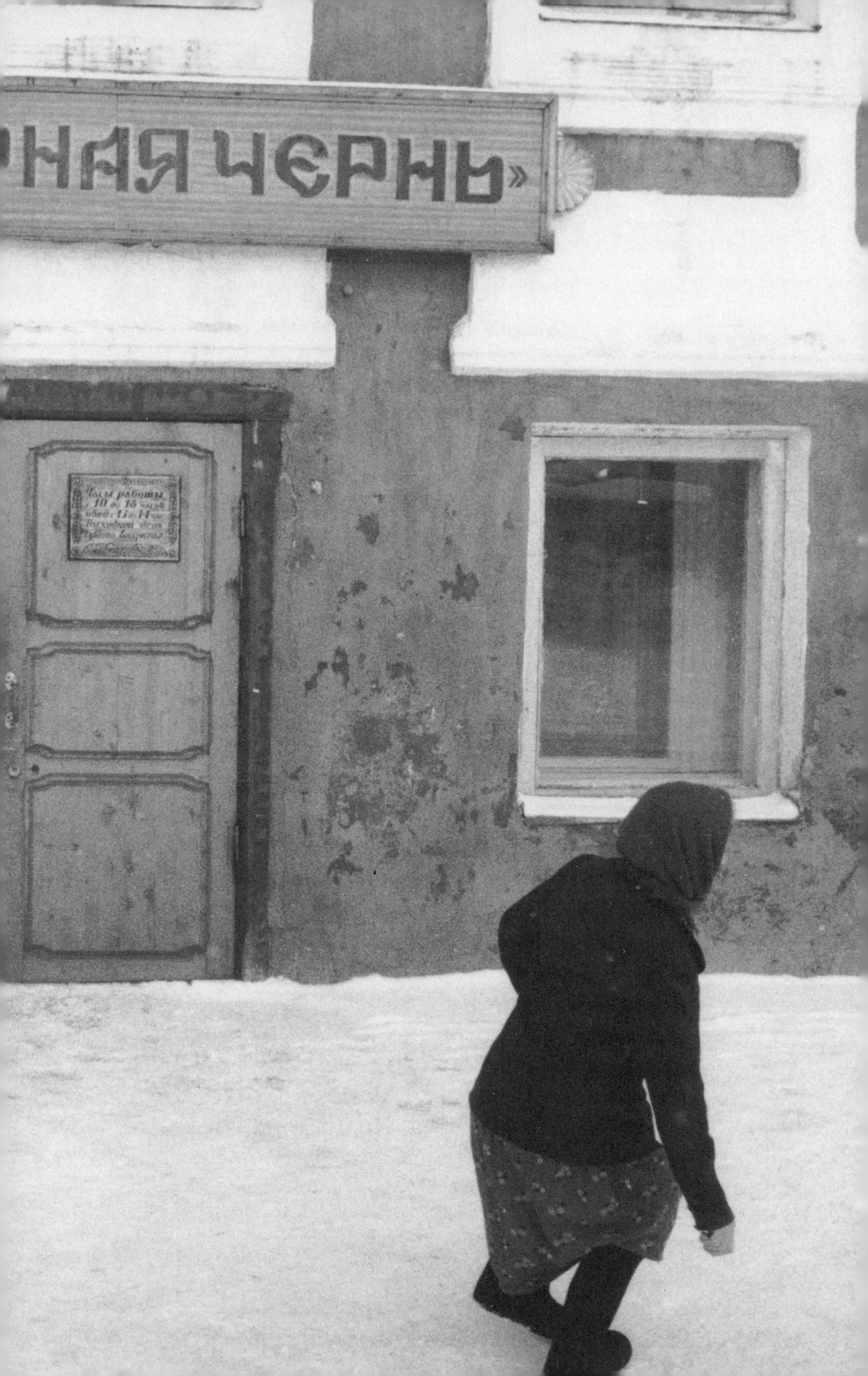
ная чернь»

WHERE THE
WATERS MEET

VELIKIY USTYUG

THE YADRIKHA STATIONHOUSE COWERED in the threadbare light. Behind it squatted a row of ragtag log cabins. Acrid coal smoke spun over the tracks. Travelers in dull dun overcoats struggled down the icy platform, hauling bags of supplies brought from Moscow.

The train suddenly clanged to a start. Wistfully recalling the warm compartment I had just vacated, I watched the cars slowly squeak and clack out of the station. I struggled to work the straps of my backpack over my down jacket, painfully aware that among the other disembarking passengers, I looked as out of place as a cosmonaut.

I made inquiries. Yes, yes, I was told, there would be a train to Velikiy Ustyug, "soon." Although my toes were already numb from the cold, I was wary of settling down inside the waiting room. If I missed the Ustyug train, I thought, it might be a long, unhappy wait for the next one.

Friends in Moscow said they had heard of Velikiy Ustyug, but could not quite recall what they had been told. It barely rated mention among the books I consulted. It seemed to be a place defined entirely by passing references: ". . . until the seventeenth century was the largest town and commercial center of northern Russia . . . interesting buildings of the seventeenth to nineteenth centuries . . . a famous silver craft is still practiced."

One day, though, in an antique shop, I found a creased and dog-eared map on which Velikiy Ustyug figured as the capital of an entire province. It was represented by a thick cluster of churches and bell towers. *Velikiy*, in Russian, means "great." It is the same word that is appended to the names of the most celebrated of Russia's tsars, Peter and Catherine.

I met Alexei, a middle-aged railroad engineer, on the train from Moscow. I first noticed him as I stood outside my compartment watching the evening bustle in front of the Yaroslavl station. He was giving a teenage girl a lecture of sorts on Russian history. It was an unremittingly patriotic exposition. One could almost hear battle axes crashing against shields, and heroic Slavs hacking their way through rank after rank of Mongol and Teutonic invaders. At first the girl listened politely. After a while, however, her attention flagged, and she excused herself to return to her berth.

At first glance, I took Alexei for a teacher. He was slight, with odd, blue-rimmed glasses and a slow, cloying manner. He noticed me eavesdropping, and came by later, once we had started moving again, to find out what I was doing on the train. He thought I was from one of the Baltic republics, or Poland; more exotic origins than that he could not imagine. After all, it was not a standard tourist route.

Alexei introduced himself with a smile that revealed several missing teeth. He was taken aback to find out I was an American. He produced a bottle of vodka; I introduced him to Fig Newtons. He was the boss of a railroad yard in Kotlas, where he directed several hundred workers. He had been a Communist — in fact, an active one. He served as the chairman of the railyard's Party committee and even held a seat on the city council. Although he insisted that he did not miss the party, he still admired, he said, the "principles" of communism.

Alexei was in despair over the growing economic distress he saw around him. In just a few months of wildfire inflation, his salary's purchasing power had been cut in half. His son, a college graduate, could not find work. The factories in Kotlas were barely operating. Alexei felt lucky to be employed at all. Only the railroads and the energy sector, he felt, had any real prospects. Otherwise, the reforms were a disaster.

Every twenty minutes or so, Alexei excused himself, got up, and went to the rear end of the railroad car. He would return a little later, looking visibly relieved. Like many Russians, he was a chain smoker. Since it is forbidden to smoke in the compartments or in the corridor, smokers spend hours huddled above the couplings, bouncing and shivering between puffs. Winter or summer, the train windows are bolted shut, impossible to open. Thus, the back of train cars gradually fill up with choking cigarette smoke from Belomors and other roughhouse Russian brands. Mixed with the unappetizing odors of the nearby toilet, the cigarette fumes encourage everyone else to scurry past as quickly as possible.

As Alexei seemed to be a history buff, I asked him what he knew about Velikiy Ustyug. It had been a long time since he had last visited, he explained. There were a lot of churches. Then, his eyes blinked and narrowed behind his odd glasses. His expression turned somber. He leaned over toward me, lowering his voice just a bit ominously. "I know why you are going there!" he exclaimed, as if my own explanation was too far-fetched to credit. "You want to find out about the silver process," he went on. "That's probably what you want to know," he repeated, shaking his head and pursing his lips thoughtfully. I asked him what he was talking about. "You know," he insisted. "But it is a secret. It is a secret process. There are guards with machine guns. They won't let you into the factory."

Despite my prodding, he refused to explain further. Instead, he mysteriously turned the conversation to spy satellites over Kamchatka and other espionage arcana he had read about somewhere. Then, he excused himself to smoke another cigarette. This time he did not return.

Before long, the Velikiy Ustyug train pulled into the junction, almost on time. It was not an express; it was scheduled to cover the sixty kilometers from Yadrikha to Ustyug in about two and a half hours. The railroad cars were the "hard," third-class variety. They were divided into low compartments outfitted with wooden benches and shelves. There was enough room in each one for six people, uncomfortably. Suitcases and homemade bundles were strewn up and down the corridor.

These cars are heated, one might say, with unstudied diffidence. If the wagon attendent feels so inclined, she has the passengers seated above the coal bin get up from their bench so she can dig out a few shovelfuls of coal. Into a tin bucket goes the coal, and the attendant waddles back down the corridor to throw the fuel into the hiccuping boiler at the end of the car. In the dead of winter, there is a long interval — about the length of any trip — between when the little furnace is fed and any warming effect the passengers may feel.

I was scrunched up in the corner of one of the compartments, blowing onto my hands for warmth, when I encountered my first gang of silver desperados. It was, admittedly, only a duo. Slava, the older of the two, looked me up and down. With a faint smile, he slid his suitcase down the bench opposite me and sat down. Sasha, his partner, had the unshaven face of a young racketeer. He quickly took the space next to me.

They both looked tired and irritable. It was obvious they had been traveling for days. Slava, in his forties, had thinning red hair and the pinched, wiry face of a terrier. One sensed that he had a wealth of life experience, some of it inspired by what an earlier generation referred to delicately as "spirits." Still, even if he was a bit frayed around the edges, he looked like he had plenty of spit left in him. Sasha was his cocky young sidekick, lounging confidently against the wall of the compartment, ready to take on the world. No one had laid a glove on him — yet.

"So, you're an American. I've never met an American before," Slava said. Sasha ran his hand over my backpack as if the nylon were the skin of a spaceship. It was time for a drink, he announced. I begged off, pleading the morning hour. We settled on instant coffee, or, more accurately, the ersatz chicory-based brew most Russians drink, with Sasha badgering the attendant until she provided a jar of hot water.

Slava described himself and Sasha as traders. He was slicing open a can of meat with a large penknife. I asked them what it was they traded. They looked at each other, then peered out of the compartment. Slava's voice turned conspiratorial. "We trade in silver," he said in a low growl.

It was an answer that for some might have conjured up images of the Hunt brothers buying and selling warehouses full of silver ingots, but Slava quickly put things in perspective. For centuries, Velikiy Ustyug was one of Russia's silver-working capitals. Thanks to its strategic position on the trading routes from Siberia, the city had ready access to inexpensive silver. Craftsmen in Ustyug specialized in niello, the art of using a sulfur alloy to create intricate black designs and patterns on metal. The niello produced in Velikiy Ustyug was famous for the durability of its blackening alloy — and for its artistry.

It was all taken very seriously. The secrets of preparing the powder were passed like a prized family recipe from one generation to another. One nineteenth-century master would begin to prepare the niello alloy only after fasting for several days and taking a hot bath. With the help of a special awl, a craftsman would make his engravings deep, shaping and flattening the metal without affecting the quality of the niello patterns. The Ustyug silverwork found its way into many applications: jewelry and snuffboxes, goblets, bracelets, reliquaries, book covers, serving plates, flasks, even the richly decorated staff of the archbishop of Velikiy Ustyug. Drawing from the Bible and Russian folklore, the Ustyug masters created whole worlds on metal, often at the order of rich noblemen and merchants.

The Bolsheviks managed to undo most of the trade, persecuting both the craftsmen and their patrons. In the thirties, though, they had a change of heart. The last local man who knew the niello formula passed the secret on to a new workshop backed by the Communist authorities. He was, according to the old-timers, a mediocre artisan. Yet he had the satisfaction of being hailed by the Party as a hero of socialist labor.

As the years went by, the "Northern Niello" operation grew into a small factory, turning out jewelry and tableware for Party bigwigs and tourists. The humdrum pieces churned out by these proletarians could not be compared with the exquisite works created in past centuries. Still, demand was high in the chaos of the post-Soviet era. In the face of runaway inflation and a rapidly depreciating currency, buying silver seemed to many a good investment.

My two companions were from Tyumen, three days by train to the east in the frozen Siberian marshes. Every few months, they came to Ustyug to buy silver pieces from a special "friend." They might spend anywhere from a few hours to a few days in Ustyug, looking over the scene, waiting for their business associate to provide the goods, sealing the deal. Once they had made their purchase, they would head for other places and other "friends" who were eager to buy their wares. Typically, they did best in port cities on the fringes of the old Russian empire, where business with the outside world had been given new impetus after the fall of the Soviet order: cities like Murmansk, Arkhangelsk, Khabarovsk, Vladivostok. Sometimes, they would sell the niello items to a seaman headed for Europe or Japan. Slava said, with obvious pride, that they had cleared over a million rubles during the past year — several thousand dollars.

I asked him if I could see what some of the silver objects looked like. He pondered the idea for a moment. "When we get to Ustyug, we can show you some," he replied. "But we will have to be careful."

I asked why. Slava weighed his words carefully. He was not sure what kind of simpleton I was. "We do not deal directly with the factory," he explained. "Our friend has contacts there, and provides us the items at a special price." Sometimes, he explained, there were "complications."

At this, Sasha opened his coat and pulled out a shiny, stubby revolver. He placed it on his lap and laughed: "That's why I carry this. For the complications." He was obviously devoted to his gun. He had pulled it out both to impress me and himself, and his feline eyes fixed on me as he looked to see how I would react. I thought of Behemoth, the man-sized, pistol-toting black cat in Bulgakov's *The Master and Margarita*.

Slava motioned to Sasha to put the revolver away. "He likes to joke," Slava said nonchalantly. The conversation drifted to American films. "Does everyone in America carry a gun?" Sasha asked. Out came the revolver again. He scratched his head with the barrel as he listened to me explain that many Americans did not even own a gun. Slava looked on with mounting disapproval. The revolver went back under the coat.

The coffee had grown cold, and all that was left of the meat was the empty can, the jagged lid wrenched open. The glasses fidgeted nervously on the table underneath the window as the train poked slowly through the forest. Sasha pulled out a pack of cigarettes, pushed one into the corner of his mouth, and lit it. The cigarette smoke smelled sour, like a trash fire in a junkyard.

Before long, the wagon attendant appeared, all indignation. "Comrades," she began, using the salutation once favored by figures of authority, large and small, in the Soviet Union. "It is strictly prohibited to smoke in the compartments. As you know. Smoke outside, or put your cigarette out immediately."

At first, Sasha tried offhand charm. "It's only one little cigarette. I'll be done in a minute."

"Don't give me that," the attendant scowled. Her grey hair was pulled back into a tight bun. Her hand, like a metronome, was tapping impatiently on her hip. "I told you to smoke out there," she continued, raising her voice and motioning toward the end of the car.

Then Sasha tried reason, of sorts. "Listen, it's cold out there. I'm not bothering anyone. No one has complained."

"I don't care," she snapped. "If you don't put that cigarette out right now, I'll get the guard to throw you off the train."

It was a showdown between the old order and the new. Sasha unbuttoned the top of his coat. "Fuck you and fuck your militiaman," he said, pronouncing each word slowly and evenly. Then he turned away from her, gazing out the window, I thought, a bit theatrically.

To my surprise, the attendant was not intimidated. "I've seen your filth before. You should be ashamed of yourself. If you think you can talk to me that way, you're wrong."

It was an ugly moment. Sasha, exuding a psychotic calm, turned back to face the woman. He pulled back one side of his coat to expose the revolver, the butt dangling out of an inside pocket. Slava, who had watched in silence as the confrontation gathered momentum, leaned toward his partner and said sharply, *"Ne nado, ne nado,"* forget it.

The attendant wheeled around. "We'll see about this," she cried out as she marched angrily down the corridor and out the door. The eyes of a passenger standing nearby followed her exit, turned toward us, and then uneasily veered away. No one said a word. I wondered whether we would see more of her. We never did.

✻ ✻ ✻

I was happy enough when the train finally pulled into the Velikiy Ustyug station. It was snowing hard. Slava was utterly solicitous toward me, his new American friend. He wanted to know if someone would be meeting me. My answer probably sounded vague. "Come to the hotel with us," he insisted. He motioned for Sasha to carry my bags. Their business partner, built like a boxer, was waiting for them in a world-weary Moskvich car. Somehow, we managed to put all the luggage in the trunk and all of ourselves inside. We left the rest of the passengers stranded at the bus stop as we skittered off over ice and packed snow several months deep.

The Hotel Sukhona — the only hotel in Velikiy Ustyug — was, in a manner of speaking, mobbed. Milling about its lobby, which was equipped with two ragamuffin lounge chairs and a plastic palm, were clusters of toughs in different sizes and shapes, all sharing the hungry, unscrupulous look of the modern Russian trader. There was something unmistakable about them; perhaps it was the no-name-brand track suits, the hefty gym bags, the gold watches, the insistent leitmotif of unshaven coolness. Here was Hollywood's contribution to Russian reform. Somehow, young Russians on the make had confused the image of sleazy drug maven with that of yuppie entrepreneur.

I wondered if they could not help looking unsavory because, deep down, they felt that what they were doing was unsavory. For at least three generations, there had been no such thing as a respectable Russian businessman. To most of their countrymen, they were still *spekulantiy*, speculators who made their way in the world by fleecing the common folk. Real, honest work was done in front of a steel furnace or on a factory floor. Manufacturing made a country strong; everything else was capitalist smoke and mirrors. The idea that profit could be justified by a middleman's effort to bring a product closer to the consumer, or to expand the range of goods available to the public, was little understood or appreciated, especially outside of the big cities. The average Russian felt in his or her bones that there was a natural, fair price for any given item. For many decades, the stilted prices of the state stores had served as the standard. To pay "more" for a given product, even if it was never available before, was still, for many people, wrong. Unaccustomed to prices in the outside world and the mischief brought on by inflation, people were tearing their hair out over ten-cent loaves of bread and one-dollar bottles of vodka.

This conservative habit of mind runs deep in the Russian psyche. It is rooted in the peasant world view: insular, parochial, and doggedly resistant to change. The traditional village was largely self-sufficient; the peasant collective held much of the village property in common, including the land. Typically, individual prosperity produced more envy than admiration.

After the revolution, wealth became for many a veritable death sentence. Both Lenin and Stalin made use of this invidiousness (along with plenty of prodding at gunpoint) to drive a wedge between the better-off peasants, the so-called *kulaks*, and the rest of the villagers. In so doing, the Party destroyed what equilibrium there was in Russian agriculture, and plunged the countryside into famine and ruin. Lenin's New Economic Policy, or NEP, which gave small-time traders some breathing room during the twenties, was soon abandoned. It gave way almost overnight in favor of Stalin's rigid central planning and collectivization. The hustlers of yesterday, the "NEPmen," were chased from the scene and denounced as "parasites." Many of them had probably thought that there was no turning back. They were wrong. And no one wept for the NEPmen once they were gone.

Scandalizing the dour ladies at the reception desk, I paid the outlandish sum of four dollars a night for one of the hotel's suites. Suites were intended for two or more people; I was expected to confine myself to a single room. From then on, I was saddled with the reputation of a profligate. Even my explanation that I wanted the room for its desk and its view of the church across the street only went so far in mollifying the hotel's management.

I was anxious to wander about the town, to admire its urban ceramics in a winter's glaze. As long as one had a warm pair of boots, walking was the preferred means of transport. There was no effort to remove the snow from the roads. Instead, it was simply pushed about from time to time by a truck with a plow attachment. In a typical year, one might go for six months or more without seeing the asphalt — or mud — underneath. In any case, there were not a lot of motor vehicles about: only a few city buses, trucks, and jeeps. It all reinforced the happy illusion that if time was not exactly standing still in Velikiy Ustyug, it was at least curled up on an old Russian *pechka*, or stove, peacefully snoring away the winter nights. It took no spectacular leap of imagination to picture horse-drawn *troikas* dashing up and down the streets, steam pouring from the horses' nostrils, the drivers' faces ruby red from the cold, their beards glistening with frost.

Velikiy Ustyug had the good fortune to be founded at the intersection of three river systems that mattered: the Sukhona, which flows northeast from Vologda and the heartland of Russia; the Vychegda, which leads down to the Russian north from the Urals and Siberia; and the Severnaya Dvina, which crosses hundreds of miles of taiga and swamp to meet the White Sea at Arkhangelsk. The first settlement was erected at the beginning of the thirteenth century near where a tributary, the Yug, flows into the Sukhona; hence the name "Ustyug," meaning "the mouth of the Yug." Appropriately, Velikiy Ustyug's coat of arms portrays a grey-bearded man pouring amphorae together.

From time immemorial, rivers were the highways of choice in Russia. They were wide and gentle, and gave access to regions that otherwise would have been virtually impossible to reach. Even when the waterways froze over, they provided a ready route for sleighs and sledges. Until the age of the railroad, which only began around the end of the nineteenth century in Russia, commerce and prosperity followed the rivers. To this day, river freighters and barges continue to ply the country's water routes.

The Mongols mostly bypassed Velikiy Ustyug, which was sheltered deep in the northern forests. Once, an official dispatched by the Golden Horde to collect tribute was given the choice of baptism or death by local residents. He hastily converted to the Orthodox faith. Likewise, Ustyug was spared many of the tribulations of Ivan the Terrible's reign and the subsequent "Time of Troubles," which sent most of Russia reeling into chaos.

Instead, with the founding of the White Sea port of Arkhangelsk in 1584, and the first Cossack forays into Siberia, Velikiy Ustyug rapidly grew into a center for trade and commerce. It was an important stop on what was then the only trade route open from Russia to Europe. Barges carrying Russian grain, furs, leather, and flax for export floated past the boom town in ever-growing numbers. Arkhangelsk saw a tenfold increase in the number of foreign ship calls during the seventeenth century. This trade was in large measure stoked by the merchants of Velikiy Ustyug. The riverboats heading back to the Russian heartland also multiplied; they were loaded to the brim with the luxuries of Europe, including wine, tobacco, clothing, and medicine. Twice a year, Velikiy

Ustyug held a fur market that attracted buyers from all over the continent. Ustyug's merchants and tradesmen became rich. Their newfound wealth they invested back in their hometown.

* * *

Light snow was still blowing across the city, but as I came up to the embankment overlooking the Sukhona River, the clouds to the south began to break up, casting down brittle rays of sunlight from just above the horizon. The embankment pitched steeply to the river's edge. The frozen Sukhona was impressive; it swept in front of Velikiy Ustyug in a long, graceful arc. Across the way, in a snowbound village, log house chimneys and stove pipes contentedly puffed out their affirmation of winter life. Nestled behind a compact stand of birch and pine trees, a pair of green-domed churches watched over the riverbank. The snow-covered ice was crisscrossed with paths leading from one side to the other. A stooped old woman shuffled along one track, dragging home a meager-looking bag. A line of schoolchildren on skis, elegant as a banking flight of loons, swept in unison past her and turned toward the southwest, upstream. Under the embankment, another woman kneeled over a square hole in the ice, splashing her laundry back and forth in the steaming water, then slapping it down into a wicker basket on a sled.

The local museum was housed in an old mansion on the river embankment. Past the darkened cloakroom, I groped my way down an unlit corridor in the direction of a rectangle of blue fluorescent light. Opening the door, I was challenged by a hefty woman whose chin was as graceless as a sentry's. After a few words of explanation, followed by a hasty conference behind closed doors, I was ushered into the director's office.

The museum director met my arrival with undisguised handwringing. One would have thought that a meteorite had crashed through the roof and landed on her desk. Her brunette hair had the cast and texture of mouse fur. Had she not tried so hard to keep them immobile, her features might have been pleasant. Until my true identity could be established with certainty through the proper channels, it seemed prudent not to smile beyond that measure required by generally accepted standards of courtesy, not to sound encouraging, not to suggest that the museum or its director could necessarily help me. The air in her office was dry, lifeless. We chatted desultorily, and sipped at tea the color of rust.

Adopting a professorial air, the museum director explained that what set Velikiy Ustyug apart from other Russian cities was the pre-eminent role the merchant class played in its development. In the north, serfdom had been practically unknown. Correspondingly, there were few landed nobles. The ensemble of churches, streets, and homes reflected the merchants' preoccupations. One example was the city's orientation toward the river, the traders' main highway. Velikiy Ustyug grew up naturally, organically, rather than as the product of some tsar's decree or nobleman's whim. The town's leading merchants oversaw where and how buildings were erected. They even ensured that land on Ustyug's principal streets went to leading citizens, people wealthy enough to erect houses of distinction. It was the rare instance, I thought, of a Russian city run by the much-maligned bourgeoisie.

I asked the museum director what had happened to the merchants after the Bolsheviks came to power. "The merchant class," she replied, "simply vanished." She said it in a tone not unlike a paleontologist, without much reference to cause or effect. Before I could probe further — to poke, in a sense, at the fossil record — she added, "the years of Soviet rule were not all bad." After all, she observed, it was the Communists who built the railroad extension to Velikiy Ustyug, as well as the bridge over the Sukhona. The local party leaders had done what they could to help the museum and the city. Now, she added, the future was uncertain. Thanks to the new phenomenon of inflation, the museum could barely cover its basic operating expenses. Materials for restoration work had become much more expensive; it would bring, she concluded, "lower quality" results.

What, I asked, was happening to the niello craft? A pained expression flickered across her face. The silver trade, she replied, was now thoroughly commercialized; artistically, it was dead. The factory workers made their designs as simple as possible in order to keep production levels up. Even compared with a few years ago, the work was crude. Paradoxically, demand for the pieces was higher than ever. In fact, she was very concerned about protecting the museum's niello collection from thieves. Recalling the faces in the hotel lobby, I could understand why.

The museum's exhibits were up a set of creaking wooden stairs, watched over by two severe grandmothers seated in straight-backed chairs. I moved from room to room, the only visitor on a February afternoon. In one corner, behind glass, were half a dozen icons gathered from Ustyug's monasteries. One depicted Christ's entrance into Jerusalem. Seated sideways on an ass, he held a palm frond in his right hand and a scroll in his left. Above, a fig tree hid a chorus of boy on-lookers. In another room was a smattering of the glories of Velikiy Ustyug's craftsmen: silver and gold pieces, enamel plates, intricate birchbark boxes.

Grudgingly, the museum director assigned me a guide. He intro-duced himself as Yuri Petrovich Ivanov, a name as common among Russians as "John Evans" is among the Welsh. He was handsome, in a country sort of way. His eyes danced impishly. He was a redhead, and his freckles heightened his boyishness. This puckish quality momen-tarily diverted my attention from the wear and tear in his face, the legacy of years of dissoluteness in the Russian provinces.

"So what the devil brought you to this *glush,* this backwater, any-way?" Yuri Petrovich asked. I explained. He shook his head in astonish-ment, slapped me on the back, and said, "Well, let's get our butts moving then." His breath felt sticky, the handiwork of the national vice.

As we pulled on our coats, Yuri Petrovich outlined our program. "First, we'll go to the Uspenskiy Sobor, the Cathedral of the Dormition. Right next to it is the Church of St. Ioann of Ustyug. Then we'll go inside the Prokopyevskiy Cathedral to see the iconostatis. From there . . ." I pretended to listen, but frankly, I was already lost in his catalog of church names. Then there was the matter of his accent and vocabulary. I had been warned about the Vologda dialect. Yuri's words bounded out like a bear on the run. His sentences would bob, weave, or simply barrel into the brush before they were finished. Slurred slang: it was the perfect torment for a foreigner with an imperfect command of the language.

One of Yuri's female colleagues walked up and a squabble broke out. He was trying to convince her to take over a school group that he was scheduled to handle the following day. She looked exasperated and walked away. He shrugged his shoulders, buttoned up his shabby pea jacket, and put on a greasy-looking beaver *shapka,* or fur hat. Out we went.

We were an unlikely pair. I was snug in my down jacket, electric green mittens, and Canadian mukluks. Yuri, the man of the north woods, walked about hunched over and shivering, slipping about in a pair of rubber galoshes.

Along the embankment a few paces, we entered a set of doors leading into a chapel. This was one of only two working churches in Ustyug. It was still a construction site; a sign reading "Please excuse us while we renovate this space" would not have looked out of place. The walls were made of plywood slapped over with cheap paint. They were entirely bare except for two or three icons hung behind the altar. A handful of *babushki* crossed themselves in approximate unison and replied hoarsely to the priest's chants. Incense hung thickly over the worshipers, drifting about under the low ceiling.

The chapel occupied one corner of an ensemble of churches dominated by the Cathedral of the Dormition, the city's best-known landmark. It is the centerpiece on Ustyug's table of architectural masterworks. The churches form an extraordinary cluster of towers and belfries; some two dozen cupolas rise up together, topped in gold leaf. The double bell tower of the cathedral, at fifty meters the tallest structure in the city, can be seen for miles. Today, the cathedral houses offices and a library, its interior stripped to make way for desks and bookshelves. A nearby church was converted into a basketball court by Communist authorities, who were presumably less inspired by the love of sport than by their desire to humble the Orthodox faith.

Yuri led us cautiously to the heavy doors of the Prokopevskiy Cathedral. A sign read "Entry Strictly Forbidden." He eased the doors open, peered in cautiously, then motioned for me to follow him, all the while tiptoeing exaggeratedly across the antechamber. He held his finger over his lips, then whispered a commentary in my ear. Behind the altar rose a beautiful iconostasis, the proud figures of the saints and the beatific Virgin framed in ornate gold. Some of the icons had been removed from their places, presumably for restoration. From time to time, voices sounded out from behind the silver-plated altar doors.

We ventured further, peering through another portal to look behind the iconostasis. A tall, ragged set of wooden shelves held dozens of icons in various stages of restoration; others lay across tables and sawhorses. Yuri waved me forward. He went ahead, walking lightly

toward a makeshift office in the back, where several people were huddled together inspecting one of the icons.

"Hello, Maria Ivanovna," Yuri began. "You wouldn't mind if I
showed this American visitor around for a few moments, would you?"

The woman scowled. "Petrovich," she said, as she swung around,
"you know you aren't permitted to come in here. Now get out."

"I just thought . . . in view of the fact that we have such a distinguished foreign guest . . ." Yuri stammered. He already sounded a bit
desperate; in no way did I look distinguished.

"Leave now before I complain to Antonina Andreevna," the
woman growled, referring to the museum's director. Someone else piped
up from behind, "Yes, Petrovich, get the hell out of here."

Their scathing use of his patronymic was not intended as a sign of
respect. We scuttled away from the atelier like panicked crabs. Outside,
Yuri was furious. "Those people think they can get away with anything!
They come from Moscow or St. Petersburg and lord it over everyone
else. They think they're so much better than we are, that they know
everything!" He raged, partly out of conviction, partly out of embarrassment.

"Are they always like that?" I asked.

"Yes, yes, they're just petty careerists. They work for the Ministry of
Culture. In Moscow. Even we who live here have to get papers signed
by ten different functionaries, *chinovniki*, before we are allowed in. It's
a scandal!"

The restorers, Yuri explained, were bitterly unhappy about having
to live in Velikiy Ustyug. "They're the second-rate ones, the ones that
couldn't get themselves positions in the big cities. They're stuck here, so
they take it out on us."

It was probably true, I reflected. From the perspective of a well-
educated Russian, living in this remote corner of the Russian north —
a thousand kilometers from any large city — was a burden, even a personal tragedy. The stores were bare; the winters were hard. For most of
the year, there was nothing to do but sit in front of the television, or
drink away the blank days and nights.

There was another reason Yuri bore a grudge against the Moscow
icon restorers. As we walked away from the church, he explained that
they were responsible for furthering a devious myth about the icons of

Velikiy Ustyug. Their unpardonable sin was this: the attribution of the work of Ustyug's celebrated masters to the "Stroganov school."

The Stroganovs, the most celebrated Russian family of traders and industrialists, made Velikiy Ustyug's neighbor, Solvychegodsk, their base of operations. The Stroganovs began to prosper under Ivan the Terrible, who gave them title to the region's saltworks. As the route to Europe opened on their doorstep, the Stroganovs expanded their operations, shifting to the production of iron, potash, and tar. In return for supplying Russian settlers and policing the frontier, the Stroganov family was awarded the exclusive right to exploit vast areas in the Perm region and the Urals. Soon their agents pushed still farther east, crossing the Urals into Siberia. There the attraction was fur, the most lucrative commodity of all.

Solvychegodsk was a company town par excellence; everyone there depended on the Stroganov family. At one point, the Stroganovs employed ten thousand free workers and five thousand serfs in their shops and industries. Like their wealthy counterparts in Velikiy Ustyug, they took a genuine interest in the welfare of their city. The Stroganov family built churches and encouraged the gold, silver, and enamel crafts. Under their patronage, Solvychegodsk's workshops produced some of the finest icons and embroideries ever made in Russia.

Still, Yuri insisted, the Ustyug icons were distinct from those painted by the Stroganovs' "hirelings." What these differences were, I never quite understood; they were too subtle to be grasped by a neophyte like myself. Yuri singled out several icons and murals that he said were obvious examples of the "Ustyug style." We paused at one icon which Yuri conceded had "certain Stroganov elements." I turned to look at him. He was grimacing. Perhaps it was in the genes. Ustyug and Solvychegodsk have been rivals as well as neighbors for five centuries.

Cossack adventurers in the employ of the Stroganovs were the first Russians to penetrate the Siberian taiga and marshes. The most famous of them, Yermak, mounted raids against the Tatar princes on the far side of the Urals. Before falling in battle, Yermak succeeded in breaking the power of the Siberian Tatar khanate, thus opening huge tracts of Russian Siberia to colonization. Although they were glamorized in later accounts, these freebooters had much in common with the Spanish conquistadors who roamed the New World in search of quick riches and adventure a century earlier. They were ruthless in their pursuit of wealth, and gave no quarter to the native peoples that stood in their way. They had their counterparts, too, in America's own westward expansion.

Near the Cathedral of the Dormition stands a statue of Semen Dezhnev, one of those swashbuckling figures. Caught up in a "fur rush" every bit as frantic as the North American gold rushes, traders and frontiersmen poured east into Siberia during the seventeenth century. They pushed farther and farther into unexplored regions, hoping to discover areas where fur-bearing animals were still abundant. Dezhnev was a soldier in government service. In 1648, from a small polar settlement, he set out in a group of seven boats to find the mouth of the Anadyr River on the Pacific, an uncharted area. After countless trials and hardships along the Arctic Ocean coast, the remnants of Dezhnev's group rounded the northeastern corner of Asia and passed through the Bering Strait, the first Europeans ever to do so. It was another fifteen years before Dezhnev was able to return overland as far as Yakutsk and report what he had seen. In fact, Dezhnev and his companions hardly knew that they had "discovered" anything. Only at the beginning of the eighteenth century did Vitus Bering sail the same waters and recognize them as the passage between Asia and America.

Dezhnev, along with many other Siberian explorers, was an Ustyug man. Another was Yerofei Khabarov. A merchant of some means, his expeditions in the early 1650s opened up the Amur River basin, which today forms part of Russia's eastern border with China. His cruelty was legendary. He liked to brag about the women and children his men slaughtered along their route. Even by the rough standards of the Siberian frontier, his methods were sufficiently brutal to have him hauled before a government tribunal. Despite his excesses, and the fact that his depredations had provoked the Chinese into mounting a retaliatory expedition, Khabarov went unpunished. Later, he was rewarded with a noble title and appointed commander of an important Siberian military garrison. His memory lives on in the name of one of the largest cities in the Russian Far East, Khabarovsk.

The Russian conqueror of Kamchatka, Vladimir Atlasov, was also born in Velikiy Ustyug. At the end of the seventeenth century, Atlasov marched down the peninsula, subduing the native Koryaks and Itelmen as he went. He returned to Moscow in triumph, and was awarded a handsome bonus. He brought with him a shipwrecked Japanese man, along with Japanese pots and textiles, the first clues that Japan lay near Russia's new dominions. Atlasov then set out for Kamchatka, this time as the Tsar's commandant. Along the way, however, he could not resist holding up a caravan laden with Chinese goods; he was jailed when he tried to sell the contraband in Yakutsk. Years later, when Kamchatka's administrators faced a native uprising, Atlasov was freed in order to bring the peninsula to heel a second time. Like Khabarov, Atlasov was nothing if not ruthless, and he quickly forced the Itelmen and Koryaks back into line. His cruelties to his own men were such, however, that they mutinied and murdered him in his bed.

Ustyug claims other sons among the Siberian pathfinders. Some of them were admirable; others were the likes of Khabarov and Atlasov. Afanasiy Bakhov was probably the first Russian to sight the northern coast of Alaska; the Ustyug merchant Vasiliy Shilov helped explore the Aleutian islands; and Mikhail Nevodchikov, a master silversmith turned adventurer, set himself up as the overlord of the Aleutians, in the process massacring a village of Aleuts on Attu Island. What is most extraordinary is that one province in the Russian north, far from the capitals of Moscow and St. Petersburg, could have provided so many historic figures in the conquest of Siberia. It is as if Daniel Boone, Meriwether Lewis, and John Fremont had all come from, say, Tennessee.

Velikiy Ustyug's special relationship with Siberia persisted into the nineteenth century. The richest man in the city in the early 1800s was Mikhail Buldakov, one of the founding directors of the Russian-American Company. For over half a century, the company held sway along the Alaskan coast, establishing trading posts like Kodiak and Sitka, and even probing as far as Hawaii and Fort Ross in California. Buldakov's estate still stands on the Ustyug embankment, guarded by two bronze gatepost lions. A sophisticated and educated man, he maintained an enviable private library. Late in life, he ceded some of his estate for the establishment of Ustyug's municipal park.

When St. Petersburg was founded at the beginning of the eighteenth century, Velikiy Ustyug's fortunes began to decline. The long route to Europe via Arkhangelsk and the White Sea was no longer the only option. It was much longer and more expensive than routing trade through Russia's new capital on the Baltic. To the south, Catherine II secured Russian access to the Black Sea, opening up trade in that direction. Thus, Velikiy Ustyug entered a long period of decadence. Eventually, most Russians were to forget that it was even there.

Although Velikiy Ustyug's economic fortunes changed, the city all the same remained conscious of her place in history. The old life that had sustained countless generations went on, much as before. The proof was on display in the Church of St. Nicholas of the Inn, in a remarkable exhibit of photographs and memorabilia from fin-de-siècle Ustyug — a vivid reminder of all that was lost in the roar of our cruel century.

The exterior of St. Nicholas had been saved, the rubble and filth of half a century of neglect swept out. Up until the seventies, this brightly painted edifice was a pathetic eyesore, its belfry half-decapitated. The patient labor of restorers and workmen had brought it back from ruin.

Yet like many of Russia's surviving churches, St. Nicholas now finds itself serving other masters than God. Officially, it is the museum's annex. One feels a certain sadness in its empty halls; even the best intentions cannot excuse the sterile, whitewashed walls, the sputtering electric bulbs, and the five-year-plan furniture. Without its believers, the church stood bare and hollow. And there simply were not enough believers left to set things right again.

The other four churches that once stood along this part of the Sukhona embankment were torn down to make way for an electric plant. They were not victims of "revolutionary excesses" of the early twenties. Rather, they were bludgeoned and bulldozed in Khrushchev's time, targets in his own born-again atheist's campaign against religion. Just downriver from St. Nicholas, behind a fence, brown soot spewed out of the plant, its dullish brick chimney the best riposte the Bolsheviks could muster to the past they so loathed. Why build it on one of the city's loveliest sites? Electrification plus Soviet power equals communism, the old slogan went. The belching, obsolete *elektrozavod* was, true enough, the embodiment of Marxism-Leninism.

The exhibit in St. Nicholas was itself staggering. By some miracle, a variety of collectors and nostalgics had managed to preserve an entire world of old photos and postcards. In them, the butchered churches breathed anew and wordlessly reprimanded their assailants. The beauty of Ustyug's old riverbank went beyond anything I had imagined. In the photographs, the Sukhona was adorned by an unbroken row of towers and cupolas. Behind soared the tulip dome of the John the Pretender Monastery, completed in 1910 and torched by a Bolshevik rabble in 1921. Another casualty was the *gostiny dvor,* the town's waterfront market-place. Once, its wide arches had sheltered merchants, workers, and peasants alike. After the Second World War, it was leveled to build cozy apartments for the local Party elite. Among the starchy but touching portraits of families and community groups, the blurry street scenes of top-hatted shopkeepers and milling vendors, the newspapers stuffed with gossip and advertisements, and the elaborately engraved business cards and invitations, there was an undeniable message: before the revolution, Russian life was normal. A glance outside was enough to confirm that this was no longer true.

All the light had drained out of the winter afternoon. It was dark, but too early to be called night. The morning would not come for a long time.

❇ ❇ ❇

Yuri wanted me to meet someone. "Irya works at the city archives," he explained. "She knows more than anyone else about what happened after the revolution."

First, we had another stop to make. Yuri tapped the back of his fingers against the side of his chin, and looked at me quizzically. In the lexicon of Russian hand gestures, this meant it was time to get a bottle. Yuri's step lightened appreciably, especially after I agreed to buy the vodka. In a poky, ill-lit grocery, he pondered his choice for several minutes — there were all of two brands — before pushing my crisp thousand-ruble note down in front of the cashier. Bottle in hand, he bounced happily out the door.

Right away, I was drawn to Irya. She was petite, pretty, engaging. She invited us in with a sweep of her arm and sat us down at her kitchen table. Far from Russia's metropolises, she crackled with urbane charm. Her twelve-year-old son was late for a music lesson. She prodded him out the door, all the while fixing up a supper of chicken and potatoes for us.

Yuri already had the bottle open, tending eagerly to our glasses. "My, it has been a long time since I was last here," he said. She did not reply; she apparently was not going to apologize to him. Teasingly, very familiarly, he needled Irya over the smoked sturgeon she had set down on the table.

"This isn't fresh. See the dark places here along the spine? That means it's old. What kind of hostess have you become, Irya? What will our guest think?"

Her reply was both playful and withering: "Keep to your chosen area of expertise. I'll worry about the food. You worry about the drinks."

Yuri sighed. Then he laughed. I recognized the signs. He was hopelessly in love with her.

A small, quiet man with greying hair appeared at the entrance to the kitchen. "I'm going out," he said pleasantly. Irya smiled and bid him goodbye. Only later did I realize that he was her husband.

Irya's eyes — green, dancing, intense — were fixed on me.

I asked her about the old Ustyug. Was anything left other than the churches and the houses?

She ran a hand through her hair. There was something very attractive about that hand, I thought. "Some descendants of the old families," she said, "still live here. You can see the same names in the census records as before the revolution. Maybe they don't even know that their forebears were once part of the elite. Following the revolution, our merchants and our intellectuals were wiped out. The Ustyug intelligentsia that spent the winter in the ballrooms and cafes of St. Petersburg, and summered here by the Sukhona — it is no more."

For months, Irya explained, the Bolsheviks did not bother with Velikiy Ustyug. Isolated from the dramatic events in Petrograd, Ustyug remained a peaceful backwater. The city still had just one policeman. A trained engineer, he spent most of his time performing housing inspections.

By the summer of 1918, however, the Russian north seemed in danger of falling to the Allied troops that were deployed off the ports of Murmansk and Arkhangelsk. In the eyes of the Bolshevik authorities, Ustyug, with its old merchant traditions, was rife with class enemies. Therefore, it had to be subdued. The town council, along with most of the city's population, at first tried to resist the newcomers. Meetings were called, only to be disbanded by armed Red Guards; the same scenario was repeated time and again.

In the end, Ustyug was brought to heel by revolutionary terror. Some opponents of the Bolsheviks fled. Others lingered too long, and were shot. By the early twenties, the houses and land of the bourgeoisie had been confiscated and the bells ripped down from the churches. A darkness was descending, although no one knew just how black it would become.

Into the thirties, a handful of prominent Ustyug residents fought to protect the city's heritage. One of them was Nikolai Bekreshov, the founder of the Ustyug museum. An intellectual of the old school, he was by most accounts a proud and difficult man. Nevertheless, he was enormously knowledgeable and fought vigorously to save Velikiy Ustyug from those who were eager to remake it in the image of the "new socialist man." People like Bekreshov were all that stood between the preservation of the city's monuments and their destruction. In the archives, Irya found the records of meetings at which Bekreshov stood up to Party officials and the secret police.

Finally, the pressure from Moscow was too much. At the height of Stalin's Great Terror, Ustyug's churches and monasteries were converted into detention centers; hundreds, perhaps thousands of people perished in them. Bekreshov himself was arrested in 1938, and executed in a camp in Arkhangelsk province. His death certificate, too, lingers forgotten in a folder in the archives.

Pitirim Sorokin's death attestation might also have found its way to the Ustyug archives. At the time of the revolution, Sorokin was a St. Petersburg university professor and a left-wing revolutionary. Although still in his twenties, he served as a cabinet minister in the ill-fated Kerensky government, overthrown by the Bolsheviks in October 1917. When Lenin dissolved the Constituent Assembly, Sorokin was one of a number of deputies arrested.

The Bolsheviks always displayed a demonic practicality. If they could not win over Russia democratically, they were prepared to take it by whatever means were necessary. A *Pravda* headline captures the mood of those days and the already prodigious capacity of the country's new rulers for slander and hyperbole: "The Hyenas of Capital and Their Hirelings Want to Seize Power From Soviet Hands." These words were not directed against some group of Tsarist generals and bankers. Rather, they were aimed at the very same socialists and democrats who had helped overturn the old order less than a year before.

After two months of imprisonment in Petrograd's Peter and Paul Fortress, Sorokin was released. He tried to resume his political activities in Moscow, but soon had to flee that city as well. He then set out, along with his wife, for his hometown, Velikiy Ustyug. Outwardly, he pretended to be on vacation; behind the scenes, he worked to undermine the Bolsheviks. Meanwhile, a delegation of commissars arrived from Moscow and issued orders for Sorokin's arrest. He and several other erstwhile conspirators left Ustyug and set out for Arkhangelsk, where they expected the Allies to land any day. Holed up in a village, they went about in disguise and tried to outwit the Red Guards who were combing the countryside in search of "renegades." Finally, they received a message: "Cargo is retarded. Continue the study of rural communes." This meant that the landing of Allied troops in Arkhangelsk had been delayed. Sorokin and the others headed back toward Ustyug.

By now, the Ustyug *Cheka,* or secret police, had begun to arrest and execute people in earnest. Orders had been issued to shoot Sorokin on sight. Half-starved and in constant fear of arrest, Sorokin drifted from one village to another in the region, somehow managing to stay a step ahead of his pursuers. At one point, he hid in a peasant's hut near the cemetery on the outskirts of town. At night, the reports from the executioners' revolvers echoed across the graveyard.

Back in the forest, Sorokin and a friend wandered about, searching for berries and mushrooms, cadging a loaf of bread from peasants when they could. As the summer gave way to the bone-chilling drizzle of autumn, their situation became desperate. "Almost all our waking hours we were hungry," Sorokin later wrote, "our bodies, and most of all, our feet in their bark shoes, were wet. We began to bloat and to feel strangely weak and tired." Always the scholar, he tried in vain to record his thoughts and sensations for inclusion in a monograph. Yet, before long, he would find his thoughts shifting "from the psychology of starvation to plans of getting something to eat."

Still, there was plenty of time for wider reflections. Sorokin recalled his mounting disillusionment with the political cataclysm he had unwittingly helped bring about:

> We continued to wander over the bosom of Nature, occasionally wishing we might see a little of civilization.

In free moments we talked much about the Revolution, and doubts which had been born in my mind at the beginning of the upheaval grew to full size. In this wild forest the utter futility of all revolution, the vanity of all Socialism and Communism became clear to me. The catastrophe of the Revolution, the deep historic roots of Bolshevism, loathed by the majority, it is true, but having as its basis and its force the passive spirit of the Russian nation, overwhelmed me with its truth. Only when the people have suffered the fullest horrors of Bolshevism, only when they have passed completely through the tragic, perhaps the fatal experience of the Communist experiment, can their dreadful sickness be cured once and forever. Only then the poisons in which Bolshevism flourished would be purged from the organism of the Russian people. Only then would this damned passivity disappear and they be transformed from a people accustomed to tyranny to a self-governing nation.

Perhaps afflicted by that selfsame Russian fatalism, Sorokin gave himself up; he had concluded that he had no other choice. The chief of Ustyug's *Cheka* informed him that he would be shot as soon as Moscow had been consulted. While Sorokin awaited his execution, he committed his thoughts to paper, ruefully observing that in the new communist paradise, freedom of speech seemed to exist only behind bars. Before the revolution, Velikiy Ustyug's prison population had rarely surpassed thirty individuals. Now there were three hundred held in the jail, along with another two hundred captive in one of the monasteries.

Each night, the guards would come to take away more prisoners. Their impending execution would be confirmed by the phrase, "No need to take your things." One night, a young man loudly denounced the Bolsheviks as he was being led out of the cell. He was shot on the spot, right in front of the other prisoners. The other condemned men screamed and wept. One fell to the floor in convulsions. But there was no escaping their rendevous by the cemetery.

Just before the first anniversary of the Bolshevik Revolution, a record number of twelve prisoners was removed. Then, for the three days of celebrations, an "amnesty" from executions was announced. In his diary, Sorokin wrote: "We all have three days to live while the Revolution is digesting its last heavy meal." Indeed, three days passed with no further victims. Then, on the morning of the fourth, the guards were back. This time, sixteen men were led out of the cell to their doom.

Rather than face the tormenting uncertainty, some prisoners tried to lie as close as possible to typhus victims, even seeking out their lice to place on their own skin. Dying that way seemed a blessing compared to waiting for the firing squad.

Once, sixty peasants were thrown into the cell, including some women and children. They were bruised and battered; they had resisted giving up their cattle and feed to a Communist requisition party. The Bolsheviks used artillery and machine guns against them. In all, three villages were burned to the ground. Within a few days of arriving at Ustyug's prison, most of the peasants were executed. One child was left, an orphan wandering about the cell among strangers.

The only bright moment in Sorokin's ordeal came when he was included in a work party sawing wood on the banks of the Sukhona. A passerby recognized him and alerted his family. A short while later, he saw his wife and a relative standing at a distance. "During two hours of hard labor, I had the bliss of gazing at them," he recalled. As the convicts filed back to prison, he passed close by. His family wept. He was overjoyed to see them one last time.

When Sorokin was finally removed from the cell, however, he was taken to his interrogator rather than to a firing squad. The official informed Sorokin that he had an order for his immediate release, signed by Lenin himself. The official repeated the words, "by Lenin himself," in awe. One of Sorokin's former students, now an influential Bolshevik, had intervened in Moscow to save him. He was being assigned to teach again at his old university in Petrograd. The day before he had been "counterrevolutionary scum"; now the Party had decided that it needed him after all.

Where did Sorokin's path lead? He was exiled from Russia a few years later, and secured a teaching position in Minnesota. In 1930, he was appointed the first professor of sociology at Harvard University, where he headed the department until the mid-fifties. Before he passed away in 1968, he wrote several influential sociology texts, giving the new discipline a strong boost in the United States. Perhaps someday a monument will be erected to him in Ustyug. The town's Harvard professor has not been completely forgotten, even though, like Dezhnev, he found fame and fortune many miles from home.

* * *

We had all moved from the kitchen to the living room. When Yuri's bottle ran out, he raced back out to buy another. After he left, Irya giggled at the idea that the museum had assigned its bad boy and ne'er-do-well to me. "They have no idea who you are," she exclaimed.

Yuri need not have bothered with the second bottle on my account. While he was gone, Irya showed me an architectural history of Velikiy Ustyug. I spent more time examining her hands than I did the text. We spoke about her student days at St. Petersburg's Repin Institute, Russia's finest art school. I discovered she had once headed the Ustyug museum and the city's cultural office. It seemed odd that she had ended up in the municipal archives. Why had she returned at all to Ustyug, I wondered? "I came back to get married," she said with a sigh. Then her voice brightened, so as not to let even a whiff of gloom settle. "But it's a wonderful, quiet place to live."

Yuri pranced back in with the vodka, shaking the snow off his coat like a happy retriever. He set it down dramatically in the middle of the table, a boyish grin breaking out over his face. Inadvertently, his arm caught the side of the bottle. Irya grabbed it before it could fall onto the floor.

For Yuri, this second bottle was the occasion for far-reaching philosophical speculation. Each toast that he proposed opened up new avenues of inquiry; for instance, why the museum director treated him so badly, or the scandalous attribution of Ustyug's best icons to the Stroganov school. I could see from Irya's expression that she was already very familiar with these topics. "I'm a rebel. I'm a bohemian," he announced. And I came to understand the true purpose of the evening. I was an excuse for Yuri to visit the woman he loved. Yuri was complaining that the museum director had once falsely accused him of being drunk and using obscene language in front of a group of visiting foreigners. I looked over at Irya. I could see that she understood that I understood.

It was time to go. Irya's hints about the lateness of the hour had had little effect on Yuri. Finally, out of fear of offending our hostess, I insisted on leaving. Yuri pulled himself up from the table, visibly full of regret.

"Perhaps we can come back tomorrow night," Yuri offered.

"You are always welcome," Irya answered noncommittally. What was she really thinking?

I am not sure I would have found my way back to the hotel without Yuri's help. The vodka was only partly to blame. I was ecstatic; I felt like a character from a nineteenth-century Russian novel. I gloried in the idyllic vision around me: the sweetly hissing snowfall sparkling against the black sky, the crunch of my boots against the road, the slumbering churches and cottages.

Yuri pulled up in front of the hotel. "Are you sure you will be all right?" he asked. I was not really certain what he meant. "Oh, I'm fine. I didn't have that much to drink," I lied.

"No, I mean the hotel. It's a dangerous place. I don't like the people who stay here."

Two young men were conversing in the darkness under the portico. "Why don't you come home with me? It would be safer," Yuri offered.

I patted him on the shoulder. "There's nothing to worry about," I said.

✳ ✳ ✳

The next morning, I tried to nurse my head back to life. Last night's exaltation had given way to reality. Outside my hotel room, a dull light like dirty gauze was seeping into the street. Grim passersby dragged themselves along on their numbing errands. I went across the street to a cafeteria. A gypsy's gaunt horse and wooden sledge stood outside; the horse's master was hawking knives to the manager. Vainly, I asked if they had pickle brine, one of dozens of reputed Russian hangover remedies. I settled instead for a bowl of sinister fish broth, tiny piscatorial heads and fins drifting about mockingly on the surface. I returned to my room, my stomach an ocean of regret.

Yuri was late. From my window, the Spassky Monastery looked serene, eternal.

After a while he appeared at my door, looking a bit frazzled. He apologized profusely, plopped down on my bed with a sigh, and went on to explain.

Yuri, it seemed, had gone to the wrong room. Without a care in the world, he knocked, heard a muffled acknowledgment, opened the door, and stepped blithely in. He opened his mouth to announce his arrival. By the time he realized that he had entered the wrong room, he was already lying face down on the floor with a man kneeling on top of him. The man was pressing a revolver to his right temple. The gun barrel felt cold; the man was strong.

"Where are you going, *khopa?*" the man growled ominously.

Yuri wanted to tell him, but somehow, the words would not come out. The pressure of the gun barrel against his skull increased.

There were other people there. The room was full of cigarette smoke. The same voice again: "I said, where are you going, asshole."

"Nowhere."

"You're right about that."

An older man was standing over him. "You screwed up. You're in the wrong room," he said, evenly. Someone laughed.

"I was looking for a foreigner. An American."

The barrel eased off his head. "You're visiting our friend? The American?"

"Yes, yes," Yuri blurted out. "I'm from the museum. I'm his guide."

The young man, whose name was Sasha, jumped up. "Hey, I'm sorry," he said, very casually. "We didn't know."

Yuri rolled onto his side. He was lying on the floor, surrounded by five men. "No hard feelings, I hope," said the older man, who had red hair and a thin face. It was Slava. "We're businessmen," he explained. "We have to be careful."

One of them helped Yuri up. They invited him to have a drink. There was a nice spread of food on the table. "Not such a bad bunch of fellows, really," Yuri commented. When he left, they slapped him on the back — a bit too hard — and told him to pass on a *bolshoi privet,* a big hello, to their American friend.

The mayor's office was just around the corner. The city hall was in a former mansion, now decrepit; it smelled of fusty overcoats. Sullen peasants lined the corridor. Yuri decided to wait in the lobby.

Mayor Frolov was the quintessential *nomenklaturist*. His desk, studded with five different phone sets, presided over a long table polished to a slavish glare. I sat down in one of the ten chairs. Frolov's wolverine deputy, after getting a glance of approval from his boss, took another.

The mayor was a Communist-era boss who had managed to hang on to his little fiefdom. His eyes had the same grey, metallic quality as ball bearings; for most of the meeting, they avoided mine. I asked him how Velikiy Ustyug was adjusting to the reforms. The potted rubber plants by the window seemed to be giving off steam, fogging over the view of the courtyard below.

His flat, bluff face replied: "Everything is fine. We make our own decisions now. We're like an independent country. Soon, we'll control an even bigger share of the taxes."

Was unemployment a problem, I wondered? Yes, a few lumberyard workers had lost their jobs. My comment about Ustyug's tourist potential brought forth a comforting answer about contacts with foreign tour representatives. Several had even visited, it seemed. Frolov added that he was looking for a private firm to convert a certain "historic building" into a hotel. It was nearby, just a block away. I racked my brain to try to figure out which of the old mansions he was talking about.

Frolov's beefy hand patted the table to get my attention. "There is one issue that we haven't solved yet," he said momentously. He looked slyly at Mr. Gladyshev, his assistant. A suitable pause ensued, for dramatic effect.

"We have too many cows," he announced, with mock gravity. Then he and Gladyshev laughed. "Our cows are putting out milk like there's no tomorrow, and we don't have any place to sell it anymore."

Later, Yuri showed me the site of the proposed hotel. To my astonishment, it was a crippled edifice with broken patches of plaster and a tin roof. The building was hardly worthy of preservation; it was as characterless as anything put up in the Soviet period. The door and windows had been sealed off with large rust-colored metal sheets. The sidewalk in front was littered with glass. "Why would anyone want to turn this place into a hotel?" I asked. Yuri just shrugged his shoulders.

It turned out that there was only one restoration project in which the mayor was really interested: namely, his own. To everyone's surprise,

Frolov had put his hands on a dilapidated old house not far from the center of town. He referred to it as his *dacha,* which in most people's minds signified a country retreat along a river or in the forest. For months, workers had been busy fixing up the place. Local wags admired the workmanship; part of the job had been completed by carpenters and plumbers on the city payroll. The finished house shone, like Frolov's desk, with varnish and fresh paint. It looked very comfortable. But why would the mayor want a second residence in town, hard by a busy street at the foot of the hill on which the old cemetery was located?

"Buried treasure," Yuri responded. Rumor had it that Frolov had somehow found out about a cache of valuables hidden under the floorboards of the house. It had once belonged to a rich merchant who disappeared after the revolution. The mayor hastily condemned the property and then had a few trusted lieutenants go through it inch by inch. Restoring the house was supposedly only a cover.

Accounts differed as to what the mayor's men had discovered. There was general consensus about the gold bars and the jewelry, however. I was skeptical at first, yet everyone I asked believed the story implicitly. Yuri insisted that over the years there had been other such episodes. In Ustyug, opinions varied about Frolov's performance as mayor. Everyone agreed, however, that he was probably by now a rather wealthy man.

After making some inquiries, I found the "Northern Niello" silver factory. In Alexei's feverish imagination, this squat cinderblock building had been the goal of my espionage mission to Velikiy Ustyug. Unfortunately, I never obtained permission to visit it. Such authorization, the mayor informed me, had to come from unnamed authorities in Moscow well in advance of a visit. It was apparent that one did not just stroll onto the fenced premises. While I did not see any machine guns, as Alexei had warned me I would, there were guards, and they did not look welcoming.

Instead, I had to content myself with a visit to the factory store, in the center of town. An hour before opening in the morning, a line of people would begin to form outside the store's entrance. The same process would be repeated in anticipation of the end of the lunch break. On this day, there were shifty young men from the hotel wearing parkas and sneakers; bovine blondes and brunettes with shopping bags like udders; even a tall, angular pensioner, looking immensely tired and sad. Like most lines in Russia, this one was anything but orderly. People jostled and argued. Each time the militiaman stationed behind the door cracked it open to let in another person, the whole crowd would shove forward as one.

When Yuri and I came back later, the sidewalk in front of the store was empty. I walked in. The store was down a few steps in a half-basement. Two saleswomen stood behind a counter, chatting. Backlit photos of niello pieces decorated the walls. I looked down into the display cases, covered in cheap black velvet. There was nothing left except for two spoons; everything else had been swept up. One of the salesgirls explained, with no hint of apology, that there were only so many pieces sent to the store each day. She knew, as I did, that only the small fry bothered to wait in the line. The real players, like my friends from the train, had the wares brought to them in the comfort of their hotel room.

Down the road from the store stood an academy for aspiring river-boat captains. The cadets, their cheeks almost vermilion from the cold, were skiing up a low hill and back down the other side. They whisked by in blue-striped middies and bell-bottom trousers.

Nearby was the Church of Ascension, Velikiy Ustyug's most beautiful. Built at the behest of a rich merchant, the church was completed in 1648. It was by no means large; it was made up of a single chapel and an adjoining belfry. Yet it appeared to bloom out of its white brick base into a thicket of petaled roof cornices, topped in turn by the dark stamens of its seven cupolas. Standing watch alongside, the shaft of the bell tower and a canopied entrance held the rest of the structure, as it were, around the hips.

There was something oddly intimate, even sensual, about the Church of the Ascension. The builders who raised the church were, no doubt, inspired by sheer piety. Perhaps, though, as new generations over the years made additions and alterations, the call of a more worldly beauty became too compelling to forswear. The exterior walls were decorated like no other church in Ustyug; they were embossed with columns and half-domes, intricate friezes and emblems. They were as affecting as a string of pearls across a woman's bare neck. Yuri was pleased when I told him that the church was my favorite. He said that we were attracted by the same things.

Before long, a workman appeared at the iron door of the church. His name was Yuri Markov, and he led us to a simple workbench next to a window. He looked like the handyman uncle I never had. His hands were brown with callouses and woodstain. The formless length of wood he was working at that moment said little to me. But, in fact, Markov was an immensely skilled artisan.

My questions must have seemed ridiculous to him. At one point, after I had asked him whether it was difficult to find the right materials, he laughed softly and replied: "Some people say it's colder here in the winter than in the summer." He had spent the last six years restoring the church's iconostasis. He would sketch a scale drawing of the wood piece he needed to replace — the wing of an angel, the hand of the crucified Savior, the crenellated frame of an icon — and then carve it. For the most part, he used local wood like birch and alder. "Bureaucratic problems" had prevented him from working in Ustyug's other churches for most of the past decade. Instead, he made furniture — and yearned to return to his real calling.

When Markov opened the doors to the main altar, I was genuinely overwhelmed. He had recreated by hand most of a fifty-foot wood iconostasis. The quality of work was remarkable; the figures of saints and angels were alive, miraculous. Velikiy Ustyug's niello craft had been gutted by decades of inflated production targets; the town's birchbark trade was tottering after being taken from cottage to factory. Here, however, was a tradition that had survived intact all of the torments of the past century.

While I admired the iconostasis, I asked Markov whether there were other wood carvers doing this type of work. He was confident, he said, that young people would follow in his steps. He had already trained one of his sons. I sensed, though, that his confidence was more rhetorical than heartfelt. "This is a hard calling," he went on. "Some of the youngsters are put off by hard work." There was also the problem of money. Building houses for the nouveau riche, for instance, was far more lucrative than restoring churches on a miserly state salary. We left him bent over a pair of benches, whittling at a board under the light of a single, bright bulb.

✷ ✷ ✷

When we arrived at Irya's apartment, great gobs of snow were tumbling out of the sky like milk spattered from some cosmic bucket. She beamed as I handed her a bottle of California white wine. Then she hugged me; her embroidered blouse was freshly starched, her hair faintly scented.

Over smoked fish, salami, and cucumber, we took up where we had left off the previous evening. Irya was even more buoyant. Each time she poked fun at Yuri, her eyes danced. She savored the white wine, the first she had had, she admitted, for years. Yuri, on the other hand, looked sadder and sadder. "I thought the wine would be sweet," he complained, turning without further ado to the more potent wallop of his vodka. She was playing up to me and teasing Yuri mercilessly. He looked more miserable with each passing minute. Under his breath, he was grumbling. He was jealous.

There was a flurry of brusque knocks at the door. Surprised, Irya looked back over her shoulder. Her husband appeared from a darkened room and headed toward the entrance. Irya, too, got up, and disappeared. Yuri and I sat there, listening, wondering at the growing commotion out of our sight.

Two militiamen, one tall, the other short, suddenly appeared before us. The short one stumbled once, then twice, his hand searching thin air for support. He was hopelessly, pitifully drunk.

I saw Yuri stiffen. I probably did, too, involuntarily. There was definitely something unsettling about the abrupt appearance of the reviled militia in the midst of our hosts' apartment.

Yuri leaned toward me and whispered: "He's a close friend of the family." Then, mysteriously, he added, "Perhaps we should be going."

Irya's face was all determination, barely offset by a mask of sweetness. She was used to being in control; she was struggling to keep it that way. The tall militiaman stood passively by the doorway. Irya's husband, too, waited in the wings, as irrelevant to the drama as a stagehand. The short militiaman, lean as a weasel, wore a spoiling look behind his thin mustache. To my surprise, I realized that he was an officer, a militia captain. Despite Irya's increasingly insistent admonitions to him to hold up, he was wheeling ominously toward the center of the sitting room, toward Yuri and me.

Velikiy Ustyug is a small town. "Yuri Petrovich, how come you don't say hello to me," the militia captain blurted out, his words muddled, bubbling out in ugly little bursts. Yuri was already on his feet. The militia captain brought himself right up, an inch or two from Yuri's face.

"How are you, Vitaliy Andreevich?" Yuri said, more composed than I had ever seen him before.

"What's a shit like you doing here, at Irya's home? And who's this with you?"

He looked over at me, obviously expecting me to answer. Yuri put his arm around him, wedging himself between the militiaman and me. The captain took another step at me. "Who are you?" he demanded, his face tense, his eyes unsteady, morbid. His breath was stale; a gold incisor gleamed. I stood up, weighing whether to answer or not.

Irya put her hands firmly on the militiaman's shoulders and pushed him down onto the couch. "It's time for you to sit and behave yourself," she scolded. He was grabbing at her, trying to pull her onto the couch with him. She pulled away. He tried to struggle up, eyeing me and Yuri. Irya pushed him back down onto the couch again, holding him there by the shoulders. Then, instead of slapping him, she stroked his cheek.

The tall militiaman was still leaning against the doorway. Yuri's hand was nudging me gently from behind. "*Poshli, poshli,* " he repeated in a whisper, "let's go, let's go." I did not need much encouragement. Irya's husband was standing by the door as we quietly gathered our things. He mumbled an apology, smiling his mild smile.

Outside, the snow had ended. A gusting wind was slapping us hard, seeking to freeze the life out of our faces. We stopped at a corner. "I didn't like that. I didn't like that at all," Yuri commented. "I don't see what she sees in that man, at all."

It was time to head back to the hotel. Yuri and his wife were taking their teenage daughter to the train station early the next morning. She was going to Tver, where she was enrolled in the university. I would say goodbye to them there.

The square in front of the hotel was deserted. To save time in the morning, I paid my bill at the front desk. While I waited for the woman on duty to fill out a receipt, I felt a tap on my shoulder.

"I know who you are. I know all about you." There was a big, balding man at my shoulder, drooling out his words. Another drunk, I thought.

His hair was plastered down in lifeless strands along the back of his skull. He was sweating in his heavy ski parka. I tried to ignore him. "You're an American," he insisted. His big paw came down on my shoulder, friendly but insistent. I was trapped.

He explained that he had heard about me from "friends." He led me over to the corner of the lobby with the chairs and the plastic palm and invited me to sit down. I did, reluctantly.

"Why are you here?" he asked, leaning in toward me. I explained. As if he had not heard me at all, he repeated his question: "Why are you here?"

I was getting impatient with the evening's surfeit of madness. "I've just told you why I'm here," I snapped. "Why are *you* here?"

He was a TV cameraman from Moscow, he claimed. He had come to Ustyug to film a report. "I worked in the U.S. for three years," he continued. Then, as if to prove his bona fides, he began to speak in an impenetrable dialect that he assured me was English. He went on in this vein for a minute or so, and then asked me, "Why are you here?"
I rose to go upstairs to my room. "I'm tired. Good night," I told him, exasperated.

"I know who you are," the fat man said.

"I don't think you do," I retorted.

"Tell me why you're really here," he demanded.

The drunk's feet kept shifting about unexpectedly as he tried to stay upright. His lunacy, whether by design or not, had finally infected me with the paranoia I used to feel in the bad old Soviet days.

"Let's go into business together," he blurted out. "I need an American business partner."

I was trying to think of a way of escaping him. "Here. Here's my business card. I've written down my phone number in Moscow." I had the presence of mind to scramble the digits.

He seemed pleased by this gesture. He smiled, then stumbled, almost falling against the palm. He asked me for a paper and pen. Laboriously, he began to scrawl across an index card I had given him. After a minute or two, he handed the card back to me.

"I'll be waiting for your call," he bellowed as I headed up the stairs. Back in my room, I looked at the index card. It was covered with strange drawings; in one corner, there appeared to be a set of church spires and a cuneiform inscription. Alongside it was what could only have been a self-portrait: a pathetic, bug-eyed creature with a storklike beak. In Roman capitals, he had written the word RAVER next to it. At the bottom, finally, appeared his name and telephone number. Someday, I do plan to call.

When I arrived the next morning at the train station, it was still dark. Yuri was there already with his family. He introduced me to his wife and daughter.

I took him aside. Had he heard anything from Irya, I wondered. He shook his head, and then paused. "You know," he began, searching for the right words. "Irya," he went on, "is a very strong person."

"I just hope she isn't in any kind of trouble. I was afraid that what happened last night had something to do with me."

"No, no," Yuri replied. He looked over my shoulder to where his wife and daughter were waiting, then back at me. "Irya," he said quietly, "has the reputation of being quite . . . voluptuous."

Inside the train, it was freezing cold. To save energy, the lights were dimmed to the faintest possible glimmer. The passengers sat huddled in their overcoats, silently breathing out little puffs of vapor. The train lurched to a start, slowly pulling out of the Ustyug station. I watched Yuri's pretty daughter, her face soft and untroubled, slip slowly into a deep sleep.

CITY OF SKULLS

VORKUTA

THERE ARE NO ROADS TO VORKUTA. In fact, apart from its ramshackle airport, Vorkuta's only link to the outside is a six-hundred-mile-long Arctic railway. One of the northernmost rail lines in the world, it crosses some of the least hospitable terrain in Russia, traversing a region that sees Europe's coldest temperatures and deepest snows. The tracks run to the very brink of the continent, and a spur line climbs over the slopes of the northern Urals to meet the Ob, one of polar Asia's river leviathans.

The railroad's true distinction, however, is that it was built at the instigation of Stalin; built, as it were, of the camps, by the camps, and for the camps. It served as the backbone of the largest concentration of labor camps in all of the Soviet Union: the Pechora basin, the main island group in Solzhenitsyn's *Arkhipelag Gulag*. Even for a time steeped in brutality and horror, the construction of the Kotlas-Vorkuta line stands out. Completed at a breakneck pace during wartime, it is said that two men died for every one of its railroad ties.

It was February, and the snow lay hip-deep in the taiga. The train ran blindly underneath the forest ramparts, a wall of spruce and birch, spruce and birch, mile after mile. Down the short embankments to the edge of the forest ran the footprints of hares, shrews, and other fretful prey. Among the trees, by logical corollary, lurked the shadow of predation.

Traveling for hours and hours this way left one feeling empty, diminished. The scenery — if that is the right word — was a forced meditation on one's own isolation and fragility. This was a wilderness defined by scale rather than by beauty.

Groaning and creaking in the bitter cold, the train stirred up a blizzard of billowing snow and brown diesel fumes. Little settlements clung to the railway's hem like unkempt toddlers. Their names were short, obscure: Tiva, Pilec, Gam. In each place there was a small store, a veteran truck or two, and a row of streetlamps on rough-hewn utility poles, still lit in the faint daylight. Otherwise, none of the villages boasted more than a dozen or so log houses. Waves of snow had washed down over the eaves and rolled up against windows and sheds. The smothering tide of white had drowned everything out-of-doors but the tips of garden fences. Occasionally, a dark figure would hurry down a path. More often, the smoke billowing out of stovepipes was the only sign of life. Always, the taiga wall stood just behind.

In Viled, the waiting room lay empty behind a set of worn doors. A bulldozer-like stationmaster scolded a drunk weaving down the icy platform, her breath leaping out in frosty barks. Buffeted by a stiff wind, the stationmaster struggled to maintain an officious pose. Finally, she waved the train forward with a green baton that looked for all the world like an oversized lollipop.

Viktor and Fyodor were just finishing up a pungent breakfast of Yaroslavskoe beer and canned fish when I first opened the door to my compartment. Viktor was pale and wiry, his eyelids black with fatigue. He wore a wrinkled white T-shirt and grimy jeans. Down his left arm ran a mad canvas of red scars and scratches. He gave me pause; he had the mean, ravaged look of a junkie. Fyodor was sitting on the other side of the pop-up table under the window. He was as big and clumsy-looking as a bruin. His cheeks were round and pudgy, his sandy hair an unkempt, curly mess, his moustache as spare as a twelve-year-old's.

Fyodor beckoned to me to share the remains of their food. He launched into what could be called the "Sears and Roebuck" line of questioning, familiar to generations of Western travelers in what was once the Soviet Union. Back then, there was something both touching and pathetic about these groping efforts to come to terms with the outside world through vicarious shopping. In the Soviet period, the price of a new TV set in the U.S. had about as much relevance to the average Russian as the latest baseball standings. Now, with Russians traveling to places like Poland and Turkey on *shopturs,* these questions had a more practical edge.

"If you don't mind my asking," Fyodor began, "how much does it cost to rent an apartment in America?"

"Well," I said, "it depends on where you are talking about."

"In New York, for example."

"In the center of New York City, in Manhattan," I explained, "it costs thousands of dollars a month to rent a two-bedroom apartment. Sometimes people pay even more than that." Fyodor let out a low whistle of surprise.

"How much does a car cost? I mean a good car, like a Volvo or a Mercedes."

"New? Maybe thirty or forty thousand dollars."

"See? Did you hear that?" Fyodor exclaimed as he wheeled around toward Viktor. "Much cheaper than here in Russia." Viktor acted distinctly uninterested.

Fyodor pressed on. "What are the most popular brands of American sound equipment?" he asked.

"It's all made in Japan. Sony has a very good reputation. There are others that cost less."

"And how much do you have to pay for a video machine?" Fyodor continued.

"You can buy a good one for less than eight hundred dollars," I replied. "The cheapest ones run about three hundred." Fyodor nodded knowingly, and, throwing out the usual script, added, "They're even cheaper in Abu Dhabi. Abu Dhabi has the lowest prices."

Surprised, I probed a bit further. "I hear that the cheapest place to buy electronic equipment is Singapore," I ventured. "No," Fyodor was adamant, "Abu Dhabi is cheaper." After a moment, he added, "I know because I've been to Singapore, too. I served in the Navy."

In fact, Fyodor had only been out of the Russian navy for six months. He had served as a boilerman on the cruiser *Petropavlovsk*. To prove it, he unbuttoned his shirt to display a large tattoo of the ship steaming through high seas.

I asked him how he had liked navy life. *"Skuchno, ochen skuchno,"* he responded, "Boring, very boring."

"But what about your travels?" I insisted. "You must have visited a lot of places."

Fyodor chuckled. "Yes, like San Diego. I sat on the ship for three days and never got to go on shore." When enlisted men did get shore leave, he went on, they had to travel in groups of six led by an officer. They never had much time or money, although that did not keep them from the shopping centers.

"In San Diego, we were tied up right next to your fleet," he recalled. "Your navy eats well! Every morning they have eggs, ham, fresh fruit, coffee. We could smell those breakfasts half a kilometer away. Meanwhile, what did we have? Lousy canned meat." Once, he was issued a can of beef dated 1935. Jokingly, I asked how it had tasted. Fyodor shot back: "It tasted just the way you would imagine!"

Much of Fyodor's time at sea had been spent in the Persian Gulf after Iraq's invasion of Kuwait. His ship had roamed up and down the Saudi and Emirates coast. It even took part in maneuvers with Western ships, until then viewed as their most likely adversaries. However cheap the stereos and VCRs, Fyodor was emphatic that the Gulf was a bore for everyone's sailors. He could not decide which had been more unavailable: the local women or cold beer.

Fyodor also recalled a visit on board the *Petropavlovsk* by U.S. Ambassador to Russia Jack Matlock while the ship was tied up in Vladivostok. When Matlock began to address the crew in fluent Russian, the sailors were flabbergasted. One sailor standing behind Fyodor remarked, "An enemy of the people, and he speaks better than our captain!" This led Fyodor into a brief digression about the idiocy of Cold War propaganda. He had been taught that America was the Soviet Union's enemy, but he always knew that it was all just *krasnopusti*, hot air.

Viktor, who had held his tongue until now, agreed. He did his compulsory military service at a frontier post on the border with Mongolia and as a lookout on the Arctic coast. If he had seen any Americans coming toward him, he said, he would have thrown down his rifle and shaken their hands. But Fyodor did not want to leave me with the impression that they were cowards. With obvious pride, he announced: "My old cruiser could outrun anything in your navy."

The two were returning home to Sosnogorsk after a business trip. Sosnogorsk lies in the taiga below the Arctic Circle, at the end of the last road in the direction of Vorkuta. After Sosnogorsk, there is only the railroad.

Viktor and Fyodor had just managed to register their company, which manufactured furnaces and boilers for everything from large apartment houses to small dachas. Pioneers on the frontier of private enterprise, they were confident about the future. "There is plenty of demand for our boilers, even now in an economic crisis," Fyodor said. Viktor described their firm, which had about fifty employees, in loving terms. What made them especially optimistic was what they described as a technological breakthrough in the world of boilers. Their boiler models, which were designed by a local engineer, would run on "almost any fuel." Even the bribes they had to pay out to government officials to complete all the paperwork had hardly dampened their enthusiasm. *"Krasnopusti,"* commented Fyodor. Their biggest headaches came from all the new taxes, which seemed to increase daily. If times got really bad, he allowed, they would just do a little "trading" on the side.

Unfortunately, I could do little to satisfy Viktor and Fyodor's curiosity about the home heating business in America. I also proved to be a poor student of the innovative features of their heating products. As it was, I had to look up the Russian word for "boiler" in my dictionary in order to understand what the two were talking about.

Luckily, I was able to steer the conversation away from boiler design. I asked Fyodor why his family had moved to the north. His father, he explained, had come to work on the railroad in the fifties. He met Fyodor's mother in Sosnogorsk. Her parents were Ukrainians, who had been exiled there in the thirties. They never talked about what happened, never explained.

Viktor, for his part, ventured not a word about his parents or background. But he did begin to talk about Stalin, about the terror and about the camps, which to this day line the railway north. He spoke with a slight stutter. Viktor described how in the late thirties, executions had taken place right in the center of Sosnogorsk, by the river. There were many unmarked grave sites in the city, he said, sometimes hidden underneath buildings or roads.

Viktor had friends who had spent time in the region's prison camps. It was vodka that had gotten them in trouble. In one instance, a young man was living with his father. One evening, both were drunk and had passed out. The father woke up and tried to rouse his son. The son told his father to leave him alone, but his father persisted, shaking him and trying to pull him out of bed. The son pushed his father away, hard. He fell over and hit the back of his head against a wood stove, splitting open his skull. The father died. The son was sentenced to six years in a labor camp.

On another occasion, two of Victor's friends were sharing a train compartment with a young woman. All three were drunk. Half in jest, one of the men threatened the other with a paring knife. In the pushing and shoving that ensued, he stabbed himself in the neck with his own knife. It sliced open an artery; he bled to death in minutes. His traveling companion got six years in the "zone," as the Soviet prison system has been known since the twenties. The "big zone" is what the prisoners called the Soviet Union itself.

✳ ✳ ✳

In Moscow, before I left, I spoke to Arseniy Roginskiy, a leading member of Memorial. Memorial is a private association dedicated to keeping the memory of the Gulag alive. It has dozens of branches throughout Russia, including one in Vorkuta. Many of its members are former prisoners or their survivors. Others are historians, human rights activists, and journalists.

A Leningrad dissident, Roginskiy was arrested in 1981 and sentenced to four years of hard labor. He served time (the Russian translates literally as "sat") in Ukhta, an oil refining center next door to Viktor and Fyodor's Sosnogorsk.

I found him in a jolly mood. He was the quintessential opinionated Russian intellectual. He drank, chain-smoked, and loved to argue. And he sought out controversy wherever he could find it, as evidenced by his choice of "the history of executions" as a research specialty.

When Roginskiy arrived at his first labor camp, he was shoved from the railroad car along with the other prisoners. Outside, they were confronted by half a dozen guards with machine guns, holding back a cluster of snarling dogs. The guards ordered the prisoners to squat on their haunches. They were told that a step to the right or to the left would be considered an escape attempt; they would be shot without warning. Then, on a whim of the head guard, the prisoners were made to waddle in the same squatting position half a kilometer to their camp.

While there were no longer any "politicals" in the camps, Roginskiy pointed out, the labor camps themselves were still open for business along the Kotlas-Vorkuta railway. He took my railroad atlas and, beginning with Kotlas, drew dark circles in pencil around each camp on the way to Vorkuta. He marked at least ten stops on the railroad, and predicted: "You will see them. They are close to the railroad. And there are many others, too."

With a few more quick pencil strokes, he sketched out the floor plan of a typical "Stolypin wagon," which to this day is used to carry prisoners back and forth along the railway. A refitted passenger car, the Stolypin has a long row of spartan cubicles, each intended for about a dozen prisoners. It also has a pair of armed guards who parcel out food and water, and, when the spirit moves them, escort their charges to the lavatory. The prisoners are crammed into their compartments behind heavy bars and grillwork. The windows have been removed, and those along the corridor are sealed off by heavy metal shutters. Roginskiy recalled once sharing a Stolypin compartment with twenty-six other occupants, squeezed in so tight that it was hard to breathe, let alone move.

No one is really certain how and why these train cars came to be known as Stolypin cars. During most of the nineteenth century, prisoners either walked or rode on horseback to exile or incarceration. In 1896, when Lenin was sent into Siberian exile, he rode in a regular third-class passenger car.

One of Tsar Nicholas II's few capable ministers, Pyotr Stolypin was both a vigorous proponent of agrarian reform and a relentless opponent of revolutionaries. Not surprisingly, this earned him the enmity of both the right and the left. He was shot at the Kiev opera in 1911 by a left-wing terrorist who was alleged by some to be a police agent as well. Stolypin died a few days later; the Tsar, who had been seated nearby at the opera, was deeply shaken.

One account attributes the Stolypin label to the fact that under his tenure, railroad cars with especially large baggage areas were used to transport peasants who wanted to settle on new land in Siberia. These cars had room for the peasants' belongings, including their tools and livestock. Nor did the prerevolutionary "fourth class" prison car have much in common with the Soviet-era Stolypin wagons. The arrested rode like normal passengers, with six persons to a compartment and room enough for luggage.

Solzhenitsyn blames the old revolutionaires — Trotskyists, anarchists, and the like — for the Stolypin label. Even as they were shipped to the camps, they still believed the "bourgeois" Tsarist minister was a greater "enemy of the people" than Stalin, the "proletarian" dictator who was sending them to ideological (and physical) oblivion. Thus, the true Stolypin car was most likely a Bolshevik invention.

The guards who worked the Stolypin cars (and the boxcars that were also used to move prisoners) were renowned for their coarseness and cruelty. Sometimes, they would not distribute the bread and salt herring the prisoners were allotted. Even the water ration, perhaps a cup a day, would be withheld by the convoy guards for days at a time. Needless to say, many prisoners expired even before they reached the camps. Some journeys, say from Kiev to Vladivostok, might take more than a month to complete. The "zeks," as the prisoners were known, figured as the lowest priority freight on the railways.

When the late Andrei Sinyavsky was taken away from Moscow after his trial in 1965, the Stolypin car was still very much part of the prisoner's life:

> All the way it was supposed to be, just what we'd read
> — German shepherds, guards with submachine guns.
> "Left, right, left. I'll shoot without warning . . ." Then
> we seemed to be pulling away. But where to? . . . South
> or north, what difference did it make? We were on our

way. Or seemed to be. I'd never been in a windowless compartment before, where there is only the clack of the wheels to soothe you with the knowledge that you're on your way!

Boiled water, bread, herring were passed out. A stretch of corridor could be seen through the diamond-pattern grillwork on the door. A guard ran by, snarling: "Who needs the latrine?" "Me, me!" They took me out. A soldier ahead of me, a soldier in back of me. "Hands behind you! Don't turn around!" Squinting to the left as I walked, I saw a wall of people, a zoo of eyes, fingers, noses. "Move it! Faster!"

✳ ✳ ✳

I had been wrong about Viktor. He was no addict. Rather, he was the father of two children and the overindulgent owner of an English bull terrier, which had playfully scratched up his arm. Whereas Fyodor's eyes were wide with the world's possibilities, from Peugeot to Panasonic, Viktor's thoughts remained close to home.

Born and bred in Sosnogorsk, he knew half the people in town by name. It was a quiet life, but a full one. He lived in a new two-bedroom apartment, in a building constructed by the factory where he used to work. His neighbors were all friends or old colleagues. Once, as a child, he had gone to the Crimea with his parents. After a few weeks, the Black Sea beaches lost their charm; he never went south again.

During the winter, he and his family skied in the woods. In the summer, they fished under the midnight sun. In those long, magical evenings, it was common to see moose, elk, and bear. Grouse and partridge were abundant, and, Viktor added, made wonderful eating. It was rare to encounter wolves, but they were there too, deep in the forests. On summer mornings, the family went off on mushroom and berry-picking excursions. There were wild strawberries, cranberries, raspberries, and the exquisite golden cloudberry, found only in the north just before the first frosts. "We have the most delicious berries in the world," Viktor boasted. He said it with such conviction that I felt sure he was right.

Not all was well, however, in Sosnogorsk. Viktor's boyhood memories of untrammeled nature had grown increasingly out-of-date. Only
twenty years before, salmon and trout had been so abundant that they
were given away by the local fishermen, or fed to house cats. Now, there
were hardly any fish left. The river, once crystal clear, was polluted.
Choking fumes from the gigantic Ukhta oil refinery regularly drifted
across the city. Nearby, in what was supposed to be a nature reserve, a
bauxite mine was being excavated. The good life was not as good as it
had once been.

The train rumbled forward in the dwindling afternoon light. I
looked at my map, with its phalanx of graphite circles running north
along the rail line, and gazed out the window. Taiga. Snow. Every few
minutes, a hut. Every ten or fifteen minutes, a village.

The train slowed as we came up to a large opening in the forest. I
guessed that this was Veslyana. In my atlas, there was a heavy pencil
mark around it. Suddenly, to the right of the train tracks, I saw the labor
camp. A high wooden fence, topped by wide loops of barbed wire, ran
for perhaps five hundred yards before turning toward the forest. At the
corner stood a low tower, with a guard visible in its cupola. Inside the
compound were rows of barracks and other buildings, black against
the snow. Perched above, like great steel raptors, were three or four
construction cranes. An ominous nest of scrap and refuse occupied one
corner of the compound.

I stood up in the compartment, mesmerized. Viktor looked at me.
"Yes, there is one here," he said simply. I pressed my head against the
window as we pulled into the village station, hoping to keep the camp
in sight. But the train came to a stop alongside a row of freight cars.
Frustrated, I opened the compartment door and walked out into the
corridor. Another set of tracks ran parallel to those we were on. I
leaned against the corridor handrail, waiting impatiently beside the
window.

The train lurched, then slowly started to move out of the station. I
began to turn back to the compartment, but pulled up short. Just below
the window, in the tracks next to us, a clump of prisoners squatted
between the two rails in a tight row of five pairs. Their faces were
young, flushed from the cold. They wore *bushlati*, the rumpled, padded
jackets known to generations of labor camp prisoners. Three armed

guards stood over them; two were stationed at each end of the row of prisoners, the other on the far side of the tracks in the middle. They had their *avtomats* trained on the group. No one spoke. The only sound was the metallic clack-clack of the wheels as the train slowly gained momentum. Without a word, the guards conveyed an unmistakable message: they were in total control. "A step to the right or the left will be considered an attempt to escape . . . " For the prisoners, the torturously drawn-out transit of the train, twenty cars long, must have inspired a silent chorus of longing: a longing for the train's warmth, for the voyager's freedom, for the joy of homecoming. Did they see me, or the other passengers, riding high above? In a moment, we had passed them by in the twilight.

The next stop was named, evocatively, Cindor. It also had a camp; it was even bigger than the one in Veslyana. Surrounded by two long wooden fences capped by dense coils of razor wire, the place was awash in light from its guard towers and rows of stark light poles. Many of the long, low buildings inside the camp perimeter were also lit; one sensed that night itself was banned inside the camp. A crane stirred and then swung eerily over a slag heap that was sloped a hundred feet above the barracks. Smoke belched out of factory chimneys. Somehow, I had imagined the labor camps as *camps* — primitive clearings in the wilderness. Instead, these were Blake's dark satanic mills, diabolically transplanted out of the way of disapproving eyes.

And so it went, for hours, as night fell and deepened. Iosser, Chinyavorik, Yarega, villages walled off by a black pencil from the life of others. The camps had a menacing sameness that suggested they were in fact numberless: infinite banks of lights, walls, guard towers, barracks. Yet just outside their confines, the villages kept up a semblance of normalcy. Children skated down the railroad platforms. Tipsy *muzhiki* in thick felt boots leaned on doorways. Dogs barked at the train and at each other. Behind one window, a woman was serving dinner from a steaming pot to a bald man in an undershirt.

We came to Ukhta, where Roginskiy "sat," and then to Sosnogorsk. I bade goodbye to Viktor and Fyodor, who urged me to visit them in the summer. It was late, and I lay down on one of the lower bunks and felt how the motion of the train mimicked the motion of the country: braking suddenly, slowing to an awkward halt, lurching forward with a banging of the couplings, gathering speed, rocking from side to side, braking again. Next door, I overheard fragments of a conversation, no doubt prompted by these haunted rails. "How was he arrested?" "Stalin understood that . . ." "No matter what you think of Stalin . . ." "My father never told us . . ." And the train rolled on to Pechora, and beyond.

✳ ✳ ✳

Early the next morning, after a restless night of stops and starts and interrupted dreams, I woke to a new world, the world of the Arctic. Sometime in the middle of the night, we had crossed the Arctic Circle. It was not just a mapmaker's abstraction. Fitfully, the taiga was thinning out to a sprinkling of dwarf spruce and birch opening out onto snow flats and rolling hills. The overcast sky was thickly blurred; it looked wrung out, casting light about sluggishly, without conviction.

We had reached a rolling plateau at the base of the Urals, which were just visible to the east. The stunted trees, coated in frost, sheltered dozens upon dozens of white ptarmigans, sitting squat on the branches, unmoved by the train's passing. Where there were no trees, the rotund birds occupied the light poles and electric lines that paralleled the tracks. Each tree, each pole, had snow plastered up along the leeward side; the region's fearsome blizzards had left their mark in the only places the wind could not sweep clean.

The waystations were desolate, ever ruder and lonelier as the train plowed north. The wood *izbas* gave way to mean brick buildings with flat roofs, bleak and featureless. It was ramshackle housing, occupied long past its intended life. Many of the dwellings were half-buried, under siege from drifts that blocked doors and crested over windows. The puny stations were decorated with worn-out Soviet slogans like "Glory to Labor," a particularly shameless formulation for settlements built by prisoners under the barrel of the gun. One doorway was guarded by a stern Lenin portrait, another unabashed icon of the old order. I wondered whether word of the Party's downfall had even reached these parts. Whereas the forest villages had a timeless Russian flavor, these places were hard-bitten reminders of the Soviet period at its cruelest.

As the tundra tightened its grip over the landscape, we stopped more and more often. The railway was now just a single track running over great expanses of snow, flanked by a double line of electric poles. They were the only feature for miles. My eyes, tired from the journey, could not at first glance distinguish land from sky. The white expanse of the tundra met the white horizon as if smeared by a great hand. Only the tufts of grass uncovered by the wind and the scrub cowering in the frozen watercourses defined where the ground had to be. It was as if the world had been compressed, crudely, to a single dimension.

Half a dozen times, we halted to let coal trains from Vorkuta roll by. Today, the city's only rationale was coal. The coal cars, glistening with frost, groaned by, full. Each one was marked in stenciled lettering: "Return urgently to Vorkuta station, Northern Railroad Administration."

* * *

After traveling for hundreds of miles across roadless wilderness, it came as a surprise to see the silhouette of a truck suddenly angling toward the rail line. For some moments, the road it was traveling on was pure supposition. Only the top of the truck's cab was visible. Soon the first truck was followed by another, and another, in a little convoy of vehicles driving from somewhere across the rolling expanse of nothingness. It meant Vorkuta was near.

We arrived with little further warning. A few sheds and warehouses appeared along the line, and then we were braking into the station. As I gazed out the window, putting my belongings together, pulling on my coat, I wondered where the city was. And then the train came to a stop.

Months of passengers coming and going through the snow had pounded the platform into a treacherous patina of gray ice. Compared to the stale, baking heat of the train car, however, the bite of the cold air outside was almost refreshing. Everyone who came off the train was carrying heavy loads, provisions from the faraway world of the capital. They waddled away to the bus waiting in front of the station. Like a broken old maid, it was hunched over to one side, the legacy of too many passengers, too many years on the road. A lucky few handed their loads to family members or friends who had the wherewithal to keep a car. Above a snow pile, a large map highlighted Vorkuta's landmarks and tourist attractions; it showed the city stretching north of the station for several miles. I found a burly, gold-toothed cab driver, negotiated a fare that would have been ridiculously low for Moscow, and headed for the hotel.

A week before I arrived in Vorkuta, the city was buried under a blizzard exceptional even by Vorkuta's outlandish winter standards. The storm was so extraordinary that it was reported on Russia's evening TV news programs. The city's airport, accustomed to almost daily snowfall, shut down for five days. Even the trains, following phalanxes of sturdy snowplow locomotives up the line, struggled to reach Vorkuta. The city registered an astounding six feet of snow in just forty-eight hours.

For a visitor, it presented a phantasmagoric sight. The wind off the tundra had swaddled the town in second-story-high drifts and whisked bulging snow curlicues, like meringue, around apartment house window frames. Hardly a street sign in Vorkuta was legible; they were all plastered over with frost. On one corner, a bank of public telephones was clogged with snow, abandoned to the elements. Walls were weirdly peppered with blots of snow, as if the population had been out pelting the city's buildings with snowballs. Even Lenin's statue, still accorded a place of honor in the central square, was scathed; the leader's gesturing underarms were stuffed with white, and his Tatar features made up into those of a ruined graybeard.

I had expected Vorkuta, too, to be a tottering place full of resentful old men. I was dead wrong. There were more young mothers and babies in Vorkuta per block than in many maternity wards. Perhaps it was attributable to the preponderance of randy miners in the population; or a shortage of contraceptives above the Arctic Circle; or the long polar nights. The moms bustled about the city streets, pushing their bundled charges over the ice in spindly prams or pulling them along in little metal sleds.

Compared with the vast majority of state enterprises, which would never keep step with Russia's market reforms, Vorkuta's mines should have been robust money machines. Everyone needed coal. Tough, proud men drawn from all four corners of the U.S.S.R., the city's miners ought to have been flush with cash. As it was, they were virtual millionaries among Russians. At least on paper, the average miner made more than fifteen times as much as the mayor, and vastly more than a pensioner.

It was this concentrated buying power that fueled the initial spurt of capitalism in Vorkuta. Private shops sprouted up all over the city, peddling the first fruits of Russia's "kiosk capitalism": Korean electronic goods, cheap German beer, American chocolate bars. Some were confined to a cramped toehold in a corner of a cavernous state-run shop. A few entrepreneurs had managed to take over entire stores.

The dirty secret behind the facade of the miners' affluence, however, was that many of them wanted to leave Vorkuta. The magnet of Vorkuta's mines was powerful as long as the pay was good and a miner could count on saving enough money to head back home sometime in the future with a fat grubstake. Otherwise, why subject oneself to the rigors of the nine-month Arctic winter and the numbing, dangerous work down in the mine shafts?

Unfortunately, Russia's raging inflation had wiped out whole lifetimes of savings in just months. Most of the enterprises that purchased Vorkuta coal could not pay their bills; the coal pits, in turn, were also confronted by financial disaster. On average, the miners received their salaries three or four months late; understandably, their mood was increasingly rebellious. Every few weeks, a strike was underway somewhere in the Vorkuta coal fields; deputations regularly went to Moscow to call on the government to resign.

Everyone agreed that tens of thousands of Vorkuta residents would move out immediately if they could. The problem was that no one could afford to. With price controls on housing lifted across Russia, the cost of apartments of all sizes and descriptions had soared. In the country's rudimentary real estate market, owners of newly privatized apartments in the big cities were free to sell or swap their places. So it was conceivable for someone to exchange an apartment in St. Petersburg, for instance, for one in Moscow. But who would want an apartment in Vorkuta? As it was, the city's housing stock was a pathetic shambles, with many people still crowded into communal apartments carved out of barracks erected in the forties and fifties. Plans to retire south to a comfortable apartment or dacha had swiftly become empty daydreams. Today, there were no guards, no dogs, no fences. Yet, for many, Vorkuta was still a place of de facto incarceration.

This was doubly true for the Vorkuta resident who remained dependent on a rapidly eroding state salary. For him, it was hard to sympathize with the miners' complaints. A typical city worker or schoolteacher was making about three thousand rubles a month, the equivalent then of six dollars. It was enough to put food on the table — barely. The other perks that the Soviet way of life had once provided, like cheap champagne from Moldova and cut-rate beach vacations in Bulgaria, had gone by the wayside. The miners, and the young hustlers out to make a fast fortune, could still go out on the town. Everyone else spent their evenings huddled in their apartments, alternately indignant or resigned.

✳ ✳ ✳

I met Vitaly Troshin in the hotel lobby. One of the founders of Vorkuta's Memorial association, he was also the city's chief architect. Troshin had just come from a meeting of the city council. Originally a Leningrader, he had lived in Vorkuta for the past decade. Vorkuta was a natural laboratory for his talents; he was a specialist in polar zone architecture and construction. Slight and intense, with a wispy red beard, Troshin looked remarkably like an Orthodox priest. As I got to know him better, I saw that the resemblance was more than skin deep.

We walked out of the hotel together across a barren, snow-covered square and turned left on Gorky Street. The city's street names remained utterly conventional: the inevitable Lenin Avenue, Red Army Street, and so forth. I commented that the center of Vorkuta looked like a museum of Stalinist architecture. Troshin smiled sadly. He had done what he could to give the city a more human face. Adding flat columns and trim to featureless edifices had helped, but only a little. Every building in the downtown area of Vorkuta could be exchanged one for another, whether office or apartment building. The only exception was the city's indoor swimming pool, which had a whimsical pair of neon dolphins flanking its entrance.

In the thirties, one Soviet architect described the essence of Stalin's socialist realism as "sincerity." Nothing could have been further from the truth. It was as much a part of the "big lie" as the camps. In Vorkuta, as elsewhere, socialist realism meant pompously overblown buildings intended to glorify the Party. It represented the triumph of the monumental over the functional; it was a style for dictators, with all traces of humanism squeezed out. Like its kissing cousins, the architectures of Nazi Germany and Fascist Italy, it was meant to awe and intimidate. Somehow, in the treeless tundra, with nothing from any earlier era to moderate its impact, the handiwork of socialist realism seemed particularly desolate. Today, after the fall of monolithic Sovietism, its uniformity was all the more anachronistic.

We stopped at the top of a bluff overlooking a small ravine. It was cold, very cold. We were buffeted by a wind blowing hard down the little valley. Troshin gestured at some shacks below. "That is where Vorkuta began, in 1933," he explained. He pointed to a clump of rusted machinery and wooden boards. "There's where the first coal mines were." My eyes followed his hand further. "This was one of the main camps for political prisoners in the thirties. Just in the area that we can see, there were thousands of prisoners. To the right, you can see the remains of the brick factory, where the executions took place. There were several mass burial sites nearby. The two apartment buildings on this side were probably built on top of the dead." The wind was blowing snow past us through the ravine. Troshin pointed back toward a power station, half a kilometer away. "That electric plant is on the site of the original power station, which was built by prison labor."

We were standing next to a guard rail. To our left was a marker, about six feet high, topped by a chest-sized boulder wrapped in coils of barbed wire. The plaque on the marker read: "In memory of the victims of the cult of personality, 1933–1953"

Why wasn't Stalin mentioned outright? At first, it seemed to strike a false note. It was Khrushchev who had first coined the term "cult of personality." After all, he was intent on condemning a single man rather than the party of which Khrushchev himself was a part. Yet the camps were also the product of a vast predatory system that masticated its prey with relish. It was inspired by Stalin and his coterie but was always dependent on millions of other hands to help it along: informers and interrogators, guards and petty grandees. They in turn relied on the willing complicity of a whole nation, gulled by a false messiah.

Troshin's office was unmistakably an architect's lair. Hung along the walls in the windowless space were designs, sketches, maps, blueprints.

Dominating one side of the large room was a map of Vorkuta, shaped unmistakably like a human head. As we sipped steaming hot tea, Troshin explained that he had been struck one day by how the outline of Vorkuta, along with its outlying settlements, resembled a skull. The center of Vorkuta lay at its base. The circular highway linking Vorkuta's mines and factories, in a long loop first north and then west, represented the back and the crown of the head. Swinging around to the south, with the town of Promishlenniy as the forehead and Komsomolskiy as the base of a nose, the route headed further down to the base of a long, Hapsburg chin at Mulda before turning back east again to Vorkuta. By the late forties, there were over eighty camps, mines, and "prison installations" arrayed around this circuit. Large and small, served by men and women alike, they were frozen hives of toil, cruelty, and death.

For Troshin, the skull motif became an obsession. After the idea had first come to him, he sat down to draw out the shape, again and again, with different variations and elements. There, in the office, it was everywhere to be seen. It appeared on copies of a Memorial fundraising letter lying on the table; it was the centerpiece of a painting set against a mass gravesite. Spread about the office were scraps of paper with barbed wire, grave markers, crowns of thorns — and skulls, hundreds of skulls. Even as we spoke, Troshin was doodling little guard towers, perimeter fences, a penciled cranium.

Remarkably, Troshin had succeeded in selling his proposal — the idea of building monuments in memory of the camps' victims — to the mayor and the city council. For Troshin, an irrepressible exponent of synergy, it was all part of the effort to bring Vorkuta out of its deep isolation. He saw an intersection of economic, cultural, and social possibilities embodied in the city's somber history and its struggle to find a place in the wider world. Investors would see Vorkuta's potential as an energy source; ecologists would be drawn to the challenges of environmental protection in the tundra; tourists would visit the pilgrimage sites of the Gulag horrors. The mayor even accepted Troshin's skull as a way to present Vorkuta to the rest of the world. It was a unique — and scary — way to promote a city. As usual, Troshin expressed his ideas with a drawing: three intersecting circles uniting such disparate goals as greater business ties, air pollution control, and scholarly conferences on the history of Stalin's camps.

I could not bring myself to tell Troshin that, however elegant, these types of intellectual conceits meant nothing in the real-life scramble for cash-laden foreigners' attention and resources. Businessmen with their eyes riveted to the bottom line would not have the patience to hear out Troshin as he spun out his seamless vision of a polar Utopia. But maybe he knew this already, deep down. By now, Vorkutans were beginning to understand that the exploratory visits of German mining engineers and Japanese investors were just that — exploratory. All over the former Soviet Union, little caravels of hungry dreamers and hustlers were appearing off uncharted shores. If they heard the tinkling of golden bells in the air, they might lower a boat, row through the surf, and open negotiations with the natives. If not, the last that would be seen of them was the top of their masts dropping below the horizon. It was beginning to be obvious to everyone, including Troshin. One could not transform a tough mining town and its unenviable past with a simple wave of the hand.

Troshin led me over to the far side of the office. On a table was the model of a large sculpture complex; chunks of white plaster were piled one on top of the other. It was the work of Russian emigre sculptor Ernst Neizvestny, who lives in New York. Ironically, Neizvestny, a former dissident, is best known for the bust that sits atop Nikita Khrushchev's grave.

Neizvestny paid a brief visit to Vorkuta in 1990, accompanied by his American daughter. He saw the camps, spoke to former prisoners, surveyed the terrain in a helicopter ride. What had come out of his experience in Vorkuta? I looked more carefully at his model. It was made up of row upon row of human heads, stacked one upon another. I imagined it larger, half the size of a football field. It would have something of the quality of an open-air catacomb. It would be powerful; it would awe, genuinely. But there were problems that still needed to be resolved. Where would the money to build it come from? Could something of that scale, in concrete, survive the Arctic winters? A Neizvestny project in Yekaterinburg, where Tsar Nicholas II and his family were executed by the Bolsheviks, had run afoul of the local authorities. Would another of his monuments fare any better here?

Neizvestny's plaster charnel house was to be just one part of an entire complex centered on the site where the first mine was opened, across from the overlook. Troshin showed me his plan. Four points, joined together by imaginary lines, formed a cross. At the base of the cross would be the Neizvestny sculpture, set at the crest of the hillside some distance from where Troshin and I had stood earlier. At the top of the crucifix, Troshin had proposed constructing a Russian Orthodox chapel. It would stand farther down the river embankment, in the direction of the power plant. The left point of the cross was the existing monument on the overlook. From there, forming the right point of the cross on the opposite bank of the river, would be a large gallery, dug out of the hillside. It would be located where the old mine had been. The gallery, too, would be in the shape of a cross. Visitors would enter the structure at its base in the hillside and walk into it as the walls rose up around them. Troshin's eyes shone as he described it. For him, it was already real, tangible.

Vorkuta had always been an oddly cosmopolitan place. Apart from the reindeer-herding Nenei, who crossed and recrossed this particular patch of tundra with supreme indifference, Vorkuta saw little of Homo sapiens before the twentieth century. Yet just before the revolution, geologists discovered rich coal deposits in the region. The first "settlers" were uprooted peasants from Russia, Ukraine, and Belarus, scattered by the tsunami of collectivization. From 1935 on, as the pace of terror began to accelerate, more and more nationalities were tossed ashore. The Vorkuta mines welcomed, if that is the right word, tens of thousands of prisoners from the Soviet republics; they included Georgians, Armenians, Uzbeks, people hailing from every corner of the empire. When Stalin purged the Comintern in 1937, even the elite of the international Communist movement found itself toiling in Vorkuta as "enemies of the people." There were Germans, Poles, Czechs, Hungarians, Chinese. For the most part, the Cominternists were starry-eyed intellectuals and agitators rather than workers or peasants; they died out especially quickly.

Each new midcentury cataclysm brought another wave of victims to Vorkuta. In 1939, Poland was dismembered by Germany and the Soviet Union; the camps filled with captured Polish soldiers. The debacle of the Winter War with Finland resulted in an influx of both Finnish POWs and luckless Soviet soldiers who had "treasonably" allowed themselves to be captured by the Finns. By 1940, the U.S.S.R. had swallowed up its three Baltic neighbors, and tens of thousands of Estonians, Latvians, and

STEERFORTH PRESS

Post Office Box 70

South Royalton, VT 05068

STEER
FORTH
PRESS

Founded in 1993, Steerforth Press is committed to publishing serious works of prose, both fiction and non-fiction. Our interests as publishers fall into no particular category or field and our only tests of a book's worth are whether it has been written well, is intended to engage the full attention of the reader, and has something new or important to say. Steerforth's books should be available at your bookstore, and most booksellers will special order any book not in stock. If you would like to know about other Steerforth books or forthcoming titles, please return this card and we will send you our catalogs twice-yearly at no charge. You may also visit our website at *www.steerforth.com*.

Name

Street Address or Post Office Box

City   State   Zip

In which book did you find this card?

Lithuanians were shipped to the *Vorkutlag,* the acronym of the Vorkuta Prison Administration. After the Nazi invasion of Russia in 1941, the German minority in the Soviet Union was deported to Central Asia, Siberia, or sent to camps like Vorkuta. During the war years, they were joined by members of other ethnic groups considered politically suspect: Crimean Tatars, Chechens, Karelian Finns.

In 1945, Vorkuta was flooded by over one hundred thousand German POWs; many were to spend the next ten years there. Their main camp in Vorkuta was nicknamed "Berlin II." Some of the houses and barracks the Germans built in Vorkuta remain to this day, admired still for their superior workmanship. But disease, hunger, and exposure were to take a heavy toll. In fact, of the three million German prisoners who fell into Soviet hands during World War II, over a third were to die in the hands of their captors.

Troshin, for one, knew how many foreigners had experienced Vorkuta's nightmare years. Survivors of the camps, mostly septuagenarians and octogenarians, were coming back to visit for the first time. Now that Vorkuta was no longer a closed city, Memorial could reach out to the associations of former prisoners in the Baltic states, in Poland, and in Germany. Working together with them, Troshin conceived a series of design competitions for "national" Vorkuta monuments, one for each country. The city would donate the site and contribute to the construction costs. The Lithuanian memorial, set beside a mass gravesite, was close to completion. Designs had been approved for other monuments, including those for Estonia, Latvia, Germany, and Armenia.

Troshin had hung photomontages of the winning designs on his walls. Typically, they featured a drawing of a monument glued to a photograph of the site where it was to be erected. The settings, photographed in black and white, were bleak. They stood in the middle of tundra, amid utility poles, with the outlines of mine shafts and smokestacks in the background. The projected monuments, noble obelisks and arches, were pasted over each wasteland scene. To me, they produced a phantasmagoric effect; the juxtaposition of the ideal and the all-too-real was just too stark. Besides, where would Troshin find the money to bring his vision to life, when the city's budget was barely sufficient to keep Vorkuta running?

I wondered about the accounts of individual prisoners. Had Memorial been collecting oral histories or written accounts? Troshin acknowledged the question, I thought, a bit impatiently. "Oh, yes, yes. We had a big conference here a few years ago. Nowadays, everyone is publishing his account of the camps. A few are worth reading; a lot of others are not."

I pressed him further. What were the best accounts of the Vorkuta camps? For just an instant, Troshin's features hardened. "It's all old hat now. These accounts just repeat the same things we already know. Each individual thinks his experiences were unique, his survival a miracle. They are all old now, and their memory plays tricks on them. So we have to move on to other things. We have to educate people, particularly the young people, about what happened. That way, it won't be as likely to happen again."

One reason Troshin sounded so cynical was that he knew the mentality of the aggrieved *zek* all too well. At the outset of the Gorbachev years, Memorial's focus was squarely on improving the lot of the Gulag survivors, many of whom were living in appalling conditions, denied even their pensions. For years, he listened to their bitter complaints about their dingy communal apartments, their declining health, their confrontations with faceless clerks and partycrats. Sometimes they even turned on Troshin, accusing him of not pushing hard enough or fast enough. Then, like a miracle, the Gulag survivors were granted what they wanted from a Soviet government turned contrite: special pensions, cash compensation, new apartments, and, for some, the most cherished prize of all — official rehabilitation.

What could the accounts of a few individuals tell us, anyway? Troshin spoke eloquently about his monuments. Yet when the subject shifted to the people who actually survived those unbelievably cruel years, he somehow seemed less interested. It was not out of meanness. It sounded callous, but it was not exactly that either. Rather, it was that Troshin was totally absorbed by the moral and ethical issues raised by the camps, their evil in toto. He thought of the camps in abstract terms. The scale of the suffering was such that it seemed to him almost foolish to talk about one or another person's saga. He was looking for something that could capture the darkness in one sweep of the arm, in one powerful symbol. He wanted to find a way to recover God from the bones and the rubble.

* * *

One peculiarity of Stalin's regime was its propensity for devouring its own children, something in which it far surpassed anything seen in Hitler's Germany. Veniamin Vasilev was a typical example. I stumbled onto his story in Vorkuta's main bookstore, in a volume of former prisoners' reminiscences. It was a cheaply bound edition; its ruble price, a year after publication, was now worth just a few cents.

Vasilev grew up in Leningrad, in a working-class family. Both his father and his oldest brother died fighting for the Reds during the Russian Civil War. His mother served on the Leningrad Soviet. In the early twenties, Vasilev led the collectivization campaign in a rural district. His methods were typical for the day; he would begin his "discussions" with the peasants by placing his revolver on the table. In his next job, he helped arrange for the shipment of the red marble used to build Lenin's mausoleum. He served as an officer in the Border Guards, then, as today, a branch of the secret police. He even named his son Genrikh, in honor of Genrikh Yagoda, Stalin's NKVD chief.

Then, in June 1936, Vasilev was arrested. He was working as the Party representative at a Leningrad factory. The knock on the door came at 6 A.M. Like so many others, Vasilev thought there had been some kind of mistake. He was not guilty of anything! At the prison a few hours later, Vasilev asked his interrogator why he had been arrested. He was told, "You know better than we do!"

Vasilev refused to sign a confession. His terrified boss was brought into the prison as a "witness" to his crimes. Still, Vasilev held out. Finally, in September, he was ordered once more to sign. A former Komsomol colleague had "confirmed" his participation in the "opposition." When Vasilyev once again refused, he was beaten. The investigator was unruffled by Vasilyev's resistence; he informed him that his refusal to sign had "no significance." He was sentenced to five years for "counterrevolutionary Trotskyist activities" and sent to the camps. It is worth noting that even in the thirties, this was a relatively short sentence. By the standards of the forties and fifties, when fifteen and twenty-five year sentences were handed out routinely, it was hardly more than a slap on the wrist.

Vasilyev was first shipped to Kotlas in a Stolypin car; his send-off, like Sinyavsky's, was a nightmare of snarling guard dogs and sobbing family. From the infamous transit prison in Kotlas, the *zeks* in his "convoy" were shipped by barge down the Severnaya Dvina River. Before the railroad was built, the journey north to Vorkuta took months rather than days or weeks; it was made by boat and on foot. But by late October, the river routes to Vorkuta were already freezing over. Another task lay ahead for Vasilyev and his companions.

Halfway to Vorkuta, Vasilyev's convoy was sent to build a road through the taiga. Trudging behind two great wooden sledges pulled by a heavy tractor, the prisoners marched out each day into the mud, and as winter swiftly advanced, into the snow and bitter cold. They were worked until they were exhausted, delirious, until the desire to simply let themselves fall down into the snow was almost overwhelming. At their base camp, they returned at night to log barracks kept thawed by a kerosene stove, to eat their meager rations of flour and groats. Otherwise, far into the forest, they huddled in sodden dugouts, slept on pine branches, supped on a thin broth of boiled bones. Before long, dysentery set in; five or six already half-dead men expired each day. Their bodies were thrown into pits, dug out of sight of the other *zeks*, and their names crossed off the camp list.

Vasilyev, too, came down with dysentery. The camp commandant walked past his cot and growled: "We've ordered a coffin for you — you son of a bitch." In fact, the camp had just three rough-hewn pine coffins, which were used over and over again; they were used to transport the dead only as far as the pits in the forest. It was a far-sighted economy measure typical of the Gulag.

Was what saved Vasilyev anything but a miracle? The commandant's orderly was a former Russian Orthodox bishop who would accompany the official on his rounds, holding a lantern. He witnessed the exchange between his master and the dying prisoner, and decided to look after Vasilyev. Although disease was spreading like wildfire in the camp, the bishop was fearless. Even after Vasilyev had soiled himself, the bishop washed and fed him. The irony that this man of the cloth, condemned by the Communists, had come to the rescue of a confirmed atheist and former secret policeman was not lost on Vasilyev.

Vasilyev had turned a corner away from oblivion; to survive, one needed just this kind of iron will and breathtaking luck. He recovered from his illness, and was assigned to build wheelbarrows in a special carpentry brigade, despite the fact that he was hopelessly unqualified as a carpenter. The work was still very hard. Yet if one were lucky enough to be spared a "general assignment" — in other words, an assignment in the mines, in road or rail construction, or in lumbering — one's chances of survival were much greater. When Vasilyev was finally transferred north, toward Vorkuta, he learned just how many of his original group of six hundred had survived one winter of road building in the taiga. Only 242 names were left on the list.

For the political prisoners, coming face to face with the Gulag's genuine criminals was one of the toughest shocks of all. In the twisted logic of the Stalinist era, the murderers, thieves, and rapists who inhabited the camps were — however misguided — still "socially friendly elements," capable of redemption. They were not "counterrevolutionaries" and "class enemies" like the political prisoners. Correspondingly, the felons had it relatively easy. They were rarely assigned the killing work. They stole from the "politicals" with impunity. Unlike the political prisoners, they were allowed to receive food packages. Some slick operators even wormed their way into camp administration roles. It was all natural enough; the hoods were more at home in the camps than in the outside world. The officials and guards who made a brutal camp system function could readily understand, even respect, the rough world of the criminals, where the strong ruled and the weak were robbed, beaten, killed. At times, that respect was even tinged with fear. There were plenty of instances in which the criminals were given a wide berth to manage their own affairs inside a camp — almost always to the detriment of the "politicals."

Rather than suffering at the hands of the reprobates, Vasilyev won them over. In border guard school, he had learned how to play the accordian. This soon came to the attention of the big boss of the camp mafia, who summoned him. A sentimental man and a music lover, this king of the thieves worshiped the gypsy folk songs that Vasilyev played. From then on Vasilyev was under his protection, a "blood brother."

Vasilyev was less lucky with the camp guards. Although most everyone recognized it as pure charade, a Gulag ritual required a camp's duty officer to regularly ask the prisoners if they had any complaints. Once, to the astonishment of his fellow prisoners, Vasilyev pointed out a guard who had stolen tobacco from him. The guard walked briskly up to him and, in front of the officer and the ranks of prisoners, punched Vasilyev in the face, knocking him to the ground. It was weeks before he could see properly again. By then, he and his group had been sent north by barge to Ust-Vorkuta, a tiny river port one hundred kilometers south of Vorkuta proper. There he spent the summer loading and unloading the barges that supplied the camps during the thirties. He and his fellows worked on a daily food ration of one hundred grams: eighty grams of flour, twenty grams of sugar.

Between the port on the Usa River and the early mining settlement ran Vorkuta's first railroad. Its nickname among the prisoners said a great deal about how it ran: the "little rocking rails." It was a narrow-gauge job, serviced by midget locomotives not much taller than a man. It pulled baby-sized flatcars north to Vorkuta, piled high with lumber and sacks of provisions, and hauled coal back to the barges for shipment south. The train also carried newly arrived prisoners to the mines. It took eight to ten hours to cover the sixty-four kilometer route. The first great wave of *zeks* to reach the Pechora Basin had built the railroad — the so-called *kulaks*. By the time Vasilyev arrived, there were practically none left alive. Even today, laying track across open, rolling tundra requires real engineering acumen and state-of-the-art machinery. These unfortunate peasants, ripped from their lands in the fever of collectivization, had to do it by hand, at gunpoint, with the most rudimentary tools imaginable.

Already, as the line's moniker suggested, the rails were coming apart. With each thaw, with each freeze, the little railroad would sink deeper into a summer bog, or pitch farther to one side or the other of an embankment. The railroad cars waddled down the track like ducks. Frequently they were actually pitched off. A clip from a blotchy propaganda newsreel I saw in Vorkuta shows a miniature locomotive creeping along the tracks, dragging flatcars full of coal. A smiling work crew stands alongside proudly, waving. The front of the engine carries a slogan: "The North will be conquered!"

Before long, Vasilyev was sent to the mines. In the summer of 1937, there still was no real town. The settlement was centered on the "Old Mine," as the first Vorkuta pit is now called; it was made up of a few canvas tents and log barracks. A large piledriver with a winch hung from the hillside above the river. Coal wagons were lined up by the entrance to the mine shaft. The ramshackle cluster of buildings, shelters, and worksites was lit feebly by the power plant just downriver. Construction on the new Vorkuta across the riverbank had only just begun. All around, there was nothing but tundra.

One became a Gulag miner the way one became a political prisoner: by being thrown in the deep end. Vasilyev was given no training whatsoever; the camp officials figured that their charges would learn from their cuts and bruises. If not, it was just one less "class enemy" to feed. Before entering the mine, everyone was searched; items on the prohibited list, plausibly enough, included cigarettes and matches. You were given a miner's pick and a wick lamp with a hook on the top — and sent in. There was no elevator down to the four hundred-meter level. Instead, you walked below on uneven wooden steps, under dank, dripping roofing, groping your way into the mine, your own lamp the only light to guide you. You reached the bottom, and the foreman, a real miner serving time in the camps, pointed you toward the shaft you were to work in. Sometimes it would be just over a meter high: black, wet, slippery, perilous.

On Vasilyev's first day in the mines, the foreman told him to pry support braces free from the loose coal left behind by the previous day's blasting. After pulling them away, he was then to haul the beams back down the shaft for reuse. With this cursory explanation completed, the foreman scampered away. Why wait to critique the newcomer's technique, when one false move might bury them both under a deluge of coal?

Alone now in the tunnel, Vasilyev tried to pull himself together. Above him, something cracked loudly, and debris clattered about nearby. He imagined meeting his end either crushed under a collapsing wall, or pinned underneath a support log. Then he heard someone moving something above him. It meant that he wasn't alone. He felt better, hung up his lamp, and began to work. He banged his helmetless head repeatedly and cut open his hands and knees. Then, after an hour or two, his lamp went out. He felt his way back out of the gallery, up the steps, until his strength gave out.

But there was nowhere else to go. He headed back down. And before long he had almost grown accustomed to life in the mines, to working like a beast day in and day out. There were no radios, no newspapers, no letters, no days off. Only a few "carrots" were extended to the prisoners. A clubhouse was erected at the mine, and some days there were concerts and plays put on by the *zeks*, even film shows. When he had the strength, Vasilyev played drums in the camp's jazz band.

Two years later, in 1939, Vasilyev was nearly killed in a cave-in. Badly injured, his arms and legs pinned under debris, alone in the cold and tomblike blackness, he was ready to die. But instead, after lying unconscious on the mine floor for hours, he was rescued. His luck had held. Nine prisoners were killed, including the mine's model worker, who had set record after record for individual production in the vain hope that he would be released early from the camps.

After two weeks in the prison clinic, his legs still in great pain, Vasilyev was sent to work in the canteen. It was one of the best assignments imaginable. The canteen served over a thousand prisoners, and all of them would have done anything to work there, close to the steamy warmth of the kitchens. To illustrate the point, the canteen was run by a tough, shrewd criminal known as "Black Sasha," who was so well set up in the camps that he surrounded himself with his favorites; he even maintained a male lover.

Unfortunately, Vasilyev's sojourn there ended after only a few months when a baby mouse was discovered in a soup pot. He and the other night shift workers were arrested; in fact, he almost received an extra sentence. Never mind that prisoners died every day from exhaustion, malnutrition, accidents in the mines, or even from an executioner's bullet in the back of the head. The culprits of the mouse scandal might be "wreckers," bent on sabotage. They had to be punished.

Not long after, though, a new, "progressive" camp commandant arrived (his predecessors had all been shot). In the mythology of Stalin's propagandists, the overarching purpose of the Gulag camps was not so much punishment as rehabilitation, correction through honest socialist labor. Most of the population, at least those whose loved ones had not been taken away by the security police, probably believed this. So, in keeping with this benevolent ethos, the new *Vorkutlag* administration decided to organize a brass band. Vasilyev's musical talent was by then well-known around the Vorkuta camps, so he was assigned to the ensemble. Even as a "professional musician," however, the prisoner retained his obligation to haul wood from railroad wagons, build barracks, and clear snow. But it was freedom from the mines, and thereby another commutation of a virtual death sentence. Half the day was spent as a regular *zek;* the other half was spent in rehearsals. The band played not only for prisoners, but also for civilians ("voluntary" miners from other parts of the Soviet Union were beginning to arrive in Vorkuta). If the band played at a dance or a banquet, the band members could sometimes wolf down the leftovers. As the new town on the other bank of the river began to grow, the free workers would even come over to the camps to dance at the prisoners' club. Soon, the band became an orchestra. Former musicians, sentenced as saboteurs, became valued soloists. A drama group was formed; it put on plays by Moliere, Chekhov, and Gorky (although Gorky's "The Lower Depths" was banned by camp authorities).

Yet there was no denying that this was Vorkuta. One night, the lead actress, a head-turning beauty, was led off the stage by a guard in the middle of a performance. She was dressed in nothing but a nightgown. She was taken away to one of the camp's NKVD bosses, who had taken a fancy to her. The curtains closed, and the prisoners waited. When she was finally brought back to complete the performance, she hid her tear-stained face behind her hands. The prisoners stood, in silence, until she came out on stage. What became of her? Her husband had already been executed by a firing squad. Within a few years, she too disappeared from Vorkuta, and perhaps from our world.

Time and time again a match was struck, flaming up brightly for a moment, only to be shaken out with a flick of the wrist and tossed aside. Albert Lucie was an African-American jazz musician, drawn from Depression-era America to the promise of a new socialist world. He toured the Soviet Union in the thirties, and decided to become a Soviet citizen. No sooner had his citizenship been granted than he was arrested and shipped to Vorkuta. He arrived, Vasilyev recalled, carrying a sumptuous leather suitcase and wearing part of his performance wardrobe: a white tuxedo jacket over a "Zulu" grass skirt. Before long, he became the biggest star the orchestra had. He was granted his own shelter along with a daily allowance of coal — unheard of luxuries for a prisoner. The women in the camp found him irresistible, including, it turned out, a female NKVD officer. Once word of that peccadillo got out, Lucie's days as a star were numbered. Subjected to "general assign-ment" work, he did not last long. His resting place is one of very few in Vorkuta that is known by name to this day: "the Negro's grave."

Only in June does the ice break up on the Vorkuta River. Each spring, the rising water and racing ice floes would wash away the makeshift bridge joining the old mining camp from the new city rising up on the opposite bank. It was a matter of considerable inconvenience, since with-out a bridge there was no way to get the coal across for shipment. Finally, in 1940, the camp administration devised another solution; the officials decided to rely on a boat pulled across the river by a cable and pulley. Its inaugural run was to be festive; the first group was made up of the entire camp orchestra along with a contingent of officials and guards. On the shore were another eight hundred prisoners under guard, waiting their turn to be served up for the experiment — to see if the vessel could be expected to carry precious loads of coal. Once in the boat, the musicians all sat down, but the camp bosses would not stoop to sit beside their charges. The vessel was hopelessly overloaded; the boatman could barely see in front of him. Halfway out into the surging river, the boat collided with a large ice floe. It capsized instantly, tossing officials, guards, and prisoners alike into the frigid water.

No one on the riverbank budged. It would have meant a bullet in the back for any prisoner who tried to help in the rescue. The people in the water were swept rapidly downstream. Vasilyev, barely able to keep himself afloat, watched as one musician, an elderly trumpeter, slipped beneath the water. Some three kilometers downriver, Vasilyev managed to reach the shore, all feeling gone in his arms and legs. Escape was out of the question; with the help of a passerby, he stumbled back through the snow and tundra to the camp. Two musicians, two camp officials, and one guard had drowned. As had the orchestra; all of its instruments were at the bottom of the river. The very next morning, the musicians were back at work in the mines.

Another year passed. Vasilyev, by now a wily survivor of camp life, had gotten himself transferred first to a railroad job, then back to the reconstituted camp orchestra. The end of his sentence was approaching. Would he be freed, or would he have his sentence extended, a common occurrence in those years? Only when the camp official asked him where he wanted to resettle (he was prohibited from returning to

Leningrad, or living in any of the major Soviet cities) did he know for sure that he would be set free. He wanted to go where it was green and warm: he chose the Cherkass, in Ukraine.

Five years before, he had left Leningrad stoically, but now, bidding his fellow *zeks* goodby, he broke down and cried. His route took him back south along the Ust-Usa River toward Kotlas. Then, he heard the news: the Nazis had invaded. It was June 22, 1941. Groups of NKVD soldiers were stopping boats and trains, pressing into military service anyone born after 1895. Released prisoners were to report immediately back to their camps. But Vasilyev and two comrades had already smelled freedom and were not about to turn around toward Vorkuta. Into the forests they disappeared.

Troshin had known Vasilyev, who died in 1992. "A nice man," he commented simply. Then he handed me a copy of Adda Voitolovskaya's memoirs.

✳ ✳ ✳

Trained as a historian, Voitolovskaya was the epitome of her class and generation: a young scholar and mother of two, with faith in a brighter future. But it was not to be. In the wake of the Kirov assassination, which set in motion the worst years of Stalin's terror, her husband was arrested. Not long after, she was dismissed from her job and exiled from Leningrad, along with her son and daughter. From then on, as she writes, her life had "no rhythm, no goals, no plans, no answers. Only questions."

She was arrested on the night of April 1, 1936. Her six-year-old son ordered the secret policemen to leave. They offered him candy, but he would not quiet down until they had left him alone with his mother. They were driven to the home of the children's grandparents in a Black Maria. There, Voitolovskaya watched as the children were led away. Her son cried out, "Mama! Hold my hand, I'm scared!"

The interrogator's first words were the conventional ones: "Now, tell me about your counterrevolutionary activities. We know all about them, from top to bottom." She was presented with a sixteen-page confession to sign, one which implicated her own mother, sister, and brother-in-law as members of "an underground Trotskyist counterrevolutionary group." She never signed, but received a five-year sentence anyway.

The same autumn as Vasilyev, she was shipped north. Eventually, she found herself in a tiny settlement called Sivaya Maska, the last camp before Vorkuta. She was part of a group of three hundred men and eight women. There was nowhere to live; the men set to work building dugouts in the October snow, dressed in the summer clothes in which they had been arrested.

At this time, the Vorkuta camps were run by Efim Kashketin, a rapacious thug even by the standards of the Gulag. To this day, the mention of Kashketin brings a hush in Vorkuta; Troshin showed me a picture of him that spoke volumes. His eyes were as terrifying as a tiger's; over half a century later, they still pounce out of his photograph with sulfurous intensity. His NKVD personnel file described him as "a good worker." It added, wrongly, "his failings have been greatly exaggerated."

Kashketin took over a large, dilapidated brick kiln and transformed it into one of the most notorious execution sites in the history of the Gulag. Before he, too, was arrested, he had thousands taken to the *kirpichni zavod*, where they were shot in the back of the head like cattle, then stripped of their clothes and valuables. He frequently joined the firing squads himself. Anguished graffiti appeared on the walls of Vorkuta's prison barracks: "It's a lie that spring brings joy. Spring 1938 brings death."

Voitolovskaya's first job was as a nurse. The men she saw in the camp's rudimentary clinic felled timber in the last stunted forests before the tundra. As the months went by, they had to venture farther and farther away from Sivaya Maska to meet their production quota. If they did not fulfill their "norm," their bread ration might fall as low as three hundred grams a day. To bring the lumber back, some *zeks* were pressed into service as "VRILO workers" — in the antiseptic terminology of the camps, "temporarily serving in the capacity of horses."

Most of the tens of thousands of women in Vorkuta's camps had one thing in common; they were mothers whose offspring had been taken away by the authorities. Voitolovskaya was luckier than many in that she had been able to leave her son and daughter with her parents. Many other mothers lost track of their children altogether. These children were the most undeserving of all of Stalin's victims; first their fathers, then their mothers, had been arrested and sent away. They were shipped en masse to orphanages and remade according to the merciless code of the time. They were given family names like Forgotten,

Homeless, and Abandoned, or simply labeled in accordance with the cities and towns from which they were taken: Orlov, Zhitomirskaya, Vladimirov, and so on. The children were to love only the Party and their country; their parents were portrayed as bloodthirsty traitors. From this frosty bosom, they went into an indifferent world to become criminals, schizophrenics, suicides.

This heartrending loss weighed heavier than anything else on the mothers. One woman from Baku had refused to leave the lobby of the NKVD headquarters until she learned the fate of her arrested husband. Days later, a clerk took her aside and told her that her husband had been defenestrated at the end of an interrogation. The clerk's advice was to flee the city immediately with her children. Instead, she fell to the street, hysterical, crying out for justice. She was arrested that very night; the children were sent to an orphanage. Three years later she died in Voitolovskaya's clinic, completely out of her mind with grief. Rather than eating, she asked repeatedly that the food be sent to her children because she was convinced that they were starving.

One of Voitolovskaya's tentmates was a twenty-year-old student, arrested fresh from the university in Saratov. Still a child, she was exuberant and fun-loving; she spoke of her parents endlessly. One day, she received this letter from her father:

> *I have only just found out that you are truly an enemy of the people, one of those who interferes, stands in the way. I can't forgive myself that I didn't detect this during your childhood. After everything that has become known to me, you cannot count on letters, nor on support from my side.*
> *P. Ivanov.*

The next day, she hung herself.

✳ ✳ ✳

Troshin bundled me and Volodiya, a young TV cameraman and producer, into a black Volga sedan. We were going to follow Vorkuta's great circle route that links the different mining communities to the city proper.

After a few hundred yards, our driver stopped the car. He got out, walked around it, and returned with a disgusted look. Throwing the

Volga into reverse, he abruptly drove us backward off the road into a snowbank. Troshin and Volodiya continued to converse, utterly unflustered. The driver got out again, opened the trunk, pulled out a shovel, and began to dig around a rear tire. Troshin paused, and then looked over at me. "You see," he explained, "there is no tire jack." Ten minutes later, the driver was sweating profusely, but the spare tire was on. We were invited outside to give the car a push.

Past the city limits, the sense of desolation grew. Empty but for an occasional dump truck skittering by, the road was glazed over with black ice. Unspoiled tundra has a spare beauty, but man had made this a wasteland. Scattered along the road were cinderblock buildings in all shapes and sizes: mines, factories, warehouses, depots, even one or two military installations. The sun had crept up above the edge of the horizon. It was almost noon.

We pulled over along a straight stretch of highway. In the near distance loomed a large mine shaft tower; behind it, a fat plume of smoke curved skyward from a tall brick chimney. I pulled the ear flaps of my hat down and stepped out of the car.

The burial site was just to the right of the road. The crosses were buried in the snow up to their crossbars. Some stood straight, defiant; others leaned and sagged from the yearly bullying of the tundra's freeze and thaw cycle. Not many of the markers were original; for years, a few caring hands had quietly replaced the crosses that had fallen over and disintegrated. Some were made of roughly hewn wood, others of wrought iron. They bore industrial letters and numbers, like bulk lots of detergent or shoes. One read A-85; another N2-3. Troshin explained that each one designated where dozens, even hundreds of prisoners were buried. The bodies had been quickly, carelessly pushed into the meager layer of earth between the surface and the permafrost. In the summer, one literally walks through the remains.

Across the way, something was clanging heavily at Mine Number 29. It was here, in the summer of 1953, that the *zeks* rose up in revolt. Like everywhere else in the Soviet Union, the news of Stalin's death in March had struck Vorkuta like a thunderbolt. Wild rumors of an amnesty raced through the camps. By July, though, no changes were in sight.

The miners' strike was well organized. Their first move was to round up all of the criminals in the camp and put them in one building, under guard. A miners' militia was organized, and food laid in. On one of the barracks, the strikers wrote in large letters: "To the motherland — coal; to the miners — freedom!"

Only in the Gulag could their demands have been seen as seditious. Permission to cut their hair, remove their prison numbers from their jackets, institute a system of incentives for good work, unrestricted mail privileges, the removal of bars from the windows of the barracks: these were the items that made up the strikers' manifesto. A special commission arrived from Moscow, heard out the miners' representatives — then ordered the camp surrounded by heavily armed soldiers. The next day, a group of officers entered the camp for "negotiations." One of them began to take pictures of the strikers. They in turn grabbed the camera away from him and smashed it against a rock. The officers marched out; shortly afterward, the soldiers opened fire. It was sunny and warm; most of the miners were outside of the barracks. Over fifty died. The others were arrested for "organizing an armed revolt against the Soviet government."

We drove on. Turning away from the main highway, the driver followed a plowed track in the snow across half a mile of open tundra. Free of the pavement, the wheels spun noiselessly toward what looked like another factory. My hosts had stopped talking; they were concentrating on locating our next destination. Moments later, we saw it.

The remnants of the abandoned labor camp were somehow smaller than I had imagined. The surviving guard tower looked like a duck blind on stilts; the outer perimeter fence posts were just birch logs jutting out of the snow. Even the leftover strands of barbed wire, hanging down limply along the fence, seemed innocuous enough. Elsewhere, it all might have passed for a pay car lot that had gone out of business.

Still, there was a lingering scent of menace. The inner fence posts were topped by a horizontal bar that jutted several feet away from the interior of the camp; the cross piece on the inside of the enclosure was closed off at an angle, presumably to deter anyone daring enough to try to climb out. From a distance, it looked, aptly enough, like a row of gallows. Slowly, methodically, I ventured out into the snow, sinking up to my waist with each step. I felt the barbed wire through my gloved hand; I was standing at the edge of the death strip, the outer edge where only free men stood. "There are only a few places like this left," Volodiya said.

Almost all of the other camps had been shorn of their buildings and enclosures; wood is precious in the tundra, both to build and to burn.

Kashketin's brick factory was pulled down long ago. The one that we parked beside was built a few years after his execution; perhaps it had never been used in the same way. The site had once been occupied by a camp; now it was a cement plant. The big kiln was all but invisible under the snow, a long mound surrounded by discarded oil drums and higgledy-piggledy steampipes.

The wind was tugging at my *shapka*, pushing at my coat. Wisps of snow snaked over the top of the kiln. Troshin pointed to an opening in the snowbank, crowned by a rusted girder. I climbed in, sliding down a chute of loose snow. Suddenly, it was quiet. I was in an eerie brick cavern, dark and somber. A gallery extended fifty yards to my left. The only light came from the opening in the roof I had clambered down and another at the end of the kiln. The floor was earth, the only earth I ever saw in Vorkuta. For longer than I realized, I stood there, out of the world above. Later, Troshin told me that he had called out my name; I heard nothing. The only sound was my breathing and the blood pounding in my ear. I held my breath for a moment. It was the most utter silence I have ever known, the silence of the grave.

* * *

On my last day in Vorkuta, it turned colder. The wind blew down the city's bleak avenues with an almost animate anger; it growled and moaned like a guard dog roused from its sleep. On my hotel window sill, the snow had blown inside in a miniature drift, defiantly refusing to melt.

My first stop was the local music school. A group of teachers, dedicated to keeping alive the songs of the Vorkuta camps, had formed a quartet called "Ballada."

They looked a bit out of sorts. One of the musicians fidgeted uneasily with his guitar. Were they simply nervous about performing for a foreigner? No, I was told later, it was the school's director that they feared. He was an old-timer who did not think much, apparently, of their peculiar vocation. Never mind that most of Russia's great folk songs sprang from the throats of Cossacks and thieves. There was still an illicit aura about these Gulag-era songs. Until a few years ago, they were only played in kitchens or around campfires. Even one of the musicians commented, in an aside, "It's not really music."

They should not have been so apologetic. Their ensemble of two guitars, accordian, and bass balalaika had the heart of an orchestra. And no language has more poetic possibilities than Russian. Who could imagine such lyrics in our businesslike English? The songs — alternately plaintive, mischievous, proud — were the real, sooty voice of Vorkuta.

One refrain went like this:

> *Across the tundra, along the wide road*
> *Where the Vorkuta/Leningrad express rushes by,*
> *We escaped, two friends afraid of the sirens,*
> *Afraid of the pursuers and the shouts of the soldiers.*

Another song, entitled "Coal From the Vorkuta Mines," had a mournful quality, like an old church dirge:

> *Coal from the Vorkuta mines*
> *Burns with a hot flame*
> *Every chunk of coal*
> *Is washed by the blood of a "zek."*

Through it all, the prisoners never lost their sense of humor. In "Song about Stalin," they even put the lie to the Great Leader's overblown rhetoric:

> *Now rain, now snow, now gnats upon us,*
> *And we're in the taiga from morning until late at night.*
> *Here from sparks you made a blaze;*
> *Thank you, I'm warmed to the bones.*
>
> *We carry our difficult cross for nothing*
> *In frost, fog and in melancholy rain,*
> *And, like trees, we fall over onto our plank beds*
> *Free from our insomniac leader.*

You appear in our dreams, when in party cap
And tunic you go on parade.
We chop down forests by the Stalin method, and the chips,
The chips fly all around.

Not everyone was ready to hear this music. Troshin had warned me about the city museum. It was a hopelessly schizophrenic shrine, where the "new" history of the camps had been grudgingly pasted onto a decades-old exhibit on the glories of Sovietism in the Arctic. When the woman who led me around spoke glowingly of the builders of Vorkuta, she meant, unfortunately, the camp bosses and party officials who oversaw the whole sham "conquest" of the tundra.

The guide seemed to have been pruned down to two emotions: resentment and fantasy. As she recounted the exploits of one of the first young woman Komsomol volunteers who came in the thirties to build socialism, her eyes — wildly smug — burned with intensity. Stern-jawed officers in NKVD uniforms, exhausted miners smiling deliriously, a meeting room packed with assenting hands: these were her heroes of Vorkuta. When a note of skepticism crept into my questions, her voice rose a few more decibels. "When people can look at the history of the city objectively again, they will understand the contribution that these figures made," she said, barely keeping herself under control. Right away, I saw that she hated me, deeply and passionately. I was an American, and for this not-so-old ideologue, that made me the enemy. It must have hurt her pride, but she tried to be ingratiating long enough to convince me to buy a scarf from a friend. I declined.

✳ ✳ ✳

It was time to go visiting. The thermometer under the portico read minus sixteen degrees Celsius, rather agreeable for the late afternoon at this time of year. What light there was came from glowing mustard streetlamps, each illuminating a wide blob of yellow snow underneath. Troshin and I trudged up and down embankments from one apartment house to another, following narrow paths pounded out of the snow by hundreds of booted feet. There were no conversations to overhear; in the winter, one does not linger on Vorkuta's city streets any longer than necessary. All one is aware of is the cold, the dark, the huffing vapor of one's breath, and the cacophonous chorale of feet scrunching and squeaking along to their destinations.

Troshin was quick and nimble, his legs as expert on the ice as an Eskimo's. Unfortunately, I tackled the downhill portions without the same aplomb. Once, I nearly bowled over a heavyset woman marching briskly up the path with sacks of groceries in both hands. Every minute or two, an impatient Troshin would stop, look back, and survey the dim courtyards and alleys behind to see whether I was still there or if I had completely lost his scent.

We entered an apartment building, walked through a dingy hallway lined with battered blue mailboxes, and climbed four flights of stairs. There was no elevator, a common tribulation in apartment blocks outside of the big cities. We knocked on a door padded with spongy imitation leather and were ushered in by a woman whom we had obviously just drawn out of a steaming hot kitchen. She greeted us warmly and motioned for us to follow her into the living room.

I was not alarmed to have a hostess order me to *razdevatsya,* or undress — it is only the customary signal to remove one's coat in an apartment's vestibule. Of course, there is more to this ritual than first meets the eye. Russians do not give it a thought, any more than Americans reflect on the inner significance of a trip to the supermarket. But one goes through an important transformation in that doorway. You remove your heavy winter coat, your fur hat, your dripping boots, your scarf, and perhaps even a sweater, and you are a new person. You are hanging up a suit of armor, and in doing so giving up the anonymity with which you joust at the hostile world outside. You put on a pair of *tapochki,* or slippers, and pad into the warm embrace of your host's apartment. In these few moments, the sullen public world outside, so unsettling to foreigners, melts into the inner world of private Russian lives, where everything that is good in Russia resides.

Vladimir Timonin outlived both Hitler's concentration camps and Stalin's Vorkuta mines — a rare distinction. Although born in the Ukraine, there was almost nothing Slavic about him. His face, broad as a bull's, seemed oddly Mediterranean. His features were as mobile as a Turkish shopkeeper's, his jet black mustache and full wiry hair those of a man half his age. Even his ample paunch did not weaken the impression of power and energy that he projected. No wonder he was a survivor.

Timonin was captured by the Germans in 1941, during the opening weeks of the war. At first the Nazis put him in a forced labor brigade. Later, after he weakened, he was consigned to a concentration camp in East Prussia. For his German captors, he felt as much pity as enmity; he could even chuckle over their organizational obsessions. He showed me a copy of his *Konzentrationslager* registration card, a model of Teutonic bureaucratic scrupulousness. The neatly typed card showed that Timonin was born in 1922. He was Catholic. He spoke Russian, Polish, and German. He had no political or criminal record.

He was "liberated" by the Red Army on May 1, 1945. Not long after, declared a traitor for having been taken prisoner, he was riding the rails to Vorkuta.

We joked, philosophized, and toasted into the night. Timonin showed no symptoms of the prisoner's pathology: no nervous tics, no faraway expression, no sudden angry outbursts. His second wife, a lively woman in her forties, plied us with *zakuski,* the appetizers that must accompany any drinking session: sausage, cheese, cucumber, smoked sturgeon, white and black bread. Timonin's daughter, a sixteen-year-old who hoped to become a journalist, sat nearby, taking in the scene. In her jeans and T-shirt, she could have been a teenager anywhere; the room she shared with her grandmother was covered with Michael Jackson posters.

Timonin was supremely uninterested in talking about his experiences in the Gulag. Instead, he wanted to know how he could send his daughter to school in the States, when I could organize a lecture tour for him, whether I could help him get his book published. Once his wife retired, he explained, the family would move to Kirov, or perhaps even to St. Petersburg. He was busy plotting, scheming, hatching plans; he acted as if he had an entire lifetime ahead of him. There was something both endearing and comic about it. Here was another quality that must have helped see him through the camps.

Vladimir Ilyin was a different sort of man. We had tea together. He was dressed in a simple, dark suit. His tall frame was topped by a full shock of white hair. He held himself with an odd elegance; he reminded me of a heron. He had none of Timonin's expansiveness: he chose his

words carefully, and his tone was matter-of-fact. He still worked drafting blueprints in the city planning office.

Born in 1925, he was only sixteen when his home town of Minsk,
the capital of Belarus, was overrun by the Nazis. Like Timonin, he was
used as forced labor in Germany. The years there were not entirely
wasted, he said, gradually breaking into a wry smile; he had learned to
be a pretty fair bookbinder.

The Minsk he returned to at the end of 1945 was an ugly shambles;
over 80 percent of the city had been destroyed. In many respects, Ilyin
recalled, the immediate postwar years were as difficult as the war itself.
There was virtually no housing; people lived in tents, or under the rubble. Food was scarce. Once, weakened by hunger, Ilyin fainted in the
street.

A few years later, in 1949, they came to take him away. He waited
for months to be charged. Eventually, the authorities settled on the all-
purpose charges of "treason to the homeland" and "membership in a
counterrevolutionary organization." Sipping his tea, Ilyin dryly commented: "My fate was not entirely satisfactory."

Thanks to his drafting skills, he was assigned at first to a secret weapons development facility in Moscow, not unlike the one
described in Solzhenitsyn's *The First Circle*. In 1951, however, it was
decided that political prisoners should not be used for sensitive projects involving national security. Ilyin and his fellow "politicals" were
sent to the camps.

It took over two months for Ilyin to reach Vorkuta from Moscow.
There were twenty-seven people in the first Stolypin compartment he
rode in. Politicals, women, and criminals were all mixed together. The
criminals stole their food and clothes; the women had to relieve themselves in the compartment. In Kirov, he was transferred to a cattle car,
his home for the next four weeks.

All three hundred prisoners from the secret facility were assigned to
hard labor. No exceptions were made. It was a policy carried out with a
single purpose — to ensure that the secrets they bore would perish
quickly and quietly along with them. Ilyin's job was one of the worst; he
loaded coal into wagons, on short rations, often in sub-freezing temperatures. The cruelty of those days sometimes had a prosaic quality.
One of Ilyin's worst memories was of standing at roll call, in winter,

from six in the morning until five in the afternoon, while the guards tried to straighten out a discrepancy in their roll-call count.

Stalin's death saved Ilyin, along with many others like him. The first news came over the radio, a year to the day after Ilyin had arrived in Vorkuta. The Great Leader had fallen ill, a bulletin announced. The barracks buzzed with excited speculation: "Is it possible that he will die? It was a reflection of the extent to which Stalin's name was held in otherwordly awe that the news of a seventy-three-year-old man's illness could have come as such a shock. Timonin had claimed that the prisoners cheered when they heard the news of Stalin's death. But Ilyin's account sounded more plausible. When camp officials read out the announcement to the camp's prisoners, there was complete silence. Everyone was afraid to react. It was the same, Ilyin recalled, when the camp officials made it known that Beria, the notorious head of Stalin's secret police, had been arrested.

Ilyin remembers catching a glimpse once of General Maslinikov, the head of the "special commission" that dealt so harshly with the strikers at Mine Number 29. Like Kashketin, his very appearance was terrifying. Ilyin chuckled and said; "If you look at his picture in the *Great Soviet Encyclopedia*, you won't be able to sleep for three days." Maslinikov tried to keep things hushed up, but word seeped back to Moscow. He was held responsible for the disturbances, and was himself shot at the end of 1953.

In the wake of Beria's death, there was a loosening of controls in the Vorkuta camps. The *zeks* were allowed to walk around freely within the camps' confines, and their rations were increased. Even little shows of defiance were tolerated. One of the oddest was that of prisoners who refused to remove their identification numbers from the back of their field jackets. To do so, they argued, was to aid in camouflaging their true status as prisoners.

The first to be released were the foreigners. Ilyin still recalls the bitter resentment the prisoners felt as they watched German and Austrian war veterans — labeled "war criminals" by the Soviet government — walk free while Soviet citizens who had fought for their homeland remained behind bars. Finally, in 1956, Ilyin was let out. He returned to Belarus, but he could not find a job. No one wanted to hire a former prisoner from the Gulag. Grudgingly, he came to the realization that there was only one place left where he could find work: Vorkuta. He returned, without joy, and found a drafting job. Now, after a heart attack, he was planning to return, finally, to his homeland. "The climate here is too hard for me. I need to go where it is warm," he said.

* * *

Afonya Sfinaris's apartment was on the ground floor, just off one of Vorkuta's main boulevards. He seemed overcome with joy to find two visitors at his door. Before we had even managed to sit down, he began to thank Troshin for helping him move from a dirty cellar room, where he had once lived, to this relatively spacious two-room suite. With undisguised pride, he took us over to his bathroom; it had a toilet and a tub! Suddenly, he was close to breaking down; a soft, rotund man in his early eighties, struggling not to blubber before his guests.

Sfinaris's days in Vorkuta, too, were numbered. He had advanced prostate cancer; his groin bulged oddly under his cheap blue tracksuit. He spoke frankly about the difficulty he had walking, going to the bathroom, keeping up enough energy to do his chores. Somehow, he managed to pad about the apartment to fetch us coffee and biscuits. He was bald except for a last fringe of hair above his temples. He looked at us from behind thick bottle-bottom glasses. Sfinaris's eyes were big and round, like those of a doe pawing nervously at the edge of a forest.

His path to Vorkuta was more improbable than most. The son of a poor Greek shoemaker who came to the Soviet Union to ply his trade, Afonya grew up making and selling sandals in the markets of Moscow. From the beginning, he displayed a real zeal for learning. "I'll eat out of your hand," he told us that night, "if you'll just let me study." His father, however, was unimpressed by such talk. "First work, then everything else," he insisted. Even as the last vestiges of the free market were squeezed out of the Soviet economy in the early thirties, and the struggle to survive became more and more difficult for the Sfinaris family, Afonya still found time to finish school, proving to be both a faithful son and a diligent student.

One day, Sfinaris's father argued with a government inspector, and the family's misfortunes began in earnest. The inspector filed a complaint. Sensing danger, Sfinaris senior went to the Greek Embassy to make arrangements to emigrate. He was told, however, that he could take only his four younger children. The two older sons, including Afonya, would have to stay. The father refused to break up his family.

For a time, they were safe. Afonya enrolled in a technical school in Leningrad, on his own in the world for the first time. Once again, however, Afonya's father ran afoul of the authorities. He was denounced for purchasing five sacks of flour on the black market, in those days a serious charge that invited draconian penalties, even the death sentence. He fled, leaving his family behind. A year later, he had moved in with another woman, yet still came to seek money from his son in Leningrad. It fell to Afonya to tell his father — on behalf of his mother, brothers, and sisters — that they never wanted to see him again.

Alongside a handful of his classmates, Afonya was arrested in 1937. But one day, just as he was being shipped away to the camps, he found out that his father was in the hospital of the very same prison where he was being held. Hearing of Afonya's arrest, Sfinaris senior had come out of hiding, walked into the infamous Lubianka, headquarters of the NKVD, and begged for his son to be released. "If he's guilty," he told the duty officer, "I'll serve his time. Let him go; he's just starting his life."

It was to no avail, of course. Afonya was sent to Vorkuta. His father, too, was arrested. Eventually, the old man was deported to Athens along with the rest of the family and three hundred thousand other Soviet Greeks — another of Stalin's whims. From the Sfinaris family, only Afonya was left behind.

In Vorkuta, Afonya was assigned as a male nurse to the city's hospital. To say that the conditions were rudimentary hardly says enough. Often there were no bandages and no medicine. Afonya's training came on the job. Some procedures he practiced on corpses; there were many to choose from. With time and bitter experience, he learned how to be of use to the handful of doctors. Eventually, Afonya was even able to diagnose tuberculosis by touch, feeling the telltale lumps of infection with his fingertips.

Stalin had been an evil man; he had ruled, in Afonya's words, according to "the old covenants." When he talked about his friends, all innocent victims of a force beyond their control, Afonya's voice shook. When he remembered how his best friend, a Greek-American named George Sviridov, had died in his arms, he cried.

Yet whatever horrors Afonya saw in the camps, he still proclaimed himself a communist. His education was a gift of Soviet schools. As the son of a poor family in Greece, he never would have had the same chance. Life was about work, about learning, about discipline. Afonya still put in half-days in the hospital's records department. He had nothing but scorn for the new Russia, its economics of chaos, its ethos of greed. Smiling his curiously childlike smile, he commented: "After all, Christ was the first communist. And the first doctor."

There was something else to it, as well. I peered into Afonya's brown and crinkled photographs, wondering at the fabric of these lives, spat upon by fate. I saw young men and women smiling, embracing, clowning for the camera. It was a summer picnic in the tundra. George Sviridov, shirtless, strutted like Apollo. They were all so alive. How could we not love the place and the time where we first knew these things? Afonya was misty-eyed. Like bright clumps of cloudberries, his youth was peeking through the snow again.

THE SONG
OF THE NORTH

ARKHANGELSK AND SOLOVKI

IT WAS ZHANNA'S IDEA, before she passed away. Firmly in the grip of cancer, she still had plans for herself and for others.

In the old days, she had worked at the Union of Composers, an official Communist organization that counted among its members all of the great — and not-so-great — Soviet composers.

For the mediocre and the politically trustworthy, it provided a comfortable enough living. Commissions for new works were handed out frequently enough to delude the composers into believing they were actually busy. That their oeuvres from time to time had to be dedicated to the completion of a new power station or the passing of some Party hack seemed a small price to pay for their tidy, respectable lives as esteemed Soviet cultural workers.

Conversely, the Union of Composers did everything it could to throttle its ideologically challenged talents — classically unreliable figures like Shostokovich and Schnittke. When historians gather one day to stir its ashes, the organization's greatest distinction may well turn out to be the zeal with which it made some of the century's greatest musical geniuses suffer under its petty bureaucratic tutelage. Years after the fall of Gorbachev and the last Soviet government, the Union of Composers was still headed by Tikhon Khrennikov, a Stalin protégé who eagerly joined the dictator's assault in the late forties and fifties against "modernists." A capable musician turned famously cynical nomenclaturist, he had ruled the roost of Soviet classical music for close to four decades, outliving many men and women more admirable than himself.

Happily, Zhanna's great love was jazz. Somehow, however bleak the political circumstances, she always seemed to find a place for American jazzmen on the modest little stage of the Union's "House of Composers." Whether it was mainstream idol Grover Washington Jr., or the cacophony of an avant-garde saxophone quartet, Zhanna knew how to work around the dour Soviet cultural watchdogs — including her own higher-ups. Even after glasnost bloomed, Zhanna was still there pulling the right strings. I remember one summer night when she helped bring pianist Billy Taylor and guitarist Pat Metheny together with Moscow's best *dzhazisti* for back-to-back jam sessions in a basement cafe. Even in Manhattan, it would have been an enviable accomplishment.

Jazz in the U.S.S.R. always represented more than just another musical genre, more than Goodman, Ellington, and Brubeck — all of whom toured there to tremendous acclaim. The sum of Soviet jazz was far greater than its parts. It stood for everything the Communist system did not: free expression, spontaneity, and the West. Stalin's men tried to stamp it out, and for a time nearly succeeded. Khrushchev ridiculed jazz, claiming it gave him indigestion. Even when jazz was not held in active disfavor by the authorities, it was still seen in Party circles as something unsavory and unworthy of a country that had produced the likes of Glinka and Tchaikovsky.

For the same reasons, perhaps, jazz found a ready audience all over the Soviet Union. It was a siren song for the free-spirited and the disaffected. Even under Stalin, jazz managed to seep in through what few fissures opened up in the wall of midcentury Marxism-Leninism, on LPs tucked into diplomats' valises or via shortwave radio broadcasts beamed from the imperialist West. Russian musicians readily embraced it, and year by year it spread, until by the sixties, bands playing Dixieland and bebop could be found from Kaliningrad to Kamchatka. For a whole generation — including Gorbachev's cohorts — jazz became the long-playing, hi-fidelity soundtrack of freedom.

Zhanna raised herself from her iron cot, propping her head up on a deathly pale elbow. After a week of confinement in the clinic, her hair — uncombed, bedraggled — had abruptly turned gray. An oversized gown fell off her shoulder without as much as a nod to Eros. Pain, the harsh chaperone of the terminally ill, hovered over her. She managed a wan smile as I pulled some yogurt and bananas from a paper bag.

She was always tiny, too small even to qualify as petite. In better days she had dark bangs, and large, vivacious eyes. Back then, she was indefatigable. In the face of all manner of cowards and fools, her Job-like patience never flagged, at least not outwardly. Only with time did I come to understand that she was capable of a toughness entirely disproportionate to her diminutive appearance and accommodating demeanor.

She was sharing a cramped ward in City Hospital #56 with five other sick women. We whispered — Zhanna did not have the strength then to speak loudly anyway — while her neighbor alternately snored and moaned. The room was dingy, the one high window caked in grime. A nurse came by and gave the woman next to us an injection. The moaning stopped. "It's awful here," Zhanna confided. "It's just a dumping ground."

Zhanna's one solace was her son, who had just graduated from the prestigious Moscow Conservatory with a degree in composition. He was engaged to be married to another musical student — so there would be someone to take care of him when his mother was gone.

Before long, however, the conversation turned to me.

"I think you should go to the North," she said, in the brisk tone I had heard before when something was left undone. "That's where you can still find the real Russia. Go to Arkhangelsk. Go to Solovki.

"A dear friend of mine — he's a jazz musician — invited me to go on a cruise to the Solovetskiy Islands," she went on. "It's part of a festival, I believe. Since I've ended up in this place," she explained, her chin bobbing in the direction of the other patients, "I can't go. But I told him you would take my place. His name is Volodiya. Here's his number. Call him when you get home."

I would make a poor substitute, I countered.

"Nonsense," she replied amiably, although we both knew that I was right. "Besides, I want you to visit Solovki."

She recalled the first time she had set foot on the islands, many years before. "I walked through this beautiful forest, it was midsummer, the birches shone in the evening light, and all across the forest floor were red — blood red — mushrooms. I've never seen mushrooms like them anywhere else. I could just feel the presence of those who perished there . . ."

The nurse, her face as impassive as fate itself, entered and drew close. "You must go now," Zhanna said, squeezing my hand. "Go, and call Volodiya." I kissed her forehead and wished her well. As I left, the nurse was pushing a needle deep into her pale, doll-like arm. By the time I reached home, I had made up my mind.

* * *

There is a reason you never hear about anyone taking a motoring holiday in Russia. Highways in Russia were always an afterthought, at best. Dam builders and airplane designers were celebrated in song and story, but who had ever heard of a famous Russian road engineer, even in Russia? Stalin sent hundreds of thousands to their deaths to fulfill his pharaonic fantasies of pushing canals and railways across unpopulated taiga. Yet he never so much as lifted a finger to have his legions of slave labor build a decent motorway between Moscow and Leningrad.

Striving to answer the question of why their roads are so bad — and no Russian would disagree with that conclusion — a Muscovite professor and a Siberian peasant would likely offer the same answer: the difficulty of building good roads in the unforgiving Russian climate. While this notion undoubtedly had some basis in fact, it did not seem as compelling when one recalled the outstanding attributes of Canadian and Scandinavian roads, laid out and maintained under much the same meteorological conditions.

Many other highly rational reasons came to mind. The economic: under socialism, there were no compelling market incentives for the development of a sophisticated highway network. The sociological: Russians were not permitted the same mobility as, say, Americans. The political-economic: there were many fewer privately owned cars in Russia than in the West, and consequently little demand for improved roads. The socio-psychological: Russians were lazy and careless when performing work that was of no direct benefit to themselves.

I found all of these explanations somehow unsatisfying. I wondered if it was not a more complicated problem. What was lacking — completely lacking, as far as road travel in Russia went — was a sense of romance. There were folk ballads about trains rushing over the tundra, riverboats cruising the moonlit Volga, even the heart-stoppingly bouncy AN-2 biplanes that crisscross Siberia's remotest air routes. Yet no Russian ever broke into song over a long-distance automobile journey or the bittersweet lure of the highway.

That summer, I was still the proud owner of a Russian jeep (later, it was stolen in broad daylight from the street in front of the U.S. Embassy in Moscow). It was a Niva, a word that means "field of grain." Indeed, its designers' inspiration was partly agricultural. The Party bosses had asked for a vehicle that could conquer the ubiquitous mud and snow of rural Russia, or at least take an apparatchik to his country dacha for the weekend. People in Moscow would often roll their eyes when I told them I owned one. "Oh, that's only for the *sovhoz*, for driving around a state farm," they would say, more than a little patronizingly. But I made no apologies. When the temperature plummeted into the frosty netherworld where the Celsius and Fahrenheit scales coincide, my faithful Niva would still start up smartly, while the BMWs and Mercedes of the city's nouveau riche sat immobilized, cold and mute under a dusting of snow.

This is not to suggest, however, that the Niva had much in common with the tonier four-wheel-drive vehicles that have become all the rage on the streets of New York and Tokyo. With a price tag of $4,000, how luxurious could it have been? The hard black vinyl seats wore out the most rugged passenger's rump within an hour, and if the steering wheel were ever to tilt, one was best advised to jump clear. Nor was it much of an exaggeration to say that the Niva handled like an armored personnel carrier. Curves, particularly on snow, could be a ticklish challenge. The brakes, too, were more than a little temperamental. Mine locked up one winter in an S-turn outside Moscow, and I will not soon forget the ensuing sensation of having been launched in a bobsled.

Nearly everyone I knew assumed that in trying to drive alone to Arkhangelsk I had taken leave of my senses. As knowingly as gypsy palm readers, my American colleagues predicted a spectacular mugging or kidnapping, or even worse. Russian friends were in some ways even more incredulous. Often, they simply guffawed: "You? A foreigner? Alone on our highways?" Even my wife, normally my most indulgent travel advisor, urged caution.

I have to admit that even I had second thoughts. On paper, it looked straightforward. Due north, six hundred miles, and I would be there. The main highway to Arkhangelsk was marked "All-Soviet Significance," the highest rating of all. Yet there were some disturbing reports in the media about motorists being robbed at gunpoint, as well as truck drivers and their cargoes simply vanishing, never to be seen again. A few days before my departure, I read a newspaper story claiming some two thousand people had "disappeared" over a twelve-month period while traveling on the roads of Kazakstan. In the United States, this item would have been treated as a come-on for a new TV series on UFOs. For the Russian reader, however, the story sounded all too real. The unfortunate victims had likely fallen afoul of the *mafiya*, and would only be located again in the next life.

One bright, lovely, and deliciously warm June morning, I drove off. My route north took me past some of Russia's most revered sites: Sergeiv Posad (known under the Communists as Zagorsk, and the site of one of the few monasteries that was allowed to function throughout the Soviet period); Petroslavl-Zalesski, where Peter the Great sailed his teenage summers away on Lake Pleschev, dreaming of building the first Russian navy; Rostov, arguably old Russia's loveliest town; and Yaroslavl, the gateway to the upper Volga and ancient rival of the Moscow princes. Yet all of these tourist map places were already well-tramped by foreigners, and I was impatient to move on. I pressed further north, into territory less visited and less coddled.

I stayed overnight in Vologda, in a hotel near the center of the city. It was after dark by the time I arrived. I remember the evening: cool, moist, and infused with twilight almost until midnight. Along with a handful of other unhappy patrons, I stood in line at the check-in desk for nearly an hour; we had all made the mistake of arriving during the hotel's shift change. While the two staffs merrily swapped stories and shopping tips behind the counter, we waited, murmurs of annoyance soon escalating to howls of protest. Yet it was all to no avail; the front desk did not reopen even a minute before the appointed hour.

I slept lightly that night, bolting from my bed to the window every time I heard a suspect noise in the vicinity of my Niva. Yet the car rested tranquilly underneath the hotel's neon-bedecked portico, none the worse for wear the next morning. Perhaps, I concluded, danger did not lurk around every corner.

Founded in the twelfth century, Vologda was long a point of transit from central Russia to the north — hence its name, drawn from the Russian word *volok,* for place of portage. The peaceful, reed-lined Vologda River loops twice through the center of the city, meandering past a thick clutch of churches and the newly renovated Kremlin. From the top of St. Sophia's bell tower, up a flight of steeply zigzagging wooden steps, one can still take in, on a clear day, a panorama of city streets fairly sprinkled with onion domes and old wooden mansions. Beyond, to the north, luxuriant meadow and forest unfold to the horizon's edge. In Vologda, the twentieth century, for all of its slogans and obsessions, had not swept everything before it.

Preparations were underway for the city's anniversary celebrations. Tractors with plow attachments scraped up a year's worth of mud from the walkways along the river. On a stage behind the bell tower, a dance troupe was warming up, with men in peasant blouses slapping and kicking their way past warbling, apple-cheeked damsels. Down the bank by the river, a pair of milk cows languidly munched at their urban pasture.

However placid the city was today, it had not always been so. Ivan the Terrible frequented Vologda in its heyday, drawn by its strategic position athwart Moscow's polar trade route to England. An English envoy passing through in 1586 praised Ivan's improbably grand stone and brick fortress, and wrote that Vologda was "a large trading city where many rich merchants live."

Ivan was also the first of many Muscovite rulers who saw Vologda and the rest of the Russian north as a convenient dumping ground for his political opponents. Those that a tsar did not have strangled or beheaded straight away were often to be found imprisoned or exiled to these parts. In the last years before the revolution, their ranks would include Lenin's sister and an intense, ruthless Georgian named Iosef Djugashvili — known among his fellow exiles by his first nom de guerre, Koba, rather than the one that in time would make an entire continent tremble: Stalin.

Like Velikiy Ustyug, Vologda watched its wealth and fame slip away with the founding of St. Petersburg, which diverted most of the Russian Empire's overseas trade from the White Sea to the Baltic. Yet Vologda remained the administrative center for a vast region, and, at the end of the nineteenth century, it figured as an important stop on the new rail line between Moscow and Arkhangelsk. If not for its robust population of political exiles, Vologda on the eve of the Revolution would have been judged a typical — if unusually picturesque — Russian provincial city, far removed from the heady drama of events in St. Petersburg and Moscow.

Then, in an improbable twist of fate, Vologda found itself, for one brief spring and summer, at the center of the international gamesmanship surrounding Russia's withdrawal from World War I in 1918. After the Bolsheviks signed the Treaty of Brest-Litovsk, the diplomats representing the Allied forces arrayed against Germany began to evacuate St. Petersburg, where increasingly it was feared that German troops, already marching through Ukraine, might occupy the city. The new Soviet leaders, motivated by the same concerns, determined to move the government south to Moscow. The Allied ambassadors, led by U.S. Ambassador David R. Francis, decided on Vologda.

Why did the representatives of the United States, Britain, France, and a dozen other countries choose a quiet backwater from which to conduct their diplomacy? The Allies were not yet reconciled to Russia's abandonment of the Eastern front, and nursed the hope of prompting the country's return to the battlefield. To move to Moscow would have implied official recognition of the Bolsheviks, whom the Allies viewed as little more than German hirelings, as likely as not to tumble from power within the year. Vologda, at a major rail junction, afforded the diplomats an escape route to Siberia should the German army move eastward, and to the White Sea should Allied forces intervene in Russia — as in fact they did later in the summer.

Whatever merits the relocation had in those terms, it was in other respects a blunder. Francis and his fellow envoys had in one stroke crippled their ability to fulfill their most important task: to keep track of developments in the fledgling Soviet state and convey them accurately to their home governments.

By all accounts — except perhaps his own — Francis was ill-equipped to handle his responsibilities. A retired Missouri politician without much grasp of diplomacy, it was perhaps not simply as a matter of etiquette that his embassy staff addressed him as "Governor" rather than "Ambassador." Isolated in Vologda while war and revolution shook the country around him, he was that much less able to size up the situation properly.

A photo of the wooden mansion in Vologda that served as the U.S. Embassy shows a group of earnest young men in ties and starched collars flanking Ambassador Francis, along with three army officers in uniform. Known as the "clubhouse," the building had a certain provincial charm. There, what little business could be stirred up in Vologda was conducted, and on Saturdays Francis would greet what meager society there was to entertain. The Brazilian and Siamese consuls argued over which of their countries had the more imposing snakes. On special occasions, like the Embassy's July Fourth reception, the Victrola would be cranked up and guests invited to dance in the garden. Francis whiled away many an evening playing cards, one of the few matters at hand for which he had an evident talent. As one English visitor remarked, "The old gentleman was no child at poker."

Francis had his finest hour as ambassador on the very eve of his departure from Vologda. Startling news had reached the embassy of the murder in Moscow of the German ambassador, Count Mirbach, and an uprising against the Bolsheviks in Yaroslavl. The Yaroslavl rebels appealed to the Allies to intervene on their behalf. Simultaneously, the Soviet leaders ordered the Allied ambassadors to proceed under Bolshevik guard to Moscow, where the new regime said it would be better able to ensure their security.

After consulting with Vologda's polyphyletic ambassadorial corps, from the French to the Chinese to the Japanese, Francis cabled back to the Moscow Commissariat of Foreign Affairs that, no, thank you, the diplomats felt quite safe in Vologda and were content to stay where they were. The Bolsheviks replied by dispatching Karl Radek — a flamboy-ant Polish Jew who was destined for the ignominy of Stalin's show trials — to induce the foreign envoys to decamp. When the diminutive Radek appeared the next day at "the clubhouse" before the assembled diplomatic corps, he brought with him his famously haughty attitude and an oversized pistol stuffed into a holster. Negotiations ensued, but Francis made it plain that the foreigners would not accompany Radek back to Moscow.

Furious at both the diplomats' intransigence as well as the evident sympathy they enjoyed among the city's Russian inhabitants, Radek contrived a scheme that was to bedevil foreigners resident in Russia throughout the rest of the Soviet period. He gave orders to the local Bolsheviks to post guards at the American embassy's gate. While they were to allow the diplomats to enter and leave as they pleased, they were also to prevent local citizens from gaining access to the premises with-out a special pass.

Not long after, the Allied diplomats, receiving word that their troops were to land in Arkhangelsk, slipped away from Vologda on a special train, ending the town's brief interlude in the annals of diplo-matic history. Yet the Volodga-inspired phalanx of burly guards soon became a standard feature outside Western offices and homes in Moscow and Leningrad, supplied, of course, for the "protection" of the foreigners.

✳ ✳ ✳

It was another fine day. As I drove out of town, I passed a gas station beseiged by cars waiting to fill up. Still, I was not particularly worried. My road atlas showed where pumps were located along my route north. Just in case, I had a full jerry can sloshing about in the back.

Not far outside of Vologda, where the road veers away from the river, stands the imposing Monastery of Our Savior-on-the-Bend. More by virtue of strategy than theology, it was founded in the fourteenth century at what was then the far northern edge of Muscovite lands.

For all intents and purposes, these lands were never sullied by the Mongols. The forests and bogs of Vologda and Arkhangelsk kept out the horseback warriors who had swept over the Russian steppes to the south. When the Golden Horde did try to dispatch its officials to these parts, they were sent packing.

Thus, the Tatar occupation, which had such a profound effect on both the face and soul of Russia, barely touched the far north. By virtue of this isolation, the north is thought to be more authentically Russian, less sullied by the "Oriental despotism" that brought the rest of the country to its knees. There was, in fact, little intermingling of Russian and Mongol blood above the taiga line. To this day, one sees the full cheekbones and lusterless eyes of the Tatar type — a Russian characterization, not mine — much less frequently north of Vologda than elsewhere in Russia. The further one travels toward the pole, the more the people resemble Scandinavians, complete with the stereotypically Nordic fair hair and blue eyes.

As it turned out, invaders fell upon Our-Savior-on-the-Bend from the west rather than from the east. Sacked on three different occasions by Catholic — read infidel — Poles and Lithuanians, the monastery's walls were built progressively higher and wider until they were, in places, yards thick. Eventually, Our-Savior-on-the-Bend was heralded as impregnable. When Napoleon reached the gates of Moscow in 1812, the Kremlin's treasures were transferred to the monastery for safekeeping. One look at the bulldog-faced bastions that guard the four corners of the complex and it is easy to comprehend why a tsar would commit his gold and diamonds to this fastness.

On a grassy stretch of riverbank at the base of the monastery walls, Governor Francis would chip away avidly at his golf balls, his aides moving wooden stakes from one spot to the next, simulating holes on a real set of links. These were perhaps the lightest moments of the century for Our Savior-on-the-Bend. By the late twenties, the cloisters had been converted into holding cells for *kulaks* deported from Ukraine and the Don. Thousands died here, starved and shot like dogs.

Now, at the end of the Soviet era, workmen were slapping new paint and plaster about the rectory, and a small circle of black-cowled nuns busied themselves with reviving the old Orthodox devotions. When not in prayer, they worked their muddy vegetable patches or walked silently about the inner grounds under the haunted inspiration of three magnificent churches — one stone, one brick, one wood. They looked at visitors with shy, undernourished expressions, their hands pale and fidgety.

A few hundred yards past the monastery, I reached what had once been the line on the Moscow-Arkhangelsk highway past which foreigners were prohibited from traveling. A militiaman strode out into the road and waved me over; he had seen my bright red diplomatic license plates. Until then, most of the highway police posts I had encountered were boarded up or converted into tire repair shops or food stands. But here the forces of order were still ensconced.

The militia station was an ill-lit cement box. I stepped inside to have my papers registered. A mildewy logbook was pulled from the desk drawer; the earnest-looking militiaman carefully wrote down every iota of information he could make out on my identity card. He noticed me looking askance at the badly cracked window overlooking the highway, and explained apologetically that his traffic post was old, "from the sixties." Proudly, he pointed out the new facility next door that he and his comrades would soon occupy. It was a converted shipping container, into which someone had cut a low doorway and two portholes with a blowtorch.

The highway, two lanes of asphalt embellished by scrawny gravel shoulders, was anything but crowded. Trucks of varying sizes, vintages, and configurations made up most of the traffic. Private cars were much rarer, and they, too, were mostly absorbed in makeshift commercial missions. I passed more than one overloaded Zhiguli huffing along the road, stuffed full of the wares of Russia's quick-calorie, low-nutrition form of capitalism: Mars bars, bacon-flavored puffs, and Bulgarian brandy.

Even where the pavement was whole rather than potholed, the Arkhangelsk highway had a curious effect on man and machine. From behind the wheel, the sensation was more like that of guiding a powerboat than of driving a car. However level and placid the highway at times appeared, it provided the motorist an eerily maritime experience, prompting cars and trucks to dip and rise as if they were plunging through midocean swells. In places, the asphalt — slapped about heedlessly by generation upon generation of road crew — looked as if it too were composed of swirling black water. Before long, my driver's seat had metamorphosed into the salt-stained cockpit of a launch, the next horizon of birch and spruce into undulating shore. The wheel I used both to steer and to keep from being tossed out of my captain's chair.

The gas gauge had slipped below one quarter, and I judged it time to fill up. I pulled over at the next station, only to find it closed — not out of gas, but rather out of electricity with which to pump the gas. There was no attendant in sight, just a hand-lettered sign on which the ink had run illegibly in the rain. I checked my map. There was another station about fifty kilometers further north. I would just be able to make it.

The way grew lonelier, emptier, even as it turned more starkly beautiful. This was taiga country, with only an occasional meadow or village to break the peculiar spell of pine-needle green and inky, amphibious marsh.

It was with genuine relief that I came up on the next set of gas pumps. The needle of the Niva's gas gauge had slipped below empty. I walked up to the pay window, placed my rubles inside a small slot, and leaned down to a waist-high grill to ask for forty liters, the maximum the tank could accommodate. The bills disappeared down a herky-jerky rubber conveyor belt through two panes of split glass. Then, to my surprise, the cash came spitting back out, and from the mouth of the woman cranking the belt, I heard the disdainful words: "Official cars only."

It was only then that I noticed the glum gaggle of motorists becalmed before the idle pumps, bemoaning this sour happenstance. I, too, stood and waited — for what exactly I was not sure. Other cars pulled up. Their drivers came up to the same window, begging, cajoling, pleading with the flat-faced woman seated inside — all to no avail. She confronted them with that particularly maddening brand of Slavic impassivity, half-listening to their entreaties, half-eyeing a black-and-white TV in the corner, calmly cracking open one sunflower seed after another between her gold-capped incisors.

I could see that I was in a bind. The next gas station was impossibly far off, some 100 kilometers to the north.

It was then that I spotted a truck driver disappear behind the station. I decided to follow him, at first from a prudent distance. A metal door in the back of the building opened to admit him, then closed. I stood by, waiting. After a few minutes the door swung back open, and the truck driver stepped out, his brightened expression conveying a sense of possibility. I screwed up my courage and slipped through the portal in his wake before the portly sunflower lady had a chance to block my way.

I was inside, but just barely. Her greeting was unpromising: "I said there isn't any gas for you." She stood before me, wide as an armoire. "Out, out," she commanded, a pudgy hand motioning me away. Having no idea what the proper etiquette was in such situations, I jumped right into a shamelessly exaggerated account of my misfortunes.

"I had just enough gas to make it here," I whined. "Now I don't know what to do. I'm just a foreigner. I'm not familiar with your roads and your regulations."

There was just a hint of thawing around the edges of her brows. "I can't sell gas to private cars. If I did, I might get in trouble. I had enough for ordinary comrades last week, but not today."

I thought to appeal to her practical side. "Of course, I understand. You must abide by the rules. Still, isn't there some procedure where someone pays" — I searched for the right word in Russian — "a penalty, an amount over and above the regular price for gas?"

She began to shake her head, but her words were less sure. "I don't know," she said with markedly less vigor. "I have to think."

I had still another weapon of subversion under my arm, and now I brought it to bear. I handed the woman two back copies of *Amerika*, a Russian-language magazine about the United States that was published throughout the Cold War years by the U.S. government. Full of glossy color photos of Detroit's hippest roadsters, Sears's latest dishwashers, and other luxuries that for Russians were either unattainable or unimaginable, *Amerika* was one of the greatest propaganda tools of modern times, and, until the Berlin Wall crumbled, worth its weight in almost anything produced in the Soviet Union. I was hoping that it still had some residual value amid the pines and bogs of Vologda *oblast*.

"Here," I said with a calculated display of casualness-*cum*-reverence, "I just happen to have a few of these. I thought you might be interested in taking a look at them . . ."

Her churlish expression melted away in an instant. "For me?" she asked. "These are for me?"

"Why, yes," I replied. "I've already read them, you see. I don't mind leaving them with you." I did not mention that I had another two hundred copies behind the Niva's back seat.

I left her skimming through an issue of *Amerika* with Wynton Marsalis on the cover, her gnawing of sunflower seeds momentarily stilled. I tried to ignore the covetous expressions of the other drivers as I filled up my tank and wheeled back out onto the road, on what had just become once again a wonderfully warm and welcoming day for a drive.

✳ ✳ ✳

I awoke in Velsk the next morning with a new plan. A mist redolent of mown hay and clover hid the Vaga River and the cottages along its banks. I strolled down the dirt road leading to the river's edge, absorbed in the rustlings of an eight-hundred-year-old hamlet rousing itself for another summer day: the raspy melody of a *babushka* singing to herself in the kitchen; the wheezy, percussive enthusiasm of the village pump being cranked over and over; the honky-tonk clatter of geese impatient to be fed.

Up above the fast-dissipating fog, the still, steady solstice sky was cloudless, suffused with a light as benign as a saint's visage. Why not improvise a bit, I thought? According to my atlas, there was another route I could follow that ran parallel to the main highway. When I reached the intersection outside of Velsk, I swung the Niva away from my all-Soviet route, into country I wanted to sample rather than skirt.

Never before in Russia had I experienced this freedom to roam, to turn down a road with careless rather than carefully studied intentions. I had no appointments to keep. Nor was there anyone shadowing me, taking careful note of where I chose to stop and start.

Here in the backwoods of the Arkhangelsk *oblast*, the forlorn scars of the Soviet era were few and far between. Seventy-five turbulent years had glided by, during which these villages barely caught the eye of the notoriously intrusive Communist Party of the Soviet Union. There were no lamentably ruined factories, no maudlin Lenin statues, no long-idle construction sites littered with broken pipes and cracked cinder block. Where there was decay, it was of a graceful, nostalgic sort, like that of a barn bent over with advancing years: the pardonable type of rural disrepair that, in whatever country, has existed in the past, exists today, and will always exist in the future.

Brightly painted cottages lined the road, along with two-story log houses weathered to the color of charcoal. Fathers split firewood, while sons flew handmade kites; mothers and daughters, their faces wrapped in flowered head scarves, strolled hand in hand. Goats and cows, dogs and cats, populated every yard, every field. Here was the preindustrial, premodern Russia that, however diminished, still filled the soul of this great country with its unenlightened, unromantic, undemocratic — yet undeniably rich and bountiful — outlook.

Even a mere passerby could feel the ancient rhythm of these places: a song of simple means, modest horizons, and a basso profundo inertia that was as immutable as a boulder at the bottom of a river. It was a folk theme made up in equal parts of exuberance, fatalism, equivocation, anarchy.

Village emotions might run high over where a cow was pastured, or how the communal vegetable plots were distributed. Yet no one was in a hurry to raise their voice, to pound a table, to make speeches over something as inherently ephemeral as politics. Therein lay the reason the Russian peasant so frustrated anyone harboring the mad ambition of remaking Russian society, whether misguided Bolshevik or naive promoter of Western capitalism. This Russia was virtually impervious to revolution; it could be ravished and abused, but not remade.

Perhaps the roads were just another reflection of this convoluted mental topography. The pavement shifted from asphalt to concrete, from concrete to hard gravel, then back to asphalt. A few kilometers later, at a clearing in the forest adorned by a long-abandoned rusty steamroller, the highway leapt back down the evolutionary scale to unimproved mud. A cut straight ahead through the trees hinted at wilted human ambition, but otherwise all signs of twentieth-century engineering had petered out. The way, black and glistening, slipped off the manmade grade toward a marshy flat.

Within minutes the Niva was drenched in ooze, not just across the grill and along the doors but all the way up and over its rooftop. Plowing blindly through mudholes the length of bowling alleys, I was never entirely certain I would emerge back into the sunlight at the other end. The faster I accelerated into the liquid stretches, the more violently the jeep was thrown about, with each rough spot spawning its own hurricane of muck and hurtling chassis.

I forged ahead like this for some time before checking the odometer. I had managed a mere fifteen kilometers. On a nearby rise, I spotted a dilapidated wooden church. I drove up to it and turned off the ignition, intending to give myself and my machine a rest while I sized up the situation.

Most of the wooden churches built before the revolution have been lost. Except for a handful that have been moved to museums, the majority succumbed over the years to a combination of neglect, fire and — most tragically — willful destruction. Here, on this knoll, I had happened upon one of the few survivors.

The church was a pint-sized affair, as humble as a worn-out shoe. Yet it mimicked, in microcosm, the conventions of all Orthodox churches. There was the inevitable belfry — before the Bolsheviks, bells were almost a defining feature of Russian faith and identity — and a tiny cupola mounted on a steeple that might have more plausibly topped a doll house. I walked off the length of the church — three lancet windows, twelve paces. Batches of wild yellow violets decorated grass as verdant as Eire.

An elderly man, poking his cane into the soft ground, hobbled up. "So you're interested in the church?" he asked. "Someone came here three years ago and took pictures, too." He invited me into his house, a hundred yards back down the hill, for a salad of green onions and sour cream and a steaming pot of tea. He and his wife, a bulldozer-faced old woman with the unsettling habit of belching at the end of her sentences, had lived there together for their entire married lives. She showed me the back room where she was born, on the day the Tsar abdicated in 1917. "Oh, people used to come to the church," she recalled. "But not anymore. The Reds took away the bells and all the icons. First the church died, then the village. Collectivization, they called it. We're the only ones left now, and after we've come to an end, there won't be anyone to look after it."

They expressed more wonderment at my travel plans than at my nationality. To them, America was as remote as Uranus, utterly unattached to their world. The road at the bottom of their hill was another matter. "You should know better than to try to drive this way," the old lady scolded, "especially now, during the summer." Her husband, too, looked askance at me. "You have to go when the weather is right," he emphasized. I looked through their lace curtains at the dizzyingly sunny fields bursting with chloroplastic life, and beyond, to the open-palmed midsummer sky. When the weather was right?

Suddenly, the totality of my miscalculation swept over me, and I burst out laughing. My host and hostess joined in, the old man pounding his cane for emphasis against the painted floor beams. "You mean, during the winter, don't you?" I gasped out. "Yes, yes, after the frost, only after the frost begins," replied the man. From the top of their hill, my stupidity must have seemed astounding. The woman's eyes filled with tears of hilarity. I could not catch everything that gurgled out in her thick peasant brogue, but I did make out her giggling "Not through the mud! Not through the *gryaz!*," repeated over and over. Yes, it was true. Around here, it was snow and ice that made the roads passable, not the tarlike summer slush.

A bit wiser, I was back on the main highway the following day. My rendevous in Arkhangelsk with Volodiya and his jazz friends loomed nearer; I only had so much time to sniff about the countryside.

With each kilometer, the landscape, the sky, the human spaces became ever more elemental, ever less trampled by the hooves of our fast-galloping era. Even where the earth had been mauled by one or another modern enthusiasm, the unhurried, unheeding configuration of life in old Russia promised its own brand of redemption, the long-standing, outlasting kind of salvation that marks its way, year after year, in frost, in mud, in flowers.

Consider the many lives of the Siski Monastery, the St. Anthony Monastery on the River Sia. For half a millenium an outpost of piety and learning in the vast northern forest, its extraordinary beauty and tranquility drew pilgrims from near and far. For other travelers, it served as a welcome way station along the arduous sledge route from Vologda to Arkhangelsk. In the years before the revolution, many a famous figure paused at Siski to rest and reflect. Here, Mikhail Lomonosov — the runaway teenage son of an Arkhangelsk fisherman — sought refuge among the monks until he was ready to continue his journey to Moscow. A pioneer of Russian science, the founder of Moscow State University, and a poet of considerable stature, Lomonosov went on to become as seminal a figure in his country's intellectual development as Isaac Newton was in that of England.

Defiled by the Bolsheviks — who rid the monastery of its monks, then converted the premises into a rest home for the party faithful — Siski was holy ground anew. The previous summer, the Moscow

Patriarch had landed in a helicopter to reconsecrate the site, and to pray for a reawakening of the monastery and its sacred mission.

On the day I arrived, the afternoon air was surprisingly sultry. The half-restored monastery was mirrored in triplicate, once for each of the lakes that surrounded it. A sandy-haired boy frolicked in the water with his dog. His barefoot sister stood on a footbridge of rough-hewn planks, carefully angling a homemade fishing rod. A long, splendid procession of billowing clouds paraded over and past the Siski churches, illuminating the still, heathen water with cumulus visions of heaven.

The monks were just completing their midday dinner, but a space was cleared for me on the long table where they had gathered to eat. They were dressed simply, some in loosely cut cotton shirts and trousers and others in Chinese denim work clothes. Without a word, a bearded brother placed before me a bowl of steaming cabbage *shchi* and a slice of black rye bread. From the rapt attention my every spooning of soup attracted, I guessed that my visit was the most entertainment my hosts had had in quite some time.

The conversation was friendly enough, but rudimentary. It recalled in no way, for instance, a meal in a Jesuit residence. I was struck by how rustic these monks' gestures were, and by the distinctly circumscribed way they spoke of their lives and their faith. I asked one brother how it was to live at the monastery during the long months of winter. "It's very gray, very cold," he replied, unenthusiastically. "But we're used to it. We hold services; we pray. And we have a lot of work restoring the buildings."

I was about to hand around a batch of *Amerika* magazines when the abbot intervened, a bit starchily I thought. "I'll put those in our monastery library," he commanded, sweeping up the copies under his arm.

I followed him upstairs to the library, which as it turned out was a bookshelf behind the locked door of his office. For someone with the rank of abbot, Trifon was surprisingly young and vigorous. He faced the world, however, with an expression in the ascetic tradition: lean, alert, and intense. In a more forthcoming manner than he had at first demonstrated, he described the difficulties the monastery faced in making its way in the post-Soviet era. His goal was to bring it back to the self-sufficiency it had enjoyed in the bygone era of a Russia governed by God and Tsar. Pilgrims and tourists, the abbot hoped, would be attracted to the region's serenity — and generate revenue for the monastery. The lands along the river and the labor of the monks' hands would provide for the rest of their earthly needs. Then he made the sign of the cross.

There was, however, the matter of the brothers themselves. Life at the monastery was hard, and Trifon feared that few had a true calling for the arduous work and discipline that restoring the Siski complex required. The novices, in particular, were not so different from the St. Petersburg architecture students who were helping during the summer with the reconstruction of one of the monastery's churches. "A couple of months working in the middle of nowhere suits them fine, but then they become restless," he observed with a forced sort of smile, "restless for your American television and cinema, restless for their family and friends, restless to do anything but stay here during our long winter."

The abbot had another struggle on his hands, one that to me was less expected. The local council had vigorously protested Moscow's decision to return the monastery to the church. The old-time bosses — now convinced followers of Adam Smith — wanted to put the place to more lucrative uses: a cross-country ski resort was one suggestion.

Before long, the affair turned nasty. First the abbot heard complaints, then threats. On the eve of the Patriarch's visit, one of the monastery's main churches mysteriously burned down. Even now, the abbot said, the church's hold on the monastery remained precarious. The former Communist *apparatchiki* had never really lost control. They were still in charge of their party fiefdoms, still running the sawmills and collective farms that were the region's economic mainstays. "They want us to fail," Trifon lamented, "and I fear that they will stop at nothing to see that their wish comes true."

On the way back out to my Niva, I passed two of the novices returning from the fields, great awkward hoes slung over their backs. They asked me if I had any more magazines. I hesitated for a moment, then had them follow me.

As I pulled away, they were gaping, dumbstruck, at an issue featuring a gyrating Michael Jackson on the back cover. It was an advertisement for the Voice of America. Somehow — across whole oceans and continents of experience — the photograph was already drowning out the gentle lapping of the novices' evensong prayers.

✳ ✳ ✳

Volodiya Turov sounded relieved to hear my voice over the phone. He had begun to wonder whether Zhanna's until then entirely hypothetical American would actually appear. And I arrived in the nick of time; the boat to Solovki was to depart the next day.

The festival Zhanna had told me about was, to say the least, an oddball event. Somehow, the director of Arkhangelsk's youth theater had wangled some money from UNESCO to stage an "international street theater festival." Like many thespians, he was fantastically disorganized and operated with an unsteady glint in his eye. Yet he also had the fanatic's virtue of never taking "no" for an answer. Against all odds, he had succeeded in enlisting in his madcap plan a gaggle of gullible foreign cultural attachés along with the threadbare collection of scribblers and dabblers that in Arkhangelsk passed for an intellectual elite.

Here, by the White Sea, it had been raining for days: a chilling, hard-hearted rain that roundly mocked the decision to steer a gathering of street performers to within a latitudinal degree or two of the Arctic Circle. I had the sad honor of witnessing the festival's concluding event in Arkhangelsk: a parade conducted in a wind-driven downpour along a waterlogged avenue.

Among the drenched, I learned, were Italian clowns, French puppeteers, and an expatriate American juggler who played flamenco guitar when he wasn't tossing fruit in the air. They were accompanied by a British radio journalist, a Norwegian photographer, a Japanese mime, and an Indian comedian. There was also a pair of Dutch street musicians who had driven all the way from Holland to Arkhangelsk in a VW bus with their two toddlers and four-month-old baby. It was a preposterous, if thoroughly lively, ensemble.

Turov was a featured player in another impossible undertaking: an avant-garde jazz group named Arkhangelsk, after the city from which it hailed. Unusually fit and trim for a musician in his forties, Turov had a handsome, smirky quality. His keyboard skills were considerable, but his charm and sense of irony were even more remarkable.

For over two decades, Arkhangelsk had sought to bring the gospel of contemporary jazz to the Russian public. Unlike most Iron Curtain ensembles, which wanted to sound as American as possible, Arkhangelsk played the standards with an eccentric edge, tossing into the mix a shot of tonal anarchism and a dash of Russian folk song.

The group had a small but devoted following in Moscow and St. Petersburg. The handful of Western jazz writers who managed to hear Arkhangelsk sang its praises in their dispatches from the Soviet music front. When things loosened up under Gorbachev, the Soviet record firm Melodiya even made a recording; Japanese and British record deals followed.

Yet this modest glory, which was about all a Soviet-bloc jazz musician could hope for, did little to pay the bills. To put bread on the table — not just a figure of speech in Russia — Turov and his fellow *dzhazisti* toured the backwoods of the Arkhangelsk region year after year, playing in unheated dance halls, dank band shells, and dingy auditoriums. Sometimes it took days of rough riding to reach the remote towns and villages where they were sent to play. Whatever the season, whatever the weather, they trudged on.

In jazz terms, some of these were gigs on the dark side of the moon, playing Coltrane before audiences of septuagenarians with folded hands and sniffling schoolchildren. Beholden for their meager salaries to the Arkhangelsk *oblast* cultural authorities, they were obliged to go where they were told, when they were told — and often enough to play what they were told. It was the quintessential form of the socialist music business: chain-gang musicians playing *po zakazu*, by order, for a handful of rubles and kopecks.

Before leaving Turov's apartment, we sat quietly on our bags in the vestibule. Russian superstition holds that travel undertaken without a minute's silent meditation needlessly tempts the fates.

Turov's wife was waiting for us at dockside on the Dvina River. The skies were clearing. We were quite a sight: two dozen or so damp *artistes* along with their Russian hosts, waving less in deference to the smattering of well-wishers assembled on shore than in unconcealed excitement over our impending adventure. The ship's loudspeaker blasted out a stentorian Russian march, the signal that we were casting off. Turov's wife waved back, her expression a wry mixture of longing to go along and relief that she would not have to keep company with the likes of us.

The *Yushar* slipped downstream from the quay and turned toward the sea, a dozen miles away. The last somber flats along the Dvina River were anything but bucolic. The muddy banks were crowded with ware-houses and factories; even the once top-secret submarine wharfs of Severodvinsk could not glamorize the pitilessly bleak riverfront.

Before long, though, the mouth of the river gave out like a bene-diction to a glimmering, brine-scented expanse of water and sky. The pilot's tug left us in a quick, expert loop around our stern. Even after the dinner bell rang, few of us could pull ourselves below deck right away. There was something mysterious afloat. The bleached waves and the ebbing gray coastline wheezed with ancient burdens and discomforts, yet the evening shone like a savior's brow.

After supper, Turov and his jazz mates gathered in the ship's lounge to jam. They had brought along some other friends, including a shy, bald guitarist from the Siberian city of Kemerovo who sat in with a lithe, dark-eyed beauty unfluently mouthing Billie Holiday tunes. The center of attention, though, was bearded saxophonist Vladimir Rezitsky, the founder of Arkhangelsk and its unquestioned genius of disorder and polyphony. He led the group first through an upside-down version of "Caravan," then a syncopated, electrified fourteenth-century Russian folk tune, topped off by a mellow rendition of "My Funny Valentine." Vodka was the principal libation, chased down by mounds of cheese and pickled garlic, and in the gentle starboard-to-port shuffle of the *Yushar,* all of us — Russians and foreigners alike — felt the walls of history and language slide past the steel-plated hull into the hum-ming depths.

Midsummer on the White Sea is all daylight or twilight; nothing truly nocturnal casts its shadow over the waves for a full fortnight, from mid-June until early July. We gathered on the poop deck as the ship's clock struck twelve, singing French children's songs and popping cham-pagne corks. The moon hovered serenely off to the east; the sun's still-beating heart hung above the western horizon, refusing to give up its place. The sea, draped in equinox purple and rose, held court. A biting wind blew down from the bow, but I had only one thought: the world was deeply, deeply beautiful.

In the space of a few short hours while I slept, dusk passed slowly but directly to dawn. By six, the church towers of the Solovetskiy Monastery could just barely be made out in the far distance off the ship's prow. Across the water was a sight that for centuries had given pilgrims and prisoners alike to ponder their mortality, and to shiver in wonder and dread at life and the manifold possibilities of each new day. For my part, I thought of Zhanna, and how her pain and confinement had transported me there, an envoy of her dying passions.

✳ ✳ ✳

A fortress of fantastic contradictions, the Solovetskiy Monastery is one of the most sacred places in all of Russian Orthodoxy. It is also one of the most tortured. From its founding in the fifteenth century to the present day, it witnessed the full gamut of human experience, from spiritual exaltation to methodical mass murder.

Turov had not made it back to our cabin that night — having found, I suspected, a more engaging bunkmate — so I decided to set off to explore the island without him. The ship was berthed alongside a concrete jetty. Beyond the Bukhta Blagopoluchiya — the Bay of Well-Being — lay the famous monastery.

Had the Solovetskiy Islands been left to the monks to run, they might well have succeeded in making it into the earthly paradise that Savvaty, German, and Zosima — the monastery's founders — had originally envisioned. The first portents were promising. At a time when bears and wolves still roamed freely about Russia, the absence of beasts of prey on the islands seemed to the monks a wondrous miracle. They soon discovered, as well, that the archipelago enjoyed a salubrious microclimate, which kept winter temperatures across the islands far more moderate than on shore.

The monks were nothing if not industrious. In greenhouses they grew fruit and vegetables unheard of on the mainland. They raised herring in an intricate network of artificial ponds built by their own hands. The monks laid out canals on which to navigate their little boats, and piped fresh water directly into the monastery. They had their own bakery, foundry, brick kiln, and print shop. By the nineteenth century, they were in every sense of the word, self-sufficient.

If only the outside world had left them alone! But here was where the Caesarian contagion lurking in Orthodox Christianity brought the monk's idyll down. From the Eastern rite's infancy in Byzantium, it had walked the same corridors, breathed the same air, broken the same bread as its temporal brother. The church and the state were different facets of the same twin-sided Constantinople, and here, under arctic rather than aromatic skies, this bitter compact betrayed the monks as surely as Cain struck down Abel.

Tragedy first swept over Solovki in the seventeenth century, when the monks rebelled against Moscow's changes to the Russian liturgy. To our skeptical late-twentieth-century minds, the dispute was as pointless as a schoolyard spat. The new rite, introduced under Tsar Alexis by his patriarch Nikon, called for worshipers to make the sign of the cross with three fingers rather than two, and introduced a series of comparatively minor redactions to the prayer books of the day.

When the reforms were resisted by the "Old Believers" — a label worn by their descendants to this day — the Tsar concluded that his Muscovite state was under threat. Those who turned their backs on the patriarch's amended rite were hounded until they renounced their heresy. Many who did not submit were put to death. The Old Believers' *ayatollah*, an outspoken priest named Avvakum, was burned at the stake in 1681. Tens of thousands of his followers, fearful that the patriarch was paving the way for the appearance of the Antichrist, did not wait to commit their souls to Heaven and immolated themselves in their own houses and barns.

Inspired by Avvakum's example, the Solovki monks refused to adopt the Nikonian reforms. In response, Tsar Alexis laid siege to the islands. Somehow, the monks held off Moscow's army for eight years, until one of the brothers treacherously unsealed a secret passageway, allowing the invaders to gain entrance to the monastery grounds. It was not the last time that blood was to be spilled inside its walls.

By Peter the Great's reign (he visited the monastery at least twice), Solovki had become a place as known for imprisonment and exile as it was for worship. Westernizers and xenophobes, court dissidents from St. Petersburg, and infidel princes from the Caucasus: within its ponderous walls, the vast, brooding fortress had cells aplenty for placid monks and political malefactors alike. Even as the Romanovs looked ever more rarely to Solovki for the incarceration of their foes — they had discovered in the interim the limitless potential of Siberia as a place of exile — the British and French obligingly kept the monastery in their sights, shelling it during a Crimean War raid.

None of this could adequately presage, however, the cruel vigor with which the Bolsheviks would wrench Solovki from its pastoral pretensions into the steely reality of the twentieth century. Their guiding spirit was Felix Dzerzhinsky, Lenin's secret police chief. The son of a Polish aristocrat, Dzerzhinsky brought a degree of dedication to his calling rarely seen outside the confines of a religious order. He combined the feverish discipline of a Dominican with the pious depravity of a Grand Inquisitor. His ecstasy lay in arrests, purges, and executions. More than one contemporary historian has concluded that he was quite mad.

In 1922, before the embers of civil strife and famine had cooled, Dzerzhinsky claimed the Solovetskiy Islands in the name of his *Cheka*, the original Soviet secret police. It was to be, he announced, a place where the revolution's enemies would either be cleansed of their sins or definitively excommunicated from the paradise on Earth being built by Lenin and his followers. Thus, Solovki was the birthplace of one of the century's least admired if most widely copied institutions: the reeducation camp.

The *Cheka's* was a peculiar regime of idealism and barbarity. One day the new masters of Solovki would crow loudly over how their charges had been transformed by honest labor and Marxist dialectics; the next, they would dispatch half-naked prisoners into the woods to be shot. Revolutionary fervor stood shoulder to shoulder with the ruthlessness of the common criminals who actually ran the camps — all proletarians, of course. It goes without saying that, as time progressed, the opportunists increasingly crowded out the true believers.

For understanding the significance of what took place on Solovki, Solzhenitsyn's account remains unsurpassed. The SLON — the "Northern Special Purpose Camps," as the installations centered around the Solovetskiy archipelago were known — metastasized across all of Soviet Eurasia, spawning what became known as the Gulag. Even the camps' acronym contained its own little sardonic irony. The word for "elephant" in Russian, SLON spawned a whole series of puns about the increasingly pachydermal dimensions of the camp system.

Inside the monastery, a hastily redone corner of the museum dealt with the horror that befell Solovki. Blurred photographs, old camp newspapers, exhortatory posters and banners, prisoners' journals: it was a sincere, but ultimately unsatisfying effort at recreating the epochal evil that gripped the islands in the early years of Bolshevism.

I followed the museum's assistant director as she led the dancers and jugglers through the whitewashed brick corridors of the monastery, into and back out of the Church of the Assumption and the Cathedral of the Transfiguration. She spoke of the architectural marvels of the Solovetskiy ensemble; the amazing industry of the monks; the monastery's heroic resistance before the French and English navies; and, with apparent feeling, of the imprisonment of the tsars' opponents within the walls of Solovki. Yet she uttered not a word about the Soviet period, and when the group came up to the panels devoted to the Gulag, she neatly steered the foreigners toward a nearby exit, leaving unaddressed two decades of foul mischief that helped give rise to even greater twentieth-century calvaries, from Auschwitz to Kampuchea.

I knew what had transpired here. I stood before the Transfiguration Gate and saw crying, stumbling prisoners wrestled out of roll call, dragged across the grass where I stood, and pushed behind the brick archway to be shot as casually as someone snapping off a light switch. It was not a matter of conjecture: this was the very place where it had all happened. The long-vanquished dead poked their heads from the ground like champignons and howled: "You see, you see!"

It was a fine afternoon, as joyous as a summer afternoon can be: bright, cloudless, complete. The foreign contingent, decked out in bathing trunks and bikinis, made for what was once the Archbishop's dacha and the bone-chilling, resin-sodden lakes that lie behind its wooded bluff. While the visitors splashed and played, calling out in mock horror at the shock of the water meeting their skin, I quizzed their guide, the same museum deputy director, about the century she had set aside.

She was an educated person, thoughtful and sympathetic in bearing and manner in a way that signaled her mainland roots. She looked me straight in the eye. "You understand these things. You live among us, and you know what we are like. They" — she nodded toward the light-hearted splashing in the water — "don't understand the first thing about Russia. Why should I burden them with the dark side of our history, the part that even we ourselves are only just beginning to understand?"

Yet she was to surprise me, just as I had perhaps given her pause with my not entirely ignorant questions about Solovki. Once everyone had dried themselves, finished their box lunches, and swatted away to the point of exhaustion the rapacious local colony of mosquitoes, she waved up a clanky old bus from the village and shepherded us on board. I asked her our destination. "The Church of the Beheading," she replied.

Twenty minutes later, after an uncomfortable ride along a rutted dirt road, the bus stopped at the base of a steep, pine-covered hill. "There is a beautiful church at the top of the rise," the guide announced, "and the best view of the Solovetskiy Islands." The visiting performers smiled expectantly, another light adventure awaiting them.

"It was also the most terrible place in the Stalinist period of Solovki," she added. "This is where they took prisoners to put them in the *izolator*, and many were tortured and murdered inside the church."

"You mean that there was a concentration camp here?" the Dutch accordianist asked, incredulously.

"Yes," my guide friend replied, "as Solzhenitsyn wrote, this is where the Gulag began."

Sekirnaya Hill was only a few hundred vertical feet high, but it rose up from the surrounding forest so abruptly that it enjoyed complete dominion over the surrounding landscape. Along with the others, I climbed the sun-speckled track that led to the Church of the Beheading, panting heavily at each knee-quaking station.

Curiously, it was only just before the summit that the church came into view. It was almost invisible, in a way that holy places are not meant to be. Its tired, pale facade seemed more forlorn than forbidding, emptied of all theology, either Christian or communist. A sightless old shepherdess sat in the shadow under a tree, a careworn smile fixed to her jaw, tending her unseen goats as they foraged for buds and berries. She was the only parishoner at the Beheading: its caretaker, its witness, its blind inheritance.

Sekirnaya Hill — Sekirka to the prisoners — was a name more feared than Solovki itself. Amid all the other fearsome sites that comprised the elephantine SLON, it was known as the place of punishment par excellence. Those who returned from their Sekirka sojourns — and they were far fewer in number than those who embarked — filled their fellows with hair-raising tales of terror.

Here sadism truly had no bounds. The inmates were made to sit all day on thick poles stretched from one side of the church's walls to the other, their feet dangling far above the floor. There was little food and even less water. Those prisoners who through exhaustion or inattention fell off the poles were beaten mercilessly by the guards, who at the Church of the Beheading were as self-consciously evil as disgraced angels, as ferocious as famished tigers. When they tired of clubbing their victims, they ran their prey out into the churchyard, tied them to logs, and pitched them down a long wooden staircase that ran from the top of the hill to its base. The monks had built precisely 365 steps, one for each day on the calendar. More often than not, the prisoner would reach the bottom in a heap of broken bones and blood. Perhaps only then did he find the bliss promised in bygone days, before the advent of scientific atheism.

To this day, the stairs fall away almost too far to see the bottom, toward a tranquil pond from which the monks once fished and drew their water. The view from the top, of blue ocean and scented pines, could only be described as painfully beautiful, a setting of alluring inhumanity.

By coincidence, it was Zosima's name day, the same Zosima who had helped found the Solovetskiy monastery. He and Savvaty were beekeepers, and according to Russian folk custom, on this day one began to collect the season's honey. It was said that when the bees flew to their hives in swarms, rain was sure to follow. When they clung to the walls of their hives, a heat wave was in the offing. Yet the humming of the bees and the hymns of their keepers were lost, for now, to Solovki, part of the leitmotif of forgotten names, ways, and sayings that once rhymed every Russian to the soil and the seasons.

✳ ✳ ✳

Later that summer, Zhanna's cancer went into remission, and she was able to go home. By fall, though, she was back in the hospital. This time, however, she gained admittance to the Botkin Institute, one of the best medical facilities in Moscow. It had been so, too, under communism, when it was reserved for the party elite and foreigners. Now Botkin was restricted only to those Russians who had amassed enough cash to pay for its services.

A Swiss admirer had heard of Zhanna's plight and covered her bill. Zhanna was elated to find that a hospital could be clean, its staff professional and courteous. Even the food was edible. When I stopped by one evening to see her, she was positively buoyant. Her new doctor had told her that they would assess her medical condition from scratch, with a whole new battery of tests. He also hinted of promising herbal treatments and salt-bath therapies. Hope had found the last bits of kindling at the back of the fireplace. "Perhaps the other doctors misdiagnosed everything," she said. "If only I'd had this type of care from the beginning!"

Meanwhile, Turov had been through Moscow a couple of times on business. By business, he did not mean jazz. In not so many words, he made it clear that he was no longer performing. Instead, he was putting all of his energy into a nebulous-sounding job selling timber to foreigners. He had "good contacts," he explained, with the Arkhangelsk authorities, and things were going very well indeed.

In my haste to return to Moscow that July from Arkhangelsk, I had neglected to stop at a place I had promised myself to visit. The saga of the Allied intervention in Russia had not ended with the stealthy departure of Ambassador Francis and his colleagues from Vologda. Troops from Britain, France, and Canada, as well as the United States, had come ashore in Arkhangelsk by the time Francis and his diplomatic colleagues reached the city. As it turned out, the soldiers were to stay in Russia for nearly twelve months of wretched, frostbitten duty that was complicated considerably by the blunders and half-measures of their commanders.

I was back in Velsk, this time in deep winter. It was the same unpretentious place I had strolled about during the summer, only turned outside in, its life having migrated from the town's leafy parks and riverbanks to stuffy kitchens and living rooms, where the cold months are lived out in front of the TV and the stove, or in vodka-inspired perorations against the vicissitudes of life.

Right on the train platform, I struck a deal with Boris, who was the proud owner of seven kiosks and the most elegant car in town, an Opel station wagon with a tape deck. He agreed to drive me north to Shenkursk, along what became known to thousands of shivering American doughboys as "the Vaga River front." In 1919 it had seen the bloodiest skirmishes that were ever to take place between U.S. troops and the Red Army.

By Velsk standards, Boris was a roaring success. He had built his fortune driving passengers from the rail station to their home villages. By working seven-day weeks, meeting trains at all hours, he had built up bit by bit enough *kapital* — that once-taboo word — to open up first one all-night kiosk, then another, and then another. First he had his family staff the booths, then friends and their relatives. The Opel was the one conspicuous fruit of his labors, and it worried Boris a bit. "I don't want to appear too rich," he confided. "I wouldn't want people to hate me."

Sad to report, Boris was a far more accomplished entrepreneur than driver. The same asphalt highway over which I had bounded the previous summer was now buried under two meters of hard-packed snow and ice. Boris was by nature impatient, and he could not fathom why he should not push a cassette into his tape deck, open a window to toss out his cigarette butt, offer up another observation about the wonders of making money, and steer the Opel, all at the same time. More than once we fishtailed wildly around curves while I gripped the dashboard, waiting for us to fly into the woods.

A day-long blizzard had just blown through, so it was easy to conjure up the inhospitable conditions under which the U.S. 339th Infantry Regiment labored as it squared off against the Bolsheviks — or the "Bolos," as the Allied troops derisively called them. I was headed to Shenkursk seventy-five years to the day after the 339th's retreat from the town, an event that did a great deal to convince President Wilson there was nothing to be gained by leaving American troops in Russia.

The muted sky, the snow-clogged fields, the ice-sated villages, the deathly still forests: the Michigan doughboys who pulled duty in Russian log stockades rather than French redoubts found themselves in an entirely different struggle than the rest of the world's Great War. In Russia, there were no trenches, no barbed wire coils, no fortified lines — only undemarcated bodies, shot, shattered, starved, strewn about willy-nilly like leaves and branches in the wake of a storm. The almost offhand execution of the Tsar marked the beginning of a barbaric era rather than the end, an anarchy as incomprehensible to the Russian Civil War's witnesses — including several thousand American troops — as the titanic clashes of armies in Europe were, in their own lunatic way, relentlessly logical and methodical.

Nearing Shenkursk, we swooped far too fast into one particularly sharp loop. The Opel came out of the curve in a panicky skid, then slid up to a militia car posted at an intersection.

One of the policemen walked up to the driver's side of the car and peered inside in an all-too familiar way. His cap's flaps were tied down tightly around his ears. "What's going on here, *tovarish?*" he asked, genuinely taken aback by the audacity of Boris' racing stop. "What's the big hurry? Let's see your documents."

Boris handed over a miserably tattered set of papers. The militia officer, his cheeks purple from the cold, flipped through them and frowned. "Your license has expired," he announced sternly. "And where's your violation card? You can't drive without your *teknitchiski talon.*"

"Oh — the *talon,*" Boris replied coolly, "it's back in my office."

"There will be a fine, a big fine," the militiaman announced. "And I'll have to confiscate your license plates." In my experience, this was an unmistakable overture for a bribe. The highway cops received a pittance in the way of a salary, so they handled their traffic responsibilities with much the same zeal as a shoe salesmen. They were only the most conspicuous state employees who worked on a commission basis.

"Have a cigarette," Boris said casually. "It's a Marlboro — not the Polish ones, but the real kind from America." He flicked one out of his open pack, a move I had only seen in the movies. The militiaman took the offering without a hint of embarrassment, and used Boris's cigarette to light his own.

Boris asked casually: "So is Sasha still with your Shenkursk brigade? I haven't seen him for years . . ."

"You know Sasha?" the militiaman asked, his eyebrow arching upward a bit skeptically.

"Know Sasha? Great guy, hell of a guy. Used to see him all the time, back in Velsk, down here when I came on police business . . ." His assertion of tribal ties hung in the air for just a moment.

"You were militia? The Velsk brigade — "

"Until my injury. Crushed my foot in a car bang-up. Chasing some hooligans. I've been out for a few years now. Miss it, miss it a lot."

The conversation went on in this comradely spirit for two more cigarettes, and then the militiaman waved us toward Shenkursk with a friendly little salute.

We drove on for a few moments before Boris tilted his head in my direction and commented: "Cops are really stupid."

"What about Sasha?"

Boris chuckled. "There's always at least one damn Sasha in every militia station."

We drove straight across the ice of the Vaga River — two wide lanes had been cleared of snow — and up a pine-covered embankment into Shenkursk. In September of 1918, with the Russian autumn already gripping the town, the 339th Infantry, like us, moved into Shenkursk unopposed.

At first, it looked as if the American soldiers had pulled a good assignment. Shenkursk was one of the larger towns in Arkhangelsk province, a summer resort of some renown, with a hotel, hospital, and other substantial buildings. More exceptionally in that lean, desperate year, there was ample food for both the doughboys and the locals. And, as one of the Americans reported home, some of the town's ladies were sophisticated enough to wear hats and other finery rather than the felt boots and shawls of the village peasant women.

Based on the first few skirmishes involving untrained Red combatants, the Allied leadership, including Ambassador Francis, came to the conclusion that the Bolshevik forces would present few complications. As the weather grew colder, the overconfident British generals commanding the Allies' joint military operations sent the Americans further upstream, along with a company of Canadian artillerymen. Before long, the Vaga began to narrow and Bolos appeared from time to time along the banks, taking potshots at the old side-wheeler the Allied troops had pressed into service. The river froze right over in a matter of days that November, and the soldiers, isolated hundreds of miles south of Arkhangelsk proper, settled down for the winter in the quiet, rustic villages that lined the way: Rovdino, Spasskoe, Ust-Padenga.

Life among the Russian peasants was an eye-opener for the small-town boys from Michigan, even if they did find some things to admire. Many of the soldiers were billeted in village homes, living for months in the very midst of Russian households. They marveled at the massive brick hearths, which were at the center of each family's health and welfare. The *pechka* not only kept the homes warm, but cooked food, boiled water, and provided the coziest sleeping platforms imaginable. As the American veterans of that Russian winter would wistfully recall in their waning years, more than one romance was consummated on these stoves.

The peasant houses themselves were perfectly adapted to their location on the subpolar brink of the habitable world. Their dark, somber
log frames were built to last for centuries, and — if spared the devasta-
tion of fire — often did. The corner joints of the big houses were hewed
by hand axe with mind-bending precision, and the ceiling cross beams
laid out so as to withstand even the heaviest winter snowloads.

The odors of Russian country life were less bearable, in what were
often crowded quarters. All winter long, the peasant kept his livestock
under the same roof as his family; the back half of the typical Arkhangelsk country house was essentially a barn. The humans did their
toiletry there as well. To make matters worse, the peasants washed
somewhat irregularly, and when they did, the process often involved a
peculiar soap made from pungent fish oil.

Still, there was an evident sympathy in the everyday relations between American and Russian that did not, for instance, characterize the
relationship between the British and the local population. The British
viewed the Russians through haughty imperial eyes. A "dos and don'ts"
sheet they produced for the edification of newly arrived Allied soldiers
warned that "the Russian is exactly like a child — inquisitive, easily
gulled, easily offended." On the other hand, the Americans shared their
rations with the needy, took local orphans under their wing, and in general treated the villagers with respect.

I would not have taken for granted these veterans' rosy accounts of
Russian-American conviviality in the midst of civil war had I not heard
the same repeated by the local dignitaries of Shenkursk. That morning,
the mayor and his entourage had waited for me to descend from the one
bus that in winter links the town with the outside world. When no curious outlander appeared, they went about their separate ways, assum-
ing that I would visit another day, if at all. They had underestimated my
spendthrift ways, never imagining for a moment that I would have gone
to the impossibly lavish lengths of *renting my own car and driver.*

My arrival, in the fabulous Opel station wagon of Boris, created a
minor stir in Shenkursk. The mayor was summoned from home, where
he was just finishing lunch; the local museum director and her staff re-
grouped and hastened to rearrange their meeting room to accommodate
a welcome ceremony; and the principal somehow rounded up the
schoolchildren he had laboriously coached to fete me.

In a matter of minutes, I found myself in an exhibit hall at a table crowned with fresh flowers, a considerable luxury anywhere in Russia in the month of January. A giggling delegation of ponytailed girls presented me with a boldly painted distaff in the region's folk style; the mayor offered a welcoming speech. I sipped delicately, self-consciously, at my teacup. Then came the invitation I dreaded — to speak before the group about my "research."

Perhaps they had imagined I was a noted historian, or an authority on what every generation of Soviet schoolchildren was told represented an unpardonable sin — namely, the intervention of the Western powers to crush the October revolution. Now they wanted to hear from an American expert. I thought of bluffing, invoking the usual banalities that come to mind on such occasions: people everywhere are all the same, we want to live in peace, never again should the armies of our two countries meet on the battlefield. Either way, I realized, my audience was bound to be disappointed. I stood up, cleared my throat, thanked the assembled citizens for the honor they had bestowed on me by attending the gathering, and sat down. There was a murmur of dismay from the adults; the children stared blankly at me, and fidgeted.

A woman standing in the back came to my rescue. She was a schoolteacher in Ust-Padenga, and she had spent years quietly talking to the village elders and collecting stories about the "winter of the Americans," as the old folks called it. "It was a difficult time," she began, "a very complicated time." At first, I was not sure what she meant, but soon it became clear that the difficulty she referred to had resided not only in the cusp of civil war, seventy-five years before, but in the intervening years, and lived in the minds of the audience itself. "Before we could not speak openly about that period. We were told what to think. The Whites and the foreign interventionists were evil and destructive; the Reds were our glorious liberators. But it was more complicated than that — much more complicated."

The mayor then chimed in: "You won't find a soul in this entire Shenkursk *oblast* who would have anything bad to say about the American occupation. Your soldiers were disciplined and correct. They were generous to the children, and they shared their rations. It was war, of course, but people liked them, and felt sorry when they had to leave. In fact, quite a few families left Shenkursk right behind your troops — some of them," he added with a chuckle, "became our American cousins, although we of course lost track of them completely following the Revolution."

Afterward, the mayor and I climbed into his official car along with one of his lieutenants. Boris followed us in the Opel. Blotted with purple and gray, the afternoon was draining away precipitously along the western horizon. We were on our way to the schoolteacher's village, to Ust-Padenga, to meet an old woman who had seen the great battle with her own eyes.

The Americans chose Ust-Padenga as a forward defensive position because it featured hills and bluffs that could be readily fortified and which offered fine views of the Vaga River and its surroundings. A second village to the south, called Nizhni Gora — Low Hill — became one stronghold. Behind Ust-Padenga, to the north, the Allied troops built log blockhouses and gun positions at the top of a ridge called Visorka Gora.

The Americans arrived in October. Their duty had been tough but not particularly dangerous. The one exception was a patrol that was ambushed in the woods, with disastrous results. Six Americans made a ferocious last stand; when their bodies were located, they were surrounded by dead Red Army partisans. In the type of barbarity that characterized the Russian Civil War, the U.S. Army lieutenant who had led the patrol was found with his arms and legs crudely severed.

By mid-January, the signs of Red Army activity were growing increasingly ominous. Bolshevik patrols drew closer and closer to the American positions, and although the doughboys rarely caught a glimpse of the white-clad troops, they swore they could hear them moving about in the forests and among the snow-covered ravines.

Alarmed, the British commander-in-chief of the Allied forces in north Russia made an inspection of Shenkursk and its forward defenses. While he felt the town's defenses were strong, he viewed the Americans' exposed position at Ust-Padenga with concern. Later, over tea with the abbess of the Shenkursk convent, he felt he could not give her the assurances she wanted against an eventual Soviet capture of the town. He returned to Arkhangelsk with a sense of unease.

One morning not long after his departure, the American defenders of Nizhni Gora woke up to a heavy barrage. Shells were exploding all too close to the log houses where they were billeted. Across the way were the Bolos, advancing steadily from the edge of the forest toward the doughboys' position. They numbered in the hundreds, far surpassing the handful of Americans holding the Nizhni Gora position. It was 45 degrees below zero.

Suddenly, another party of Reds came charging up the hill. A frantic firefight ensued, with the Americans holding off successive rushes with heavy machine-gun fire. Yet the pressure was too great. A group of Cossacks fighting with the Whites arrived to bolster the American defenses, then broke and ran when their commander was cut down.

With a number of his men already wounded, the lieutenant in charge of the U.S. troops gave the order to retreat back into the village of Nizhni Gora. The Bolsheviks, however, already controlled the main street, and the Americans were forced to scramble under fire through the deep snow behind the village houses. Corporal Guiseppe De Amicis died behind his Lewis gun, trying to cover his retreating comrades. Corporal Victor Stier, who had been struck in the jaw with a bullet at the opening of the engagement, was wounded again, this time fatally. Even those doughboys who made it out of the village alive faced a gauntlet of enemy fire across an open snowfield before they could reach the relative safety of the American position on Visorka Gora.

In all, only seven of the original forty-seven members of the platoon managed to make it back to their lines that day. The next morning, two other soldiers stumbled into camp. They had found refuge in a sympathetic peasant's closet, then bayoneted their way past a search party that stumbled onto their hiding place. They were the luckiest men on the battlefield, notwithstanding their frostbite.

I recognized the place even before the mayor's car came to a stop. Ust-Padenga lay right beside the main Moscow-Arkhangelsk highway. In fact, the road actually traversed Nizhni Gora and its higher neighbor, Visorka Gora, a bluff over the Vaga River that I had admired as I passed by the previous summer, oblivious to the place's uneasy significance in U.S.-Russian history.

Now, muffled by heavy snow and geriatric light, its beauty was starker, more equivocal. The schoolteacher led us along an icy footpath at the top of the ridge, and pointed to the centuries-old timbers of the village houses. They were pockmarked with bullet holes, and here and there, larger craters the size of angry fists. "Here, you can see the shell holes.

These were made in 1919, when the Reds bombarded the American positions." She gestured toward a level area just outside the cluster of homes. "That's where the Americans were buried. In the summer, you can still make out where the graves are. A few years after the battle, they came to take the bodies away, but some may have been left behind."

The Americans, shielded by their log blockhouses, held out along the top of the rise for a couple of days. They were seconded by two artillery pieces, manned by hardened Canadian veterans of the Western front. During the abbreviated daylight hours, the Red troops mounted repeated infantry assaults against the bluff, but to no avail. Many of the attackers were cut down by the Canadians, who demonstrated considerable skill at firing short-fuse shrapnel into the Bolshevik ranks. Their losses were appalling; hundreds of Reds fell under the Allied guns.

Just as incendiary shells began to fall on Visorka Gora, the order came to withdraw. The Allied commanders had concluded that the attack on Ust-Padenga was just part of a broader thrust designed to dislodge the foreigners and their White Russian allies from Shenkursk itself. Now the Americans on Visorka Gora were in danger of being cut off. They organized their retreat in the light of a burning house struck by a Soviet shell.

The Allied wounded were hastily loaded onto pony sledges. The other men followed behind on foot, stumbling on despite the predatory cold of night. After an uneasy daylight halt in a village known for its Bolshevik sympathies, the exhausted troops took to the road again after dark, praying that they would be able to evade the enemy patrols they knew were in the vicinity.

The next day, in Spasskoe, the company made another stand, once again under heavy bombardment. The doughboys took up positions in a churchyard cemetery, crouching for cover behind gravestones and crosses. The captain in charge of the one remaining Canadian gun was killed by a Bolshevik shell, and his American counterpart nearly so. The men fought again during the brief hours of daylight, then pulled back under the cover of darkness, this time to the relative safety of Shenkursk.

They did not have much of an opportunity to rest. The situation in Shenkursk was growing increasingly desperate. By all accounts, the town was nearly surrounded. From the monastery's church towers, the gunflashes of the Bolshevik artillery were visible from almost all points of the compass. There was little time to spare. The order was given after nightfall; the troops would pull out immediately, bringing with them only what they could carry on their own backs.

The main escape route north in the direction of Shegovary and Arkhangelsk was already blocked by the Reds. The Allied troops — British, American, Canadian, and White Russian — had no choice but to march out along a narrow forest track which their scouts had reported was still open. It was a windless, bitterly cold night. The wounded went first, carried on sleds behind hardy Russian ponies. Next came the able-bodied soldiers, about a thousand in all. It was hard going; the snow on this forgotten route was hardly broken. It was worst of all for those who had taken part in the fighting in Nizhni Gora; for six days, they had had virtually no rest. Before long, the soldiers began to jettison their belongings in the hope of lightening their load: boots and belts, Bibles and bottles all went by the wayside. Some of the men collapsed and had to be revived by their fellows, who shook and slapped them or rubbed snow in their faces.

Bringing up the rear were some five hundred townspeople — those who had no confidence in the mercy of the advancing Bolsheviks — carrying with them as many of their belongings as they could manage to throw onto their sleighs. Most of them were never to return to Shenkursk.

The column of soldiers and refugees, which stretched along the road for a mile, somehow slipped away undiscovered, making ten miles by dawn. With the first light, the Bolsheviks unleashed another artillery barrage on Shenkursk, a sign that they still did not realize that the Allies had abandoned the town.

Nor, as it turned out, did they pursue the retreating Allied units. In strategic terms, the Red Army had already made a powerful statement. The retreat from Shenkursk put an end to the Allied ambition of playing a direct role in bringing down the Bolsheviks. In the face of vastly superior numbers, there was no hope of linking with the White Russian armies then advancing on central Russia from Siberia. By summer, all of the Americans would be gone. Not long after, the British and French, too, held up their hands and departed, leaving the hodgepodge of Russian monarchists, socialists, and nationalists — united only by their hatred of Bolshevism — to sail away into exile or make their peace with the new Soviet masters. So it was that we in the West forgot this episode entirely, while every Russian schoolchild learned how the foreign interventionists were flung back to their ships and the Union of Soviet Socialist Republics was saved.

✳ ✳ ✳

Evgenia's son was waiting for us by the door of her house, one of perhaps two dozen homes in Ust-Padenga. Although it evidently was built well before the revolution, it was in reasonably good repair. I asked him if his mother, at eighty-three, was the oldest resident of the village.

No, he replied, there was a man who was older who lived a few doors away, as well as a woman at the other end of the road who was nearly one hundred. But his mother, he added, was the person who remembered the Americans best.

Evgenia was seated on a worn green divan. A table and two or three spindly chairs rounded out the furniture. The walls were painted white, with a somber, sooty Madonna of Smolensk perched in one corner. I might have called it the house's only decorative touch, but in the mind of the peasant, an icon's role was as utilitarian as a hoe or a ewe. In the gentle eddies of the old Russian north — unlike the rest of the country — many icons never left their places of honor, nor ceded their space to the graven images of the Bolshevik heroes: Lenin, Stalin, or lesser dieties like Brezhnev.

I was directed to sit next to Evgenia, and within moments she took my hand. Hers felt damp and shapeless, clammy as a fallen leaf brought back up from the autumnal ground. She had heard an American was coming to visit her — the first she had encountered in seventy-five years — and her eyes sparkled oddly against her wrinkled skin and high, fragile cheekbones. Like an abandoned orchard tree animated by a passing gust, something girlish and strong-legged was stirring, something long-buried by the gerontological processes of decay and senility. My entourage leaned over expectantly. Evgenia's son looked a bit apprehensive.

"Bill," she began, "lived with us." Her smile had widened and brightened even more, to the point where she looked a bit unhinged.

"There were two American soldiers that were billeted here with the family," the son interjected, half-whispering. "She's talking about one of them. She was seven years old at the time."

Unmindful of her son, and ignoring everyone else in the room but me, Evgenia continued. "Bill was a very nice boy," she recalled. "He used to help with the chores. He brought us food, too. He gave us children chocolate. It was very good chocolate, I remember that." She gripped my hand tighter. "I wish I knew what happened to him. We never knew if he got away after the fighting."

"Tell him about the battle, Evgenia Nikolaevna," the mayor urged. "He's come a long way and he wants to hear about what happened."

This was a topic that seemed to interest her less. "It was terrible, just terrible. They fired right over the house, toward Visorka Gora. Momma made us hide in the root cellar. There were explosions from morning to night, and we were all frightened." But she did not have much else to offer in the way of battlefield lore. It was the account of a seven-year-old, not a military historian. Even now, her mind was on something else. "You look like Bill," she said, peering more closely at me. "Momma and Pappa never heard what happened to him, whether he escaped or whether he died. I wish I knew."

"What did your parents think of the Americans?" I asked.

"They liked them. Everyone liked them. They weren't afraid of hard work. And they paid for their lodging, and for their meals. They were *much,"* she emphasized the word almost vehemently, *"much* better than either the Whites or the Reds." She paused, then added, "I'm sorry, but it's the truth, by God. The Whites, the Reds, they never did a thing for the peasant. They just took what they wanted and they didn't care if they left anything for you or not. Things just got worse and worse. There was never enough food again. And there were more killings."

Her hands, stifling as a shroud, reached up my forearm. "We had such a time, such a gay time. Bill could pick me right up and put me on his shoulders. And he taught all the girls — even me — how to dance. He would turn the handle on his machine — he called it the Victrola — and we would listen to the music, and dance. I never heard music like that before. I never ever heard that music again, either."

Then she looked at me, and asked very simply, directly and lucidly: "Do you know what happened to Bill?" Before I had a chance to answer, she began to hum something to herself from very long ago, *la–dee–dee–dah,* a tune that sounded a great deal like a foxtrot.

✶ ✶ ✶

Not long after I returned to Moscow, I heard that Zhanna had passed away. I found out the night before the burial; the news came in a call from a saxophonist who had known her very well and me only slightly. But he was in a hurry, I had already made plans for the next day, and somehow I did not find the time, as the expression goes, to attend her funeral. I still feel ashamed, even now as I write these words.

I was told later that it was a raw, moody affair, attended by music people from all over Russia, and a few from even farther away. Zhanna adored flowers, and there were many bouquets for her leavetaking. A group of old jazz friends had an impromptu jam at the foot of her grave, but it was too frigid for the horn players to keep their lips pressed to their instruments for long. I heard that Turov was there too, serving as one of the pallbearers. The funeral broke up in a dark, blustery snow shower, with toasts and tears all around.

I still think of Zhanna — in fact, not so infrequently. That people like her awoke under Khrushchev, rebelled under Brezhnev, and clearly saw what they needed to do under Gorbachev: that is what brought change to the big, burly, boisterous landmass we call Russia. She saw her country for what it was, and loved its appalling prodigal ways, as they say in Russian, *bez sentimentalnosti* — without sentimentality.

We foreigners, on the other hand, cannot help but be sentimental about Russia. John Cudahy, a young U.S. Army lieutenant who fought in that same winter of 1918–19 wrote some lines that have not been surpassed by any of the legions of American journalists, diplomats, and chroniclers who have since tried to capture what it was about the country that both fascinated and afflicted them:

> This is Russia of the American soldier, a cluster of dirty huts, dominated by the severe white church, and encircling all, fields and fields of spotless snows; Russia, terrible in the grasp of devastating Arctic cold; the squalor and fulsome filth of the villages; the mou-

jik, his mild eyes, his patient bearded face — the grey drudgery and gaping ignorance of his starved life; the little shaggy pony, docile and uncomplaining in winds icy as the breath of the sepulcher; Russia, her dread mystery, and that intangible quality of melodrama that throngs the air, and lingers in the air, persistently haunts the spirit, and is as consciously perceptible as the dirty villages, the white church, and the grief-laden skies.

THE WIDOWED
MOUNTAINS

KABARDINO-BALKARIA

THE SUMMER MORNING took a first, supple, waking stretch, rolling gently over to reveal the bare shoulders of the distant range, wrapped in lavender and rose mist. The supine fields, the cypress-lined lanes, the baby brick houses bordered by whitewashed walls — all lay motionless on the slumbering plain. Breathless from its rush south across the dusty Russian steppes, the train slowed, as if it, too, were awestruck. All the light, all the glory of this opulent dawn belonged to the Caucasus.

I was hardly the first traveler to be moved by the sight of these peaks. Many arrived with more aggressive intentions than mine. Scythians, Persians, Macedonians, Romans, Parthians, Arabs, Cumans, Mongols, Turks: all had come before me, indomitable conquerers seduced by this notoriously passionate topography.

By contrast, the Russians were arrivistes, eleventh-hour pretenders to the maiden's hand. Only in the eighteenth century did they reach the ancient divide between Europe and Asia. Yet they soon made up for lost time. As conquerers go, the Russians proved to be unusually obsessed, and doubly morbid. Whatever the geopolitical rationale for subjugating the Caucasus — securing Moscow's borders, bringing the Turks to heel, countering British expansionism — Russian men under arms seemed to exult in the bloodstained exoticism that came with making war in these parts.

In the early nineteenth century, hunting down Chechens and dispatching Circassians was all part of the rite of passage for dashing young officers from St. Petersburg. Some of Russia's greatest writers also found inspiration in Caucasian bloodletting. Playing at cavalryman rather than pacifist, fledgling author Lev Tolstoy helped raze native villages, all the while coveting the St. George's Cross and the garrison whores. Outside of Grozny, which was in Tolstoy's day a solitary Russian fortress surrounded by enemy redoubts, the humanitarian-to-be once reveled in his narrow escape from a party of murderous Chechen horsemen.

Mikhail Lermontov's audacious, blackguard talent found its muse in the bittersweet Caucasus wars. A Guards officer who was exiled to the frontier for having criticized the tsar, his poetry overflows with a morose bravado. Killing, loving, reciting verse all ultimately brought in him much the same reaction: ". . . Life, if you really look at it, is such a dull, such an empty farce . . ." He admired his Muslim foes the way a big game hunter loves the elk, seeking — while slaying the object of his admiration — to stoke his own nihilistic romanticism. In an eerie presaging of a death as pointless as it was inevitable, Lermontov wrote these lines in 1841, a few months before he was gunned down in a duel:

> In noon's heat, in a dale of Dagestan,
> With lead inside my breast, stirless I lay;
> The deep wound still smoked on; my blood
> Kept trickling drop by drop away.

Little by little, by sheer dogged persistence and the dumb logic of vastly superior numbers, the Russians wore down the mountain peoples, progressively bringing larger and larger portions of the Caucasus under their control. Tens of thousands died resisting the Russians; hundreds of thousands of the vanquished fled to Turkey and beyond. Some of the tribes, from the Adygey to the Tsakhur, were reduced to little more than musty folk costumes and nostalgic place names. Yet a century and a half later, after the relative quiet of the Brezhnev era, the same twisted dance of seduction and subjugation had still not run its course. Even now, the Caucasus held a fatal attraction for Russia.

✳ ✳ ✳

It was a Friday in August. Sunlight began to spill down from above the surrounding hills into the city of Nalchik, still dozing, fresh and virginal, in the morning quiet. The taxi galloped along wide and empty boulevards flanked by gently swaying shade trees. A bearded old man in gray overalls and a blue beret was sweeping a sidewalk, attentively, in short, self-assured strokes. He looked up, and I remembered. This was once a nation of warriors, not street sweepers. The Caucasus made for proud people.

They sang the praises of the Hotel Nalchik — back in Moscow, that is. I was assured it was the finest the capital of Kabardino-Balkaria — a "republic" within the Russian Federation — had to offer. Yet my room reeked of cigarettes and something indescribably more taboo, something animal, corporeal. Even after I opened the windows, the stench would not go away. Had the last guest who stayed here ever checked out, I wondered? I opened the bathroom door cautiously, half-expecting to find a corpse in the tub. But there was no body, and in fact no tub. Instead, a gurgling showerhead hung gloomily over a dank, greenish slab. While I shaved, a cockroach swaggered over my toothbrush, then took refuge underneath a towel.

I went out onto the balcony. Across the avenue in front of the hotel stood a statue. The figure wore a turban. I was tired, I realized, bonetired. I closed the curtains, lay down as best I could on the Hottentot-sized bed, and fell fast asleep.

When I awoke, a halfhearted breeze was brushing the bottom of the drapes back and forth along the floor. It was suffocatingly hot, the summer of dry steppes and parched horsemen. I returned to the balcony and parted the curtains. The square below broiled in the full sun. A group of men had gathered around a bench; they wore dark homburgs and black cotton jackets. Nearby, a grill smoked and spluttered beneath a rack of shish kebabs.

Why had I come to this place? In part, because I knew nothing about it, because as far as the outside world was concerned, there was almost nothing to know about it. The papers were full of headlines about the Chechens and their mounting defiance of Moscow. The Georgians to the south were immersed in their customary fratricide. Cholera had struck with a vengence in nearby Dagestan. Ingush was killing Ossetian, and vice-versa, next door. But Kabardino-Balkaria was a quiet eddy on the map of the Caucasus, or so it seemed from afar.

The Balkars, though, had an unquiet history. Along with the Chechens and several other mountain peoples, they were deported from their homeland in 1944 by a vengeful Stalin, who accused them of collaboration with the Nazis during the brief period the Germans held the North Caucasus. In the late fifties, under Khrushchev, the Balkars were permitted to return, but a cloud of shame, it seemed, still lingered over their lands. The standard Soviet reflex of secrecy, coupled with the outside world's utter indifference, had consigned the Balkars to deep shadow. What was left of them? Did they have a language, a culture, a separate identity? Or like other peoples swallowed up in the vast Soviet space, had they ceased to exist as anything more than an ethnographer's footnote?

A few weeks before my arrival, I had sent a telegram to the Ministry of Culture of the Republic of Kabardino-Balkaria, asking for help. From my hotel room, I called to arrange a meeting. Had they received my message? There was a long pause, and the reply seemed to come from far away, rather than just a few blocks up the street: "Yes, yes, we received it."

Perhaps it was a mistake to set the meeting for 11:30 A.M. I had reasoned that it would be better to meet before lunch than after, since the minister and his staff might leave early for the weekend. As it turned out, Nalchik's "Government House" was already devoid of life by late morning, its lobby somnolent but for the flies orbiting the head of a snoozy guard. He pointed me up a flight of marble stairs, which led to a long corridor. The high ceilings and mirrors magnified the impression of a vast emptiness, a bureaucratic Gobi.

Eventually, I found the minister's office and knocked. There was no answer. I tried the doorknob. With a little push, the door opened to a reception room. Only there was no receptionist. There was no one at all.

After a moment, I heard a hearty burst of laughter. It came from behind the minister's door. I waited, hoping someone would appear. Finally, there was nothing else to do. I knocked on the door and walked in.

The minister and the man who would be introduced to me as the vice-minister were, it appeared, enjoying a good chuckle over a bottle of cognac.

"Is this the minister's office?" I asked, already fearing the worst.

The taller of the two, who was rising to his feet as ponderously as an ox, looked annoyed at the interruption. He was too large a man to be a convincing Minister of Culture. He looked like a stevedore, only pretentious.

"I am the minister," he pronounced solemnly.

We all shook hands, the minister, the ferret-faced vice-minister, and I. I was motioned to sit down. They did not seem surprised to see me, yet they were anything but welcoming. There was not a hint of bonhomie; in fact, the audience had all the cheer of a forced march. As I explained what I was interested in seeing and doing, my words were met with perfunctory nods and grunts. Five minutes into the meeting, and my interlocutors had hardly ventured a word. Officialdom had evidently obliterated all expression from their faces. Only their eyes searched and probed, like the eager glare of lions waiting for a wildebeest to start and stumble.

"I'm particularly interested in the history of the Balkars, including their deportation after the war," I was saying.

Just then, the minister interrupted. "They were deported *during* the war. It was wartime, you see."

I explained that I had heard about a retired general who was the leader of a Balkar nationalist party. Was there any way I could arrange to meet him? The minister shrugged his shoulders. "Lieutenant-General Beppayev? I've never heard of him," he said blandly. He looked over at the vice-minister. "Have you?" he asked. The man shook his head solemnly.

I wondered whether I could speak to any Balkar elders, those who had survived exile in Central Asia.

"Well," the minister began, "you've come at an awkward time. You see, it's already Friday, and there's nothing that we can do until next week."

I volunteered to make my own arrangements if the minister would provide me with some names and phone numbers. "No, that would not be possible," the vice-minister shot back.

"On Monday, I will call you personally to talk about the arrangements," the Minister said. This, I took it, was meant to be reassuring. In truth, I had been given the cold shoulder. Then the minister stood up and extended his dockside hand. His grip was strangling, like a well-oiled rope. It was time to go.

I was a bit taken aback. I knew no one, had no leads. My carefully worded telegram, so ingratiating, so self-important, had not even merited a cup of tea.

Slowly, I walked back down Nalchik's main avenue in the direction of the hotel. Raven-faced women promenaded arm in arm, clucking over the day's events. Their hirsute men strode behind, absorbed in schemes, disputes, and reveries. A clutch of gypsies begged on one corner; a second group sold gold chains and rings on the next. Alighting beside a donkey cart, a tinted-glass Mercedes raced its engine out of a stoplight.

In retrospect, I can say I owe everything I was able to do in Kabardino-Balkaria to the Nalchik phone book. In Soviet days, a city's telephone directory — if it existed at all — was as hard to get one's hands on as a code book. People collected phone numbers over the course of decades, painstakingly committing them to notebooks and scraps of paper. Now, canny young businessmen had seized upon the idea of publishing telephone directories for profit. As luck would have it, they were available at almost every Nalchik kiosk. I tucked one under my arm gratefully; I had my first break.

In my travels, I would also sup at the bookshops, gulping up virtually anything put out by local publishing houses. Nowadays, among Russians, these titles had few takers. The Russian public — as devoted a culture of readers as there is in the world — was too enthralled with imported pulp fiction and sex manuals to bother now with homegrown tomes about history and culture. This was the impact the opening to the

West had on the Russian book market, leaving both intellectuals and right-wingers fuming at the disappearance of the country's great classics from the bookshelves. Today, across most of humiliated Russia, it was easier to buy Tom Clancy than Chekhov.

This was not to say that literature in Kabardino-Balkaria — that is, literature in the broadest understanding of the word — was dead. According to the Nalchik papers, there was to be that very evening a gala celebrating the sixtieth birthday of the greatest living Balkar poet, Tanzilya Zumakulova. "Flowers on the Stage," one headline proclaimed. In a front page sidebar, fellow writers had fallen over one another to lavish praise on her. "Tanzilya is truly an outstanding poet," waxed one, "the pride of her native literature, a splendid master of Soviet poetry." The President of Kabardino-Balkaria had decreed Tanzilya a "People's Artist of the Republic of Kabardino-Balkaria." In fact, as I read further, I realized that Tanzilya had by some fantastic coincidence captured all of the local papers' front pages. Obviously, this was to be a landmark event.

The reputed bard of the Balkars — "whose wisdom is as great as a man's," according to one columnist — was seated stage right, several meters back from the footlights. I was squeezed into one of the back rows of the auditorium, chockablock with giggling schoolgirls and sweating functionaries in coats and ties. From where I sat, at least, Tanzilya did not bewitch. She looked uncomfortable, like a frumpish typing teacher dragged out in front of a school assembly.

For an evening celebrating the poet laureate of the Balkar people, there was surprisingly little Balkar spoken. There were, instead, a great number of flowerly speeches in heavily accented Russian. A relentless procession of notables in all shapes and sizes came up to the microphone, paying homage to Tanzilya in terms that might have led even a sovereign to blush.

However, it was soon apparent that the words mattered less to the audience — and perhaps to Tanzilya as well — than the speakers' deeds. The head of the Writers Union presented Tanzilya with a set of china. The minister of agriculture offered up a boom box and a carpet. The presents began to pile up in the commodious environs of Tanzilya's feet. Each factory manager, each collective farm director, each district chief came forth, leading delegations bearing microwaves, TV sets, dining-room tables.

True, there were brief cultural interludes. Men in black boots and karakul hats leaped across the stage, their *kinjal* daggers slashing high through the air; svelte young women with braided hair whirled and beat goatskin tambourines. Soon, however, another videotape machine would be laid before Tanzilya. "Tanzilya, Tanzilya . . ." began all of the tributes; the typing teacher smiled and applauded absently, wordlessly.

The hours went by, the testimonials uncounted. This was, I thought, a recondite medieval ritual. Each speaker unveiled his gifts by declaiming their modesty, but the gasps and clapping of the audience told a different story. There was dishonor for those who had the bad luck of bearing a gift that had already been unveiled by a predecessor — but after all, how many different brands of tape deck were available in Kabardino-Balkaria?

The greatest *coup de theatre* was pulled off by the speaker of the republic's parliament. He complimented the quality and good taste of the preceding gifts, apologized for being able to offer so little, then drew from his vest pocket the keys to a new car. The crowd roared its approval.

It is written in the Koran: *"The life of this world is but a vain provision."*

The pageant had gone on well into the evening, almost past the supper hour. Still, Tanzilya was mute. Now the master of ceremonies announced that there was time for only a few more speeches. A tall, vigorous man leaped to his feet and approached the microphone. "Stereos are good," he began, "video machines are good, cars are good — but Tanzilya is better." His remarks had a purposeful ring; his voice soared rather than wafted. "And thus, it gives me great pride," he went on, "to announce that Tanzilya has made an important decision, the decision of someone who loves her country, her motherland. She has concluded that in view of the desperate condition of the state today and the crimes of Yeltsin and his clique, she will join the Central Committee of the Communist Party of the Kabardinian-Balkar Republic." So much, I thought, for the conscience of the Balkar people. The apparatchik poet smiled faintly as the lights in the house went up. There was no poetry to be heard that night.

Outside, the night air revived my spirits. I walked back across the square to my hotel, past the turbaned figure on the pedestal. When I got back to my room, I picked up the phone and called a number in the telephone directory. Professor Musukayev — the author of a modest booklet entitled "Traditional Hospitality of the Kabardinians and Balkars" I had bought earlier in the day — answered the phone. After we had spoken — and it was a good conversation — the line went dead.

* * *

Sanctioned by the minister of culture or not, I was determined to see Elbrus, the mountain soul of the Caucasus. The next morning, I found a taxi driver in front of the hotel and struck a deal.

We headed south, into the first foothills. The roadsides were dusty and potholed, but as we climbed, the hot shimmer of the plains freshened bit by bit into a bright, angular clarity. The sullen brown of the sunburnt fields around Nalchik gave way to trim backyard orchards and verdant upland meadows. The Kabardinian villages, sturdy and neat, displayed a decided pride of place. Their houses were crowned by tin crescents and gleaming filigree that shined like toy minarets — the first shoots of Islam's reascent. Even the village cows looked scrubbed and well-fed.

My driver, too, was Kabardinian. He evinced a certain dignity uncommon to his Muscovite counterparts. He guided his cab like the skilled cavalier he no doubt was, holding the wheel with a single practiced hand. He was courteous, dutiful, but without even a hint of servility.

I asked about his family. He admitted — with no trace of discomfort — that he had only laid eyes on his wife on one occasion before they were wed. "I wasn't sure how pretty she was," he chuckled, "but I knew that she had just graduated from a cooking institute. So at least I was going to eat well!"

In the end, his wife had given him three sons; he was, he said, completely satisfied. He described her as *ochen poslushnaya*, very obedient, an expression that I had only heard used before by dog owners. Now the time had come, he added, to find a mate for his oldest son, who had just completed his obligatory military service.

"We thought that with *perestroika* we would become rich," he went on. He shook his head, and there was a note of irony in his voice. "Not so long ago, all of the Soviet Union came here for vacation. But now the tourists have stopped coming. If you have dollars, you go to Paris or

New York. If you don't, you stay at home planting potatoes for the winter. Besides, everyone thinks that the Caucasus is dangerous, that it is all robbing and shooting and killing."

Below, a chalky river frothed in the narrowing valley. The route began now to meander back and forth across the valley as the way steepened. With a gnashing of gears, the car's engine deepened an octave.

Why had things remained quiet in Kabardino-Balkaria, I asked, when neighboring lands, from Georgia to Chechnya, were so troubled?

"We want peace. The Kabardinians, the Balkars, we are the same people." The answer was too smug, I thought.

"What about last summer? Didn't the Balkars demonstrate? Didn't they say they wanted their own republic?"

From the awkward pause that ensued, it was obvious no one had posed him these questions before, at least not in this precise juxtaposition.

"There was trouble," he began, "but the government put things right again. The Balkars came to their senses." Now the fat was in the fire. "Besides, this idea, a Balkar republic, it's . . . it's ridiculous."

He turned toward me, taking his eyes off the road — something I by no means wanted to encourage. "How could they feed themselves? How would they live? Look at these rocks, these mountains," he continued, gesturing at the walls of the ravine we were approaching.

I pressed him further. "But the Balkars used to live in these mountains. Why couldn't they now?"

"They lived terribly," he blurted out derisively, "in caves! All they had were their sheep. As it was, they depended entirely on the Kabardinians. Besides," he added heatedly, "there are many more Kabardinians than Balkars. Why should they have their own republic when there are so few of them? What would be next? Would every family have its own republic? Every house?"

Before long, we reached Zhankhoteko, where for generations — perhaps centuries — there has been a wool market in the village square. Here, the absence of tourists was evident. I had the wares of thirty women all to myself: thick sweaters, shawls, and blankets. I did not have to haggle; the prices plummeted audibly as I walked from one stall to the next.

We climbed with the valley, winding ever higher underneath bare, stony escarpments. The firs and pines melted from the landscape. Along the way, we passed through Tyrnyauz, a mining town clutching the mountainside for dear life. The place had all of the ugly quirks of provincial Sovietism: crumbling prefab apartment blocks and a thicket of belching pipes, chimneys, and vents. Somewhere out of sight above, the heights were being plumbed for tungsten and molybdenum, two metals prized by the Russian space industry. Gargantuan chutes ran thousands of feet down a sheer rock face and into the river.

South of Tyrnyauz, the high peaks and glaciers of the main Caucasus range came into view. The summer sun was warm, almost too warm inside the black Volga sedan. Still, the snow-grizzled mountains had an aloof quality, like a distant, silently admonishing parent.

As much as the summits and glaciers might have passed in a photograph for someplace in the European Alps — the Swiss Engadin perhaps — a single glance around the valley floor was enough to debunk any alpine conceit of pristine air and prim habitations. Even here, a mile and a half above sea level, the motif was decay. We had entered the sanatoria district, a once-exclusive playground of the Communist Party's rich and famous. These spa buildings, while never luxurious by our standards, were plum vacation spots in the Brezhnev era. Now they had fallen on hard times, or worse. At the few that had managed to stay open, pensioners padded about on unkempt walkways in cheap print dresses and baggy cotton shirts, ghosts of the Soviet Union's unself-consciously gauche past.

The rest of the sanatoria were closed, even now during the high season. Those places overseen by the blindly optimistic were at least locked and shuttered; the owners still hoped for better days to come. We stopped for a few minutes at another sanatorium, left in the hands, apparently, of a confirmed pessimist. The buildings had been simply abandoned to the elements, and both nature and her human consorts had proven unforgiving. I walked through the shattered doorway into what must have been a dining hall, picking my way carefully over glass fragments and broken furniture. I had the place to myself — or so I thought — until I saw a cow and her calf lolling about in the lobby. Perhaps they were on their way back to the tennis courts, which had already reverted to elaborately fenced pasture.

Up the road, we were flagged down at a militia post, which commanded an arthritic-looking metal gate. I offered up my documents. After a few moments, I was invited in for a chat. In Soviet days, the valley was open to the occasional party of foreigners lured by the novelty of Russian mountains and socialist skiing. Now, though, this spot was only a few miles from the international border with the newly independent country of Georgia. To the bitter regret of many Russians, the warmest Black Sea beach resorts, the loveliest orchards, and the best vineyards were now out of their grasp, no longer part of their empire. Instead, the same people Russians had once referred to optimistically as "our Georgian brothers" had reduced much of their nation to a shell-pocked shambles, a pitiful carcass of what it had once been.

After a hurried consultation in a back room, I was permitted to proceed. "But you must leave by nightfall," the officer in charge warned me.

We passed through a fragrant grove of pines on the valley floor. At the far end of the forest the road suddenly burst into the open, seemingly just under the base of Elbrus, its twin cones radiant with ice high above. My driver, too, was pleased. "Elbrus! There's Elbrus!" he exclaimed.

We pulled up at the base of the aerial tramway. The cable cars were bedded down in their base station, all but the one, that is, which lay crumpled on the hillside some ways up the line. "Last winter, one of the trams fell," the driver said casually. "Eighteen people killed. Now the cable cars don't run very often." The rust blooms on the pylons were even more eloquent; "not very often" clearly meant never.

"What happened? Was there an investigation?" I asked.

My companion laughed heartily. "It wasn't the first time. Who knows what happened! Things happen! Who can say why?"

His was, I realized, the voice of Asia. Who can say why, indeed? Meanwhile, my Western eyes were fixed on the broken carcass of the cable car. I visualized the swinging car, the flutter of fear turning to panic, the long, muffled screams, a metallic smash of life to rock. After a few moments of reflecting on that horror, contemplating the why, I turned away. My driver had meandered back down to a stone retaining wall, where he was absent-mindedly urinating on the walk.

It is written: *"Every misfortune that befalls the earth, or your own persons, is ordained before We bring it into being."*

The two of us drove back to a lodge at the foot of a double chairlift. I resisted the temptation to inquire about its safety record. Swallowing hard, I bought tickets for both stages up the side of Mount Cheget.

The chair swooped me up into the edges of Russian airspace. True, the lift clanked rather than hummed, but in the thrill of seeing the high Caucasus, I left my unease behind. It was a magnificent day; not a single cloud obscured the view. Elbrus, as ancient as Ararat, was built like a sturdy wet nurse, all mammary folds and glands. In Persian, its name means "Two Heads"; the Balkars called it simply Mingi-Tau — "Thousands Mountain", as large a number as they could imagine. More spectacular still, to the west, was Donguzorun-Chegetkarabashi, a towering mountain edifice with a sheer glaciated face worthy of the Eiger. As I watched, wisps of snow and vapor whipped down its cliffs, driven by a mischievous wind from Georgia. Far below, Donguzorunkyol Lake gave off an otherworldly emerald glow.

Along this narrow cleft between the two peaks, the Nazis tried to breach the Red Army's lines in the winter of 1943, seeking to punch through to the Caspian oilfields and Iran. The crack Edelweiss mountain division managed to plant the Nazi flag on the summit of Elbrus, and fought to within a few thousand feet of the top of the pass, but in the end was beaten back in ferocious combat. Some of the soldiers' remains — German and Soviet — were never buried. Their bones rest undisturbed in winter and spring, under the deep snow in the pass. The rumors of unexploded mines keep the curious out during the rest of the year.

At the top of the lift, over two miles high, the air was brittle as a wafer, the wind unyielding as flint. I climbed toward the summit of Cheget, then walked back down to the midstation. The path was deserted; perhaps the other tourists feared the mines even more than I did. Facing southeast to the Georgian frontier, the ridge cascaded away in an undulating carpet of green. Tiny incandescent rivulets rushed off the mountainside.

I came to the ruins of a stone hut, reduced to little more than a weary square of stones in a flat patch of grass. The eerie waters of Donguzorunkyol shimmered below; the clouding summit of Donguzorun-Chegetkarabashi brooded above. In summers past, before the war, before the deportations, this spot must have known the shepherd's steady gait, the sheepdog's insistent bark, the bleating of Balkar flocks.

On the way back to Nalchik, it rained.

✳ ✳ ✳

The professor drew hard on a cigarette, and waved his hand disdain-fully. "The minister of culture! Don't bother with him. He won't do a thing for you." I was seated on his couch, sipping at a glass of Georgian cognac. My phone call had brought me an invitation for "a little some-thing to eat." The professor's wife, a teacher herself, fussed over me re-lentlessly; a plethora of plates soon crowded the frontiers of the table and spilled over to a neighboring buffet.

"Hospitality," Musukayev was explaining, "used to come naturally to people. It was a great honor to be the host; it was a solemn obliga-tion. The folk beliefs spoke to this hunger. If a Balkar saw the shadow of a bird cross the walls of his hut, or a dog roll on its back, a guest was to be expected." Musukayev leaned back in his chair, reflecting. He was slight and balding, but agile. "In olden times, if a traveler with cholera appeared at your hut, you were obliged to feed him, to offer him shel-ter. The same if your wife or your oldest daughter had just died, and was lying unburied in your home. Even if the scoundrel who murdered your eldest son came to your door, demanding a meal and a bed, your role was to provide it. There were many instances like these, some recorded by foreigners. There is a Balkar proverb: 'Treat to bread he who struck you with a stone.'"

The professor was a prolific writer. He brought one work after an-other down from his shelves. For the most part, they carried the anti-septic titles of the Soviet era: *On Balkars and Balkaria, About the Origins of Last Names, Habits and Customs of the Mountain People.* He presented me with a copy of each and every one, even titles that I knew must have been long out of print and difficult for the author to part with. I protested, to no avail. It was, I realized, the code of the mountains in action.

I assumed an ethnographer would make much of the differences be-tween Kabardinians and Balkars. Yet Musukayev was insistent; the two peoples had a great deal in common. Although their languages, Circassian and Turkic, were unrelated, the Kabardinians and the Balkar Turks had lived side by side for many centuries. After generations of in-termarriage, it was often impossible to say, at first glance, whether a given person looked Balkar or Kabardinian; physiologically, there was no single Balkar "type." Both populations were thoroughly Islamicized (and partly Russified) long before the Bolshevik Revolution; their clothing, customs, food, and traditions were similar enough to be indistinguishable to a casual visitor. If there was any difference, it was between the image of the urbane horseman of the steppes — the Kabardinian gentleman — and the plain-speaking man of the mountains — the Balkar shepherd.

I asked the professor if he knew of General Beppayev, the self-styled leader of the Balkar nationalist party. He smiled in a nebulous way and said: "The General lives somewhere around here, but I don't know him. I don't have much to do with that circle." There was to be, it seemed, no introduction.

Besides, Musukayev continued, it was simplistic to attribute all of the Caucasus' uncounted conflicts to national differences. Better to ask about a man's family, his circle of relations and friends, his village. Each valley had its own character, its own call on its sons and daughters — and its own enmities toward neighbors far and near.

Tellingly, Adam was admonished in the Garden of Eden by Allah: *"Go hence, and may your descendents be enemies to each other."*

However fratricidal, many of the Caucasus peoples, including the Balkars, were also celebrated for their longevity. Some attributed this to a wholesome, athletic lifestyle without the stress of modern society, others to diet. As recently as the 1970s, almost one out of every ten Balkars was over ninety years old. I asked Musukayev why it was that among the local delicacies laid in front of me, there was no sign of any yogurt, celebrated in America as the secret to the mountaineer's long life.

This prompted a hearty laugh from the professor. "Yogurt? You say Americans think we live a long time because of yogurt?!" Musukayev, who had also written about the "long-lifers" among the Balkars, had a different theory. "The old people used to enjoy long, healthy lives because they felt needed. They were treated with respect; they had real authority. This gave them life."

It was hard to survive in the mountains, Musukayev pointed out. Life there was a relentless struggle on the margins of sustainability. Relations clustered together rather than dispersed; within these local clan groupings, cooperation was the sine qua non of self-preservation.

Even bandits had to work their trade in groups. In this light, it made sense to vest clear, indisputable authority in the elders. While the oldest male ruled the roost, the senior woman in a family grouping or village also enjoyed special status. Relationships among brothers, sisters, and even wives were also governed by the rigid hierarchy of age. A younger brother had to defer to his older brother, and so on.

All these rules and customs were, for the most part, strictly observed. Out of deference, younger men ceded the right side of the road to their elders. They were to avoid overtaking someone older on a road, crossing his path, or looking back at him. They were to avert their eyes from someone senior unless directly addressed by him.

At home, too, the clan patriarch had important privileges. His chair faced the entrance to the house; neither it nor the elder's bed could be sat upon by others. To place a hat or a glove on either was considered an unpardonable insult.

The twentieth century was not kind to the village elders. Already, before the revolution, they had to get used to taking orders from tsarist sergeants and file clerks. As elsewhere in the Russian empire, the Bolsheviks set out to destroy the old ways in earnest. Many greybeards were rounded up as "oppositionists"; some received a bullet behind the ear for their contrariness. The mullahs, too, were quickly disposed of, along with their mosques. Before long, not one place of worship was left standing in Kabardino-Balkaria. The campaigns against the "feudal exploitation" of the former order went on in fits and starts throughout the twenties and thirties. Each time a village council or a *Sharia* court was overturned in favor of a "people's tribunal," the old ways skipped a beat. Industrialization, collectivization, the War, exile — all of these proved to be enemies of Balkar traditions. So many enemies . . .

"Now," Musukayev concluded, "our elders die younger and younger every year. All we let them do is make toasts and dress up in funny costumes."

✳ ✳ ✳

So it was that I fell into the welcoming hands of Professor Musukayev rather than the chokehold proffered by the government of the Republic of Kabardino-Balkaria. At his instigation, a Russian military-style jeep hauled me up to a collective farm in the foothills south of Nalchik. There I was joined by the jolly Idris, the farm director's assistant, and Mukhamed, the headman of Verkhnaya Balkariya — a mountain village, the professor had assured me, where I would find what I was looking for.

Until the Soviet era, the upper Cherek valley was practically inaccessible. The Balkars who lived in this remote corner of the Empire were only nominally subjects of the tsar. Most of their trade and contact with the outside world ran south to Georgia and the Black Sea. In the 1920s, the footpath north past the Cherek chasm to Nalchik was widened enough to accommodate horses. Later, it was blasted with dynamite to create just enough room for one rather hypothetical lane of vehicle traffic. An incautious hoof or a wayward tire meant a cinematic tumble to oblivion.

As we slowly motored up the side of the gorge, I was struck by the intrinsic drama of all things Caucasian. The Russian milieu was flat, pastoral, at times even suffocating; the Caucasus knew only how to tower and plunge. It was a landscape for *beau geste*, for wild theatricality.

In front of an earthen tunnel sprinkled with loose rock, the driver pulled the jeep up against the cliff wall. We got out and stepped to the edge of the precipice. A golden eagle shot by below us, screeching a warning. Since at least the Second World War, everything beyond this point had been closed to foreigners and ordinary Soviet citizens alike. Only a special pass would have taken you farther, into the heartland of the Balkars.

We reached the top of the gorge, and the way leveled out into a broad valley flanked by saw-toothed peaks. The blue of the sky had deepened with the altitude. The high peaks, glittering icily at the very end of the valley, appeared oddly close at hand. We stopped to chat with a mustachioed peasant, who sported a dark jacket and a fedora. An enormous scythe was slung over his shoulder. He was out cutting fodder for his cow.

Along the meadowed slopes above us, it looked at first as if some perspicacious vintner had built terrace after terrace in stone. Then Idris explained: all around us were the remains of Balkar villages, reduced to walls, foundations, an occasional shrub or tree. Once, five thousand people had lived here. Now these terraces were overgrown, not with vines, but with sorrow.

Across the river, another abandoned settlement covered the hillside up to an apron of cliffs. All that was left standing was an ancient watchtower, condemned for the rest of its days to a pointless vigil. The cultivated patches and plots in the valley bottom were the only puddles of life, the last counterpoints to the detritis of a whole people.

Outwardly, at least, Idris and Mukhamed were unmoved. They had grown up with the knowledge of this loss; it was as much a part of everyday life as the dust that whirled down the road or the limp of the neighbor's mare. We walked slowly up a once-cobbled lane to the foot of another guard tower, perched impossibly on top of a great boulder. As we passed one gutted, overgrown foundation after another, I sweated unreservedly; the air had fallen limp, dead.

One evening in late November 1943, a knot of soldiers from the NKVD's 11th Division appeared at the top of the pass behind where we now stood. The Red Army was on the run, bruised and battered by the determined advance of German troops east and south toward the oil fields of Azerbaijan. Already, Nalchik had fallen. As Soviet troops retreated into the foothills of the Caucasus, they came under fire from an unexpected quarter: hillsmen eager, perhaps too eager, to banish Sovietism from their lands once and for all. In the Party's lexicon, they were "bandits." Indeed, a few may have been in the employ of the Germans, who were closing in fast. Others had taken to the hills years before, after losing their herds to the collective farms. Still more were Red Army deserters who faced the death penalty if returned to their units. The rest were perhaps dyed-in-the-wool thieves. But after everything that these lands had suffered under Soviet rule, was it any wonder that there were men who took up arms willfully, joyfully, to liberate their valleys and villages?

As it fell back, the 11th Division traded fire from time to time with snipers, losing half a dozen men in all. Stung by this defiance behind his own lines, the commanding officer of one of the Division's detachments, a Captain Nakin, sought and received new instructions: "With the receipt of these orders . . . liquidate bandit groups located in the village of Verkhnaya Balkaria. Take the most decisive measures, right up to executions by firing squads, the burning of homes and property." A second order went still further, calling on him to "annihilate the bandits and their accomplices, completely burn buildings and property, liquidate everything that might give shelter to banditism. Under no circumstances show pity even to indirect accomplices . . ."

That fall, there had been no bandits — no men at all but the old and the infirm — in the villages of Verkhnaya Balkaria. Anyone able to carry a rifle had either been sent away to fight with the Red Army or was hiding out in the remotest reaches of the mountains, keeping a distance from Russian and German soldiers alike.

A little before midnight, after the valley had grown quiet, the NKVD troops left their positions overlooking Verkhnaya Balkaria and quietly slipped into the little hamlet of Sautu. Without warning, the soldiers broke down doors and tossed grenades through the windows of the stone huts, driving the terrified inhabitants outside. In groups of a dozen or more, the villagers were executed by firing squad. Then their houses were set on fire and their bodies thrown back inside to mix with the embers.

Ali Misirov, a wounded veteran invalided home from the army, cowered in his family's potato cellar after the first explosions. As he hid, he heard screams and bursts of machine-gun fire. At first he assumed the invaders were Germans. Only when he heard Russian being spoken did he understand that the attack was being carried out by Soviet troops. Children who tried to run away were shot in the back. Even the village cripple was gunned down. Misirov lost all of his loved ones: his wife, his son, his sister, and his two nephews.

According to the NKVD's own files, published for the first time a half century later, 310 inhabitants of Sautu were murdered that night, 150 of them children.

From Sautu, the soldiers moved on. In Glashevo, they executed another sixty-seven people. In Verkhny Cheget, one of their victims was Kabul Kadirov, the father of four sons serving with the Red Army.

Tani Baysieva was only seven on the day the soldiers came. When the news of the massacres began to spread across the valley, her family fled to a neighbor's home. All told, there were sixty people in the house when the soldiers caught up with them. They were invited outside for a "meeting" by the officer in charge and told to line up against the hut's stone wall. When several of the old people tried to slip away, the shooting began. Tani heard the grown-ups chanting a Muslim prayer as bodies fell all around her. She found herself pinned under her mortally wounded mother.

Tani lay motionless, trying to ignore her mother's feeble cries for water. Nearby, the soldiers had paused for lunch; she watched one slowly, carefully peel an apple. After the soldiers finished, they prodded the bodies again for signs of life. Miraculously, she went unnoticed. Tani stayed there, under the stiffening body of her mother, for three more days. She survived her own four gunshot wounds to see her entire family buried: mother, father, grandmother, sisters.

Rauzat Kuchukova's stepmother also died during those terrible days. The soldiers came to the door of their hut — her father was away that day — and asked for water. Rauzat was only six, but she remembered that there were many men in uniform, and they were thirsty. They passed the cup of water around the room. Then they shot Rauzat's stepmother and left.

Captain Nakin, who led his men into the Cheget valley, proudly reported to his headquarters that they had done away with fifteen hundred people, of whom ninety were "bandits," four hundred "men," and the rest "supporters of the bandits."

Before long, Nakin's superiors sensed that something was very wrong. They knew that the scale of the opposition came nowhere close to the numbers of dead Nakin provided. Furthermore, Nakin's unit had suffered virtually no casualties itself.

Once the generals came to the realization that a massacre of Soviet civilians had taken place at the hands of Soviet troops, their reflex was the conventional Soviet one: remove all traces, and blame someone else. Nakin was ordered to bury the dead. Yet there were too many, and time was short. The official "line" was concocted: "On the 6th of December 1943, a group of German-fascist occupiers, under the leadership of a German Army major, whose name it has been impossible to establish, and with the active help of traitors to the motherland . . . robbed, harrassed and committed violence against peaceful inhabitants, burned homes, executed by firing squad peaceful inhabitants, old people, women and children . . ."

By the time German troops actually arrived in Verkhnaya Balkaria, most of the villagers had run away. Yet once it became apparent that the soldiers were not mistreating those who had stayed behind in the village, the surviving Balkars returned. The Germans even helped the villagers bury their dead, dragging the corpses behind their skis to the graveyard. All told, some seven hundred bodies were laid to rest.

* * *

A trial of a different sort awaited me when we drove into Verkhnaya Balkaria. Despite its magnificent setting, it is today a cheerless, Third World moderne sort of place, with concrete and cinder block houses erected one beside another along a treeless street. The village had a crumbling, transient look; it appeared to be merely biding time until a natural catastrophe, an earthquake perhaps, reduced it completely to rubble. Only one edifice stood out among the sheet metal rooftops. At a jog in the road, a red brick mosque was under construction — paid for, Idris told me proudly, by the residents themselves. Two domes on the roof were beginning to take shape, although there was still more to be done.

> In the Koran, it is written: *"Worship your Lord and do good works, so that you may triumph."*

Idris's parents lived in a plain, one-story house behind a metal gate. I was ushered in with some ceremony to meet his father, a spry man who still had a spring in his step despite a wholly disheveled appearance. He was hearty enough, in fact, that he and his village cohorts, despite their half-hearted avowals of Islamic rectitude, were about to put on a prodigious display of imbibition.

Idris's father, as the eldest male at the table, served as toastmaster. Various local luminaries, of all ages and girths, joined us. The littlest guest was Idris's five-year old nephew. The boy was known to all as "the wild one," a mocking yet respectful reference to the fact that he was half-Chechen. The women appeared with plates, then left; their place was in the kitchen.

There were no familiar culinary safe havens on this table: no spongy black bread, no hearty cabbage soup, nothing familiar to the Russian, much less American, palate. Instead, the dominant — in fact, only — theme was meat, with just a handful of variations: mutton, lamb, and cow hoof, the latter something of a rarity in these parts. A steamy broth contained what looked like a petrified claw; I sipped noisily from the top, hoping that ostentatious slurping might compensate for the fact that the volume in the bowl never diminished. When the women returned to clear room for the next course, I could see that I was in trouble. Rather than asking me if I were finished, they simply left the soup bowl beside me.

Whatever one may have imagined about partaking in a feast of freshly slaughtered sheep is probably true. Eager diners around you yank at hunks of flesh and gristle boiled to the color and consistency of gray canvas. The sheep's head grins sardonically as it is placed before you — as the guest of honor — with a grand flourish. It would be unseemly to hide or to crawl away. The choice is to cause insult or injury: the former to one's hosts, the latter to oneself.

I still believe that my strategy of surreptitiously dropping pieces of mutton into my soup bowl — until it neared the point of overflowing — would have worked out admirably had it not been for one other factor: namely, the vodka. All that there was to eat apart from the dearly departed sheep's innards were a few desultory french fries. They were hardly enough to tide over a mewling tot, much less a luncheon guest at a table of swigging Balkars intent on proclaiming their hospitality as avidly as Baptists giving witness to their flock.

There were toasts to the American people, to the Balkar people, to friendship between our peoples, to peace among all peoples. There were toasts to the eldest, the youngest, the handsomest, the bravest. There were toasts like speeches, and toasts like half-completed puns. There were toasts of offering and toasts of thanks. And there were toasts in less than perfect Russian — including mine — and toasts in what I surmised was inestimable Balkar Turkic.

No one seemed to recall that *in the Koran it is written: "Believers, wine and games of chance, idols and divining arrows, are abominations devised by Satan."*

Vodka, especially for those who keep a distance from it under normal circumstances, has an unforgiving nature. How I managed to remain on my feet, much less snap off a series of group portraits of the lunch party, I will never know. I was also still lucid enough to put some questions about the exile of the Balkars to the elders. The table, until then light-hearted, turned somber.

Idris's father's eyes, I noticed, were the color of slate. He was on his feet now, standing rigidly. He raised his glass, a bit theatrically, a bit emotionally, and said, "May we never forget the losses of the war and the dead we Balkars left behind in Kazakstan."

By the end of 1943, German troops had given up the ground they had won in the North Caucasus and were steadily being pushed back toward Eastern Europe. Unlike in Russia, the return of Communist rule was no occasion for celebration in the Caucasus. As the mountain peoples would soon learn, the Party had returned to these heights with sword in hand and fury in heart.

Beria, Stalin's Georgian secret police chief, proposed banishing from the North Caucasus and southern Russia whole nations he deemed to have proven treasonous during the months of German occupation: the Karachay, the Kalmyks, the Chechens, the Ingush, the Balkars. In November 1943, the Karachay were the first to be herded off their lands and dispatched to Central Asia. The Buddhist Kalmyks came next, destined for Siberia. Some were exiled as far away as Sakhalin, the somber island off Russia's Pacific coast.

On February 23, 1943, Zuber Kumekhov, the First Party Secretary of Kabardino-Balkaria, was asked to sign a document prepared in Moscow by some of Beria's henchmen. It called for the immediate deportation of the Balkar people "beyond the borders of the Kabardinian-Balkar republic." The document had already been signed by the heads of the Nalchik interior ministry and the secret police. Only Kumekhov's signature was missing.

At first, he hesitated. It was an appalling quandary, even by the twisted standards of the day. The chief of the Kabardinian-Balkar NKVD, a Russian named Filatov, urged Kumekhov to sign: "The issue of exiling the Balkars has already been decided in Moscow. Our signatures in reality mean nothing. But Comrade Beria must know what our attitude toward banditism is. We've already signed the document. In the event that the First Secretary doesn't sign it, wouldn't it look like political" — he paused — "shortsightedness?"

In the end, Kumekhov added his name to the document. In later years, he tried to explain that he feared worse, that if he had not gone along, Beria might have exiled the Kabardinian nation as well. Some people claim that had Kumekhov been a Balkar rather than a Kabardinian, he might not have agreed to sign. The only certainty — and it must have been the most compelling reason on that day in February — was that without his signature, Kumekhov would have been executed, carelessly flattened by the treads of the system that both he and Beria served.

On the same day that Kumekhov was asked to witness what stood to be remembered as the death certificate of the Balkar nation, the entire Chechen and Ingush populations were rounded up and transported away from their homelands, and the territory they had occupied was divided among the Georgian republic, the Russian federation, and other neighboring regions.

Beria's personal train, bristling with guns and armor plate, arrived in Nalchik on March 2, fresh from supervising the Chechen and Ingush operations. Kumekhov offered Beria an inspection tour in a chauffered car. Beria refused the offer, and instead had his own bulletproof sedan and escort jeep unloaded from one of the train's wagons. All day, they toured the unsuspecting republic, from the ruins of Nalchik — which the Nazis razed as they pulled out — to the Elbrus valley. Kumekhov could not believe that this most feared and powerful man, seated next to the driver in his custom-made limousine, was so unimposing, so obscure-looking. Beria did not utter a word during the entire tour. Only when he returned to the train did he turn to Kumekhov and say: "The operation must take place smartly and without a hitch. And within the alloted time. I wish you success."

The deportation of the Balkars began before dawn on March 8, 1944. It was to be a beautiful, sunny spring day — ironically, a Soviet holiday, International Women's Day. For each village, the experience was practically the same. First, a line of Studebaker trucks appeared, packed with troops. The troops disembarked, and took up positions around the settlement. Instructions were given by an officer; no explanations were offered. Families were allowed a half hour or less to pack what belongings they could carry and load aboard the trucks (built with pride in places like Detroit, and shipped to Russia under the Lend-Lease program). What survivors remembered most were the hellish sounds of those thirty minutes: women wailing, dogs barking, orphaned cows bellowing. The crippled and the dying were simply left behind. Down dirt roads and rocky tracks, the Balkars, from stoic centenarians to bawling babies, were brought to the bombed-out railroad station in Nalchik. Special freight trains awaited them, ringed by heavily armed NKVD troops. People were herded right and left; parents were separated from children, families dragged apart, never to be reunited.

The cattle cars set aside for Beria's ugly errand had already been used for his earlier deportations; they were caked in old feces, and smeared in dried blood and urine. With practice, the NKVD had perfected these sinister operations to a ruthless science. The secret police had learned that it was possible to increase both the number of cattle cars in each train and the number of bodies packed into each car. The latter could be brought about thanks to a more efficient mixing of children among adults, enabling loads of 45 people or more in a space much smaller than a standard American boxcar. It was not long before typhus and dysentery set in. Hundreds, if not thousands, died en route.

By March 11, Beria was able to report to the Politburo that 37,103 Balkars had been deported to Central Asia. That same day, First Party Secretary Kumekhov was removed from his post. Within a few years, almost a third of the Balkar nation would perish of hunger, disease, exposure, and despair, abandoned in an alien wasteland, ostracized as traitors.

The Koran exclaims: *"How many cities have We laid in ruin! In the night Our scourge fell upon them, or at midday, when they were drowsing."*

I bid farewell to my hosts and passed out dreamlessly while the jeep bounced and jolted back down the narrow road to Nalchik. Later, we stopped to rest at the bottom of the pass beside a moody body of water called, evocatively, the Blue Lake. Credited by the Balkars with the power to erase pain and grant wishes, it was said to receive its water from dozens of underground springs, and, by some, to have no bottom. It was also taboo; no one dared swim in the Blue Lake. There we met a woman with a dark mane of hair and a knowing look, along with her two consorts, dressed in black shirt and pants. I told them I was looking for a certain retired general, and they nodded their heads wordlessly.

✳ ✳ ✳

To reach Chegem, one must pass — as it were — under the mountains. The route snakes along the base of a wild gorge, the sides of which rise higher and steeper with each twist and turn. At its narrowest, there is just room enough to accommodate both the lone road to Chegem and the river that bears its name. The bottom of this canyon is one of Kabardino-Balkaria's best known beauty spots, a shade-drenched, moss-cool sanctuary where nearly everyone pulls over to stretch, to smoke, and to take in the sight of the waterfall that flutters down into the middle of a decidedly Caucausian tableau.

Verkhniy Chegem was Professor Musukayev's *aul,* the village of his ancestors. I was handed over for the day to the professor's friend Akhmat, who was driving his eldest son, on leave from his military service, up to his grandmother's place. The boy's uniform, crowned by the distinctive forest-green cap of the Border Guards, did not camouflage his obvious relief to be back home among friends and family.

The phlegmatic Akhmat spared me a reprise of the extravagant bouts of hospitality I had endured the day before. When I discovered that there was no fresh sheep boiling in the kitchen, I could scarcely suppress a sigh of relief. In comparison, the salted mutton shreds his mother had heated up in her skillet were child's play; I managed to chew at them quite convincingly. Even the obligatory vodka toasts were moderate in comparison to the previous day's alcoholic maelstrom. The conversation drifted in and out of Russian, with the best gossip, I suspected, tossed around in the choppy, clucky syllables of the Balkar language. Everything was in order; the men, young and old, held court while the women bustled about in the kitchen, offering up a comment from time to time while they chopped and stirred. I asked them about General Beppayev. "He is our leader," one of them said simply.

After lunch, we sat outside sipping mint tea, our heads stroked by the underboughs of an apricot grove that had no right to prosper at this altitude. My hosts picked the fruit carelessly, tossing the pits into the long grass at the back of the yard. As an outsider, I was not so blasé. To me, the stubborn little orchard was a type of benediction, a reminder of how an unmindful world can be redeemed by tiny acts of devotion.

The neighbors across the street were putting on a new galvanized roof. The woman of the house, a sturdy old matron with a ready smile, hung her Balkar carpets out for us to admire. Patched together from brightly colored pieces of felt, they were direct, bold splashes of color, a far cry from the devious geometries woven by the lowland Azeris and Turkmen. Next door, someone's uncle — I never quite understood whose — had a hot charcoal fire stoked; his anvil, planted as firmly as a fist onto an ancient stump, lay ready for the clang of hammer on horseshoe. These were, after all, tough and independent people. Traditional craftsmanship — an occult art in much of the former Soviet Union — still held true in this remote valley.

Kaisyn Kuliyev's home in Eltyubyu, a few kilometers away, was one of the last stone huts left standing in all of Balkaria. Long before the stolid Tanzilya found herself on the stages of Nalchik, there was Kuliyev. He had died a few years before, a poet genuinely beloved by all.

Kuliyev's verses often recalled the Balkar world before the deportation. He must have chosen this spot, I thought, to stoke his memories to the fullest. Eltyubyu owed little to Mother Russia; it was Bosphoran, not Muscovite. The village houses were dressed in pastel pinks and blues splashed on stucco and topped by sun-scoured tile roofs. A tower with crenellated ramparts commanded the village's dirt crossroads. Olive-skinned little girls with great round faces and sky-blue eyes skipped past, unabsorbed by us.

Kuliyev's refuge sat behind the village, at the base of a scarred and screed canyon as venerable as Sinai. Massive cliffs rose like tablets above a stream and a talus-strewn expanse of pasture. I would have said that it was the most beautiful spot in Russia, had it really been in Russia.

Outwardly, Kuliyev's was a rough sort of house, half dug out of the hillside, with whitewashed stone walls covered by a sod roof. Inside, wooden beams kept the structure from collapsing onto the bare dirt floor. I understood how a Kabardinian might have labeled such a house a cave. Yet it was completely at ease in its surroundings. A wind as mercurial as a jinn startled, then settled the dandelions by the outer gate. The hens pecked at the ground nonchalantly, oblivious to our footsteps.

Kuliyev wrote the words to this folk song:

> *All of this could be forgotten*
> *Forgotten the insults, bitterness and suffering,*
> *If the dead — certainly not killed by the war —*
> *Were to return from exile;*
> *Once, when I went to listen to the songs of the cliffs,*
> *I saw at dawn,*
> *A gray-haired Balkar kiss the rocks*
> *In his disgraced brown* beshmet *hat.*

Up the mountainside, on soil too thin to sustain more than the meagrest grasses, stood a cluster of odd stone structures: dark, otherworldly cones. After lunch, Akhmat invited an old school chum of his to accompany us to the site, along with his friend's two young sons.

Some say that these structures date back to within a few centuries after the birth of Christ. The vaults have no doors; hence the theory that they served as mausoleums rather than dwellings for the living. Legend has it that plague victims were left to die here among the remains of the dead. Professor Musukayev had a dissenting opinion; he placed the earliest at the beginning of the sixteenth century, not long before the arrival of Islam in the mountains — some of the few surviving shrines of the lost credos that once held sway in this part of the Caucasus. One way or another, they are among the last worldly reminders of peoples whose very names hover on the edge of mythology rather than history: Khazars, Alans, Huns. It is to these lost tribes that the Balkars owe their ancestral allegiance.

Beneath these ancient crypts, my culinary luck ran out. The boys sat on their haunches, each greedily devouring a pear. For the grown-ups, however, Akhmat's friend had brought along an even more delightful little snack: half a sheep's head and a bottle of vodka. The head had been neatly sawed down the middle; it still boasted one eye, one ear, and precisely half its nostrils and teeth. The sheer tenderness with which Akhmat unwrapped the cellophane from around the head signaled to me that I was being treated to an indubitable delicacy. Had the demi-skull perhaps retained a bit more of its skin and fur, I might have petted it. But its macabre expression, grinning nearly down to the bone, left me contemplating a mad dash back down to the road. No culture that would serve up such an item to its guests, I thought in bitter panic, deserved to survive. Then, with a cold chill down my spine, I remembered my mother's own peanut butter and dill pickle sandwiches.

✵ ✵ ✵

The sun, still glowing with ruddy enthusiasm at the end of another summer day, strode regally off dusk's backlit stage. From the wings sprang a chorus of swallows, chasing their evening meal across the scarlet sky in Byzantine dips and whirls. After a final flurry of feasting, they gave way to a lugubrious corps of bats that flapped about the streetlights and cypress trees, oblivious to the murmuring pedestrians below.

The phone rang, jangling me out of my reverie on the balcony. "I understand that you want to meet the General," the voice said. It was not a question; it was delivered as a plain statement of fact.

The voice gave me instructions: the street name, the number, the entrance. The voice would be waiting for me in the street. I began to ask something, but the phone line went dead again. It stayed dead for the rest of the time I was in Nalchik.

The directions appeared simple enough to follow. My taxi driver, however, was not convinced. We drove back and forth from street to street, looking for an address that he insisted to me did not exist. After ten or fifteen minutes of fruitless cruising, he offered to take me back to the hotel. I paid him and got out instead.

I wandered down the block, following the street numbers as best I could in the dark. I walked past a pair of militiamen, one tall, one short. As I passed them, one called out brusquely, "Where are you going, buddy?"

I turned, not quite sure that they were talking to me. "*Chevo?* What?" I replied.

The two cops swaggered over to me. "Documents," the little one snarled. I was carrying a small bag over my shoulder with my notebook and my camera. "Let's see what's in there," the tall one added, motioning me to hand him the bag.

I paused for just a moment to drink down fully this hearty draught of nostalgia. The militiamen had approached me just as they would have before words like *perestroika* and *glasnost* began to undermine the self-confidence of the forces of order. No doubt, it was a slow night. Mistaking me for a local, they were going to give me the once-over in the time-honored style of gendarme and peasant.

I played my trump card. "Here is my diplomatic identity card," I said, watching the corners of their mouths arch downwards as they realized that I was a foreigner. Their fun had come to an end almost before it had begun. They took several steps away to peer at my ID under a wavering streetlight. "An American!" I overheard one of them exclaim. Then they turned to face me — and I do not exaggerate — one bowed to nearly oriental depths while the other walked up respectfully and handed my *kartochka* back to me. Then they both saluted. It was the eternal Russian waltz of rank and servility, only they had ended up unexpectedly as coachmen rather than courtiers. The surprise denouement only highlighted the mystifying deference that visiting foreigners can still induce in an otherwise xenophobic Russia.

A bit farther down the street, at the back entrance to a large office block, a man was gesturing at me. I walked over to him. He shook my hand, introduced himself as the person who had phoned me, and led me past a metal gate and through an empty parking lot. As we entered a dark hallway and headed up a set of narrow stairs, he apologized. "This is the only location they would give us," he explained, ". . . the headquarters of the tax police."

What kind of national movement was this, I wondered, occupying space provided by the authorities it ostensibly opposed? It was not the only anomaly of the evening.

The leadership of the National Council of the Balkar People, perhaps twelve men and women in all, had gathered around a makeshift rectangle of tables, arranged conference style. Lieutenant General Beppayev presided, a hand-stitched flag hung slightly askew on the wall above him.

The general called on his colleagues one by one. His looked to be a far-fetched sort of shadow cabinet. The melon-faced lady with the mildly crossed eyes was to run the economy of the future Balkar republic. The awkward, rail-thin intellectual was to take charge of foreign policy, and so on. The general tapped his fingers impatiently as one particularly long-winded minister-designate introduced himself. I was not the only person to notice, and the pace of commentary quickened appreciably. It was obvious who was in charge.

Yet there was nothing particularly severe about General Beppayev's countenance. Like many retired military officers, he was built powerfully but by no means athletically. On a lazy summer day on a back porch, he might have come across as someone's good-natured uncle: wavy silver hair, alert gray eyes, an easy chuckle.

Yet his mild looks belied a tough childhood and a problematic career. His early years were spent on the dusty steppes of Kazakstan, an exiled Balkar adolescent scrambling to survive. He joined the Soviet army, where he must have shown some talent. He worked his way up to hold several top military posts, serving as deputy commander of the Hungarian military district and the Transcaucasian military zone. Then, his career fell apart ignominiously. He was said, variously, to have traded in drugs, arms, or cigarettes, or to have stirred up national tensions, or all of the above. He returned "home" to Kabardino-Balkaria — although he had never actually resided there before — and soon outflanked the more moderate leaders of the National Council, forcing them to resign and taking the organization's reins into his own hands. Before long, he was urging his followers to hoard food and to keep up their sharpshooting skills just in case clashes with the Kabardinians broke out.

Tea was served. The general was in an expansive mood. He catalogued the horrors of exile: the families left to fend for themselves on the steppes without food, shelter, or medicine; the hostility of their Kyrgyz and Kazak neighbors who had been told that the deportees were traitors; the deaths of countless Balkars, young and old alike. Meanwhile, back in their homeland, everything they had owned was confiscated. Ostensibly turned over for safekeeping to the state, in practice their houses, their livestock, and their personal possessions were often expropriated by unscrupulous officials.

The "rehabilitation" that took place in the fifties, the general argued, had set right much less than it had left undone. For one thing, thousands of Balkars still languished in Central Asia. Today, following the independence of the former Soviet republics from Russia, these stragglers were more cut off than ever.

While some returned exiles managed to claim their former homes in the mountain villages, most found that impossible. As I had seen, the old settlements were bulldozed into rubble by Communist officials eager to see the returning Balkars stay in towns or on collective farms where it was easier to keep tabs on them. "Our land lies empty, barren as an old widow," the general exclaimed, pounding his fist on the table for emphasis.

What was the National Council's program? I asked. There was no lack of specificity; the smaller the political group, the more extensive its pretensions, worthy or not. The general's followers were no exception. The council members all joined in with the recounting: the immediate return of Balkars still living in Central Asia; the restructuring of the local parliament into three chambers, one for Kabardinians, one for

Balkars, and the other for Russians and other nationalities; the restoration of the Balkar districts that had existed until 1944 instead of the postwar units with ethnically mixed boundaries; increased federal funds for Balkar development. New factories would be built, world-class tourist facilities would be planned, funding for environmental clean-ups would be provided. On the cultural front, the program called for the construction of a Balkar national theater (to be named for the poet Kaisyn Kuliyev); the creation of a "folkloric-ethnographic ensemble"; the founding of a Balkar ethnographic museum; the publishing of a Balkar encyclopedia. And so forth.

The flag above Beppayev's head displayed the outline of a mountain with two peaks; it was Elbrus stitched into cheap blue satin. I asked the general about the Kabardinians. Would they be willing to allow the Balkars their independence?

"They will have to," he answered all too confidently. "They are afraid of us. That's why they put us here in this miserable building, so the militia and the KGB can keep an eye on us. They know what our demands are." His face had grown severe, brazen. He jabbed the air for emphasis. "These are reasonable demands. But if they are not met by this fall, when we have our next congress, the situation will become very, very tense."

I brought up the matter of the local legislative elections that had taken place six months before. The Balkar nationalist candidates had failed to win a single seat. General Beppayev looked at me patronizingly, if sympathetically. "Since you are an American, it must be difficult for you to understand," he said. "But here we do not have real democracy. Here the elections are always won by the people who have the power. So elections are a sham, although once we establish the Balkar republic, we will have true democracy, with free elections. Just like you have in America." The shadow cabinet, one and all, beamed.

I was running out of questions suited for irrefutable answers. Yet I sincerely wondered how the general thought he could keep an independent Balkaria solvent. His eyes twinkled as he replied, as proud as a schoolboy; "We have the strategic minerals."

He began to talk about the fantastic potential of Tyrnyauz and its tungsten and molybdenum mines. The Russian aerospace concerns could not do without them; there were no other such deposits anywhere in the Russian Federation. There was enough mineral wealth in the mountains, he went on, to make the Balkar republic another Switzerland, a Saudi Arabia in the Caucasus. And there were "very reliable reports" of gold deposits, the general added. Only now the wealth would go to the Balkar people instead of the bureaucrats and bosses in Moscow and Nalchik. The eyes of the ministers-designate shone.

It had been a long day. I pocketed my souvenir Balkar national flag and left.

✻ ✻ ✻

The next morning, I reported to the airport for my flight home to Moscow. Swarthy traders wearing sunglasses — notwithstanding the drab overcast skies — lined up to have their bulging nylon duffel bags weighed on the terminal's baggage scales. Every single bag was grotesquely overweight, but cash flew at the cashier's window and hence so did the traders' luggage. There was more pushing and jostling in the waiting room as it became apparent that the flight was oversubscribed. The ticket agents were firm. "You, you, and you will not board," they insisted. Yet a few minutes later, all eight of the unseated yous were on board, standing in the aisle as the plane taxied for takeoff. The vituperation they poured on the aircrew's heads made the bottom line clear enough. In this era of full-blown anarchy, it was imprudent to trifle with cash-rich, patience-poor passengers.

I could not help noticing, as I walked across the tarmac to the TU-134, that its Aeroflot markings had been obliterated in a clumsy swath of black painted across the fuselage. The jet had been privatized and was now owned by one of the more than one hundred "Babyflots" operating across the skies of the former Soviet Union. Infelicitously, one such fledgling carrier had dubbed itself, in English, "Touch and Go Airlines." But as to this plane's new operators, there was not a single clue. Was it now in the hands of Air Ingushetia, Air Nalchik, even Balkaria Air? Somehow, the nameless flight managed to take off safely, overweight, overwrought, the question of nationality left unanswered, at least for the moment.

In the Koran, it is written: *"The judgment of Allah will surely come to pass: do not seek to hurry it on."*

STEPPES OF
THE SHAMAN

TUVA

IN THE HANDS OF A RUSSIAN HOST, it is only prudent to expect the unexpected. And so it was with Misha.

Little did my wife and I realize when we agreed to vacation one summer in Tuva — an otherworldly appendage of Siberia opposite the Mongolian border — that we had signed our lives over to one of the most fanatically organized Russians on the planet.

We gave our assent to the trip by bellowing over the static in our phone, praying we would be heard across the transcendental distance separating Moscow and Kyzyl, the capital of the Tuvan Republic. It was all necessarily a bit vague. "We'll meet in Krasnoyarsk," Misha yelled, "and I'll take care of the rest."

People in my parents' generation knew more about Tuva than I did, and even that was not necessarily a great deal. For them, it was the Tannu Tuva of their 1930s grade-school geography book, a mysterious eddy of yurts and bareback horsemen drifting placidly amid the torrent of revolution and change in China and the Soviet Union. Tannu Tuva's postage stamps, the country's only export, depicted a place so exotic that it seemed the little serrated diamonds and triangles might leap to life at any moment. Nomads riding reindeer, camels chasing locomotives: the stamps left an indelible mark on budding philatelists like my father, growing up five thousand miles away in Depression-era America.

Yet Tannu Tuva disappeared from the atlases after the Second World War. Obsessed by the Bomb and the bikini, the world had too many other things on its mind to notice. One newly decolonized country after another was being added to the ranks of the United Nations. Did it really make any difference in the meantime if some backwater territory was crossed off the ledger of independent states by a larger and more powerful neighbor? As far as the rest of the planet was concerned, the Tuvans had dropped completely from sight, inhabiting what a Cold War scholar once labeled "one of the most insular and obscure places on earth."

We landed in Krasnoyarsk to find Misha pacing outside the VIP lounge. His son Sergei and his niece Yulia waited nearby, chewing gum and looking bored.

Stumbling across the tarmac, we were still woozy after our overnight flight. We had taken off from Moscow almost half a day late, for reasons we were never quite able to surmise. An overnight stay in what was the closest thing to a metropolis in this part of Siberia would have been welcome. Misha, though, was aching to be gone; he had a schedule to keep.

It was my first encounter with Misha's self-tutored motoring skills. He worshiped his humdrum Sputnik sedan with totemic adoration. He bragged about marathon weeks-long expeditions across the back of the Russian beyond, trips undertaken, as it were, on a whim and a prayer. And what he lacked in good driving judgment, he fancied he made up for in reckless velocity and numbskull endurance. My wife did not mind so much; she was cozily ensconced in the back seat, chatting with Misha's teenage charges. I had the misfortune of being assigned to the front, an unwilling eyewitness to the unnerving miles that lay ahead.

After a bone-rattling ride over the cobblestones of Krasnoyarsk proper, Misha pulled over to allow us a quick view of one of Siberia's — and the world's — grandest rivers: the Yenesei. Rushed as we were, it was still much more than I had ever imagined seeing in the bad old days of U.S.–U.S.S.R. confrontation. Closed, closeted Krasnoyarsk had achieved fame, of a backward sort, through its legacy of late Soviet secrecy. Somewhere downriver was an ABM radar array that for years had bedeviled arms negotiators. Nearby lay one of the most secret Soviet nuclear facilities of all, Krasnoyarsk-26, reputed to include a city-sized bunker supplied by an underground lake.

We crossed the Yenesei on a mile-long trestle bridge high above the river's shrub-dotted islets and riffles. The Arctic Sea lay a thousand wilderness miles due north. Misha swung the car south, toward Mongolia.

We roared past unbroken stands of birch and pine, climbing steadily until the river had disappeared behind us. Then the highway, too, plunged down, dropping precipitously into Ovsyanka, an old-fashioned hamlet hard by the Yenesei gorge.

Ovsyanka was the longtime redoubt of the Siberian writer Viktor Astafiev, one of Russia's so-called "village writers." For decades, they roamed the margins of Soviet literary legitimacy, only gaining official approval in the twilight years of Brezhnev. Yet even as democracy and free speech flowered in Russia, the village writers — who range in ideological coloring from mystic environmentalist to proto-Fascist — remained controversial. What they did share was an abhorrence of the new Russian oligarchy of capitalists and criminals that was commensurate to their distaste for the former Communist system.

Their measure of earthly paradise was, instead, the Russian peasant and his lost world of folk allegiances and pagan ritual. Ovsyanka looked the right place from which to conjure up the memory of a village utopia — one that, at the same time, assuredly never existed. The sturdy log houses with cracked windows and rusted tin roofs; their exuberant, unkempt gardens of blue irises and scilla; haggard dogs scratching their ears for fleas and little girls dressed like pansies: everything that was timeless and threadbare about Russian country life was gathered here, in a simple *derevya*, one among the thousands of villages perched at the gates of the country's precariously uncertain future.

I longed to pull over and look around, but it was not to be. Our next designated rest stop was still some distance ahead, under the insolent glare of the Divnogorsk Dam, which had backed up hundreds of miles of the once-wild Yenesei into a sluggish reservoir. We parked at an observation point facing the dam's spillways. As hot tea from a thermos was passed around, Misha extolled the heroic sacrifices made by the dam's builders. What a hackneyed bore, I thought. I did not then realize how completely I had misjudged him.

We were not keeping up with Misha's schedule, and the afternoon was quickly fading toward evening. He was calculating the liters of gasoline in his tank carefully — whether from thriftiness or some more obscure mania I could not tell. After a while, he took to turning off the car's engine on downhill stretches. At the top of each rise, Misha would cut off the motor with a decisive click and whip the gearstick into neutral. The car would roll, at first humbly, then faster and faster.

Misha was familiar with the road. Yet he seemed determined, even on the longest stretches, not to succumb to the temptation of restarting the engine and regaining control over the car's velocity. The bottom curves — and they were plentiful — he negotiated with what bordered on suicidal equanimity.

"What happens if you have a problem with the brakes?" I asked, enunciating the words as calmly as I could while I held tight to the oval grip above the passenger door.

Misha thought for a moment, and replied with another question: "You're not afraid, are you?"

I did not have an honest answer for him. I swallowed hard and decided that I had no choice but to submit to this desperate form of petrol rationing.

As it turned out, it was not nearly desperate enough. Therein, perhaps, lay our salvation. Rather than having to pay cash, Misha had passed up one gas station after another, seeking to find a place that would accept his "official" Tuvan government gas coupons. Near the bottom of a hill, the Sputnik's tank finally ran dry. This time the motor would not cough back to life, and we crawled to a stop on the shoulder of the highway. I imagined momentarily the night that lay before us: cold, hunger, ravenous mosquitoes, and the impossible gymnastics of five people trying to doze off inside a cramped car.

Yet Misha was nothing if not fantastically fortunate. While it had been many miles since we had last sighted another vehicle, our Sputnik rolled up directly behind another, smaller car. I saw that it was a tiny Zaporozhets, a model originally designed for the use of invalids and the elderly, and later embraced by pennywise Soviet citizens as the cheapest form of automobile on offer.

Painted an amusement park green, the Zaporozhets was not much bigger than a bumper car, with the same playful lines and pointless chrome trim. Short of a gypsy wagon, there was probably no more humiliating rescue craft for a proud Russian driver like Misha. It was as if a well-heeled yachtsman had to be rescued by a Welshman's coracle.

A stocky, barrel-chested man emerged from the cockpit, looking as if he had been quite asleep. He and Misha got to the point quickly. Before I had a chance to ask how the negotiations were going, the good Samaritan, stained T-shirt and all, was pouring the contents of his spare fuel can into our gas tank. Moments later, we were waving goodbye. He had not asked for even a kopeck.

Soon, the wooded hills gave way to the rolling steppes of Khakasia. The claustrophobia induced in us by mile after mile of unbroken forest evaporated almost instantly in the spare, arid clarity of vacant range. But there was no mistaking this exotic prairie for Kansas. In at least half a dozen spots along the highway, stone petroglyphs poked out of ancient burial mounds. Once again, I would have liked to stop. Yet Misha — in a hurry to outrun the oncoming darkness — was not about to indulge my curiosity.

Night pounced on us from the east, abruptly swallowing up the odd luminescence of the hills flanking the road. Our companions in the backseat had fallen fast asleep. The car's headlights sliced open the darkness, stampeding a cloud of moths and grasshoppers up into our path. I pressed my face against the car window and peered out into the darkness. The stars blazed with adventure, just as they had from my parents' old Plymouth, on the wondrously untroubled automotive expeditions of my childhood.

We overnighted in Shira, a dusty town in the middle of the steppe, parched but for its two lakes, one fresh, the other salt. Misha had arranged a room for us in the local sanatorium, where his friend, a prominent member of the Khakasian parliament, was staying. The

Khakass — a synthetic label dreamed up by the early Soviet state to lump together a variety of Turkic-speaking groups living along the Yenesei — now made up barely ten percent of their own "autonomous district."

Some of the local government's ceremonial posts in the capital of Abakan were still held by non-Russians, but the indigenous peoples of Khakasia — the Kachins, Kyzyls, Sagays, Beltirs, and Koybals — had long since been pushed aside by wave after wave of Slavic settler. The process began well before the Soviet period. Douglas Carruthers, an English adventurer who passed through Khakasia at the outset of the twentieth century, was pleased by the evidence of assimilation that he saw. "The Abakan Tartars," he observed, "are a good example of the ability Russia shows in westernizing the Eastern. Here you may see Tartars of ancient race turned into devout members of the Orthodox Faith, dressed more or less in Siberian aspect."

An Austrian ethnographer who passed by on his way to Tannu Tuva in 1929 took a different view of the fate of the Khakasian population. "Only their faces betrayed the men as Tatars," Otto Manchen-Helfen wrote. "They understood Russian, spoke Russian, and dressed like Russians. True, they did not deny their nationality when asked about it, but their response, 'We are Khakass,' sounded more sad than proud." Even if the demographic realities had been less conclusive, other issues would have come into play. The fact that Khakasia held rich gold and aluminum deposits only made Moscow that much more determined to have the region pressed to Mother Russia's bosom forever.

We spent the next morning splashing about the margins of Shira's nearer lake, just down the hill from the sanatorium, even rowing a boat out to the middle where Misha's son impetuously flung himself over the side, nearly swamping us all. It was obvious from the sizeable colony of sun-martyred matrons, sprawled on the water's edge like walruses, that this was a popular vacation spot. To be sure, the ungainly Shira beach set would have scandalized the French or Italian Rivieras with its unabashed potbellies and cellulite. Likewise, the cuisine at the sanatorium would have left gourmands gasping for relief. Mutton soup, kasha, and a mare's-milk cottage cheese was served barracks-style in a vast dining room. "It's wonderful for the gall bladder," Misha's Khakasian friend assured us.

Meanwhile, under the omniscent sky of middle Asia — unmarred by haze or clouds — the waters of Shira barely rippled.

The midday heat, along with the heavy lunch, had left us languorous in the extreme. Still, we ventured out in two cars to the salt lake several kilometers beyond town. Here, the effect of water and steppe was bleak rather than benevolent. Not one tree shaded the shoreline. The lake surface had a faintly green hue, the product of the high saline content, which our hosts told us was — like our repast of mutton and kasha — marvelously therapeutic. Other bathers had gathered lakeside, crunching across the narrow, salt-glazed beach to bask in the weirdly buoyant water, floating with their heads and feet becalmed like sloops at anchor.

It was time to part company with our Khakasian hosts. We climbed back into the Sputnik, sated from the sun and the lake's torpid massage.

Beyond the steppe lay more steppe. The parching July sky had boiled away all points of reference; the landscape was empty even of mirages. I was grateful for the air rushing over me from the open window, but my arm, unaccustomed to these solar climes, reddened and burned.

For a long while, we traveled in silence. I happened then to glance over at Misha. The heat, the food, and the salt water had proved too much. To my very real consternation, I saw that he was struggling, with less and less success, to stay awake. His eyelids would narrow, than flutter shut, his chin suddenly plummeting toward his collarbone until by some happy reflex he would awaken and bring his head back up again to the level of the windshield.

Undeniably, it was time for action. But Misha's suggestion the day before that I was not man enough to be his passenger made me hesitate. There is no delicate way to grab the wheel out of someone else's hands. I had to think of something else.

"Misha," I began, in as loud a voice as I dared adopt short of shouting, "tell me about your — your parents!"

He looked over in my direction hazily. Then he yawned. "My parents? What about my parents?"

"I don't know exactly," I replied, stalling. "I was just curious about how your family ended up in Tuva. When did your parents go there? And why?"

While Misha's brain foggily pondered a response, the right front tire rumbled off the shoulder. Not a moment too soon, he yanked the wheel hard to bring us back up on the asphalt.

"Actually, I was born in Pechora," Misha explained. His face was still flushed from the heat, but the drowsiness was lifting. "My father had finished his sentence in the camps the year before, the year after Stalin died. My mother went there to be with him — he wasn't allowed to move back to Leningrad. There was a list of twenty-four cities which the former prisoners could not move back to. So it was not just Leningrad. It was 'no' to Moscow, to Kiev and to any of the other big cities in the Soviet Union."

Thus it was, on the day I discovered his father had survived the Pechora camps, that I began to know the real Misha.

His father, by Misha's description, was a man who liked to speak his mind. An engineer, he was also a Communist Party member. But one day, he made the mistake of commenting too openly about the short-comings of the Vozhd, the Leader. Someone informed on him, and he was arrested for "anti-Soviet agitation." He received fifteen years, a typical penalty for political offenders in Stalin's waning years. When Misha's father was taken away, it had all the finality of a death sentence.

Somehow he survived. Then the impossible, the unimaginable happened: the immortal Vozhd expired. Not so long after, the ghoulish Beria was executed. And the gates of the Gulag swung open, at least for some. His father had bent and buckled like a board left out in the open, yet he still managed to produce a son, then a daughter.

Misha was nine months old when his parents took him away, leaving Pechora on the same train line that serviced harsh, hard-bitten Vorkuta. His parents wanted to find a place where the stigma of the camps would not weigh so heavily, and where Russian colonists with skills and education were in demand. One of Misha's uncles had been assigned to a faraway district along the border with Mongolia. If it were possible to make a fresh start anywhere in the Soviet Union, it seemed like the right spot. In this way, based on what it was not rather than what it was, Misha's mother and father chose Tuva as their new home.

We crossed the Yenesei again, skirting the capital Abakan, and entered the Minusinsk Valley, with its pleasing mix of woodland and pasture, village and farm. One of the oldest settled areas in all of Siberia, it was a place where the rigors of Russian rural life were mitigated by good land and a comparatively mild climate. It was country that might gladden the heart of a city dweller: green, rustic, comparatively unspoiled.

Thus it was doubly incongruous to encounter, after countless muddy and potholed crossroads along the long route from Krasnoyarsk, a carefully engineered cloverleaf intersection. A four-lane highway, devoid of traffic, led off into the distance. Misha pointed out an idle airstrip nearby and commented laconically: "They can even land passenger jets here." Once upon a time, this had been a place of pilgrimage in the Communist faith; the fumes of diesel tour buses — a sort of proletarian incense — swirled in the streets. All of these blessings were for the greater glory of Shushenskoe, the village where Lenin was exiled for three years beginning in 1897.

In Soviet lore, the Bolshevik revolutionaries banished to Siberia under Tsarist rule faced impossibly cruel conditions. Yet Lenin's stay in Shushenskoe was something of a lark. "Apart from hunting and swimming," he wrote home, "most of my time is spent on long walks." In fact, we now know that both Lenin and his mother pleaded with the authorities to assign him — for the sake of his ostensibly fragile constitution — to what was then known as the "southern Yenesei province," as pleasant a destination as there was east of the Urals.

It was in Shushenskoe that Lenin was persuaded to marry his fellow agitator Nadezhda Krupskaya, even after her mother had made it plain that she wanted them to legalize their status — Lenin and Krupskaya were both fervent atheists — in a church ceremony. The couple found a comfortable enough house in town, and never wanted for food and supplies.

Nor did the authorities cut off Lenin's ties to the outside world. What a plentiful supply of books and magazines could not provide in news from beyond Shushenskoe, the rest of the exile community and the occasional visitor from European Russia did. In fact, Lenin's time in Siberian exile was to prove among his most productive; there is no dearth of articles and letters penned while he waited out this rural interlude. Whatever protestations his official chroniclers made to the contrary, he fared far better than the other early Bolsheviks, many of whom spent years in barren, remote outposts of the Russian Empire instead of in Paris and Zurich — among the comfortable European cities where Lenin was to reside over the next twenty years.

Shushenskoe did not unduly suffer from its accidental association with the demiurge Lenin. By the late twenties, the town had already developed into a mecca for revolutionary-minded tourists. Otto Manchen-Helfen commented wryly that "the neighboring villages are burning with envy, and cannot forgive the czarist government for not sending Lenin in turn from one village to the next."

Before long, the hospitable farmland of the Minusinsk Valley gave way to a pitched terrain of larch and pine. We had reached the Sayan Mountains, the range that separated Tuva from the rest of Russia. For miles on end, there were no signs of human habitation. When we came upon cabins or shacks, they appeared singly or in pairs. In fact, one family of terrified Old Believers hid out from Soviet authorities on a remote mountainside for more than half a century — and were only discovered accidentally by a party of geologists in the late seventies. It was a zone of obstinate solitude, as far removed from the Leninist manscape of apartment towers and factory chimneys as could be imagined. The Sayans were also the very essence of borderland: a point beyond which the fiber of one nature and culture gave out, and another assumed shape. It was doubly ironic, then, that the only line of verse that Lenin was ever known to pen — in an uncharacteristically sentimental moment of his exile — was devoted to this very region: "In Shusha, at the foot of the Sayans . . ."

In fact, had it not been for the mutterings of the autumnal snowstorms and the rustle of aboriginal feet and hooves, little would have ever impinged on the unearthly quiet of these mountains and passes. The caravans of yore that ferried silk and furs between the Manchu and Moscow empires followed less taxing routes. Nor did the Cossacks, who pushed through even more arduous terrain elsewhere in Siberia, bother to cross these high places. Even the Russian Civil War, which found Reds hunting down on horseback the fleeing Whites, only left behind its mangled victims hanging from the brush for one flood season. Tackling these same passes in a tarantass, Manchen-Helfen commented: "There are still stretches where it is advisable to jump out of the wagon before being catapulted out."

Carruthers, too, was struck by the untamed qualities of this country. Reaching the last Russian village before his party headed into the unmapped mountains, he saw that he was standing at a dividing line that had so far endured all of man's worldly ambitions. "The dark wall of pines," he wrote, "rises in an unbroken line beyond the meadows and corn-field. It remains the same to-day, as it was a thousand years ago. The villagers fell the timber on the outskirts for their own use, the hunters penetrate into its innermost depths . . . but its borders are inviolable as yet from the rapid march of man across Siberia." Almost a century later, his words still rang true. The Sayans were, to a surprising degree, a quarter empty of man and modernity.

As for Soviet scholarship about Tuva, Carruthers's account of his expedition was to unwittingly achieve the status of holy writ. In contrast to some of his English contemporaries wandering about the likes of Central Asia and Tibet, Carruthers was perhaps less enamored with the pungent East than he was with Eaton. For him, prerevolutionary Russia — for all of its injustices and deformities — was still an apostle of Western science and Christianity. He quite rightly saw the enfeebled hand of the Chinese as a waning influence on Tuva and Mongolia. The idea of Tuvan self-government apparently did not occur to him; he judged the "Uriankhai," as the Tuvans were then known, as utterly unsuited to the challenges of "the hurrying march of civilization."

Thus he was to pen a passage about the geopolitical place of Tuva that would appear in countless Soviet tracts justifying the territory's incorporation into the U.S.S.R. "I realized that this region," he wrote,

> although within the limits of the Chinese Empire, is essentially Siberian in character. It is an integral part of Siberia, its drainage flows to Siberia and the Arctic, the conditions . . . as well as the climate, are Siberian rather than Mongolian. . . . The flora and fauna of Siberia have overflowed across the border ranges and given the basin a northern character. Physically, politically, and economically, the basin should belong to Russia, and not to Mongolia, and the inevitable absorption of this region by the Siberian element could easily be imagined.

More careful observers would not have extrapolated a civilizing mission for Holy Russia out of a naturalist's observations — observations that were in any case flawed. Doubtless with no more gravity than with any other page, he put these thoughts to paper for his audience of English bibliophiles in the lighthearted months before the outbreak of the Great War. Yet for the rest of the century this passage was to echo over Tuva like a lamaist's mournful temple horn.

We had climbed for more than an hour, and finally the high, rocky summits, dappled with ice, came into view. Between November and May, the pass we were ascending was often blocked by snow. Misha pointed out a spot where an avalanche had once swept a passenger bus off the road, dropping it a thousand feet into a ravine. Yet, however un-reliable, this was the only major road link between Tuva and the rest of the world. Reflecting on the twisting highway and Misha's esoteric braking theories, I was thankful Misha had picked us up in July rather than January.

We reached the top of the col, with the car's engine whining through an elongated hairpin turn, and marveled at the gale galloping down the peaks and rattling the stunted spruce clinging to the pass. Like a rumpled saddlecloth, Tuva — finally — lay spread out before us.

It was a view worthy of meditation. My own reaction came closer to that of Manchen-Helfen than to Carruthers. Just past the makeshift border post, where the Tannu Tuvan soldiers lolled about in Red Army uniforms under the watchful portraits of Stalin and Voroshilov, Manchen-Helfen nevertheless exclaimed: "Siberia has ended; Central Asia has begun."

The wind shook the car in earnest as we began the long descent down the other side of the pass. Misha slowed to take in the view, but did not stop. Yet to the south, to the very edge of the horizon, another world had been cast open for our appraisal.

✳ ✳ ✳

Misha and Zoya lived well, at least in comparison with their neighbors. He was the deputy chairman of the Tuvan parliament; she was an ethnographer who studied relations between the Tuvan and Russian communities. Their apartment building was new and comparatively spacious, a rarity in sleepy, shabby Kyzyl. They had their own kitchen and bathroom, and even an extra bedroom for their son Sergei.

It was also a family of very contemporary, beyond-the-border en-thusiasms. Both Zoya and Misha had managed to travel abroad, she to Europe and he to America. Misha's heart was set on purchasing a four-wheel-drive vehicle of foreign manufacture: Jeep, Land Rover, it almost did not matter what brand as long as it was not Russian. Zoya was still less discriminating in her reverance for all things Western, from German kitchen gadgets to French perfume. And in a town with only one legitimate basketball court, Sergei was more devoted to Michael Jordan and the Chicago Bulls than to any sports team on his own side of the Atlantic (or Pacific).

Zoya and Misha's love story was odd in that it began under the aus-pices of the Communist youth organization, the Komsomol — a fact that would have seemed to forestall passion as a motive. Yet a special yearning did bring them together, even if it first took shape in a setting as mundane as a stack of manila folders.

I had no trouble picturing Zoya as the beauty that she must have been. Tall and regal in bearing, she had the high steppe cheekbones and almond eyes of a Mongol heroine. A bright girl whose parents were low-level Party officials, Zoya asked permission to join a delegation of Tuvan youth headed for a destination that must have been almost too exotic to even imagine — Czechoslovakia. Her overprotective institute head (was he also secretly infatuated with her?) declined to approve her exit papers; in those days, all requests for foreign travel were vetted by a prospective traveler's employer as well as by the militia and the KGB.

Desperate not to miss out on this opportunity to experience the outside world — the world, as Tuvans say, "beyond the Sayans" — Zoya went to the headquarters of the local Komsomol, and asked to see the person in charge.

She was ushered into Misha's office. She was struck by how youth-ful he was — and how handsome. To this day, Misha has kept his boy-ish good looks. But what impressed her the most at the time was his easy manner and his willingness to help.

After she left, Misha picked up the phone and called the director of the institute where Zoya worked. Even back then, he was not shy about using his authority as a Communist official. Within the hour, Zoya had her papers in order. It seemed only fair that she would agree to see him once she returned.

Interracial courtships were few and far between among Russians and Tuvans, two peoples that had had precious little in common before the two countries' shotgun marriage was officially consummated in 1944. For centuries, the forerunners of the modern day Tuvans lived under the tutelage of the Mongol khans, even taking part in the vast military campaigns of Genghis and Kublai. To this day, the Tuvan language, which is of Turkic origin, contains many words of Mongolian origin. Ethnically, Tuvans and Mongolians are, to an outsider, barely distinguishable. They also share the same brand of Tibetan Buddhism, which began to penetrate both Mongolia and Tuva in the mid-sixteenth century.

Eventually, the Mongols came under the sway of the Chinese. The Manchu dynasty had adroitly exploited the many feudal rivalries among Mongol chieftans. After decades of ruthless struggle, Chinese troops conquered the Oirot empire, of which Tuva was a part. They are thought to have slaughtered as many as a million Mongol and Turkic tribespeople in 1755–56.

By the beginning of the eighteenth century, another geopolitical player had emerged on the scene in Inner Asia: the Tsar's Russians. From the Chinese emperor's perspective, Uriankhai was an impossibly faraway province about which even his wisest counselors knew very little. It lay beyond even the assiduously labeled Outer Mongolia. For Russia, the Tuvan lands were much closer, only a week's hard ride past the same Minusinsk Valley that later would so charm Lenin.

In the eyes of the first Russian colonists, the Tuvans were dirty, disheveled, and fantastically ignorant. Their flat, Mongol features whispered of the Golden Horde. The racial memory of the indignities suffered at the hands of the Tatar still simmered darkly in the Russian heart. Besides, what could have been more antithetical to dialectical materialism and the other truths of scientific Marxism than the ravings of Tuvan shamen? Or so the Party leadership reasoned.

Nor was the average Tuvan necessarily bowled over by his new Russian overseers. First, there was the matter of vodka. Alcohol consumption was never a major feature of Tuvan life (although Tuvans did imbibe *arak,* a much milder drink made from fermented mare's milk). The propensity of so many Russians to spend their free time in the cups struck Tuvans as a sign of decadence. Russian learning and science was admired, but the open disdain the Slavic immigrants evinced for Tuvan culture wore thinner as the years went by, just as the manifest failings of communism became ever more apparent.

In point of fact, Tuva's quarter century of independence came about as much by accident as by any grand design. The chaos accompanying the fall of the Chinese imperial house in 1912 had allowed the Mongolians to declare their independence, albeit as a Russian "protectorate." In 1914, Tuva was annexed by Tsarist Russia, which dispatched a wave of Slavic settlers onto the steppes below the Sayans.

However, the fall of the Romanovs, coming just a few years later, left the question of Tuva's status up in the air once again. Tuva was swept up in bloody skirmishes on the margins of the Russian Civil War, including fighting among Chinese, Mongols, and the half-crazed Estonian Baron Ungern Sternberg, who treated everyone within his grasp with the same manaical cruelty. The Chinese were finally vanquished in 1920; the last units of White irregulars were driven off by the Red Army at the end of 1921. Amid this confusion, some Tuvan leaders conceived a vision of an independent Buddhist state, closely aligned with its neighbor Mongolia. Other Tuvans — especially the young — were inflamed by the ideals of Marxism-Leninism, and naturally looked to the new Soviet state for inspiration and comfort. The two camps, although both ostensibly wedded to socialist ideals, were to come into bitter conflict.

Quietly, Soviet Russia took up where Tsarist officials had left off. Moscow established diplomatic relations with the People's Republic of Tannu Tuva, in large measure to discourage any competing Mongolian claims of sovereignty. At least one historian has argued that a majority of Tuvans at the time would have opted to become part of Mongolia. Meanwhile, through the Comintern, Soviet agents patiently built up their influence on the ground. Young Tuvans were brought to Moscow for ideological and military training; a "Tuvan People's Revolutionary Party" was formed under Comintern auspices.

Throughout most of the twenties, Tannu Tuva's Communist leadership was as much nationalist as Marxist-Leninist. The form of government still had some recognizably pluralistic features, including an elected legislature. At that time, preservation of the country's Buddhist traditions and closer relations with Mongolia carried more weight with

Tannu Tuva's political leaders than, say, intensifying the class struggle. In fact, the country's parliament, the Khural, passed legislation limiting the rights of Russian settlers, and anti-Russian disturbances in 1924 prompted the Soviet ambassador to call on cavalry from Minusinsk to intervene. In 1928, the Tuvan Prime Minister Donduk went so far as to promulgate a decree declaring Buddhism as the country's official religion and outlawing antireligious propaganda.

All of this was to be for naught. A small circle of newly-minted Stalinist revolutionaries took control of Tannu Tuva. They were led by Solchak Toka, a graduate of the Communist University of Toilers of the East (KUTV), and self-styled poet. By coincidence, Manchen-Helfen was accompanied to Tuva by Toka and four other students who had just completed their studies in Moscow. About their alma mater, the visiting ethnographer had no illusions. The KUTV was housed, he wrote, in

> an inconspicuous two-story building where human bombs are manufactured. Hundreds of young Orientals — Yakuts, Mongols, Tuvans, Uzbeks, Koreans, Afghans, and Persians, are trained there for three years to explode the old ways in their homelands. In three years, shamanists are turned into atheists, worshippers of Buddha into worshippers of tractors. Equipped with soap, toothbrushes, and meager Russian, these fine fellows — crammed with catchwords and slogans and fanaticized, as missionaries surely must be if they are to accomplish anything — have the mission of pushing their countrymen straight into the 21st century.

Toka and his entourage were steeped in both the theory and practice of Soviet-style communism, and no sooner had they grasped the reins of power than they began a series of brutal purges to rid the country of their opponents, real and imagined. To further the cause of building socialism, Tuvan society had to be turned upside-down. The population was made to understand that its future lay in embracing its fraternal Soviet brothers to the north. Pan-Mongolianism was rooted out as the most sinister of heresies. A cultural revolution was unleashed in order to ensure the "liquidation of feudal chiefs as a class." Between 1929 and 1931, Toka and his followers reduced Tannu Tuva's twenty-five Buddhist monasteries to a single *khure*, the ranks of the country's lamas from over four thousand to just fifteen traumatized survivors. The shamans, too, were hunted down; the wave of persecution was interdenominational. Most were subjected to what was known in NKVD parlance as "active methods of interrogation."

It is a testament to the degree of control that Moscow exercised over nominally independent Tannu Tuva even before its formal absorption into the Soviet Union that the traditional Mongolian alphabet was replaced as early as 1930 by the Tuvan vernacular written in Roman script, then superseded in the late thirties by a Cyrillic version.

Most astounding of all was that Toka and his entourage felt compelled, in a land geared since time immemorial to nomadism and open-range pasturing, to ape Stalin's reckless collectivization campaign. Within a few years, three-quarters of Tuva's population had been rounded up into state farms, and the number of cattle, sheep, and reindeer vastly diminished. Toka's grasp of Marxist theory — and that of the Comintern — was flexible enough to apply it to the Tuvan context: owners of fewer than twenty head of cattle were construed as the "people," owners of more than 120 the "kulaks," with the latter designation denoting vermin to be exterminated.

What did the starry-eyed Marxist-Leninist idealism of the young Tuvan revolutionaries and their blind faith in Soviet benevolence bring? Collectivization was one blow. When the backwash of Stalin's terror struck Tuva, the luster of world proletarianism dulled further under the familiar pattern of early morning arrests, beatings, and muffled gunshots in cellars. The final straw was Khrushchev's misbegotten "virgin lands" campaign, designed to up lagging Russian agricultural production by bringing huge expanses of untilled land into cultivation. No sooner had the Tuvan steppe been plowed up by Russian tractors than its topsoil blew away toward the Mongolian border. Communist-style science had brought forth another economic and ecological disaster. But by then, in the late fifties, it was far too late to change course. Tuva had long since "voluntarily" joined the ranks of the uneasy nations held captive in the Soviet Union. There was no turning back, or so it appeared.

✳ ✳ ✳

Every morning we awoke to find a freshly typed schedule for our day's activities waiting for us on the kitchen table. For Misha, the eternal *komsomolets,* everything short of our toilet stops needed to be laid out in advance. One day he had arranged a picnic next to a salt lake. The next would be devoted to picking mushrooms in the taiga. A third would take us to the Mongolian border to inspect the nomadic lifestyle of yurts and camels. I recall some negotiation on the last point. We demurred on Misha's offer to let us fire AK-47s from one of the Russian army border posts (he was a friend of the detachment commander). Leery of seeing a photograph published in the Moscow press of two U.S. diplomats strafing one of Russia's neighbors, I said no. My refusal did nothing in Misha's eyes to shore up his faith in my manhood, and he cajoled me for days to reconsider.

Kyzyl — a Turkic word for "red" — was not the authentic Tuva. After all, the very notion of a city rubbed against the grain of a people that until midcentury had spent its days drifting about inner Asia, keeping company with the likes of reindeer and camels, rather than file clerks and tram drivers. Founded in 1914 under the name Belotsarsk, or White Tsar — a label that did not last long once Bolshevik insurgents took control of the town at the end of the Russian Civil War — Kyzyl was even now an ungainly intrusion of cement and brick on the vast Tuvan panorama of steppe, mountain, and river. The city's one hundred thousand or so inhabitants looked for all the world as if they had stumbled upon the place by happenstance. They wandered about in ill-fitting suits and awkward dresses, roaming from half-empty store to half-occupied office, living out a life that was still not fully their own. Kyzyl, too, was a place thronged by the idle young. Every corner seemed to harbor a teenage drunk, every street a cluster of bored and morose youth.

Even in the city, most of the faces were Tuvan; overall, less than a third of Tuva's population was Russian. In Khakasia, for instance, the idea of declaring independence from Russia would have been met with universal derision. In Tuva, on the other hand, it was not so improbable a notion. Demographically, Tuvans were in the majority; in fact, it was the only place in the Russian Federation where Russians were so thinly

represented. Tuva bordered Mongolia, making autonomy a viable propo-
sition geographically compared to "autonomous regions" located in the
heart of Siberia. And Tuva had, in living memory, been independent —
at least theoretically.

On the first day after our arrival, Misha walked us past some of the
homely landmarks of Tuva's fleeting era of sovereignty. We set out from
the stern, obdurate likeness of Toka located just off Kyzyl's central
square. There had been talk of removing the old Stalinist from his
pedestal, but somehow he remained.

At a quiet street corner nearby stood Moscow's former chancellery.
Here, the U.S.S.R.'s representative, whose role was more that of procon-
sul than diplomat, passed on instructions to Toka and his followers.
Only recently did it come to light that Toka had remained a member of
the Soviet Communist Party even while serving as the leader of his
nominally independent country. Tuvan nationalists called that treason,
but in the context of the times, it was hardly surprising.

That Soviet officialdom would play mentor to the Tuvan People's
Revolutionary Party was a foregone conclusion, with or without Toka.
To put it delicately, the two peoples in the twenties were at vastly different stages of development. When the Comintern greeted the first
delegation from the new Communist government of Tannu Tuva, the
Tuvans entered the Kremlin's Red Hall in great wool shepherd coats
and hats. They heaped every sort of abuse on the old order in Tuva, in
particular bemoaning the tyranny of first-born males, who by tradition
inherited all of their father's herds and worldly possessions. It soon became clear that the group was made up, one and all, of second, third,
and fourth sons, who saw themselves, in an odd birth-order variation on
Marxist doctrine, as an exploited class.

As Tuva's history would bear out, the tough-minded Comintern
types would make small work out of their earnest little charges from
Tannu Tuva. Yet sometimes even Moscow's honest gestures would go
awry. When the Tuvans commented on how awed they were by the
Russian capital's tall buildings, an American Communist named
Samuel Adams Darcy innocently showed them a photograph of a much
taller Manhattan skyscraper. After consulting with their translator, the
Tuvans replied that they were not so easily fooled. They could recognize
a pigeon coop, they sniffed, when they saw one; eighty-story buildings,

they reasoned, simply could not exist. Surely such an edifice would be perpetually full of clouds, or the moon would become impaled on them.

Continuing our stroll, we passed by an unassuming wooden house, which had served as headquarters for the Tannu Tuvan secret police. The NKVD had schooled it well. One former employee of the Tuvan Interior Ministry recalled how around-the-clock interrogation sessions might last for days on end, with the prisoner kept on his feet for the whole time, deprived of sleep and food. This approach, he remembered, was effective; it "paralyzed the nervous system and [the prisoner] replied to all questions affirmatively and signed whatever was put in front of him in the way of a report."

Not long before our arrival in Kyzyl, one of the last survivors among Toka's entourage, Oyun Polat, had given a local newspaper his first interview in nearly half a century. He was, as the Tannu Tuva interior minister, a type of Tuvan Beria or Yezhov — his very name had once struck fear in the hearts of his countrymen. His argumentation had a scarcely disguised Nuremburg quality. "I do not completely deny my guilt," he wrote. "But I was merely one of the actors . . . To find the truth after so many years is today, of course, difficult. This is especially the case in our country since they want to either label you a hero or a criminal . . ."

The building was now badly run-down and overgrown; the bitterly cold Tuvan winters had long since stripped the whitewash off its log walls. Yet the cellar, where Toka's enemies were beaten and tortured, was said to have changed little from its heyday. Misha lowered his voice as we walked by, mindful perhaps of the unhappy spirits that were still said to swirl about the ruins. Most Tuvans made a practice of avoiding altogether the sidewalk in front of the old cottage, just as Moscow passersby even today will cross the street in order to keep a safe distance from the walls of the KGB's infamous Lubianka prison.

There was also Tuva's regional museum, a large wooden mansion of decidedly Mongolian inspiration. Behind its swooping roof and sky-blue window frames, the Little Khural voted to join the Soviet Union in August, 1944. The parliament's request to enter the U.S.S.R. was ridiculously grandiloquent. "Fulfilling the undeviating will and burning desire of the whole Tuvan people," the resolution read, " . . . there is no other route for us than the route of the Soviet Union." The official

minutes record that a vote was taken (although today's Tuvan nationalists insist no balloting ever took place), and the assembled delegates
nodded in unison, muttering their deeply ambigious *chak-chak,* a "yes,
yes" that could have just as easily meant "maybe" or "never." On paper,
the decision was unanimous. Yet it is safe to assume that more than one
Tuvan heart lay heavier that night with the knowledge that the future
might bring less rather than more comfort for the Tuvan people.

We ended up that hot, dusty afternoon where all walks in Kyzyl
seemingly culminate: the "center of Asia" obelisk on the banks of the
Yenesei. The promenade was deserted except for one leggy schoolgirl,
who was perched gymnastically over the metal railing, reading a newspaper in the vernacular. Tuvans reckoned — and no one had ever risen
to dispute them — that their republic occupied the precise geographic
middle of the vast continent. Here, the river still bucked and snorted, a
headstrong colt to the wide, worn packhorse we had first crossed in
Krasnoyarsk. Beyond the river, a flat plain ended abruptly in a black,
treeless massif. Except for a line of telephone poles stitched across the
steppe, there was nothing to suggest that the twentieth century had
made any inroads east of Kyzyl's proud monument.

Still, the post-Soviet world in all of its perplexing ambivalence was
little by little insinuating its way into Tuva — to reverse the local
expression — from beyond the Sayans. The television in Zoya's kitchen
blared throughout our supper the mangled Russian overdub of a third-
rate horror flick. For half an hour, from the arrival of the *manti*
dumplings until the teapot had gone tepid, our hosts sat spellbound by
an all-too-typical postmodern American export: a film featuring one
after another twisted aria of teenage screams, punctuated by a full-stage
production of slashings, pummelings, and impalings.

My wife and I tried to ignore it; by birthright, we were inured to
the trash. Yet, enthralled as adolescent glue sniffers, Sergei, Zoya, and
even Misha — who should have known better — wolfed down the food
on their plates without once glancing away from the television. No
wonder they and their compatriots had come to the conclusion that
America was a place where everyone wore a gun, where murder and
mayhem stalked every home, every street.

The immediate culprit was something called Tuva TV, which in the
space of a year had supplanted in the hearts of the local populace the

numbingly staid official television station. The new channel burst onto the scene with an unapologetic stew of pirated movies, kidnapped sports broadcasts, and hijacked music videos. It was part village crier, part circus ringmaster, an electronic medicine man to those apartment dwellers in Kyzyl lucky enough to be able to plug into its cable broadcasts.

Tuva TV was the brainchild of a n'er-do-well Russian actor, the apex of whose theatrical career was a drama award from the Tuvan Komsomol. Viktor Kuzin was lean, sardonic, his gestures lively and emphatic. He projected a type of energy that was thoroughly Russian. It was dynamism that hinted of excess, a maximalism that was trimmed with unscrupulousness.

Kuzin's best-remembered role in Tuva had been as the lead in a pot-boiler about rough-and-ready Bolsheviks liberating Siberia from Kolchak's counterrevolutionaries. Back then, he had made a dashing railroad worker-*cum*-Red partisan. Then his hairline began to recede, and the illusory salary Kyzyl's Music and Drama Theater paid under what was euphemistically known as the "new conditions" — the low-wage, high-inflation crunch that followed on the heels of the Soviet Union's collapse — barely sufficed to keep food on the table. After I paid a call on him, I felt the only wonder was that he had waited so long before taking his considerable impresarial talents beyond the stage.

Tuva TV operated out of a makeshift studio on the third floor of the Soviet-era "House of Fashion," where more booze was now sold than blouses. A few racks of Chinese-made raincoats were the only offerings of women's garments I saw. Upstairs, Kuzin ushered me into the control room, where a rouged and mascaraed Tuvan woman was running through a videotape while a technician sat smoking in front of a bank of monitors. The woman eyed me suspiciously, then turned away.

The studio, it turned out, was across the hall and a few doors down. It was bleakly functional. There was a single TV camera, one light stand, and a chair and table where one of Tuva TV's rotating cast of female announcers was usually seated. All were young, provocatively beautiful, and far too heavily made up. During programming breaks, they read the paid announcements and personal greetings that were the station's only livelihood. Otherwise, Tuva TV ran everything from Elsa Klensch's CNN fashion show to old Tom and Jerry cartoons — a clumsy potpourri of Western kitsch. One of the few programs that the station produced on its own was a twice-weekly primer on American slang, in which two local English teachers tried to explain for their audiences the hidden meaning of lyrics penned by the likes of Meatloaf and the artist formerly known as Prince.

I asked Kuzin what criteria he used to choose the programming he aired on Tuva TV.

"None," he replied breezily. "Absolutely none. We broadcast everything that we can get our hands on."

Normally, I might have found his candor refreshing, but having sampled his wares over supper the night before, I felt far less indulgent. Tuva TV did not even bother to remove a film's FBI antipiracy warning before airing it.

"You know you're breaking the law," I said. "You don't have the right to show most of what you're putting on the air."

He waved his hand impatiently for me to cease and desist. "I've heard that all before. I'll stop showing the films and the rock videos and the NBA games just as soon as all the other people who do exactly the same thing stop. Until then, it's hardly fair to ask me to be some kind of martyr to all the greedy millionaires in Hollywood. Everyone," he repeated the word for emphasis, "positively everyone in Russian television does the same thing."

Was he worried about subjecting his Tuvan audience to a steady diet of violent films and trash TV, I asked?

"I'm a businessman," he replied. "I want to make money. If I put on a show about some long-dead Luxembourg balletmaster, the kind of thing they run on the state-owned channel, I'd go bust in three hours. I'm giving people what they want. Isn't that what capitalism is all about?"

Why would Kuzin look at things any differently, after all? All he knew about television — and all he knew about capitalism — he had made up as he went along. He had never been outside of the former socialist countries. And a highly flexible moral code was one hallmark of the Soviet era, which in the end had conjured up — for all of its elaborate lip service to the joys of collectivism — some of the world's most cynically self-centered citizens.

Kuzin was Russian; I understood him. But the Tuvan personality was something else again. I sat down with one former Tuvan Party official from the early days of "Soviet power" and quickly found I had lost my bearings. He was a bald, heavyset man in his late sixties; he resembled nothing so much as a geriatric Chinese Politburo member. His speech, his mannerisms, were so slow and ponderous that even his breathing and the movement of his prunelike lips came off as the product of long-ingrained ideological caution. He labored visibly over my questions, partly from my unfamiliar accent, partly from what must have seemed to him to be a bizarre line of inquiry on the human costs of collectivization and repression. More than once he paused at length before saying, "I understand your question," then summoned up replies that were so bloodless and opaque that I wondered whether I was confronting a singularly heartless monster or a Zen master of understatement and indirection.

His trajectory as a local party functionary was unexceptional: a training course at a Moscow party institute, middle school instructor, inspector of agricultural products, chief of a district-level party committee. Oddly, he was proud of Tuva's prewar self-sufficiency, even though he had devoted his life to the system that had summarily brought it to an end. "We were once wealthy," he announced, citing livestock figures in the millions, a figure never to be reached again during the Soviet era. "We sent fifty-eight thousand horses to the front," he related, "and twenty-five thousand cows to Ukraine at the end of the war." For once, his features betrayed a trace of animation.

But with the end of the war came the second wave of collectivization, along with more repression — this time directed against "nationalists," presumably people who displayed a lack of enthusiasm over the fraternal coupling of Tannu Tuva to the Soviet Union. "There were disturbances. Our herds were decimated. The country was ruined," he stated blandly, matter-of-factly. He persistently refused to fill in the whys and wherefores. "By the early sixties," he recalled obliquely, "all of the issues were resolved."

I asked him how, in retrospect, he viewed the Soviet experience in Tuva. "What was positive was their culture," he began. "Before the Soviet era, Tuvan culture was at a very low level. Until the thirties, almost no one could read or write. The Communists mounted a literacy campaign." Then he added, "I was one of the first graduates of the Kyzyl *lycee*, in 1942. And I went on to become a teacher." He was, I realized, one of the many children who at Toka's orders were taken from their families to attend school in the city. Toka's brave new world required functionaries, not herdsmen. "What I heard . . . was shocking," Manchen-Helfen related after visiting Tuva's first school. The world described by the teachers, he reported, was divided into the Soviet Union, a land of utter enlightenment, and the rest of the world, cast as a "realm of darkness." I had no trouble believing Manchen-Helfen's characterization of learning dominated by *agitprop*. A book on Misha's shelf entitled *Soviet Tuva*, published in the nineteen-seventies, offered up the following awful doggerel:

> *Lenin is the air we breathe;*
> *Lenin is the mountain which we ascend;*
> *Lenin is the wisdom that is behind our entire people at work*
>   *and in our accomplishments;*
> *Lenin is our teacher, our very best . . .*

"Was there a bad legacy as well?" I asked the old pensioner. His observation about what was positive in the Soviet experience had implied a negative, a yang to match the yin.

He pondered the question, perhaps for as long as a dozen heartbeats. Then, wordlessly, he shrugged his shoulders.

✳ ✳ ✳

Misha kept us busy that summer week, but not without sharing with us some of the delicious pratfalls of provincial life on the farthest edge of empire. As we packed one morning for a lakeside lunch many miles beyond Kyzyl, he chuckled over a handwritten note that one of his Tuvan assistants had sent in to the local headman in advance of our visit. It read: "Gennadi Anatolevich! Take your boat and wash it and show the people in question around the lake. Clean the shore immediately so that we are not put to shame in front of the Americans."

While he might poke fun from time to time at the natives, Misha delved into Tuvan culture and society with the passion that only a serious amateur can bring to a vocation. No doubt it was partly a matter of political survival. Although his constituency was for the most part made up of ethnic Russians living deep in the forests of northeast Tuva, the vast majority of deputies in the legislature were full-blooded Tuvans. During the Gorbachev era, Misha's was a voice for reform. When anti-Russian disturbances broke out in the early nineties, he called for moderation. As the Soviet Union fell apart, he aligned himself with a leading Tuvan nationalist, and gave up his Communist Party membership. In both post-Soviet polls, he was elected to his seat handily.

Yet Misha's sympathy for the Tuvan qualities of Tuva was more than simple political expediency. At a time when ethnic Slavs were rushing to leave this poorest corner of the Russian Federation — among them many of Tuva's best doctors and engineers — Misha remained stubbornly committed to his odd, exotic homeland. It did not seem to matter to him that Tuva was so economically dependent on Moscow that nearly ninety percent of its budget came from the Kremlin; that Kyzyl had one of the highest crime rates in all of Russia, especially if statistics on horse-rustling were included; and that the current generation of Tuvan youth had acquired a disastrous taste for the vodka and cognac that their elders had forsworn.

Nor was he especially judgmental about Tuva's unorthodox faiths and traditions. True, he was dismissive of the cult of Tuva admirers that had cropped up in the United States under the banner of a "Friends of Tuva" association, and he made withering comments about visitors from Marin County who made pilgrimages to Tuva to chant alongside the shamans. Yet when we stopped one afternoon by a spring tucked inside a cleft in the mountains, Misha had us tie lengths of cloth to the branches of a prayer tree overhanging the water's source, a sign that he at least meant to respect what his Tuvan countrymen held sacred.

More than once I heard Zoya, the Tuvan ethnographer, speak disparagingly of her own people's "lack of culture." Her son, half-Tuvan, half-Russian, left no doubt that he found everything about Tuva backward and boring; he steadfastly refused, for instance, to learn any of the Tuvan language. "I'm Russian," he reminded me more than once when I tried to call into question his single-minded determination to leave Kyzyl behind forever.

It all stood in sharp, and somewhat disconcerting, contrast to his father's relentless intellectual curiosity. Misha knew enough to admire what there was to admire about Tuva; his marriage to Zoya was evidence enough. He was wise enough to respect its people, who had somehow withstood the travails of a century long on demands from afar, of an epoch impatient to throw aside unhurried traditions wherever they might be found. Two generations worth of Soviet life were not quite enough to change a simple fact; Tuvans continued to know who they were. They were still tied to their heroic history, to their lonesome land.

We took the waters one blisteringly hot afternoon, Russian-style, at a salt lake bubbling with tiny bloodworms. I waded cautiously through black ooze toward the middle, following Misha and Sergei with more than a little skepticism. High on the opposite bank, a bareback rider galloped on his mount across the silver steppe, headed to a yurt just within our line of sight. As our hosts had promised, we felt the lake's seething denizens rise to meet us from the bottom, pricking us with what we did not know. "You'll feel wonderful afterward," Zoya said. She, however, had sense enough to stay on shore.

I remember the picnic that day with special fondness. The clear sky of inner Asia was a pure, bright blue; it enveloped us with a feeling of expansive well-being that I could barely recall having ever experienced in Moscow. And what a talent Russians have for improvisation! The barbecue was lit with a blowtorch; a tarp was hung between the doors of our two cars to provide relief from the sun. A pop-up aluminum table held our repast: fresh farmer's cheese, *lavash* bread warmed on the car's trunk, a salad of tomatoes and cucumbers hand-picked that morning in Misha's mother's garden. A posed photo of our little party reminds me that there was grilled beef and lamb too; we men hold long meat-laden skewers above the women, like crossed sabers over a wedding party.

At one point, Misha grabbed me by the arm and pointed toward the heavens. "See that?" he asked. All I could make out was an anonymous jet and its vapor trail, far above at cruising altitude.

"Precisely," Misha continued. "That's the daily flight to Singapore. Did you realize that we're almost exactly halfway between Moscow and the countries of Southeast Asia?" He went on to describe one of his pet projects: the construction in Kyzyl of a modern airport and refueling stop for long-haul flights across Eurasia. Landing fees and transit lounges would fill the Tuvan government's coffers. Misha had even made up his mind about the wares that would be sold in the terminal's duty-free shops, shops that in his fertile imagination had already gone from ribbon-cutting to million-dollar sales. I nodded with all of the tacit agreement I could feign.

The shadows lengthened across the steppe, bringing into relief every ridge and mound between us and the far-off Sayans. We drove across the open grassland to the other shore of the lake, toward the yurt we had gazed at from the water.

A bare-chested young man greeted us with a nod. He was seated on a chestnut Tuvan pony; a single bridle rope was looped around its face and neck. The yurt, which from afar had looked magnificently rustic, turned out to have more than its share of modern amenities. Rather than felt, it was covered in standard-issue canvas. Jeans and T-shirts were stuffed in between the yurt's support lines, drying out in the summer sun. Across the way, a wooden corral penned several more would-be free-range ponies. A large pig, too obese to have kept pace with a nomadic existence, snorted out a warning at us. Most sobering of all was the sight of a Sputnik automobile not too unlike Misha's, parked immediately behind the back of the yurt.

Without a moment's hesitation, the yurt's owner, a tall man in his fifties, waved us inside. He and Misha were mildly acquainted — both worked for the Tuvan government, and they passed the time sharing news of colleagues on the make and on the mend, as well as a variety of intramural teapot tempests. We passed around a chipped cup full of fermented mare's milk, which tasted astoundingly cool and refreshing considering it had been drawn from a wood barrel in a corner of the sun-beaten yurt.

As we conversed, three or four preschoolers in varying degrees of undress huddled next to an old brass bed, watching the adults with a mixture of awe and mirth. The littlest of them, a baby girl of no more than nine months, had been given the name Isaura, in honor of a sultry Brazilian soap opera character whose tropical misadventures had become famous even here, on the arid plateau of middle Asia.

So it turned out that the noble primitivism we had imagined still flourished in the far reaches of the steppe was more our Rousseauist fantasy than Tuva's hinterland reality. Our hosts did not sit down around a campfire to offer up throat songs to the heavens, nor to wonder awestruck at the glow of the night sky, which in Tuva harbors more stars at midnight than many city dwellers see in a lifetime. No, a black and white television set was plugged into the car's cigarette lighter, and the natives gathered under the yurt's canvas to marvel at the world beyond the mountains. It twinkled with a peculiarly absorbing ingenuity, filling the screen with fin-de-siècle portent and pathos.

*   *   *

For months, I had the feeling that I had missed something important in Tuva. It filled me with a surprisingly intense uneasiness. My wife and I had had a wonderful time. Zoya and Misha had been the most devoted of hosts, almost to a fault. The scenery, the water, the weather: it had all been glorious. What was gnawing at me? I wondered.

Eventually, I came to understand. Unconsciously, Misha had choked the happenstance out of our visit; in his mania to organize every moment of our stay, he had wrung out most of the spontaneity, all of the waywardness of discovery. I could not help myself; I resented his controlling nature even though I recognized I had no right to expect anything else. It was the Russian way to smother toddlers — and all the more so foreigners — with a surfeit of attention.

This impulse to swaddle visitors with shopworn platitudes and morning-to-midnight itineraries long antedated the likes of Intourist and the Soviet Peace Committee. To whom or what could this insistence on embracing outlanders with an all-too-firm bear hug be attributed? Was it a byproduct of the stifling conformity of the village commune, or the trauma of Mongol domination, or of something even more antique and inexplicable?

The Marquis de Custine quickly had his fill of this brand of Russian hospitality during his nineteenth-century travels through the heartland of Russia. "It is a civil pretext for restraining the movements of the traveller," he wrote, "and for limiting the freedom of his observations . . . the observer can inspect nothing without a guide; never being alone, he has the greater difficulty in forming his judgement upon his own spontaneous impressions . . . In this manner they tyrannise over us in pretending to do us honour."

I broke the news to Misha and Zoya as gently as I knew how; I would not be staying with them when I returned to Tuva. His reaction was uncomprehending; hers, I think, a bit resentful. But I insisted. I would stay in a hotel, I explained, so that I might get more work done.

Once again, the flight to Krasnoyarsk took off well past its scheduled departure time. Over the intercom a few moments after takeoff, the captain blamed our delay on "a *complete* hydraulic system failure," leaving at least one nervous flyer to speculate that a "partial" failure of the plane's controls might not have kept us on the ground for long.

I also hypothesized that a glutton for gunshots and squealing tires had chosen the in-flight movie. Since there were no headphones to be distributed, the sound was broadcast throughout the cabin at a volume sufficient to jolt a Bedlam resident into sanity. Any mental process more ambitious than catatonia — including sleep — was simply out of the question.

Hours later, the plane descended through a thinning cloud bank. The airport at Krasnoyarsk was decorated in deep new drifts, its runway only half-scraped clean of the latest blizzard. In these parts, February is the most bountiful winter month, when the snow hangs heaviest in the forests, and a cornucopia of frost fills cottage windows with the full harvest of the season's unremitting subzero temperatures. Yet the Siberian can already feel the days lengthening. He dreams of the other season when the sky blooms wide with light and warmth and the fields and meadows push up in a pageant of green so exuberant that the ground unfolds from mud and slush in days rather than weeks, and the whole sullen land blossoms to summer exuberance in a matter of weeks rather than months.

A YAK-40, the pride of Aeroflot's backwoods fleet, sped us over the Sayan mountains to Tuva. Misha was on hand to greet me as I deplaned, and I saw for myself how far removed from reality was his dream of a new jetport in Kyzyl. The city's aerodrome was just that; a relic of a bygone era when biplanes were the acme of aviation and overgrown shacks made do as terminals. Never before had I walked through an airport lobby over creaking, weathered floorboards.

Misha had also arranged for a room at the former Communist Party guest house. It remained closed to ordinary tourists, who were obliged instead to stay in the city's one hotel, a rundown tenement. I should have been grateful to the Tuvan government for having accorded me a quiet suite behind the walls of the old party residence — it had a desk, sofa and hot running water — but I sensed that once again I was being enveloped, octopus-like, by Misha's meta-hospitality. Since there was no restaurant at the guest house, my meals were to be taken at what I came to refer to as "Café Zoya," that is, at Misha and Zoya's apartment. In a city where restaurant fare was barely identifiable, Zoya's cooking was a godsend. Yet culinary satisfaction came at a price; it meant I was still beholden to Misha's schedule.

I had timed my arrival to coincide with Shagaa, the Tuvan New Year celebration. Like many other religious festivals — including the Orthodox Christmas and Easter observances — Shagaa was suppressed during the Soviet period, albeit with varying degrees of intensity. Even before Tuva's incorporation into the U.S.S.R., Toka's Marxist-Leninist zealotry had forced Tuvans to observe Shagaa quietly, if at all. For a people building a socialist utopia, the more scientific European calendar was the one to emulate, not the retrograde lunar calculations of astronomer-monks in Lhasa.

Only in 1988 did the authorities in Tuva permit Shagaa to be celebrated again openly. Almost immediately, it became a focal point for Tuvan cultural manifestations, including both Buddhist and shamanist rituals. Shagaa also gave new impetus to Tuvan nationalism, and it is probably not coincidental that the first anti-Russian disturbances of the Soviet period took place just two years later, in 1990.

In an all-too-typical gesture, Misha invited me to welcome in the Year of the Blue Dog in the most ambitious fashion possible: by climbing at dawn the mountain overlooking the confluence of the Yenesei's two branches, the Biy-Khem and the Ka-Khem.

He was there, knocking on my door, well before the winter sun had peered above the horizon. Outside, it was a characteristic February morning in Kyzyl: a lung-rattling, boot-crunching rhapsody in cold, with the temperature registering dismayingly close to the thermometer's bulb.

We walked briskly along the riverbank. Just as the sky began to lighten, we came upon a group of thirty or so Tuvans standing on an ice-pile above the frozen Yenesei. An elderly shaman in a bright red vest and peaked fur hat slowly circled a two-foot-high pile of stones, pounding a wide, flat leather drum with a mallet. He was summoning the spirits that were needed to welcome in the new year properly. A meager stand of branches protruded from the *ovaa*, the stone shrine; they were festooned with strips of colored satin. One after another, the

Tuvans who had assembled — from giddy schoolboys to solemn grand-mothers — stepped forward to tie cloths to the branches and to place offerings at the base of the *ovaa*. I looked over the crowd and realized that Misha and I were the only Caucasians in sight.

A white-haired, bespectacled man with a scholarly mien had observed us from the margins of the ceremony. "That's Professor Kenin-Lopsan," Misha whispered, "He's our leading authority on shamanism." We greeted him, and a conversation of sorts ensued.

Misha introduced me with a degree of formality that I had not seen from him before. "He is here to learn about Tuva," Misha explained. "I've told him that the old traditions have not been lost, thanks in large measure to your work, Professor."

"I'm old," Kenin-Lopsan replied. "I'm really not in very good health."

"You look fine," Misha insisted.

"No, I don't have much energy anymore. I have arthritis and back pains. Sometimes they are so bad I can't even get out of bed. And I have dizzy spells." The professor was still peering at me from behind his glasses. He was dressed entirely in black: black coat, black trousers, a black fur cap. He leaned to one side, propped up by a waist-high wood cane.

Kenin-Lopsan had done more to preserve the myths and sagas of Tuvan shamans than anyone else alive. Over three decades, he criss-crossed his homeland, searching for people who recalled the period when animist beliefs were part of the everyday fabric of Tuvan life, and the prestige of the shaman went unchallenged. While outwardly he adopted a posture of scholarly detachment toward the folk practices he studied (a matter of professional survival during the Soviet period), it was widely thought that Kenin-Lopsan could himself communicate with the spirits of the land and water, and heal the sick and infirm.

We left him behind and followed a path over the gray-green ice to the foot of the mountain across the river. Dozens of Tuvans had already assembled on the opposite bank. Some were clustered around a roaring bonfire; others tried their hand at lassoing from some forty paces a toy horse's head mounted on a stick. Halfway up the mountainside, an oversize painted dog's head gazed goofily down upon the merrymakers.

I would have been content to take in the goings-on at the base of the mountain, but Misha, ever the man of action, motioned me to follow him up the hillside. An impromptu trail of icy bootprints led toward the summit. Soon we were climbing briskly — almost jogging, really. I sensed that Misha's competitive spirit was getting the better of him. Rather than deferring to his out-of-town guest to set the pace, he pressed ahead, faster and faster. It was a bare-knuckled challenge to my manhood, and I churned my legs upward through the snow in hot pursuit.

Twenty minutes later, we both stood panting at the top. Three young Tuvan men — Misha knew them too — sat at the edge of a precipice that overlooked the two arms of the Yenesei, many hundreds of vertical feet below. They had hauled wood all the way up from the riverbank, and were standing before a lively fire that leaped and cavorted with every rush of wind down the valley. From this height, Kyzyl, still slumbering under a low mist, looked like no more than a fleeting encampment. Outfitted in arctic mufti, Misha posed for me at the brink of the cliff, flanked by two grinning spirits chiseled from blocks of ice.

We turned to go back. A few meters below the summit, just out of the wind, a figure sat outlined against the snow, leaning comfortably against a stout cane, gazing contentedly toward the brightening sky.

Misha was flabbergasted. "Kenin-Lopsan," he called out. "How did you get up here? We just barely arrived ourselves!"

The shaman's "second soul," it is said, moves through space and time in communion with other spirits, leaving behind the cumbersome impediment of the body. It was difficult to believe that the teetering old man with whom we had conversed, who had so insistently decried his ill health, would have managed to reach the other side of the river, much less matched our pace to the top of the mountain. We had seen no one else behind us on the treeless ridge. And there was no other route up.

As for Misha's question, the black-clothed figure in the snow just smiled. If there was an answer, it did not pass through his lips.

Back in the town square, the Tuvan national theater was hung with gaily-colored sashes and banners. As it was the Year of the Blue Dog that was being celebrated, it seemed only natural to see a dog show taking place in one corner of the square. A pantomime between the outgoing year's rooster and a yipping, pawing, collie-masked actor brought laughs and cheers from the crowd in the square. Then, with a howling, barking fanfare of horns and drums, a twenty-foot-long blue dragon-dog burst through the theater's main doors, and danced down the main steps, leading a parade of other animal-actors (corresponding to the Chinese zodiac) through the crush of Tuvan onlookers.

Not everyone's mind was on the celestial, however. I stood beside a troop of silk-jacketed boys on horseback, conversing with the chairman of the modern version of the Great Khural. Like Toka, he was an intellectual of sorts. He was also Misha's closest political ally. He had made his name in Tuvan politics by calling for autonomy from Russia; wisely, perhaps, he had since moderated his tone. In fact, his stridency had diminished with every month that he had been in power. I admired his realism, yet I was not sure that it was of an entirely selfless variety.

"You must understand," the chairman of the Khural was saying, "we can't just let anyone who calls himself a singer travel abroad. We have to protect our culture from unscrupulous people, both yours and ours. I have the artistic integrity of the music to think about."

The chairman had buttonholed me about one of his pet peeves: the booming market for Tuvan throat-singers abroad and the fact that he did not control it. In particular, he was angry about an American musicologist whom he claimed had cheated a group of Tuvan performers that had toured the United States not long before. His reasoning was by our lights obtuse, and he offered no evidence of fraud or chicanery. Instead, he hinted darkly of surreptitious royalties kept under the table, as if Tuvan *khoomai* sold as many units as a blockbuster rap album.

"He won't be welcome back here," the chairman went on, speaking still of the unlucky musicologist. "He can forget about signing any contracts without my approval."

Misha noticed that the chairman's soliloquy had fallen on deaf ears, and diplomatically eased me away. We circled the square several more times as I eagerly snapped photographs. One of the most popular attractions was a pillow-fighting contest among schoolboys, who battled each other from opposite ends of a sawhorse to see who would be knocked to the ground first.

I was taking in a particularly heated bout, with dozens of Tuvans standing about, rooting for their favorite pint-size gladiator, when I felt a tap on my shoulder. I turned around to a scrawny, gap-toothed smile, and the words, in broken, stilted English, "You want? You buy?"

My heart sank. My annoyance at being so readily identified as a foreigner was the least of it. As I peered at the three Poloroid photographs that were being held up to my unwilling face, the realization sank in. The hunter in the picture holding up the pelt in some barebones apartment was the same thin, pockmarked face that was now addressing me. And the ghostly gray-white fur he was displaying over his couch was that of a snow leopard.

"Eto snezhnaya barsa, ne tak li?" I growled, filling rapidly with indignation. "It's a snow leopard, isn't it?"

"Da, da," he replied in Russian. *"Ochen tsennaya veshch,"* he continued, "it's a very valuable item." As if to infuriate me still more, he added: "The snow leopard is very rare. It's in the *Krasnaya Kniga."* The "Red Book" is the official Russian list of endangered species.

"So you shot it yourself?" I inquired.

"Yes, near the border with Mongolia."

He paused. Perhaps he saw the look in my eyes, because he began to edge back a step or two into the crowd.

I was angry. I called him a criminal.

The poacher melted away, with a look as hurt as a chastened pup.

Misha, too, looked at me oddly. "It was wrong to shoot that snow leopard," he said, in an even tone. "It's a protected animal." Yet he did not sound very convincing. There was not one murmur of shock in his voice.

That night, at Café Zoya, there was another guest at the table. He was a big, formidable Russian in his late forties, with a square-jawed face stamped by a shady, off-putting sort of gregariousness. The man was dressed casually but tastefully; he found a way to mention in passing the provenance of his English wool sport coat and Italian leather shoes. At another point, he effused over a particular hotel in Paris and its impeccable service, while disparaging another such establishment in Amsterdam. To hear such talk in the Russian provinces could only mean one thing: new money, fast money, under-the-table money.

Misha's associate described his line of work variously as importing and exporting, mining, and tourism, and I guessed that whatever he actually did for a living involved in some measure all of the above. From what I could gather, he was in charge of something large and lucrative located many miles outside of Kyzyl.

Throughout supper, Misha and his guest exchanged a series of verbal nods and winks. "And the asbestos?" one might begin. Asbestos was one of Tuva's very few commodities.

"Never mind. On Tuesday. Like we discussed before," the other would answer.

My role that night, I discovered, was that of college counselor. Misha's guest had sent his son to a boarding school in Cyprus to learn English. Now he wanted him to attend a university in the States. He had plenty of money, the guest assured me. His boy, too, was smart. He just needed some advice. What was a good American university?

I launched into an overview of U.S. higher education, followed by a verbal treatise on the difference between private and public universities. I explained that some colleges specialized in liberal arts, others put more emphasis on science and engineering.

"What does your son want to study?" I asked.

"*Biznes,*" came the swift reply. "I want him to work for me. He needs to understand American companies, how they function, how they make profits."

I asked more questions, eventually too many. Did his son want to study on the East or West Coast? Did he prefer a large or small university? Did he want to live in a city or in a more rural area?

The man's interest was flagging rapidly. "The boy doesn't have to learn to write poetry," he interjected suddenly. "All he needs to know is business, business, business."

When he got up to leave, Misha followed his guest to the vestibule, closing the door behind them. From the other side of the glass partition, I watched the two men converse, the meaning of their traded words and gestures as clear as the day's headlines.

✳ ✳ ✳

I had a jeep for the day, courtesy of the Tuvan taxpayers, along with the company of one of Misha's parliamentary aides, Kim Danilovich. A quietly officious supernumerary couched behind oversize glasses, he was a man of indeterminate age and views. From what I had seen of him in Kyzyl, he normally kept his peace, notwithstanding the silent avidity with which he followed the twists and turns of other people's conversations.

The road to Samagaltai was, I think, the most desolately beautiful I have ever traveled. In the ethereal light of the winter dawn, the snow-laquered steppes lay before us in leonine defiance of anything civilized, anything man-touched. It was a world of drifting, undulating white-ness, where the wind had had its way since before the shaman's deep, warbling song was first heard at dawn. The black asphalt of the high-way was the only intrusion, and as such it was the embodiment of the bleak lyricism that is so much a part of travel in the empty reaches of inner Asia. Here in this thin dark ribbon is the role of man, it said; the rest belongs to the endless steppe, to nature and to the spirit.

I could never quite manage to lure Kim Danilovich into small talk. His years under the mastery of Russians, I suspected, had lent him a form of caution as inscrutable as it was multilayered. He parried every inquiry I made, save those about his family and the weather. Least of all was he will-ing to speak about relations between the Tuvan and Russian communities.

In those settlements that we did pass through, however, Kim Danilovich seemed to have a wealth of contacts and endeavors. All along the way, we stopped to ferry villagers from one place to another. And my chaperone was anything but reserved with his fellow country-men. He spoke confidently to our Tuvan passengers, and they re-sponded with obvious deference. At Misha's side, Kim Danilovich was an obedient, self-effacing cipher; among his own people, he was a re-spected figure. It was a dynamic that would have been familiar to past colonial subjects the world over, from Bantu to Bengalis. Tuva was, after all, still a dependency of Russia, even if it had achieved a slim measure of autonomy in the new post-Soviet conditions.

I wanted to visit a snow-covered yurt, even though Misha had has-tened to inform me that my wish was largely anachronistic. During the cold months, modern Tuvans preferred Russian-style wood cabins to felt. Yet I had heard that in a few places, the family yurt remained up year-round. Kim Danilovich had promised to see what he could do.

We had already crossed the last barrier of mountains before Mongolia, and entered a wide, flat, treeless basin that I knew stretched on for many hundreds of miles past Tuva to the fringes of the Gobi Desert. We passed a sign, and Kim Danilovich motioned to the driver to turn down a snow-covered track that was barely distinguishable from the surrounding steppe.

We drove for another hour, stopping frequently to check our bearings or puzzle over another anonymous fork in the road. There were no points of reference: no names, no places, nothing that the human mind could readily encompass. In fact, it was the steppe's unbending, unadorned character that threatened to overwhelm the conscious mind, not vice versa.

Finally, we arrived at the outskirts of a tiny settlement. A boy on horseback galloped across our path, the muzzle of his shaggy Tuvan pony encrusted with ice. The driver steered in the direction of a house on a small rise. Beside the house was a large yurt, its stovepipe spewing white smoke.

Inside the house, a communal meal was unfolding. The women wore their Mongolian silk jackets, a festive touch for what was this family's New Year's meal. Kim Danilovich and I sat down with the other men at a long wooden table. We slurped down a *lagman* soup larded with mutton grease, and talked over the merits of the herdsman's life. Alcohol and isolation, they said, were the main problems. That, along with the thievery of their Mongolian neighbors, added one man. It was a sad commentary on the abject poverty in Mongolia that Mongolians would sneak across the border to steal from their "rich" Tuvan cousins. No other lesson had done so much to discourage Tuva from setting a course toward independence. Better to keep food on the table, Tuvans reasoned, than to opt for self-reliance — and empty stomachs. I pondered this wisdom as I nibbled at a local cheese that looked something like a chunk of crumbled cinderblock, and wondered: how could the Tuvan diet get any less appetizing?

After lunch, we were ushered into the yurt by the family patriarch — I was never able to sort out most of the relationships around the table — and his eye-catching daughter. The interior was arranged as meticulously as a museum display; the colorful painted chests were placed in exactly the correct positions according to ceremony and tradition. In fact, there was no sign that anyone actually made use of the yurt. I looked over at Kim Danilovich, and he smiled and lowered his head with unmistakable embarrassment. "We raised the yurt in your honor," the father explained. "Normally we don't erect it until the summer." I have a fine photograph of that visit as a souvenir, a "Tuvan Gothic" portrait of the gravely serious old man, his ample wife, and their bewitching daughter, standing proudly in the ankle-deep snow before their unseasonably assembled yurt.

We stopped at the *khure* in Samagaltai, one of only a handful of Tuvan Buddhist monasteries that had so far been rebuilt. People in Tuva spoke with genuine emotion about the visit of the Dalai Lama in 1992, almost certainly the first of his line to ever set foot in these mountains and valleys. Yet if lamaism was in revival, it was a quiet, unostentatious one. One of the first — and grandest — monastic centers in the Tuvan lands, Samagaltai's post-Soviet *khure* was just two small buildings, a temple and a combined classroom and office.

Kim Danilovich and I sat before the head monk; as far as I could tell he was the only monk in Samagaltai, and a part-time one at that. He served the Lord Buddha, he explained, each morning until lunchtime; in the afternoon, he dispensed with his saffron cloak and donned the garb of the shaman, dispensing his healing advice by appointment in his home. His dual role reminded me of an old saying about Haiti, and the surprisingly comfortable relationship between its two longstanding faiths. "Haiti," the expression went, "is ninety percent Catholic, and one hundred percent voodoo."

It was time to read my fortune, and I waited cross-legged before the lama. Part of his brief was blatantly astrological; he quizzed me at length about the exact time of my birth, and had me subtract the time difference between Tuva and Washington, D.C. He lit more incense, then took my pulse. Where did Buddhism end and animism begin, I wondered?

He peered at length at my palm. His nails, I noticed, were black with dirt. "You will have more adventures," he began. I nodded, thinking that observation a very safe bet with so many months in Russia still before me.

"Have you been experiencing back trouble?" he asked suddenly. I had, in fact, slept badly the night before, and my neck was painfully sore. He had noticed my stiff posture, I concluded.

The monk drew a box of snuff from an altar and raised a pinch of it quickly to his nostrils. He looked at me intently again, and put another question to me. "Are you angry about something? Do you have a problem with anger?"

"Not particularly," I stuttered. Here, I thought, he had gone down a blind alley.

He regarded me quizzically again, and I felt I needed to explain further. I was a person who prided myself on my self-control. "I really don't lose my temper very often," I volunteered. "Anger isn't a very big problem with me."

The lama seemed not to have heard me. "Here," he said, handing me a small package of snuff wrapped in newsprint, "keep this with you, and you will find those feelings will diminish."

Our audience was over, and as we returned to the jeep, I saw the monk hurriedly change from his robes to his street clothes. No doubt he was anxious to get home for lunch. My encounter with lamaism had been anything but a mystical experience. I might just as well have had a friendly chat with the local grocer or pharmacist. It was religion at the retail level, with no pretense of theology or grand spiritual design.

And yet, on the long ride home across the awesomely diffident steppe, I found myself pondering the monk's words, and having second thoughts. Had I been too quick to dismiss his questions as the missteps of a second-rate soothsayer? Repressing anger was not the same as not experiencing it; had the monk actually seen something I had ignored? At one point, I leaned over to Kim Danilovich and commented that perhaps the lama had been right after all, that it was possible I had a problem with anger, deep down.

Kim Danilovich blinked, and allowed a slow, wise smile to form on his lips. "You see, we're still our own people. That's something that the Russians don't fully understand. Even Kozlov doesn't realize just how Tuvan we still are." Kozlov was Misha's last name. It was the only time that Kim Danilovich spoke about himself, about his own anger. Needless to say, I never mentioned it to Misha.

High above the mountains, in the fading afternoon light, a jetliner mutely crossed Tuva on its helter-skelter civilizing mission, its contrail bright against the darkening sky. From the backseat of the jeep, I watched it fly over and past the mountain peaks, and the vapor clouds melt and dissipate until they were indistinguishable from the steppe, the dark ribbon of highway, and the meaning of Kim Danilovich's quiet demeanor.

LIVING ON
THE VOLCANO

KAMCHATKA

EIGHT AND ONE-HALF HOURS IN THE AIR, on a jet plane, nonstop, and you land in the same country you left behind. Nowhere else in the world can you take a marathon flight like this without facing passport control and customs at the other end. Count on four or five hours to cross China, Brazil, or India by plane; it is still only about half the time spent on the Moscow to Petropavlovsk-Kamchatski route. One can imagine a comparable flight from, say, Miami to Anchorage or New York to Guam, but no airline actually flies routes like these, certainly not without stopping somewhere in between. The exception only serves to prove the rule. Paris and France's Indian Ocean dependency, La Reunion, are about as far apart as Moscow and Kamchatka, but you have to fly over most of Africa to reach St.

Denis, the island's capital. Anywhere you might land on the way to Petropavlovsk would be Russian.

Despite the loss of its Soviet empire, Russia remains the world's largest country, a major power with longstanding strategic interests and — let there be no mistake — armed forces capable of backing them up. For Moscow, despite the end of the Cold War, Kamchatka is still a vital outpost in the North Pacific region.

Until the early twenties, Kamchatka's Russian population numbered only a few thousand; it was perhaps one-sixth the size of the indigenous Koryak and Itelmen communities. By midcentury, though, successive waves of Slavic immigrants had overwhelmed Kamchatka's native community. Demographically, Kamchatka is today no more Asian than St. Petersburg.

Under Communist rule, Kamchatka took its marching orders from Moscow. Party bosses, economic planners, and military commanders barely lifted a finger without first checking with their superiors back in the capital. Even today, it is easier to fly from Kamchatka to Moscow than it is to neighboring cities in the Russian Far East like Vladivostok and Khabarovsk. In the airport at Petropavlovsk, the clocks are set on Moscow time, nine hours behind.

The authorities in Moscow were anything but eager to ease the peninsula's isolation. On the contrary, until the end of the Soviet period, ordinary Russians had to seek special authorization even to set foot in Kamchatka. No one dreamed of going there on a lark. If you did not have relatives there, if you were not a geologist or an ethnographer, if you did not serve in the military, you simply were not welcome.

Yet some geographical realities are irreducible. As Kamchatka residents wake up to the new day, their compatriots in the Russian capital are still tuned in to the previous night's news programs. Likewise, many Petropavlovsk inhabitants are already asleep by Moscow's lunch hour. To most Russians, Kamchatka is a watchword for being lost on the periphery; unlucky sports fans and concertgoers relegated to the seats farthest from the stage are said to be stuck "out in Kamchatka."

For years, the flights between Moscow and Kamchatka constituted a veritable lifeline, an air bridge between outpost and metropole. It was not uncommon for people to fly to the capital just to undertake a weekend shopping expedition, or see a new production at the Bolshoi. Now, many of the flights took off practically empty. Instead of $20 round-trip, the same journey cost over $350, and the price was still headed upward.

The result was that I could revel in the impossible luxury of having three seats to myself all the way to Kamchatka. Never mind that the Ilyushin-62's four rear-fitted turbines scream on takeoff like a coven of witches — and have been known to catch fire while airborne. Rather than being assaulted by plump, unfragrant neighbors rummaging through oversize carry-on sacks, I gratefully dozed off. Even the notorious Aeroflot food was in this instance edible. I left inviolate, however, the trademark blue chicken leg.

The plane rode the chill, morose air over the Arctic Sea coast, following the barren curve from Vorkuta to Magadan. Lifeless gray clouds drifted by underneath, as rumpled as discarded trousers; down below, the short, glorious Russian summer was well over. Already, in late August, a wispy fall of snow lay on the tundra, powdering the rich rouge of the autumn bogs and tussocks.

Over the northern coast of the Okhotsk Sea, mute to the outside world for generations, the clouds gave way to an astonishing panorama of onyx blue ocean, aloof as polished stone, and a jagged island swept clear of everything but rock and grass.

Seeing the Okhotsk Sea with my own eyes struck me as something of a miracle. For half a century, any foreigner who flew in these skies was judged an intruder. The air charts still carry an ominous caption: "Unauthorized aircraft in this airspace may be fired upon without warning." I thought, too, of the barges full of doomed "class enemies" scuttled in these waters during the thirties and forties. Even the Nazis did not imitate that particular form of barbarism.

Before long we crossed over another shore, over Kamchatka. The coast of this most flamboyantly shaped of peninsulas looked comparatively flat, a long sash of forest and marsh intersected by dozens of roundabout rivers and streams. Soon, though, the land rose up into the Sredinniy Khrebet, or Middle Range. Five hundred miles in length, north to south, it forms the backbone of Kamchatka. It was obvious that this was rugged country; there were no roads, no houses. Dark pines lined the watercourses and intermediate slopes. On the higher ground, they gave way to low scrub that petered out into open rock and tundra. Some of the peaks were rounded, unextraordinary. But scattered

234 ♦ LIVING ON THE VOLCANO

about, in all directions, were the snow-covered cones of the peninsula's volcanoes, rising up in exotic greeting, in dazzling menace.

The IL–62 swooped in over Avachinskaya Bay, whining loudly as it banked past Petropavlovsk and the Koryak volcanoes behind it. The airport was tucked into one corner of a vast military complex. Instead of passenger jets and hangars, the runway was lined with Migs parked inside blastproof bunkers. One olive-green fighter, emblazoned with a large red star on its fuselage, warmed up its engines in front of a bunker door, the pilot standing up in the plane's open cockpit. From this air-field, ten years before, other airmen took off into the night to intercept a Korean airliner lost somewhere overhead. They failed. Unfortunately, their comrades based on Sakhalin Island did not.

The civilian terminal, all dank and corrupted concrete, sat at the end of a long taxiway. Erected as an afterthought, the terminal was probably never adequate for the number of people it serviced.

The passengers basked outside under the late summer sun, wait-ing patiently for someone to bring the baggage up. On a vendor's table, a newspaper headline read "Turn Out The Lights: Electric Rates Increase By 1300 Percent." According to the article, Kamchatka had chalked up the highest prices in all of Russia for twenty of twenty-eight basic foodstuffs. Once, everything in this remote corner of the Russian Federation was subsidized. Now it cost real money to transport goods here — real money that many consumers simply did not have.

On the long bus ride into the city, my seatmate explained that she had given up on Kamchatka. She had just spent ten hours selling rasp-berries in front of the airport terminal. It was a job that, on a good day, earned her a few dollars. She was remarkably cheerful under the cir-cumstances. I guessed, too, that she had once been pretty, but her looks had wasted away under the Halloween conventions of Soviet fashion. Her hair, dyed a shade of electric lavender coveted only in Russian beauty salons, bobbed about next to the bus's open window. Her co-quetry, while heartfelt, came across as parody.

Despite her upbeat veneer, her world had fallen apart. Everything, she judged, absolutely everything, had worsened since Yeltsin came to power. Life had been much better under Leonid Ilyich, she said, mean-ing Brezhnev. In those days, she had held a real job working in a candy factory. Back then, a loaf of bread cost only five kopecks. These were not really political statements. She never mentioned the party, the revolution, or Lenin. Instead, she was clinging with all her might to the halcyon days of her youth, an era she could fathom, a time when everyone knew where they stood.

Her husband, a hopeless drunk, had died years before (I resisted the temptation to ask whether this was Yeltsin's fault as well). Her son, recently graduated from a technical institute, could not find work. Her own pension was barely enough to feed her cocker spaniel. There was no future in high-priced, dead-end Kamchatka, she insisted, adding that she was far from the only person desperate to leave.

A few months before, her daughter had invited her to come live in Nizhny Novgorod. Although she had never laid eyes on it, that faraway city above the Volga — which she still referred to by its Communist-era moniker, Gorky — was a place dripping in milk and honey. She might have been speaking of Paris.

When our bus pulled into a terminal at the edge of the Petropavlovsk, she galloped over to a neighboring bus, her hands weighed down with her berry buckets, to see if it was the one I needed to take. Chatting up the driver, she carved out a place for me in the front row of seats. I wished her well. She smiled, waved, and was gone.

When George Kennan arrived in Petropavlovsk in August 1865 (he was a distant forebear of this century's diplomat and scholar of the same name), it was a modest village, home to perhaps three hundred souls. As seen from the deck of his ship, Petropavlovsk was dwarfed by its surroundings; it was, in his words, nothing more than "a little cluster of red-roofed and bark-thatched log houses; a Greek church of curious architecture, with a green painted dome; a strip of beach, a half-ruined wharf, two whale-boats, and the dismantled wreck of a half-sunken vessel."

Sailing into Avachinskaya Bay after an arduous crossing from San Francisco, Kennan had expected to see a barren, inhospitable country. He was surprised to find, instead, a land of lush vegetation and unforgettable vistas. "It may be imagined with what delight and surprise," he later wrote, "we looked upon green hills covered with trees and verdant thickets; upon valleys white with clover and diversified with little groves of silver-barked birch; and even the rocks nodding with wild roses and columbine . . ."

Kennan did not come to Kamchatka by pure happenstance. A young Western Union telegraph operator bored by his deskbound duties, he volunteered to take part in a risky expedition charged with surveying an overland telegraph route linking Europe and America via the Bering Strait. Earlier efforts to lay a cable under the Atlantic Ocean had been frustrated; the land route across Siberia increasingly looked like the only option. Along with a handful of other hardy adventurers, he was to spend the next two years traveling across Kamchatka and Eastern Siberia, enduring starvation rations, bitter cold, and more than one brush with death.

In the end, the survey work conducted by the self-styled "Russo-American Telegraph Company" came to naught; the Atlantic cable was successfully laid and the Siberian project abandoned. Kennan's book about his experiences, however, was a smashing success. *Tent Life in Siberia*, first published in 1870, made him famous. Kennan became nineteenth-century America's leading authority on Russia, returning later in life to Siberia to write an account of the Tsarist penal system.

The first known photograph of Petropavlovsk, taken in the 1880s, portrays a settlement much as the elder Kennan described it: shabby log houses bordered by picket fences and intersected by muddy footpaths. Not one structure from the last century has survived to the present day, a consequence, in part, of Kamchatka's harsh climate.

Yet however primitive and isolated Petropavlovsk was in Kennan's day, it was also surprisingly cosmopolitan. Perhaps the pattern was set from the beginning; the settlement was founded by Vitus Bering, a Norwegian explorer in the service of Russia. Petropavlovsk was named for Bering's two ships, the St. Peter and the St. Paul, although by the time of Kennan's visit, the village's mostly illiterate inhabitants had apparently forgotten how their settlement was christened.

During the nineteenth century, Petropavlovsk was a regular port of call for whalers from the U.S. and Europe. Later, the Japanese fishing fleet would join their ranks as well. By the time Kennan arrived, there were already American and German fur traders living in Petropavlovsk. Kennan was also surprised by the foreign luxuries on display in the residence of the Russian captain-of-the-port; he owned not only a piano but also a stereoscope, as unusual a plaything for its day as a videophone is in ours.

No one seemed to pay much attention to the question of citizenship. A thrice-elected village mayor was an American citizen named Edmund Sandalin. Decorated by the Tsar, his medal and the accompanying citation still hang in Petropavlovsk's museum.

By the turn of the century, foreigners were commonplace in Kamchatka. However many marine mammals they slaughtered, whatever diseases and vices they propagated among the natives, the traders and seafarers also left more positive and enduring traces. Old Winchester rifles and Currier and Ives prints are still to be found in Kamchatka villages. The sturdiest homes in Petropavlovsk were built with North American cedar and spruce. Only in the past couple of decades were some of these minor landmarks, including the interwar headquarters of a Japanese firm that was crowned in pagoda-like towers, torn down. In Kamchatka, people still use the word "progress" without irony.

The village church, where Kennan attended a bumptious Cossack wedding, is also no more. Somehow, it managed to stay open until the thirties, when the Communist authorities finally confiscated its bells and appropriated the building. The church was then converted into a movie theater, a "people's temple" preaching through cinema a gospel of class struggle and five-year plans. Finally, the old church was leveled to make way for a still more important project — the bunkerlike local Party headquarters, which in turn was vacated at the end of the Soviet era.

However, plenty of dilapidated wooden barracks do still stand in the center of Petropavlovsk. At first I judged them abandoned, but a closer look revealed signs of a squalid sort of life. Behind one place on Sovetskaya Street, a worn-out drunk sat propped against an entrance, while children cavorted nearby in a garbage-strewn back lot. This particular building, like the others, was divided into communal apartments, where thin walls, steamy kitchens, and odoriferous bathrooms were shared by strangers living off a common corridor.

Ever since the early twenties, when the country's housing stock was divided up willy-nilly by the triumphant Bolsheviks, life in the *kommunalka* had provided grist for books, plays, and movies. It was, to some extent, a symbol of all of the idiocies and frustrations of life in the Soviet Union: a numbing existence of crowding, callousness, and conformity. Even under Stalin, the housing crisis was so acute that it could not be ignored. In fact, it was one of the few failings of Stalinism that could be openly discussed while the dictator was still alive.

Across one wall on Sovetskaya Street, a rebellious resident had painted in bold letters a perfect sendup of Communist sloganeering: "Power to the Soviets; Housing to the People," "Rats, Roaches and Bugs: Our Neighbors," "Welcome to the Tsarist Museum." The young woman who had authored the lines spotted me photographing them. She leaned out of her window and asked me what I thought. I gave her a thumbs-up. She smiled as she stroked her cat, obviously pleased with herself.

What was amazingly international in the last decade of the twentieth century were Petropavlovsk's roads. Fully half of the cars on the city's streets were Japanese. From all appearances, their new Russian owners were still busy verifying their vehicles' performance specifications. They posed questions to themselves like, "Can this car really attain a velocity of 180 kilometers per hour as the speedometer suggests?"

Lacking a world-class test track anywhere in Kamchatka, these issues had to be sorted out within the city limits. The marvels of Japanese motor engineering were especially appealing to drivers heretofore accustomed to the lunking characteristics of Soviet cars, which were never noted for their acceleration or handling. The "envelope" of a Russian Lada, to borrow an all-too germane term from the world of supersonic air combat, was never too formidable. A Nissan sedan, on the other hand, offered ample opportunities for disastrous miscalculation. It turns out that a little bit of performance, like knowledge, can be a dangerous thing.

The fact that Japanese cars had their steering wheels on the right — in other words, on the wrong side of the road for Petropavlovsk's motorists — was a further complication. Driving in Russia was perilous enough when a car was properly configured for Russian roads. When it was not, a driver's life expectancy fell off the actuarial tables into the select company of blind rock climbers and emphysemic pearl divers.

The Toyotas and Mitsubishis that ended up in Kamchatka were the castoffs from the bottom of the Japanese used-car heap. They were either going to be bought by a Russian sailor or by the junkman. This type of automobile, with its new paint sprayed about so injudiciously that it commonly spilled over the bumpers and wheels, was known as *metalom* in Russian auto parlance — literally, scrap. If something less than indispensable broke, like a windshield or a muffler, one would ignore it. After all, there were no dealerships yet in Kamchatka. If the automobile did not run, it was simply abandoned. Riding in one of these vehicles, I found, brought one back into contact with one's core theological beliefs. The local GAI, or traffic police, complained that there were now more accidents in Petropavlovsk in one average weekend night than there used to be during an entire month.

On his first morning in Petropavlovsk, Kennan hiked to the top of the Nikolskaya Gora, the steep hill separating the city's original port from Avatchinskaya Bay proper. The harbor that he described as a "land-locked mill pond . . . within a stone's throw of the nearest house" is still there, but it would be barely recognizable to him. The little village along the waterfront gave way long ago to tiers of mean, grey buildings rising up the slope behind the port. The miraculous inlet that had sheltered Kennan's ship — and Bering's — was filled in and replaced by a crowded mishmash of warehouses, piers, cranes, and drydocks.

The same Nicholas Hill, however, had changed little from Kennan's time. It was still a sharp climb on a path that wound up through marsh violets and luminous birches. The top of the first knoll afforded a breathtaking view over the entire bay and the volcanoes to the southwest. The bluff overlooking the water dropped off precipitously to a thin beach of black pebbles. From afar, it looked inviting. Yet I had already discovered that it was littered with the inevitable detritis of *Homo soveticus* on holiday: rusted cans, smashed bottles, even human feces.

It was here that the Cossack defenders of Petropavlovsk repelled a Crimean War landing party of French and British soldiers in 1854. Many of the invaders fell to their deaths at bayonet point. The French admiral who planned the operation, only to see his troops slaughtered by the ragtag Cossacks, promptly committed suicide — a point reported by Kennan. A pair of monuments honoring the Cossacks guard the ridge; one of them is decorated with over a century's worth of graffiti. Farther along the ridge are the remains of gun emplacements and trenches.

On this beautiful afternoon, it was as if all the city's life had gravitated here. Little clusters of people were sunbathing, picnicking, drinking. A child ran back and forth past the old cannons overlooking the bay. In a nearby clearing, a gravel-voiced coach badgered three young boxers to greater exertions; they punched and jabbed at the air, grim and determined. Under a silver birch, in a glade of undulating grass, a couple was entwined so passionately that I winced with envy.

I kept walking, now up a steep dirt road leading to a point overlooking the harbor and the bay. The breeze was waxing; gulls cackled in the airstream overhead.

I had left the strollers and lovers behind, yet I was not alone. A very ordinary looking man in a pedestrian brown windbreaker had followed me up and over the hill. Whenever I caught sight of him, he feigned a devout interest in botany or zoology. He gazed intently at invisible songbirds. He poked at bushes, combing the shrubs for nuts and berries that I surmised were not there. At one point, he sliced some branches off a low tree with a penknife, examined them meticulously, then dropped them once I had strolled farther on.

I approached a gate. Behind it was a radar station. To the right of the gate was a large dog house, with a sign reading *Zlaya Sobaka,* literally "mean dog." While I saw no signs of any menacing canines, it seemed prudent not to proceed any farther. I turned about, nodded at the amateur scientist as I walked by, and headed back into the city center. He followed, but this time at a more discreet distance.

✷ ✷ ✷

The *crème de la crème* of Petropavlovsk hotels was the Oktyabrskaya. Oddly, most people in town that I met had no idea where it was located. The Oktyabrskaya still shunned the bourgeois notion of advertising itself with a sign at the door. There was absolutely nothing on the outside of the three-story building that distinguished it from its neighbors. I learned to direct taxi drivers to "the building across the street from the jewelry store."

Why the mystery? Yes, the Oktyabrskaya was once the Communist Party hotel, and the right to book a room there had by no means been granted to everyone. Under the *ancien regime,* you would have needed a party card or the intervention of someone who had one. Now, however, any foreigner with dollars could walk in off the street and command the best suite — if he was willing, that is, to pay the premium room charges expected of non-Russians, often five times higher than the "local" rate.

Cash-strapped Russians, however, still needed some special *blat*, or pull, to guarantee themselves a place. When I arrived, a meeting of the Kamchatka regional legislature had just gotten underway. Yet even these local bigwigs were elbowing each other at the reception desk to get the last spaces left in the hotel. One waved his deputy's credentials; another tried to flatter the sullen ladies at the desk. The only one whom I saw get a room quietly consummated the deal — with cash — in the smoke-filled telephone operator's booth behind the reception desk.

Later, when I tried to clarify how much I would have to pay for my room (as a diplomat, I was entitled to pay the much lower Russian fee), a trader from the Caucasus chastised me for not forking up the $50 foreigner's room rate. "You can pay the foreigner's price. Where in your country," he added, indignantly, "could you have such a good room for so little, for $10?"

He was a short man in a cheap leather jacket who needed a shave. He looked half melon merchant, half terrorist. Unwittingly, I had punched his envy button. Standing in front of the reception desk, I did not feel comfortable offering too frank a critique of the hotel's inadequacies. "I think that the price would be the same in the States," I replied, as evenly as I could.

This brought forth a guffaw from him. "You have a good room. They cost $200 a night in America," he protested. I bit my tongue, knowing that nothing I could say would shake his view. Someone had told him once that hotel rooms cost hundreds of dollars in Manhattan. He could not imagine anything better than what the Oktyabrskaya offered.

The luxury penthouse in question was a third-floor walk-up with no hot water, no heat, no soap, no towels, no toilet paper, no toilet seat, and a TV with a hallucinatory picture. In addition to a basement café that was anything but chic, the hotel provided the following services: check-in and check-out. Always mindful of my location on the planet, I was perfectly comfortable; besides, the telephone and the refrigerator did work. But how could I explain that most people in the West would have refused to take the room at all? It was the best that Petropavlovsk could offer, and yet it would not measure up to many of the worst flop-houses and brothels in Europe, Asia, or America.

In the course of his soliloquy, my melon salesman friend had also uttered the new refrain heard all across Russia: *teper, u nas vsyo* — now, we have everything. For those Russians who themselves had never laid eyes on a shopping mall, it seemed as if the whole world's cornucopia was already available in the kiosks and street stalls that have sprouted up across the land. After all, there were dozens of different types of imported booze on sale, where before there had only been Soviet vodka and cognac. Imported chocolate was also a fixture; Russian kids liked the same candy bars that have seduced children everywhere else.

Supposedly, if one haunted the country's kiosks long enough, one could find just about anything: a pirated Clint Eastwood video, a Victoria's Secret silk negligee, a portable fax. It certainly was not true in Kamchatka. Walk past a few kiosks, with their smattering of bored or inebriated vendors, and rather than feeling a rush of enthusiasm for the miracle of entrepreneurship, one sometimes felt a bit sad. One might pity a people so badly misled, so intractably penalized by their years of forced isolation and mendacious ideology. At moments like this, it really did seem that Russia was a Bolivia with writers, a Bangladesh with rockets.

Outside the Morskoy Vokzal, the city's cavernous sea terminal, I watched an overcrowded lighter bring in the crew of a returned freighter. The crew members were dressed in almost fashionable sports gear; they were loaded down with new computers and VCRs rather than duffel bags.

Inside the terminal, however, the atmosphere was more akin to a mausoleum. The previous year's yellowed shipping schedules hung limply on the walls. They bore witness to what had once been a busy roster of boat arrivals and departures, linking the coastal towns and villages of Kamchatka with the capital. Shipping routes had also connected the peninsula with the remote Kuril and Komandorskie islands. A passenger liner from Vladivostok, over a thousand miles away, had called in Petropavlovsk every two weeks.

The magic of the market, and open borders, had put a swift end to all that. The oversized painted map of Kamchatka's sea routes in the terminal lobby was now a mockery, humbled by the turn of events of the past year. The ships that for decades had dutifully kept up the intracoastal service along Kamchatka's littoral had drifted away to the far more lucrative trade with Japan and Korea. Rather than hauling people and supplies back and forth among the far-flung settlements on Kamchatka and the neighboring islands, these ships, now in private hands, carried timber, furs, and fish to Asian markets and returned with cars and other Western consumeralia. The less sturdy craft unsuitable for longer sea crossings were in mothballs; the derisory returns of the coastal trade were insufficient to cover the mushrooming costs of fuel. Much to the displeasure of local officials, a spit of land outside town replete with beached ships had become a sort of mecca for visiting photographers. Every time an article about Petropavlovsk appeared in a Western newspaper, it would feature the same forlorn scene of Kamchatka's abandoned rustbucket fleet.

The ticket clerks, blue-uniformed women absorbed in their knitting, were apologetic. "It's a scandal," one said. "But that's the way everything is now," she added. *"Polnoe razval,* a complete collapse." It boded ill for the isolated settlements along the Kamchatkan coast that depended on summer shipments of food, fuel, and supplies to make it through the winter. Most of these places had no road links whatsoever. The peninsula's small fleet of light airplanes could never fill the gap. Unless the shipments were made by the end of October, the towns and villages would have to wait until the following spring. For once, the grumbling from some Russians about famine and doom under the new democracy did not come across as overly alarmist.

Beside a closed ticket window was a hand-lettered schedule for service to a place called Rybachi. I consulted my map of Petropavlovsk and environs and another in the terminal's waiting room; Rybachi was nowhere to be found. Although the hand-lettered ink had been smeared into minature Rorshachs, I was able to make out that it was a current schedule rather than a historic document. Rybachi could not be too far away, I surmised. According to the schedule, a round trip could be made in a little over two hours. The first sailing the next day was scheduled for 6 A.M. By all appearances, it was the only chance I would have to view Avachinskaya Bay from the water. I resolved to drag myself awake in time to make it.

Overnight, it rained wildly; the morning was raw and wet. A heavy wind shook the trees in the Nikolskaya Gora, still obscured in the predawn gloom. Except for a pair of slumbering drunks sprawled out under a bus stop shelter, the streets were deserted. I walked briskly down the hill to the Morskoy Vokzal, its outline just visible in the port's ghostly perimeter lighting. All that marked the entrance to the terminal was a feeble fluorescent gleam; otherwise the building was dark. Inside the waiting room, a few more desolate figures lay asleep on hard wooden benches; the only sign of life came from an all-night kiosk in a corner of the lobby.

Although it was already ten before six, the ticket booth was closed. Puzzled, I asked a pair of acned vendors in the kiosk whether the ferry to Rybachi was operating. "We don't know anything about the ships," one of them replied.

I headed back outside, walking through a set of gates to the pier. Only one ship was manned. It was a sleek little cutter, about fifty feet long. I walked up to the prow of the boat and asked a crewman whether it was headed for Rybachi. He looked at me a bit quizzically, and replied that it was. An officer came up behind him; he was wearing what looked like a Russian Navy uniform. To my surprise, he leaned down from the bow and asked me whether I had authorization to go to Rybachi.

"Why do I need permission?" I asked.

"You're a foreigner," he stated.

"Yes."

"Rybachi is a closed military zone. There's a submarine base in the town. You have to get a pass."

There were not supposed to be any closed areas any longer, although a military base was obviously another matter. "I just wanted to take a look at the bay," I insisted. "It seemed to me that this was the only boat there was. Is it possible for me to go over and come right back?"

The officer, in turn, chewed on this for a while. He looked me over, and shrugged his shoulders. It was early; no one else was around. "OK. I can sell you a ticket. But come back later, at 9 A.M. It's dark now, and you won't see anything anyway."

I thanked him. It was a long walk up the hill in the rain. Back at the hotel, I lay down to catch some sleep before the next boat. When I overslept, I was not too worried. I would wait to take the cruise after I returned to Petropavlovsk. The weather, I calculated, could only improve.

* * *

Kennan set out with his companions in early September to ascend the Kamchatka peninsula. My plan was to retrace his route. From four thousand miles away in Moscow, I had plotted my adventure step-by-step on a rudimentary road map. From Petropavlovsk, Kennan's party ascended the Abacha River in a whaleboat; climbed over the mountain range beyond the capital on horseback; rafted down the Kamchatka River to Klyuchi, a village at the foot of Kamchatka's highest volcanoes; trudged over the high ridges of the Middle Range; struggled up the trackless west coast of the peninsula; and then wintered among the nomadic Koryaks, who carried Kennan and his companions across the frozen tundra in dogsleds, sheltering them in sooty teepees.

Before arriving in Petropavlovsk, I, too, had imagined myself following mountain paths astride a hardy pony, or paddling a canoe downstream beside a native guide. It was not long, however, before I came to my senses. I saw that all of the painstaking reckonings I had made back in Moscow, poring over books and charts, were utterly unrealistic. I was hopelessly outclassed by the colossal dimensions and rigors of Kamchatka.

The president of the Kamchatka backpacking club, Vladimir Menshikov, shook his head glumly when he heard what I was proposing. "It would take three months, not three weeks, to do what you want," he said, his hand whisking over a topographic map of the peninsula as if he were chasing away a fly. "And that's if you could manage it in the first place," he added, none too charitably. For one thing, he explained, there was no public transport overland past Milkovo, which was only a third of the way into the Kamchatka valley. A river expedition could be arranged, he went on, but it would require a great deal of planning — and money. After a moment's hesitation, he added that the trail that Kennan followed to cross the Middle Range had been out of use for many years. Since there was already snow at the higher elevations, crossing the mountains was out of the question until the following spring.

Menshikov, a deceptively unimposing man with a cool, dispassionate manner, then proceeded to recount a series of "foolhardy adventurers who came to a bad end in Kamchatka" stories, most of which culminated in the unlucky party being devoured by bears or scalded to death in volcanic sinkholes. Rather than attempting to follow Kennan's route, he suggested, I ought to tour the valley behind Petropavlovsk, taking no fewer than two guides with me. A party of three, he explained, was the minimum for venturing into the wilderness.

As an aside, he mentioned that even on this "uncomplicated" route there had been a fatal bear attack a few weeks earlier. More and more such incidents were being recorded, which Menshikov attributed to the slow but steady encroachment of humans and their dachas into domains heretofore considered by the bears to be their own. In this instance, a man had been fishing in a stream also favored by the ursine community. Rather than abandoning his catch at the first sign of the bear, he had foolishly tried to wave off the beast. The bear, in turn, opted to dine on him rather than endure yet another tedious repast of fresh salmon. Still, Menshikov tried to console me by observing that "statistically," it was "rather unlikely" that another attack would occur in the same area anytime soon.

Bears, like volcanoes, were an important part of the Kamchatka story. The peninsula is thought to have one of the largest concentrations of brown bears anywhere in the world. Kamchatka is known as a *med-vezhonaya uglya*, literally, "bear corner." As opposed to other Russian regions that have earned the label more out of their utter remoteness than from any special abundance of ursine inhabitants, the expression in Kamchatka is meant both literally and figuratively.

More remarkable still are persistent reports in Kamchatka of a mammoth black bear, weighing up to a ton. The locals treat its existence as an established fact. A Swedish bear specialist supposedly concluded after measuring a series of giant paw prints that the big bears do, indeed, exist — although he, too, never actually saw one.

Until recently, the peninsula was by every standard a paradise for bears, with abundant food, great expanses of pristine wilderness, and — most importantly — few humans to interfere with a bruin's unabashed, even hedonistic lifestyle. On the rare occasions when the native Kamchadals killed a bear, they feared the vengefulness of the bear's spirit and prayed for his forgiveness. The Kennan party's haphazard encounter with a bear alongside the banks of a river was more comic than mythic. In Kennan's account, "the only calm and self-possessed individual in the entire party was the bear," who "surveyed the situation coolly for a few seconds, and then started at an awkward gallop for the woods."

During the Soviet period, occasional parties of bigwigs and generals would take potshots at bears during unofficial hunting excursions. Brezhnev himself is said to have raised gun to shoulder in pursuit of a Kamchatkan bearskin. Yet it was a sport reserved for the most privileged Soviet nomenclaturists and military men only. Otherwise, Kamchatka's status as a closed region, backed by all the security that the armed forces and secret services could provide, made it de facto one of the largest nature reserves on the planet.

Remove one closed, totalitarian regime, replace it with an ostensibly democratic, market-oriented one, and the equation for *Ursus arctos* was quickly turned inside out — and infinitely for the worse. The bears' Achilles' heel lay a bit further up in its anatomy than its back paws. For the sake of human male potency or whatever other ill-founded reasons, the gall bladders and livers of bears were fetching thousands, even tens of thousands of dollars in places like Hong Kong and Singapore.

Inspired by the prospect of overnight fortunes, and unimpeded by local authorities, who had run out of both the will and the resources to counter them, poachers were taking to the air in small planes and helicopters, shooting bears wherever they sighted them. Equally destructive were custom bear-hunting expeditions offered to well-heeled foreigners, who flocked from all over Europe and North America to join in the slaughter. For the most part, the authorities — covetous military officers and corrupt local officials — aided and abetted the sorry spectacle. The few people who pushed the cause of ecology too far found their lives bedeviled in ways large and small: a slashed tire here, a trumped-up corruption charge there.

People like Menshikov knew what was happening, but what could they do? Even the handful of park rangers and biologists officially charged with protecting Kamchatka's wildlife were stymied. The regional environmental authority, unlike the poachers, could no longer afford helicopter flights to monitor the bear population and combat the lawbreakers.

The truest friend the peninsula's bears had was Vitaliy Nikolayenko. I met him in the den of the Kamchatka hiking club, deep in the basement of a Petropavlovsk apartment block. Nikolayenko had devoted a quarter century to documenting the life of Kamchatka's bears. Spending much of the year alone in a simple cabin in the Kronotsky Biosphere Reserve, he had compiled an astounding archive of thousands of photographs: an unmatched family album of the life and times of an entire ursine community.

As he untied his moldy cardboard binders of photographs, spreading the black-and-white images across a long wooden table, I saw that his own bearded features, burly yet affecting, also had a certain ursiform quality. "I'm no scientist," he bluntly admitted. By his own admission, he was anything but dispassionate. Irresistibly drawn to his bear neighbors, he had built his archive on his belly and his knees, without all of the high-tech paraphernalia of his Western counterparts. Nor were there the same financial rewards. Occasionally he sold a photograph or two, but otherwise all that sustained him was his meager salary as a park employee.

Nor was Nikolayenko an accomplished conversationalist. Yet as hesitant as he was to talk, his outrage over what was happening was apparent. He tossed one photograph after another toward me: a bear rubbing his back against a tree with a snowy mountainside as a backdrop; another wading through a stream with a salmon dangling from its mouth; a third seated lackadaisically on its haunches, looking for all the world like a child's cuddly, if oversized, playmate. "Can you tell what all three of these bears have in common?" he asked, his bushy eyebrows arched upward as if to land a heavy blow. I could not, but the answer came charging up behind my moment of hesitation. "They're all dead, killed by poachers."

Two years before, on the eve of the collapse of Soviet power, there had been by Nikolayenko's estimate at least ten thousand brown bears in Kamchatka. Now there were as few as five thousand left. The arithmetic was worse than alarming; it was a headlong plunge toward extinction. How could things have gone so far awry? I wondered.

"It's your so-called democracy," Nikolayenko replied. "Democracy is *chepukha*. It's pure nonsense. What you call democracy — maybe it works in your country — but here it's just an excuse for the greedy to get rich at the expense of the people."

He had not raised his voice, but he looked at me coldly, with undisguised disdain. "I'm a Communist," he continued, "and I'm proud of it. Under the old system, nature here in Kamchatka was left alone. Once

Gorbachev came to power, things started to go to hell. It's not just the bears. The logging firms are cutting down the forests and selling the logs to the Koreans and the Japanese. The logs that they miss end up in the bottom of the rivers, fouling the water and killing the fish. The salmon catch used to be regulated; now so many fish are taken illegally that the runs have stopped in some rivers. It's every man for himself, and no one can stop the poachers and the polluters."

✳ ✳ ✳

It had rained again, all day, in a sopping procession of squalls driven north from the Sea of Japan. The storm so completely engulfed the city that Petropavlovsk appeared to have been buried, Pompeii-like, under a veritable lahar of misty precipitation. Pirate noir clouds bolted ashore from the ocean, while drainpipes and gutters spilled water down from the hillsides in overbrimming rushlets. Nightfall came more as a wet amplification of darkness than a reversal of the day. I waited in my hotel room, eager to be gone, anxious to pursue Kennan's footsteps deeper into the wilderness.

It was just before ten, and all I had was a name and an address. A truck was headed north to Klyuchi that night; a friend of Menshikov's knew Klyuchi's state assemblyman, who was hitching a ride as well. The arrangements did seem, well, a bit precarious. Even my cab driver disapproved; he insisted on accompanying me all the way upstairs to the door of the apartment. When it opened, neither of us were reassured, but I thanked him and walked in anyway.

The entryway was stacked high with identical cardboard boxes, dozens upon dozens of them, moist from the rain. There was barely room to set my backpack down. Across the floor of the living room, which had been stripped bare of furniture, lay stacks of antlers, stretching from one wall to the other, along with piles of animal skins, neatly dressed and bound according to size and color. The man who answered the door, broad-chested, bleary-eyed, reeking of vodka, pointed me to another figure across the room. "That's your Sasha," he said, "go sit by him."

Sasha had a sorrowful expression, one that never quite left his face as long as I knew him. Even now, at our first meeting, it hovered around his worn but sensitive eyes, his wrung-out intellectual's forehead. He was well past his youth, and his frame, although still lean, had a run-down cast to it. His cheeks, too, had hollowed; they matched a morose little beard, as wispy as the hair at the end of a donkey's tail.

Sasha greeted me quietly, incuriously, as if he were distracted by something far weightier than my arrival or my slightly nervous, probing questions. He had come down to Petropavlovsk for the very same session of the Kamchatka parliament that had attracted the other deputies to my hotel. Now he was hitching a ride back; he did not have enough money, he explained, for the airfare. The political responsibilities, he added, were just a sideline; by profession, he was a volcanologist.

I asked him about the antlers. His reply was cryptic: "Oh, those are just for tourists."

The door opened again, and several figures, soaked to the bone, began to carry the boxes out. One man walked up to Sasha, eyed me, and said: "Let's get going. We're already late." We obeyed.

Although the purpose of this expedition was still a mystery to me, I could already see that there were problems. For one thing, the truck that was supposed to take us north had broken down; the flatbed waiting for us in the parking lot was only on loan for the night. We embarked in a driving rain, huddled behind the cab on the steel floor. The truck roared through the city's empty streets, churning up a geyser of inky runoff.

Before long, it became apparent that we were lost. We made several splashy U-turns, then stopped, the rain pouring down upon us. The driver climbed out of the cab and came back for a parlay with Sasha. We were supposed to rendezvous with the other truck near a beer stand, but no one remembered how to find the way.

The exchange with Sasha turned acrimonious: "You live here, and you don't know your way around," the driver yelled, exasperated.

"I live in Klyuchi — not Petropavlovsk," Sasha replied evenly.

We turned back from where we had come. After half a dozen more soaking miles, the flatbed turned into a thicket of low apartment buildings, rattling and bouncing down gloomy, deserted drives and alleyways.

Finally, we pulled up alongside the other truck. A man looked up from under the hood of the broken-down rig. His face, his jacket, his trousers were all drenched in oil, black even against the murky night. Upon spotting us, he waved, then let out a torrent of obscenities. He was working over an open oil pan with a cigarette dangling from a corner of his mouth. Even in the dark, I could make out the line where he had held his cigarette between his tar-covered fingers.

The disabled truck was a ZIL, the acronym for the Soviet Union's best-known auto plant: literally, *Zavod imeni Lenina,* "the Lenin factory." Yet rather than being known as a "Lenin," three generations of Russian truck drivers had called it only one thing: a Truman. Turned out by the tens of thousands, the Truman was based on a wartime Studebaker model sent to Russia under Lend-Lease. From an American's perspective, the truck belonged on a World War II movie set. Coated in a dozen layers of olive-green paint, its toothy grill beamed with nostalgia. Two rotund headlamps topped fenders that bulged like zoot suits. Despite all the Soviet-American enmity of the Cold War years, in this one instance the name of an American president from Missouri had managed to hold sway over the otherwise ubiquitous sobriquet of the genius of Marxism-Leninism.

The grease-smeared mechanic, I learned, was Kolya. He had first learned to drive a Truman in the army. Groping about in the dark, Kolya poured a two-liter glass bottle full of lubricant somewhere down into the engine block. "The filthy bitch drinks oil like champagne," he explained. Yet even as he pounded at the motor, Kolya commented: "No one knows why, but these Trumans just run and run."

I stood back under a tree and watched the others pass the boxes from one truck to the other. Sasha hovered nearby, dripping quiet misery in his flimsy baby-blue anorak. Our companions — if that was the right word — worked by the light of the flatbed's headlights, fiendishly cursing the Truman, the rain, the night, their misfortune. I thought to myself: "Only soldiers or criminals could swear like this."

The man seated in the cab of the flatbed pumped its accelerator every few moments, trying to keep its engine, too, from petering out. Despite the commotion, not a word of complaint came down from the apartment blocks around us. It was as if the residents had sensed, one and all, that any group of profane, brutish renegades willing to turn a residential parking lot into a nocturnal repair shop and loading dock were best left to their own devices.

Suddenly, with a rasping metallic cough, the Truman came to life. I, too, let out a damp, hoarse cheer. One by one, we climbed up a ladder into the back of the truck. The cabin was about a dozen feet long, with small oblong windows running along both sides. The interior bristled with rusty Rube Goldberg gadgets and broken electrical leads. On one wall, I was just able to make out the words "Emergency Services." The floor was taken up, two and three deep, with the much-portaged boxes, the precious cargo that had been the inspiration for so much nighttime drudgery and frustration.

The gearbox gnashed, and the truck lurched forward, laboring up a hill. I did the best I could to settle in. Five of us were crowded into the back. Two people were stretched out on a raised shelf directly behind the cab. Sasha and I, along with the heifer-faced Grisha, had to make do as best we could on top of the boxes.

By now, it was well past midnight. The Truman groaned and grunted up a mountain road far beyond the lights of the city. As we climbed into a cloudbank, a steady rain enveloped us. The cool night air smelled of pine needles and dank moss. The road surface, too, suddenly reverted to nature, dropping back on the evolutionary scale from asphalt to hard, pitted gravel.

It was then that I came to grips with another of the Truman's qualities: the absence of shock absorbers. When it hit a bump, the whole undercarriage jumped. When it hit a series of bumps — and the road to Klyuchi was nothing but a long, staccato run of potholes and washboard — the Truman banged up and down with uncanny ferocity. It was a bestial way to spend the night.

The first order of business was to repair Kolya's flashlight, which had conked out just as he was finishing the engine work. He bent the wiring back and forth and hammered the assembly against the wall of the compartment, all to no avail. A candle was found, but no matches. Perhaps there were some up with the driver, someone suggested. Pounding on the back window of the cab, yelling at the top of his lungs, Kolya could not get the truck to stop; the roar of the old engine and the rain hammering on the roof were too much.

So our grand banquet took place in the dead of night, without the slightest illumination. I heard several of the boxes being ripped open. "What's in the cartons?" I asked, a question of some import since at that moment I was bouncing hard up and down on top of several of them.

"Red caviar," came back the reply. "Thousands and thousands of jars of the stuff." Just then someone shoved a glass of vodka into my hand and proposed a toast.

I could inspect nothing that I drank or ate that night, and with hindsight it may have been just as well. Judging from what met my lips in between the toasts, I was handed a damp chunk of farmer's rye paired up with a crunchy green onion, another piece of bread slathered with an oozy imitation of liver pate, and a gritty slice of "doctor's sausage" that tasted as if it had been dropped on the floor of the truck before it found its way to me. Was *doktorskaya*, a distant relative of bologna, so named because it had been created at the inspiration of a physician, or — as seemed more likely — because it described the likely destination for the unfortunates who ate it?

In conversation, I soon discovered that my companions were smugglers, although they — Russian patriots to the man — would have objected mightily to the label. They were, as well, pilot, copilot, navigator, mechanic, and loader in the Russian air force — I did not believe for a minute their assurances of being "retired" — who had flown a transport plane into an airfield in Klyuchi on something a bit more irregular than an official mission. They had obtained an illegal truckload of red caviar *na levo* — literally, "on the left" — and were planning to fly a circuitous route back to their home base in Krasnoyarsk, alighting in six or seven other locations where they could sell the goods at a considerable markup.

And thus the haste and insistence on traveling after sunset. Despite what Sasha had told me, the all-night drive was not necessitated so much by the prospect of a storm spinning up the Kamchatka peninsula — it was already upon us — but rather by the smuggler's preferred modus operandi: moving his wares in darkness and foul weather out of sight of cranky, avaricious police officials. Indeed, the various roadside checkpoints we passed that night were shut tight, their guards napping snugly to the lullaby melody of the storm bending down the treetops. I imagined, too, that the longer the plane was absent without leave, ferrying salmon eggs to new-money sybarites across Siberia, the more likely that some fool commanding officer might start to ask questions.

I was drunk, I was exhausted, but sleep proved to be beyond me. Even after the questions had subsided about whether life in Russia was better or worse than in America, along with my companions' bathetic — and bottle-induced — speculations in pure philosophy, there were still the bone-jangling jolts of the road. The others in the truck snored, or sang, or sloshed down glass after glass of spirit, all within the unmitigated netherworld of the back of the truck. It had turned cold and dank, and I tried to push down ever deeper into my sleeping bag. I sought to forget, as well, that I was spending the night among utter strangers, on a deserted road, with nothing between me and oblivion but the statistical improbability (that expression again!) of someone wanting to do me in.

When I finally dozed off — for what must have been only a matter of minutes — the truck dissolved into hemlock green. I found myself walking alone in the forest; I felt a tingling of unease. I rang a schoolbell in my hand. My eyes searched the unnervingly fragrant undergrowth. Something rustled, and I started. Kolya the mechanic stepped from behind a bush into the trail. I wanted to run, but he moved too fast. He grabbed me with a paw and swung me overhead. Strangely, I felt nothing when his jaws closed around my shoulder. The other bears had gathered around. The truck lurched heavily to one side; I was saying, "He's eating me," as I woke up, sweating, wondering what lay ahead.

Some time before dawn, we stopped so that the party could relieve itself, en masse. It seemed to take a long time, standing there in the fathomless dark beside the deserted road, hearing the deep-voiced wind intone under our feeble chorus of tinkling. I was offered the passenger seat by Igor, the driver. Thinking it a high honor, I accepted somewhat self-consciously. Yet I discovered that all I had done was trade an uncushioned box for a springless seat.

Igor strained to see in the headlights' feeble beam, fighting to keep himself awake by chain-smoking and vigorously thumping himself from time to time in the forehead. Soviet economics had dictated that there be only one wiper on these trucks. My side of the windscreen collected mud and flattened insects to the point where what little I could make out of Kamchatka I saw through a dribbling patina of road muck.

The vintage look of the Truman's cab only heightened my disorientation. Rather than a single gear stick, three oddball cranks and levers protruded up through slots in the floorboard. The dash, too, was anything but high-tech. At seemingly random intervals, Igor would pull a knob out or press his finger down impatiently on a button. The gas gauge looked more familiar, but it, naturally, did not work. Each time one of the truck's dual gas tanks went dry, Igor would pull over, tap on the tank wall to confirm that it was indeed empty, fill the tank out of a jerry can, and then goose the carburetor to get the engine restarted. In sum, the only truly reliable point of reference for a late-twentieth-century driver was the steering wheel.

The dawn stumbled into daylight. A charcoal overcast the length of the horizon dominated the morning; it was the kind of somber weather that gnaws at the human spirit. The road ran flat and straight now, lined on both sides by a dense, scrubby forest of conifers and birch. From the highway, there were no signs of the "fields of rye and neatly fenced gardens" of which Kennan wrote, nor the proliferation of primroses and irises he saw in his late summer of the last century.

What mountains were visible trailed far off to the east of the valley, veiled miserably in low cloud. Outside Pushchino, I waited bleary-eyed in a frigid drizzle while Igor argued with the attendant over whether we could purchase gasoline from a pump reserved for official cars. Over a century before, Kennan had reached Pushchino sufficiently exhilarated to comment that no "previous journey . . . had ever afforded me more pure, healthy enjoyment." I could not say the same on that cotton-mouthed, red-eyed morning.

Later, we passed Milkovo, where Kennan was mistaken by the villagers for Tsar Alexander II (they had received notification of the visit of a "Yagor Kennan, Telegraphist and Operator," and mistook the word "operator" for "imperator"). As we passed by the town, the rear-view mirror on my side fell with a muffled crunch to the road. Igor shrugged his shoulders and commented, "Who cares? It's not our truck."

Every kilometer we traveled farther north seemed to take us deeper and deeper into a world that despite its proximity to nature was half-derelict, half-depraved. Implausibly, the road worsened yet again until it was little more than a mud track. The villages we passed looked empty, abandoned. At one bend, the carcass of a flatbed that had slid off the highway lay on its side, its cargo spilled out into a bog.

In mid-afternoon, we came to the banks of the Kamchatka River. A black barge with a matchbox pilot's cabin was beating back toward us against a churning, clutching current. Swollen with rainwater, the river gave out an ominous crackle as it dragged whole branches and trees along. A grimy roll call of vehicles had gathered on the riverbank along with us: trucks, jeeps, even one or two cars. Kennan's acquaintance with the Kamchatka River had been more bucolic than this. "Nothing was real," he rhapsodized, "but the tranquil river which flowed at my feet, the birch tree which dropped its yellow leaves upon my head, and the far-away purple mountains."

I walked down to the water's edge. The muddy slope was littered with cans, bottles, tires, oil drums, and even a refrigerator. A man in a wrinkled and stained nylon jumpsuit — there were only men on this route — spit in my direction. One of his eyes was swollen and lacerated. "The shitload of a boat will never make it," he said, without emotion. Then he spit again.

The makeshift ferry raced its motor and charged straight for the shoreline. With every last ripple of horsepower it could muster, the barge careened ashore with a sickening crunch, driving its bow several meters out of the water. Down came the vehicle ramp, and the trollish figures on deck began to wave the waiting vehicles on board while the captain frantically worked the engine and the rudder to keep the vessel lined up perpendicular to the bank.

With an insouciance so profound that it was more magical than frightening, the waiting vehicles one by one careened down the mucky river margin, aiming at full speed for the ramp. One after another they crashed and clanged onboard, wheels flying on the bounce, then screeching to a stop inches from disaster. Within moments of the last truck's daredevil landing on the deck, the crew had winched the ramp back up, and the barge was spinning out into the main channel. I knew then, as if Charon were at the helm, that we would reach the other bank, Elysian or not. Klyuchi lay just ahead.

✻ ✻ ✻

It was a long time before I woke up. Sasha had deposited me without fanfare on the grounds of the Klyuchi volcanological station, in a cottage a few doors away from his own. My leave-taking from the caviar boys was fraught with feigned bittersweet hugs and slaps on the back; more telling, I thought, was the careless way they tossed my backpack to the ground as the truck pulled away. I had just enough energy left to drag myself through the door and drop onto a bearskin-covered divan, my sleeping bag hurriedly unrolled over me.

Klyuchi, seemingly content in its antediluvian obscurity, lives and breathes in the shadow of Kamchatka's grandest and most obstreperous volcanoes. The Klyuchevskaya Sopka, whose central crater is all of twenty miles from the town, is one of the largest active volcanoes in the world. Three miles high, it towers over all of central Kamchatka — weather permitting. Along with the equally menacing Sheveluch volcano on the north side of the Kamchatka River (its top half blew up in 1963 in a spectacular "directed blast" similar to the eruption at Mount St. Helens), the two peaks account for more than half of the rock and ash thrown up in an average year by all the volcanoes in Kamchatka and the Kuril Islands combined. As a whole, the Klyuchevskaya group comprises twelve large volcanoes, one or more of which is usually belching smoke or letting out subterranean growls, whether or not an eruption is imminent. Even during its "quiescent" periods, the summit of Klyuchevskaya is in constant flux, changing form seemingly at will.

Kennan duly reported "the boldness and picturesque beauty of its situation," but found still more remarkable the cosmic unconcern of Klyuchi's residents, going about their business untroubled by the obvious peril looming above them. "Its inhabitants have come to regard with indifference the occasional mutterings of warning which come from the depths of the burning craters," he observed, "and the showers of ashes which are frequently sifted over their houses and fields."

In some winters, Kennan related, the snow around Klyuchi was so blackened by cinders and ash that it was impossible for sledges to move about. One eruption had not grown dim in the villagers' memory: "Far up in the dark winter's sky . . . blazed a column of lurid flame from the crater, crowned by a great volume of fire-lighted smoke. Amid loud rumblings and dull reverberations from the interior the molten lava began to flow in broad fiery rivers down the snow-covered mountain side, until for half the distance to its base it was one glowing mass of fire which . . . illuminated the whole country within a radius of twenty-five miles."

After my truck ordeal, I roamed about my new accommodations — in reality, just one side of a modest little duplex — basking momentarily in a crazy sense of luxury. The most prominent feature of the one large room was a bookself crammed with books and volcanic artifacts. A framed black-and-white photograph depicted scientists urging a dogsled up a near-vertical slope, a smoldering volcano in the background. There were chunks and slabs of igneous rock in grays, greens, and blues; photos of volcanoes in various states of eruption; and memorabilia from trips abroad to Japan and Europe, including a handsome collection of name tags from international scientific conferences and carefully preserved Aeroflot ticket stubs. The walls were adorned by elk skins and a painfully amateurish oil painting of the Montmarte. For a few moments, it felt like home.

Outside, though, it was pouring rain, in miserable, wind-whipped gushes. The grand tour of my accommodations began to sour, as well; there was no electricity, and thus no hot water. No tea was to be had, either, from the electric samovar. The kitchen sink, strangely, had no drainpipe; I never did quite figure out how it was supposed to be manipulated. The Bulgarian-made toilet bowl tremored uneasily when enthroned.

Before long, Sasha was at the door, offering lunch. We all sat down at his kitchen table, his young wife and their new baby, the twentyish daughter from his first marriage, and her admiring graduate student friend from faraway Bashkortostan, where they both were studying. The soup, lip-scalding hot, brimming over with bits of fresh salmon, potatoes, and dill, rallied my spirits again. We negotiated, too, my rent for the week. Sasha proposed $120, which struck me as a bit outlandish. I came back with an offer of $35, expecting to split the difference. But Sasha accepted with nary a grumble.

Back home, Sasha came across as more at ease, but he was no more of a convivial host than before. My questions tailed off in the face of his phlegmatism. He was ready, though, to talk about the essential fact of this moment in his life: Klyuchi's volcanic research station, once a magnet for some of the leading geologists in the Soviet Union, was near ruin.

Over half the station's specialists had left during the past year, most on "multi-year" contracts for parts overseas, unlikely ever to return. Australia, Argentina, Mexico, and Brazil were among their destinations.

Included among the departed was the owner of the bric-a-brac in my cottage. Meanwhile, the scientific work at Klyuchi had ground to a halt. The station was out of money. The last time Sasha and his remaining colleagues had been paid was five months before. A split among the peninsula's volcanologists had only made matters worse. Kamchatka now had two warring volcanic institutes, and they were absorbed with their in-fighting rather than finding ways to keep the Klyuchi station operating.

Hunched over the kitchen table, Sasha allowed — and here a touch of bitterness prompted his sad eyes to shimmer a bit — that he no longer had the wherewithal to buy new clothes for his family, or to take them on vacation. He was, in short, out of money. When the job offers first began to come in from abroad, he recalled, he viewed his fleeing colleagues disparagingly, as weak-willed dilettantes. He could not imagine then that things would turn out as badly as they had for the volcanic station, nor for him.

Perhaps no one would have invited him anyway; he only spoke Russian and a little German. Unfortunately, English was the lingua franca for geologists the world over. Now, had there been any foreign jobs for the taking, he would have left in a minute.

How did the remaining volcanologists get by? Sasha dryly noted that a few of his colleagues continued to take measurements at the monitoring stations high up on the flanks of the volcano — but they did so only irregularly, when the spirit moved them. By implication, he was not among them. Others moonlighted as guides, leading parties of hunters or tourists into the backcountry. Still, this required a lot of contacts, and you had to know something about business.

The baby began to cry, then wailed louder and louder until conversation became impossible. Sasha motioned to his wife to take the girl into the back room, and then shook his head in wordless despair.

That afternoon, under a chill, misty drizzle, I walked past a knot-holed quilt of weathered village fences and down to the riverbank to watch Sasha earn a living in the new Russia. Instead of a scientist, his partner was a local trapper, overweight and undershaven. A cage full of snarling *laikas* threw themselves at me, wildly testing the solidity of their enclosure. Swearing menacingly at the dogs, the trapper greeted me with a rough hello. He wore a dark-spattered outfit of khaki and oilskin; his forearms were covered to the elbow in blood and innards. A few steps farther into his back yard, and we came upon Sasha, clad in a deeply smeared set of canvas overalls and crude rubber Wellingtons.

The salmon were running in the Kamchatka River, and the men had brought in bucket upon bucket of the fish. They worked swiftly, expertly, slicing the salmon open with one deft motion of their black-handled knives, scooping out the egg sacks lodged in the fishes' bellies with their bare hands, and dividing the spoils into three troughs: the heads, tails, and entrails for the dogs, the pale flesh for home, the luminescent orange red caviar — the mother lode — to sell, in order to put bread on the table.

The steam rising off the two men in the rain added a feverish aura to their labors. The salmon run is a frantic affair that lasts but a week. The trapper's flat, brutal features, red from exertion, burned with a dervish intensity. Yet the hard-hearted yelping of the hunting dogs, the fast, moist slap of the salmon being flipped onto the cutting plank, the slick, sickening drip of guts into a metal pail — this was not Sasha's world. His weary gray beard, his gentryman's eyes, telegraphed his disdain for the slaughter and his role in it. For this, too, was an illicit meal ticket, punishable by a hefty fine or even imprisonment — although it was anything but unusual for the townspeople in these days of savage economic dislocation. Sasha worked long after I left that afternoon, long into the night, until he could stand up no longer. Then he slept for twelve hours, woke up to his stinking work clothes, and began all over again.

At first glance, Klyuchi did not seem like much of a town. There was a gritty dormitory (the locals insisted, for some reason, on calling it a hotel), a cracked-plaster movie theater, and a handful of stores and kiosks with little to offer beyond candy bars, soft drinks, and booze. A single bus ran all of the town's routes, one after the other from morning until night.

From the top of the research station's wooden observation tower, however, I glimpsed a bigger truth about Klyuchi, one that was to shape the rest of my stay in Kamchatka. About a kilometer south of the town stood a large military installation. From afar, army bases look the same the world over: row upon row of khaki-green barracks, a sprinkling of parade grounds and athletic fields, and a perimeter topped with razor-wire fence. This one also boasted an impressive array of satellite dishes and bulbous radar arrays. I had no idea why it was here, hundreds of miles from anywhere in Kamchatka — itself one of Russia's most famous nowheres — but I knew right away that it was not good news.

I decided then to call on Ivanov. I still half-entertained the notion of pushing deeper into the wilds, even walking part of Kennan's route into the mountains. Sasha's trapper friend had spoken of Ivanov in awed tones. He was the best tracker and hunter in Klyuchi, he explained. He knew more about the region's history and traditions than anyone else. He had a sixth sense about how the weather behaved, about how wild game thought — insights that no white man had. "You know," the trapper explained, "Ivanov is one of our last *Itelmeni*. He knows things that civilized men have forgotten."

Ivanov's wife, a cherubic Russian woman with frizzy tufts of rust-colored curls, invited me into their sitting room. I lowered myself with all the dignity I could muster onto a lovingly pampered couch. She set down a tray of aromatic tea, wild strawberry preserves, and bite-sized buttered red caviar sandwiches. A wall clock patiently ticked off the minutes.

"Hello," a voice suddenly ventured. A figure in a soiled cream cardigan and dark cotton pants stood before me. He was shorter than I had imagined, but he held himself very erect. We shook hands. "I am Ivanov," he announced. "Please consider yourself my guest."

His face was remarkable. I had been told that Ivanov was in his early sixties, but he did not appear to be a day over forty. True, his brow was deeply wrinkled, but his cheeks had a vibrant rose cast, and his eyes leapt with life and vigor. He retained a full shock of wavy brown hair, combed roughly back from his forehead. I was reminded of a daguerreotype I had once seen of a nineteenth-century Apache chief; Ivanov's expression had the same combination of pride, sagacity, and fiber. In fact, an American geneticist has found a shared marker between our Native Americans and Kamchatka's indigenous peoples.

Ivanov set our encounter in motion with a gift-giving ceremony, a formal offering toward friendship. "The Itelmen were always very hospitable, very generous," he commented, handing me a forlorn-looking Kamchatkan tree squirrel he had trapped and stuffed. "But they could never abide by a breach of trust. One betrayal, and the friendship was at an end." I reciprocated with the best I had to offer: a U.S. Embassy Moscow–emblazoned ballpoint pen. Luckily, it was the gesture that counted; the bond of friendship had been sealed.

I asked him what was left of Kamchadal culture. He confirmed that it had almost entirely died out. "The only full-blooded Itelmen live in the villages around Tigil, on the west coast. A few still speak the language. But otherwise, our people, our way of life, have passed from the earth."

Their downfall had begun centuries before under the likes of Ustyug's butcherous Atlasov, but it continued quietly into the twentieth century through intermarriage and disease. The decline of the Kamchadals accelerated with the influx of Slavic immigrants onto the peninsula beginning in the thirties. While the first Bolsheviks were generally indulgent toward the "little peoples" of Siberia and the Far North, bringing health and education to groups previously cut off from the modern world, the emphasis swiftly changed under Stalin, from understanding of the unique character and needs of the native peoples to a heavy-handed insistence on conformity with Marxist-Leninist models — models of dubious value in European Russia, much less among the forests and tundra of the Russian north. Stalinism brought collectivization to Koryak reindeer herders, proletarian consciousness to Itelmen sable hunters. It did them a great deal more harm than good.

Despite all of that era's dislocations, life in Klyuchi still revolved around the seasons and the traditions of Kamchadal and Russian alike until the early 1960s. That was when the Russian military arrived in earnest. Suddenly, the little town swarmed with outsiders. Its age-old rhythms fell by the wayside, overtaken by laws, regulations, restrictions — and, if there was any question about the above, the iron hand of the base commander. I sat astounded as Ivanov described to me what lay up the hill from the town. The installation, he explained, was the largest missile tracking and testing facility in the Russian Far East. Rockets were fired from points west of the Urals and Kazakstan onto a test *polygon* just north of Klyuchi.

"Why here? Why Klyuchi?" I asked.

"There were so few people living in these parts . . . only Itelmen and a few crazy Russians," Ivanov reasoned. "Besides, they say that the trajectory of the rockets is the same as if they were launched at America. So it was the best place to fire them."

Thus, Klyuchi doubled its pyrotechnic rating. Even when the neighboring volcanos were not putting on a show, Russian ICBM tests filled the entertainment gap. During the Cold War, Ivanov recalled, there might be as many as a dozen tests a year. Sometimes, when a missile came over, one would be aware only of a faint whistling, followed by a dull thud far off in the distance. Other times, particularly in the bone-cold graveyard hush of a still January night, the incoming rocket would announce itself from the west with a shattering boom, cometing across the black sky, scattering green and orange sparks down upon the town's surroundings, and impacting with an earth-shaking roar. The old-timers, Ivanov pointed out, usually knew beforehand when tests were in the offing. Planes would suddenly appear overhead; the wind carried with it the growling agitation of trucks moving heavy loads out of sight.

When the Soviet rocket forces took over Klyuchi and its surroundings, they made vast areas to the north and west off limits to the hunters, trappers, and fishermen who had made their livelihoods off the land. Why had Menshikov, as experienced a mountain guide as there was in Kamchatka, responded so elliptically to my question about the route that Kennan followed over the mountains? The reason was that the track up the Yolovka Pass, along with the villages along the way, lay within the boundaries of the closed military zone; the inhabitants had been removed, on occasion forcibly, the village huts boarded up or torn down. It was not just my imagination at play along the road to Klyuchi; the deserted settlements I saw were genuine Cold War ghost towns.

Harchina, where Kennan and his party located a guide to take them across the mountains, was no more. Nor was the Kamchadal settlement of Yolovka, where one of Kennan's boatmen broke out singing a particularly ridiculous version of "Oh, Susanna" he had learned from American seamen, keeping time on a skillet. Beyond a few rotting floorboards and fallow apple trees — this, according to Ivanov — there was nothing left to see.

We got up to take a tour around Ivanov's yard, which ran down from his bright sky-blue and white house to the river's edge. His wife's garden sheltered a great, cluttered bouquet of wildflowers, untamed, profuse, profane in their luxuriant excess of hue and shade. Here were Kennan's cowslips, his iris and larkspur.

It was also soon apparent that Ivanov never threw anything away. His workshed was piled high with tools, scraps of wood and iron, old crates and boxes — more than could have ever been counted or cataloged. "I'm a collector," he acknowledged with a modest grin. "And what interests me the most," he added, "is the history that no one else wants."

He led me around a corner of the shed to point out one of his prize possessions. "Do you know what this is?" he asked. I did, in fact. It was the broken half of a dugout canoe, nine feet of narrow and rough-hewn log felled and worked generations ago. It looked as if it had risen out of the waves from another world, the world that Kennan glimpsed as he traveled up the peninsula.

"It's one of only two left in all of Kamchatka," Ivanov said. "The other one is on display at the museum in Milkovo. One of my neighbors was about to saw this up for firewood; I exchanged it for a tin of tea. The fellow still takes me for a complete fool."

Ivanov had read everything he could put his hands on about his forebears. He had hidden away all manner of other artifacts of the lost ways of the Kamchadals: deerskin tunics, arrowheads, a bear's skull. He had also spent a great deal of time empathizing his way backward in time, seeking out places along the river and in the mountains that had carried special significance for his people, where Ivanov felt their spirits still lingered, however fitfully. Sometimes it was a grove of silver birches, or a rock outcropping, or simply a fork in a forest trail. It was not entirely clear how he came to his conclusions, even after he had patiently explained his method to me. Part of his knowledge stemmed from stories he heard as a child; the rest seemed to be an unfathomable process of "locating the scent" from the land itself.

It was growing dark, and the clouds had lowered again, the wind rattling down the muddy alleyways and slamming ill-hung shutters first open, then shut. I stopped to talk to an old lady, bundled up against the elements in a heavy black shawl, a tattered print dress, and calf-high wading boots. Her name was Revolutsiya — yes, Revolution. She was born in Klyuchi in 1919, even before the Bolsheviks had reached these parts. Yet her parents had heard about the promise of the new society, the bright future that would be their baby daughter's to inherit. She laughed at a little joke of mine, or perhaps at my funny Russian accent, and I saw that she had not one tooth left. I took her photograph in the fading light, with her seated on a simple wooden bench — a single board perched on two logs — in front of her gate. How many well-worn board benches were there like it across all of Russia! When I explained that I was an American, Revolutsiya appeared unbelieving, then uneasy. "Do you think that they will arrest me now?" she asked, without the slightest trace of irony.

Back at the volcanic station, the plat du jour at Sasha's had not changed with the day. The fish soup was beginning to look a bit too familiar — although not as yet contemptible. Sasha's wife, likewise, waited on me dutifully, but unenthusiastically. Her husband was asleep again, resting in between his piscine labors. When I left, I tiptoed lightly around their ill-tempered mongrel — but, happily, the dog was far too absorbed in his salmon dinner to pay any heed to me.

As I walked back home, I was startled to see that the lights in my cottage, heretofore without electricity, were blazing brightly. In my absence, the population inside its modest walls had grown substantially. To be precise, there were nine new residents. They were part of a Swiss climbing party, along with their Russian guides, just in from an expedition to the principal summits around Klyuchevskaya. They looked their part to the carabiner: athletic, cocky, triumphant. I must have seemed an odd figure to them, like a drab little sparrow lost far beyond its established range.

Comparing notes with the climbers and their Russian caretakers, I realized that there were one or two matters about Klyuchi that Sasha had somehow neglected to bring to my attention. One bit of news that attracted my interest immediately was that Klyuchi was officially closed to foreigners. One of the Russians, a geologist moonlighting as a travel agent, explained the townspeople had been able for the past year or so to bring in European hikers and climbers on the unspoken understanding that they did so quietly and out of sight of the military. Still, the by-the-book commanders did not make it easy; just a month before, a group of Germans had been sent packing on a few hour's notice. There was no love lost between the locals and their uniformed neighbors.

"Can you imagine?" he railed. "We have world-class mountains, unique attractions, and those army creeps won't let us make something out of this town!" Unfortunately, I could imagine.

✳ ✳ ✳

The next morning, the rain had ceased, and the bleak cloud cover was slowly easing its way up the slopes behind the volcanic station. For the first time since I had set foot in Klyuchi, the weather had taken a promising turn. The Swiss and their entourage, sated by adventure, were headed home to the tedious orderliness of their Berns and Basels.

I sat at the wobbly table by the window, mulling over my next move. Based on what I had heard the night before, it seemed prudent to move on. But when, and how, and in what direction?

I watched a diminutive woman open the door of her house and step out cautiously into the light. She looked about warily, then let her stout hands drop to her side, as if in profound relief to see no one about. With the hobbled gait of a horse waiting to be put to rest, she trod uneasily down the hill in the direction of town.

A khaki military jeep pulled up in front of Sasha's house, and an officer and a man in civilian clothes went in. Slouching down behind the curtain, I waited. Twenty, thirty minutes passed by. I heated up another batch of instant noodles and a fresh pot of tea. Then, the officials came back out. The civilian got into the back seat of the jeep, but the officer walked to the next house along the road. As I watched, he proceeded from door to door, introducing himself — politely, it seemed — and stepping inside for a few minutes. He repeated this routine four or five times, then turned a corner beyond my line of sight, the jeep following him. There were dozens of possible explanations, I said to myself, but at least one of them did not bode well. I made up my mind to leave Klyuchi as soon as I could.

Down in town, on the main street, I asked passersby where I could catch a bus to the airport. My plan was to buy a ticket for the next flight back to Petropavlovsk, with the idea of then doubling back to another town on Kennan's itinerary like Palana, the capital of the Koryak peoples' so-called "autonomous district." A bus pulled up, and I got on. It roamed well past the outskirts of Klyuchi, but at no point did the airport come into sight. An hour later I was back where I had started, no more the wiser. I asked again, and was directed back to the same spot to wait.

After a while, the bus reappeared. This time, it turned uphill. It charged up a road carved out of crumbly black pumice, avidly wending its way through a series of switchbacks, the tightly packed passengers leaning first left, then right with each successive turn. I watched with growing apprehension as the base drew closer and closer, the toy apartment houses and antenna arrays I had seen from the observation tower on the volcanic station growing ever larger and more tangible through the front windscreen.

"I'll just hop out at the last stop before the base," I said to myself. Only the bus was not making any stops; not a soul moved to get off. I eased my daypack, which contained a camera and telephoto lens, down from my lap to my feet. Frantically, I looked around for signs of an airport. I had expected it to be located on the gentle flats alongside the river, not the pitched mountainside above town.

Suddenly, we pulled up to a set of gates. A soldier strode over from the guardpost and climbed up the bus steps. My heart was pounding. He looked up and down the aisle casually, said something to the driver, and then briskly hopped off. The bus door closed, and we roared onto the base.

Now, finally, the bus began to discharge its passengers. With each stop, what had started as an overflow crowd quickly thinned out. Before long, the bus was down to its last half-dozen riders. I began to wonder — what if the route ends in the middle of the base? We drove past a section of apartment blocks, then by a depot full of camouflaged vehicles, then what was apparently a laboratory. I did not want to look; instead, I tried to will myself invisible.

The road spun around unexpectedly, and off to one side I spotted the airport. Parked at the end of the runway was a large Hind helicopter, bristling with guns and rocket pods. We drove past a row of forest-green planes, all sporting large red stars on their fuselages. The airport, I realized, was really a military airfield. In a flash, I understood that this was where my smuggling companions had landed and taken off. No wonder they had been able to do so without attracting attention. Another moment, and we were once again out of the gates of the base. The relief I felt as I rode the bus back down the hill to Klyuchi gave way to a gnawing sense of foreboding.

Back at the volcanic station, I went to see Sasha. He was having lunch; his wife offered me soup. I asked him why he had not told me that Klyuchi was closed to foreigners. He waved his hand dismissively. I was not to take it seriously, apparently. "We've had a hundred foreigners here this summer. There were French, English, Belgians, Canadians, even a couple of Turks. No one made any fuss." Then he looked at me a bit more intently and asked, "Is there something special about you? Is there any reason that someone would have a special interest in you?"

I dabbed my spoon around the soup for a moment, stirring up chunks of salmon and dill. "No," I lied. "I can't think of anything special." "Besides," I added, "there aren't supposed to be any closed cities anymore. Our government signed an agreement with your government. We're allowed to travel wherever we want."

I made it clear to Sasha that, one way or the other, I wanted to leave town. I did not mention my abortive effort to buy a ticket at the airport earlier in the day. The ridiculous excursion through the base, if found out, had the potential to get me kicked out of the country, or worse.

"I'll see about getting you a ticket," Sasha said, adding that he would try to go by the airport later. I felt reassured; after all, if the local parliamentarian did not have enough pull, who would?

The sun's pale disk flirted with the ebbing clouds, and it almost seemed warm. I grabbed my camera and headed outdoors, hoping to finally catch a glimpse of the magnificent Klyuchevskaya volcano. A murmuration of purple-mouthed children had occupied a berry tree outside my door. They insisted that I try their "prince berries," and giggled when I unceremoniously spat the acid fruit out.

About halfway across the open field in the middle of the volcanic station, a man stopped me short and asked if I knew where he could find "the American." His face, peering at me quizzically from under a little cloth cap, struck me at first as wholly innocuous, inconsequential. Yet the more I got to know him, the more I began to see something else revolving behind his pale cheeks, his pasted-down manners, his starling eyes.

He introduced himself as Leonid. He had stopped in to see a friend at the militia station, he explained, when he overheard someone say they were looking for an American who was staying on the volcanic station. Apparently, the American's father was trying to reach him. The father, he added, had something to do with the American Embassy in Moscow.

Needless to say, this got my attention. Although the reference was badly skewed, hearing my CIA veteran father invoked in the middle of

Kamchatka by a complete stranger — even without any reference to his former employer — was odd in the extreme. The message was obviously garbled, but what was really behind it? Was my father ill? Was the Embassy trying to reach me? Or was the issue really me and where my own two feet were planted?

I pressed Leonid for more clues, but he insisted that we go to the militia station together to talk to the duty officer. Whatever trepidation I felt, following Leonid seemed to be the only reasonable course of action. As he led me down into town, he jabbered about his business affairs and the awful weather of the past weeks. As if to emphasize the latter point, a dark wedge of cloud shifted overhead, and it began to sprinkle anew. My mind, however, was elsewhere.

My new acquaintance showed me through the door. "So you found the American, Leonid Ibrahimovich," the militia captain remarked from behind the front counter. "Good. Thank you. Wait here for a few minutes." Staring at me, he said, "Come back into my office." I did. He closed the door.

"Understand," he began, "I don't give a damn who you really are and why you're here, but we have had" — he paused at this point — "certain inquiries about you from Moscow. I think that you can understand what I am talking about."

"I suppose I do," I replied.

"They have been looking for you for several days. They thought that you were in Atlasovo or Kozyrevsk."

I started to explain about Kennan and his route through Kamchatka.

The militia captain was unmoved, and, holding his hand up, interrupted me. "It is my responsibility to inform you that the town of Klyuchi is closed to foreign citizens. I must advise you to leave the town immediately since you are in violation of Russian law. If you do not, there may be serious consequences."

What consequences? I asked.

"This matter is outside of the competency of the militia and the Ministry of the Interior. I can't say what the competent organs will do, but I may tell you that we ourselves have no objection to your presence here. Others, however, do."

There was something else I did not completely understand. "Your friend mentioned something about my father. Was he trying to reach me?"

The militiaman shrugged his shoulders. "I just made it up. So you would come down to the station." Then he added, more enigmatically, "There was something about your father in the message from Moscow."

Leonid was waiting to walk me back up the hill to the volcanic station. He wanted to know what I had found out. His all too solicitous concern was already rubbing me the wrong way. Something told me to play dumb: the American innocent abroad.

"The militia said that Klyuchi is closed to foreigners," I began. "I had no idea. There was a whole party of Swiss climbers here just yesterday. I haven't even been able to take any photographs of the volcanoes."

I was worried about my father, I explained. Why would he have been trying to contact me? Leonid, wiping his brow at the top of the hill, nodded sympathetically. "I'm staying here at the volcanic station," he interjected. "Why don't you come by for tea later on?"

I found Sasha in his odorous fish gear, preparing for more piscatory evisceration on the riverbank. He ran a hand down his spare, graying beard. The bleak circles under his eyes looked bleaker. His baby daughter was sick, coughing in baleful wheezes behind the kitchen wall. "The next flight to Petropavlovsk is the day after tomorrow," he explained. "Give me your identity card, and I'll make the arrangements." The day after tomorrow — it echoed mournfully in my ears like a guard's footsteps down a prison corridor.

Outside, the raindrops fell in cold, ugly gobs. To contain my frustration, I traversed the volcanic station's common, soaking my boots and pants cuffs in the dank, drenching grass. The weather had closed in again. It was the remnants of another Pacific storm.

Leonid came out to meet me in a cheap windbreaker that clung, dripping, to his pullover. He renewed his invitation to tea. I decided that it would be too impolitic to decline.

It was warm, even stuffy, inside the cabin, which served as a makeshift dormitory for Russian visitors to the station. The place would not have done for Westerners, what with its droopy fixtures and exposed plumbing, its soot-black pantry and its single, seatless toilet planted directly underneath a leaky overhead water reservoir. Clustered around the kitchen stove, nursing cups of tea and a loaf of black bread, the residents had taken cover from the raging wet outside. One man was a geology teacher from Siberia; two women had come to pick mushrooms and berries in the forests around Klyuchi; the others were unchaperoned high school students from Petropavlovsk larking about in the mountains on their last days of summer vacation. As for Leonid, was it a business trip, or vacation, or the obligation to nurse a sick relative? His visit had so many angles and purposes, by his own description, that it opened in me a sulfurous vent of caution, even — as the truth sank in — a debouchement of alarm.

It was not far into the conversation before Kennan's name came to the fore. The geology teacher found a reference to Kennan's passage through Klyuchi in his lovingly thumbed chronology of Klyuchevskaya's eruptions. The reference helped establish my bona fides with the group, which I sensed had eyed my arrival in this corner of Kamchatka dubiously. The teenagers wanted to hear my opinion of the latest Western rock groups; the mushroom ladies doted on me as if I were a long-lost nephew, pushing tea and and plates of gingersnaps at me. It was one of those marvelous interludes, when the traveler in Russia senses the epochal gulf in history and language and experience narrowing to a crack in the floor, and the whole country purring at his feet like a fat, languid feline. Only Leonid sounded a note of agitation, here and there interjecting comments and observations that appeared most of all calculated to remind us that he was there, he was present.

The geology teacher from Siberia came to Klyuchi whenever he could; he had a consuming passion for all things volcanic. Over the years, he had gotten to know most of the researchers at the volcanic station. He bemoaned how the place had fallen in the world. Ticking off on his hands who had gone where, he observed that the remaining few volcanologists were at the end of their rope. The saddest case, he added, was Katia. Who was Katia? I asked. "You know," he replied, "Katia Zhdanova, Stalin's granddaughter."

Leonid leaned forward from the radiator and glared at the geology teacher. But it was too late. "Stalin's granddaughter lives here? Here in Klyuchi?" I probed. "I didn't know that Stalin had a granddaughter."

"Katia was the daughter of Svetlana and her second husband, Andrei Zhdanov," the geology teacher explained. "It was an unhappy marriage, from beginning to end. Zhdanov was the son of one of Stalin's ministers — one of his worst, in fact. They say that Svetlana only married the son to please her father. The two divorced even before the old bastard died. Anyway, when Svetlana decided to stay in the West, she simply abandoned her children. I think Katia was only about ten years old at the time — it came as a complete shock. They say she hates her mother, even though they were reunited for a time. Who can blame her, after all?"

"Why in the world is she living here?" I asked, my incredulity left undisguised.

"She is a geologist. So was her husband. He committed suicide, right over there," he gestured with his thumb, "in that house." He paused, then added, "He had been ill for a long time. They say that it was quite a mess. He used a shotgun."

Did she ever talk about her grandfather? I wondered. "No, she lives alone, she keeps to herself. After the Twentieth Party Congress, of course, it took on a different meaning, being the granddaughter of Stalin. There were still privileges, but there was also opprobrium. She's a very unhappy person. So is her mother. You know, they look quite a lot alike. This tragedy, all that misfortune — it's something, I believe, connected to her family. Maybe it's a curse, or *kismet*."

"Maybe you talk too much," retorted Leonid, barely able to contain himself now. "Do you really know what you're talking about?"

Leonid's outburst had a dampening effect on the conviviality around the kitchen table. Russians have exquisitely sensitive antennae when it comes to provocateurs, and Leonid was not even a particularly subtle one. Soon, the geology teacher excused himself, and the ladies slipped out of the kitchen with their baskets of wild blueberries and *podberyozoviy* fungi — named for where they are normally found, "under the birch tree."

On the other hand, the teenagers, veering toward adulthood without the chronic impulses of caution and circumspection bred into their parents and grandparents, lingered on, far more absorbed in their own frivolities than in anything we adults had to say. The first day of school — September 1 throughout Russia — was just around the corner, and the students were trying to make arrangements to return overland to Petropavlovsk on the back of a truck. Swallowing hard — I had never dreamed of reprising my murderous ride up the peninsula — I asked whether there might be room for me. A girl with a long, thick blonde ponytail smiled encouragingly. She agreed to wake me up that night if she and her classmates found a ride. Leonid scowled.

I spent the night restlessly, half-awake, listening to the rain's wordless ranting as it admonished the windowpanes and the roof shingles to give way, to succumb to the slumberless storm. Each time I rose to look out under the lightpost onto the puddled grass, the muddy lane, nothing had changed, nothing had moved, nothing had cried out, even in the dark shade of the house of Stalin's granddaughter.

"She is a gay, open, artless creature," Svetlana Alliluyeva Djugashvili — Stalin's daughter — wrote about her child. Years after abandoning her Katia, something — perhaps the cold, ruthless eye of the Leader himself — imbued the mother's pages with a voice both shrewd and vile: "Novels bored her . . . it is a pity that artistic feelings are so weakly developed in her . . . she has no flair for clothes . . ." The mother could affirm, with an assurance that in time would not match her father's steely depravity: "It is good for the children to spread their own wings. My heart will always miss them, but I am not indispensable to them . . ."

The ponytailed girl never came by to wake me, and in the hours that lay ahead, my own fate was sealed.

✳ ✳ ✳

"I'll take you up to the airport this afternoon. Then you'll pay for the ticket and take the flight," Sasha was explaining to me. It was another chill, raw day that bore no resemblance to summer in other, more civilized atitudes. Sasha's wife offered me more soup. I declined, perhaps not as politely as I should have. My backpack was ready. I was ready. It was just a matter of hours, now.

One last time, I walked through the town, past its blank, dreary storefronts, its toothless drunks, and its scruffy frame housing. I was more than happy to leave, but inside me nagged my failure of failures: I was to depart Klyuchi without ever having laid eyes on Klyuchevskaya.

Sasha was waiting for me, straddling his motorcycle, his morose eyes hidden behind a ludicrous pair of rubber goggles. He motioned me to the sidecar, but when I went to sit in it, he told me that I was to put my backpack there and climb onto the back of the cycle. I did as he said, a bit embarrassed at my lack of sidecar savoir faire. With a spurt of blue exhaust, the motorcycle lurched and bounded down the volcanic station's rutted access road. I clung on to the motorcycle's frame as best I could, my hands clutching the back of the vinyl seat, my legs flirting with the griddle-hot exhaust pipe and the churning rear wheel.

Retracing the route the bus had followed a few days before, we bounced up the washboard-like gravel inclines, slowing to a walking pace at the steepest points and the sharpest curves. Notwithstanding our modest speed, each dip and rut was a challenge. I grimly held onto the seat, fully expecting the backpack to tumble out.

It felt distinctly colder as we reached the crest of the ridge above town. The motorcycle sputtered noisily past the unguarded back gate of the base and gurgled to a stop in front of the tiny wooden terminal. Anywhere else, it would have been described as a hut, a shack. Here it was check-in counter, cashier's window, baggage hold, transit lounge, and tower, all crammed into two rooms and a dirty corridor.

A battered Aeroflot sign presided over the ticket booth. I felt relieved. It was not just a military facility, after all. I presented my ID card and paid for a seat on the flight. The clerk behaved as if she sold tickets to foreigners every day.

It was only then, as I turned away from the counter, that I realized Sasha had slipped away, wordlessly.

Two men walked up to me. One of them was a militiaman, in uniform. The other wore a long, black leather jacket. He flashed an official-looking identification card at me and said, matter-of-factly: "Please come with us." As I was being led away, I saw, unmistakably, the pudgy profile of Leonid, leaning quietly against a wall, watching.

It was more than vaguely Hollywood, however seedy the set. Only this time, I was the one being detained by the authorities, not some thespian in a trenchcoat. I followed the two men into a back room, which had a desk and a table. There were two other figures standing at the back. The door was closed. I was invited, politely but firmly, to be seated.

The man in the leather jacket — the Russian secret policeman's fatigues — spoke first. "We are from the special section of the militia," he began, using one of the enduring — if not entirely endearing — euphemisms for the Russian security services. His face, like that of a celluloid villain, was cruel and repellent. With his squinty brow and frosty expression, he might easily have passed for Charles Bronson's evil, or at least badly hungover, twin. A dark fedora hinted faintly of Goebbels or Capone. It was as if central casting had dispatched him all the way from Tinsel Town — or from the studios of Mosfilm in the Russian capital — just to confirm my every preconception about the vampires who had terrorized generations of Soviets. Was it possible, I wondered momentarily, that creatures like these are brought forth from the human bosom?

"Klyuchi is a closed military zone. No foreigners are allowed here," he stated. "Why don't you tell us the purpose of your mission?"

I ignored the obvious implications of his use of the word "mission." "I'm retracing the route of an American explorer from the nineteenth century, George Kennan," I explained. "He was a famous expert on Russia." To make my point, I pulled the copy of *Tent Life in Siberia* out of my backpack and passed it across the table.

The book quickly found its way down to the end of the table, un-opened. "This is a military zone," my interlocutor repeated. "Would I be allowed into an American military base? No, of course not. So why are you here? Why don't you show any respect for Russian laws?"

"I had no idea that there was a facility here. No one in Petropavlovsk told me. I didn't know until after I arrived in Klyuchi."

"If you hadn't used a subterfuge to enter the military zone, you would have known. A foreigner cannot buy a plane ticket to Klyuchi." Obviously, one of the things that was bothering the forces of order was that I had fallen off their radar scope, hitching a ride on an anonymous truck rather than appearing at the airport to try to book a seat on a flight to a destination denied to foreigners.

"It was no secret I was going to Klyuchi," I insisted. "I must have told a dozen people in Petropavlovsk. I even mentioned it during a TV interview. No one said anything. No one said: 'Don't go to Klyuchi because it's closed to foreigners.'"

There were more stern looks across the table. The uniformed man was tearing apart little squares of paper. "You are located on the territory of the Russian Federation," the big boss again intoned. "You are obliged to conduct yourself in accordance with our laws. You have entered a military zone without the permission of the competent au-thorities." Then he added, with an unnecessary rhetorical flourish, "It is a very, very serious matter."

There was something else I felt obliged to mention, if only for the record. "You know, our two countries signed an agreement that states that our citizens can travel wherever they want in either country. It's called the 'Open Lands' agreement." Trying not to sound too smug, I added, "Perhaps you haven't been fully informed yet, here in Kamchatka."

This last remark was not appreciated. "I know the laws and regulations of the Russian Federation," the Bronson look-alike thundered, "and you have violated the Law of June 24, 1981 on the Rights of Foreign Citizen Visitors to the U.S.S.R." The irony of his juxtaposition of the two sovereign entities, one which had ostensibly been interred once and for all, the other which had theoretically replaced it, was lost on him and his colleagues.

"You can make a military base off limits. But you can't close an entire town," I parried. "Klyuchi has been here a lot longer than your base."

"I am informing you that the entire Klyuchi region is closed to foreigners. That is the law, Russian law."

In this situation, I realized, I was not going to win any arguments. I decided to try contrition. "I'm very sorry. If I had known Klyuchi was closed to foreigners, I wouldn't have come in the first place."

"So, you admit that you violated Russian law, then?"

"That's what you are telling me, isn't it?"

"Exactly."

We sat, in silence, for some five or ten minutes while one of my interlocutor's flunkies laboriously filled out paperwork connected to my crime. At several points, he appeared to be having a hard time of it, whispering his questions into the ear of the boss, who replied with a frown and whispered explanations.

After further discussion, the paper was passed across the table to me.

"Sign it," the man in charge said.

"May I first read it?"

"Read it, then sign it," he huffed.

It was what is called in Russian a *protokol*. Hovering in the realm of jurisprudence somewhere between a parking ticket and a sworn affidavit, it was the most common legal instrument for fixing blame in the old Soviet Union — from the most trivial infractions to flagrant crimes against the state such as political agitation and black-marketeering. The authorities filled it out for you, citing the law in question, the nature of the violation, and the "explanation of the violator." The Soviet citizen was expected to sign, acknowledging his guilt.

I refused. It was an impulse buried deep in my own personal Cold War wiring. In those days, when we diplomats expected to be hassled, framed, or worse, the first phrases that we had to memorize in Russian language training were "I protest! I have diplomatic immunity." Before I could ask how to find the Bolshoi Theatre, or where the bathroom was, I had learned by heart a line designed for run-ins with hostile Soviet authorities. And one lesson above all others had been drummed into us, time and time again: "Don't sign anything, ever."

My determination not to sign the *protokol* was, for my secret police minders, another development outside of the usual script. With a Russian citizen, I gather, they would have repeated, perhaps with greater feeling, the order to sign. That usually worked. Traditionally, they had other means — very convincing means — at their disposal.

"I'm sorry, but I don't want to sign the paper," I was saying.

"What do you mean? You have to sign it."

"I have been instructed by my Embassy not to sign."

"How can that be? You *must* sign."

Things went on in this spirit for some minutes. Then one of the underlings found inspiration in another tack. "What about the fine?" he asked triumphantly. "Who's going to pay the 2,000-ruble fine?"

Four dollars did not seem an astronomical price for violating Russian national security. By paying, however, I would be admitting "guilt" without my signature. So I said no again.

"Well, the money will have to come from somewhere," exclaimed the man in charge. "Perhaps if you don't pay it, we'll have to take it from an orphanage. Or from the city clinic. You Americans have plenty of cash. Why don't you just make it easier for everyone and pay?"

The part about cash-bloated Americans, the same argument I had heard the week before in my hotel in Petropavlovsk, strengthened my resolve. "Paying the fine," I countered, "is the same as signing your *protokol*."

Charles Bronson's twin as much as confirmed my observation with his next offer. "I will forget about the signature," he ventured, "if you pay the money."

Just then, an airport employee stuck his head through the door. "The plane's not coming. No fuel in Petropavlovsk."

I groaned. My interlocutors groaned. The scene would have to be reshot the next day.

"Here's your copy of the *protokol*. Go back to the volcanic station," the chief policeman said. "And stay off the military base."

One of his supernumeraries grasped me by the arm. "What about the fine?" he inquired.

"I'll think about it," I replied. Then I rode back down the mountain with Sasha.

✳ ✳ ✳

There was not much to say to Sasha. On the one hand, I was concerned that he might suffer for having brought me to Klyuchi. On the other hand, I knew that he had been a willing enough accomplice in the airport charade, never once opening his hand to me in the days that led up to my detention.

Leonid displayed no embarrassment for having been at the airport. On the contrary, he sought me out again, fairly wringing his hands with concern over my situation. He had come to the airport, he hastened to explain, to see about buying a ticket. Then he happened to spot me being led away. He considered intervening, vouching for me, but thought better of it. He had a family, you see.

"Will you be in serious trouble now?" he inquired.

"You tell me," I responded.

"What about the fine? Are you going to pay it?"

I could not believe that he had the gall to ask. Angrily, I said, "What business is it of yours?"

"My militia friends are afraid that they will have to cover the fine out of their own pockets. They hope that you will find a way to pay."

The hardest thing to do in a language that is not your own is to swear. Too often, obscenities come out muddled, leaving the intended recipient doubled over in laughter rather than in shame. Or a phrase you thought only mildly provocative erupts into a blood feud. So I kept my reply as direct and unadorned as possible. I looked him in the eye and said, "Go to the devil."

With this, Leonid realized that our relationship had clouded over irretrievably. With a shrug of his shoulders and a mocking expression, he walked away.

Rather than stewing alone at the volcanic station, I sought out Ivanov. I found him in his shed, tinkering with a venerable outboard motor; he was making preparations for his first autumn hunting expedition. A rifle lay nearby, shining with new grease.

After hearing of my travails, his only comment was, "What else can you expect from these people? They are the same as always." Then he led me to the back of his outbuilding, along a grassy path, and through a door to his private bath. It was lined with dark tile, and a set of steps led down to a tiny pool filled with faintly shimmering green water.

"During the Khrushchev era," he chuckled, "the authorities tried to make me tear my little bathhouse down. They said that it was built without authorization. Meanwhile, they were leveling whole villages of my people, laying waste to thousands of hectares of peaceful forest, bringing their people and their filth to my quiet corner of Kamchatka. For years, the struggle went on. Orders and edicts and other useless pieces of paper flew back and forth. They even came once with a bulldozer to tear the bathhouse down. But I never bent my head to them, and eventually they gave up. You can't respect these people; they only have respect for themselves."

On Kennan's last day in Klyuchi, before he and his party headed west to force their way over the Middle Range, Kennan partook in what he wryly called "the black baths of the Kamchadals." In the dim light of a single candle, he was subjected to the fierce heat of a Russian bath, presided over by "a long-haired, naked Kamchadal [who] proceeded to throw water upon the pile of red-hot stones until they hissed like a locomotive, and the candle burned blue in the centre of a steamy halo."

Once Kennan's very bones seemed to be melting, the Kamchadal completed the rest of the ritual. "I was scrubbed, rolled, pounded," Kennan related, "drenched with cold water and scalded with hot, beaten with bundles of birch twigs, rubbed down with wads of hemp which scraped like brick-bats, and finally left to recover my breath . . ." While describing the whole experience at one point as an "ordeal," he has the reader understand that it was by no means an unwelcome experience.

In the waning hours of that complicated afternoon, Ivanov's bath, which had survived many a Klyuchi military commandant and party hack, was, for me, a wholly welcome refuge. While Ivanov was not about to play the role of Kamchadal masseur, he let me rub and splash away my cares in steamy splendor, in his own personal monument to the triumph of one over many.

The next day, I returned to the airport on the back of Sasha's motorcycle; I had by now grown quite proficient at riding the back of his bronco seat. To the south and east, the sky was beginning to clear. The same welcoming committee was on hand again; the big boss in the dark fedora was at the front of the receiving line as I walked up with my backpack. Leonid was nowhere in sight.

I was not quite sure what to expect. Yet I noticed right away that the atmosphere had changed dramatically from the previous day. There were handshakes all around, and even a fatherly pat on the shoulder from the man in charge, who identified himself for the first time as Colonel Moskalenko, chief of security for the rocket base. We chatted for some minutes about his Ukrainian last name — his grandparents were *kulaks* deported to the Far East — and he apologized for his "brusque" behavior of the day before. Perhaps, I thought, some further consultations had taken place with Moscow after all. Moskalenko scrupiously avoided any more references to the security of the Russian state having been violated; he only mentioned my failure to provide my complete itinerary in advance to the Foreign Ministry, something which I had, indeed, not done.

The YAK-40 from Petropavlovsk dropped down suddenly onto the tarmac, darting out of the breaking clouds like a dragonfly. It was time to wave goodbye and be off; the turnaround time for the plane in Klyuchi was just a few hurried minutes. As I turned to bid farewell to Colonel Moskalenko, he reached into his satchel and handed me a black-and-white photograph. It was a panoramic view of Klyuchevskaya, in winter.

"I know that you haven't had the best weather since you came," he began, "and you weren't able to take many photographs. So here's one that you can have, as a souvenir. We didn't want you to leave with any hard feelings." Sasha stood a few yards back beside his motorcycle, as always a silent extra in a film far bigger than he. I called out goodbye; he nodded his head.

The jet roared skyward, gaining altitude rapidly. It swung full circle back south, following the Kamchatka River valley I had descended in the Truman truck the week before. I looked down in time to see the hoary, ragged cone of Klyuchevskaya breaking free from the clouds, its eternal ice flickering red in the late sun. It reminded me of some beast of my childhood imagination, magnificent and terrible, a great bear of a mountain.

Later, as we approached Petropavlovsk, high over its bay, the pilot put our plane into a sharp, banking dive. The angle of descent was so steep I could feel my body being pressed forcefully into the back of my seat and my feet sliding out uneasily from the floor. The child in front of me was even more uncomfortable; I heard him warn his mother that he was going to be ill. It is a rare Aeroflot flight that features airsickness bags. Cursing, the woman searched frantically for a receptacle — any receptacle — to contain the mess, all the while admonishing the poor unfortunate boy to buck up and hold it in. In desperation, she unzipped the hood from her parka and held it over his chin.

The pilot dipped the wing another few degrees, and it was all over, in just a moment or two of awful, squishy barfing. No one said a word, but I imagined the other passengers had the same horrified reaction as I.

By now a little concerned about this precipitous approach dive, I pressed my face to the window to try to figure out why the pilot had put the plane's nose down so steeply. And then I saw it. Off our left wing, a Mig, amazingly close, rocketed by. Hereabouts, the Red Air Force still ruled the skies. We leveled off, and I heard the mother — furious, mortified — say to her little boy, "You're not man enough to live in Kamchatka." I think it was the cruelest remark I ever heard. I last saw them descending the ramp of the plane, the child still crying, his mother clutching the anorak hood, bulging with its vile contents.

For my part, I was relieved to set down again in Petropavlovsk, gratified that there were no more welcoming parties at the airport. Back at the Oktyabrskaya Hotel, there was still no hot water, but I was well beyond caring. I felt lucky to be there at all. There is an expression in Russian that substitutes nicely for our "skating on thin ice"; it is *zhit na vulkan,* to live on the volcano. I had pushed my luck far enough for one trip.

As I readied myself for bed, the phone rang. It was a man's voice, and he already knew my name. "Mister Taplin," he began, "I understand you are interested in visiting Rybachi, across the bay. I can provide a boat for you tomorrow. It will not cost much — it will be very cheap. When would you like to go?"

"Where did you get the idea I wanted to go to Rybachi?"

"A friend of mine told me."

"Not Leonid, by any chance? Is your friend's name Leonid?"

"Yes, yes, that's his name."

I smiled to myself at the sheer brazenness of it, all the while starting to set the receiver back down on its hook. "Thank you," I told the caller cheerily. *"Eto ne nada,* it won't be necessary. My mission is accomplished."

BARBARY COAST

VLADIVOSTOK

ALL I HEARD BEFORE I WENT TO VLADIVOSTOK was how completely unlike the rest of Russia it would be. It was as if the city were marked on some weathered chart by sea serpents and a goddess mounted on a scallop shell. "Why, it's closer to Manila than it is to Moscow," one of my Muscovite friends said in awe. "It's like Mars. All the animals and plants are different," added another. Perhaps the most fanciful description was the one I heard most often. "It resembles your San Francisco," people would say, "built on hills above the ocean."

For all of the improbability of that comparison, I did expect to find Vladivostok at the very margins of the Russian milieu, a dim sum–flavored neighbor to the wildly eccentric North Korea and a billion Chinese. Nothing could have been further from the truth. Vladivostok was more than just another Russian city; it was a veritable bastion of Russianness. A garrison town at the edge of empire, it was aggressively, self-consciously, exaggeratedly Russian. Nowhere did the melodramatic perfume of the Orient infiltrate its streets. Instead, the scents of Vladivostok were thoroughly Sovietesque: cigarettes, diesel fuel, over-ripe cabbage in soggy crates. All of the new Russia's agony and opportunity was on display: a future framed, at least for now, by commerce, crime, and chaos.

The airport terminal, located an hour's drive from the center of Vladivostok, was another of Russia's countless dysfunctional edifices, a glass-fronted incubator of grime and body odor. The highway into the city, too, was altogether characteristic: a contorted stretch of crumbling asphalt terrorized by speeding luxury sedans and militiamen lolling about checkpoints, their *avtomati* loaded and cocked. I longed to see something non-Russian along the route. A lush stand of bamboo flew by, then a handful of lacquered dachas. Was this the Orient, after all?

The very prosaic outskirts of Vladivostok were my answer. Drab apartment blocks with damp stains across their facades; an overcranked bus struggling up to a stop and disgorging a slurry wall of passengers; pensioners lined up outside a market, hawking their silver and underwear like grizzled carnies: sadly, there was little doubt I was on familiar ground. Why should I have been disappointed? Lenin himself had once commented, "Though Vladivostok is a long way off, it is, after all, one of our own towns."

The road swung up and over a ridge overlooking the port. There was no glittering city on a hill. Even under a flattering August sun, Vladivostok was gray and sullen, maimed by a proletarian manscape of decaying flats, belching smokestacks, and rusting wharves. Only the Golden Horn, the city's elbow-shaped harbor, managed a few aqua sparkles.

Once upon a time, the land where Vladivostok now stands was as Asian as Assam. Through force of arms and clever diplomacy, the Russians wrested it from the Chinese in the nineteenth century, at a time when the equally rapacious European powers were preoccupied with the Ch'ing emperor's treaty ports farther south. When an over-reaching naval officer claimed Vladivostok and the lands around it in the name of the Tsar, Nicholas I is said to have upbraided his more cautious advisors with the pronouncement that where once the Russian flag had flown, it was never to be lowered. Until our own decade, his words were honored by Russian and Soviet leader alike — excepting Lenin, who acceded to the Treaty of Brest-Litovsk's territorial losses in order to save the fledgling Soviet state.

Thus, Vladivostok — its name, Lord of the East, still echoes with the jingoism of the period — was founded comparatively late, in 1860. It grew rapidly, and by 1900 had already become the largest Russian city east of the Urals. However rough-and-tumble its lifestyle — throughout its history, Vladivostok has invariably been described as chaotic, filthy and dangerous — it stood apart. Boasting the finest harbor on Russia's Pacific coast, along with the eastern terminus of the Trans-Siberian railroad, the city seemed destined for great things.

At the turn of the last century, Vladivostok remained very conspicuously part of East Asia. In 1877, four of five civilians in the city were either Chinese or Korean, a proportion that did not change markedly until after 1900. Nine of ten workers on the Vladivostok wharves were Chinese. Three thousand Japanese immigrants made up the bulk of the city's tradesmen; there were Japanese barbers, carpenters, jewelers, photographers, and — unsurprisingly, in briny Vladivostok — prostitutes. While Vladivostok proudly flew the Russian colors, and Slavic xenophobia was palpable from the governor down to the peasant, Vladivostok was nevertheless a colorful and exotic gateway to the rest of the Pacific rim.

Along Semenov Street, named for Vladivostok's first Russian settler, stood a red brick Buddhist temple. Not far away was Peking Street, where Chinese and Korean merchants plied their wares, and the pungent aroma of noodle shops spilled out onto the cobblestones. On a nearby corner, the Lotus Cabaret featured traditional Chinese theater and dance — and, for the less culturally minded, plenty of gambling in the back rooms. Likewise, there were Korean clubs down the hill in the celebratedly nefarious Millionka neighborhood, which was centered, naturally enough, around Korea Street.

In contrast to the Chinese and Japanese, however, the Koreans readily adopted many Russian ways. A considerable number converted to the Orthodox Church, and more than four thousand fought on behalf of the Tsar during World War I. Even in the twenties, after the trauma of civil war and revolution, as many as three hundred thousand Koreans remained in the Primorskiy Krai (the Maritime Region, of which Vladivostok is the capital), along with close to one hundred thousand Chinese.

Yet this Asian Russia was destined for oblivion. It speaks volumes about how completely the Chinese and Korean presence was liquidated during the Soviet period that the Lotus Cabaret was converted after the Bolsheviks took control of Vladivostok into a "house of revolutionary defense," then the Dzerzhinsky Club of Culture; the Buddhist temple was torn down in one of Stalin's antireligious campaigns; Korea Street became Border Guard Street; and in 1964, Peking Street was rechristened, in the wake of the Sino-Soviet schism, in honor of a Russian admiral.

On the eve of the twentieth century, there was a growing awareness around the world of Russia's potential, of its vast resources, both human and material. Writers on both sides of the Atlantic spoke of Siberia as a vast treasure trove of lumber, furs, and mineral riches. The Japanese, too, were not unmindful of their gigantic and increasingly assertive neighbor. Americans, British, French, Turks, Dutch, Danish, and Italians all came to the new Russian entrepôt in Vladivostok, opening consulates and trading houses, sensing that they would have an important stake in Russia's eastern gateway.

Then came a series of blows to the Russian polity and people such as few societies have had to face this century: the stinging humiliation of the Russo-Japanese War; the unsated ferment of the 1905 uprisings; the dark plunge into World War I and its awful bloodletting; and the dual revolutions of 1917, one so amateurish that it bordered on the comic, the other driven forward in deadly earnest, with millions of corpses offered as a down payment toward the whole cruel Soviet period.

The Vladivostok that greeted General Graves's American troops as they disembarked in 1918 was already in its dotage. It was a swirling confusion of idled tsarist officers and nobility, hot-headed Cossacks, impassive Japanese sentries (there were thousands of Nipponese soldiers posted in Vladivostok and its surroundings), stampeding coolies and *droshky* drivers, and, as time went on, a mounting tide of Russian refugees fleeing the atrocities of the civil war to the west.

Thousands of tons of war materiel that the Allies had dispatched to Russia after the outbreak of World War I lay open to the elements on the city's docks. Such was the disorder in the country even prior to the Tsar's abdication that much of what had been off-loaded in Vladivostok never made it past the wharves. The atmosphere was alternately delusory and desperate, depending on the latest rumor sweeping the city.

Kolchak, the White Russian leader, was marching on Moscow; Kolchak and his troops were falling back on Omsk. Such was Vladivostok's erratic pulse as the old life of Russia ebbed away.

Eventually, everyone who could do so fled. The celebrated Czech legion, which had fought its way across Siberia rather than allow itself to be disarmed by the Bolsheviks, declared its work in Russia done. Disillusioned by the collapse of the Whites and the cynicism of America's European allies at the Versailles Conference, Woodrow Wilson announced in January 1920 that U.S. troops would be coming home. The last Americans set sail, appropriately enough, on April Fools' Day. Nothing if not realists in everything that concerned Russia, the British and French had left the year before. Even the Japanese army, which doggedly fought alongside its Cossack allies for another two years, eventually evacuated home, abandoning Japan's dream of establishing a protectorate on the Russian mainland.

Once the Bolsheviks tightened their grip on Vladivostok, the disenfranchised Russian rich packed their steamer trunks with their jewelry and gold and set sail for Europe and America, most never to lay eyes on their homeland again. The actor Yul Brynner, whose Swiss grandfather presided over one of Vladivostok's most successful trading houses, was one of those refugees. His family's art deco home still stands on a rise not far from the port, a barely recognizable fossil from an earlier epoch. Others fleeing the chaos migrated south to Harbin and Shanghai, where large Russian exile communities grew up, only to be obliterated in the cataclysm of World War II. By then, there was little of the Far East left in the Russian Far East.

At first, the Revolution treated the region benignly, almost absentmindedly. When the Bolsheviks gained control of Vladivostok for good in 1922, the worst of the Red Terror and famine had already run its course in the rest of Russia. Lenin and his associates called a breathing space in their draconian plans of socialist construction, and trading centers like Vladivostok benefited.

Nearly all of the Koreans in the Russian Far East chose Soviet citizenship rather than return to their homeland, which was then occupied by the Japanese. In 1925, Russo-Koreans still made up about one-quarter of Vladivostok's population — and, intriguingly, three-quarters of the local Komsomol Communist Party youth organization. They were judged sufficiently loyal, in those early, naive days of Soviet communism, to merit their own Korean National District, in a region along the border where close to ninety-five percent of the inhabitants were ethnic Koreans.

On the other hand, Chinese migrant labor was only grudgingly tolerated, both before and after the Revolution. When there was an outbreak of cholera, or a downturn in the local economy, the Chinese more often than not were blamed. Sometimes they were evicted from the city, or even deported back to China. Yet a 1926 census revealed that one in five Vladivostok residents was Chinese.

Then came the thirties. Japan invaded Manchuria, carving it off the rest of China. In response, Stalin rushed tens of thousands of troops to the Russian Far East. Meanwhile, economic conditions in Vladivostok and the Primorskiy Krai deteriorated rapidly in the wake of Moscow's harsh policies. Collectivization invariably meant the application of brute force, even among the submissive Koreans, and tensions rose rapidly. By the mid-thirties, private enterprise had been definitively rubbed out in Vladivostok.

Then, as the Great Terror spread across the Soviet Union, what was left of Vladivostok's Asian population came under attack. An article in *Pravda* denouncing Japanese spies and Trotskyites among the Chinese and Koreans set the purge in motion. Some sixty-three thousand Chinese simply vanished into the frigid maw of the Gulag. The city's Chinese newspapers, schools, and theaters were boarded up, along with a special "Oriental worker's faculty" at the University of Vladivostok. Henceforth, there would be no more Chinese coolies to haul water (few of the city's houses had running water or indoor plumbing), nor Chinese-grown fruit and vegetables in the markets, nor smuggled luxuries like satin and foreign cigarettes.

The Koreans fared a bit better. They were deported, one and all, to the steppes of Central Asia, where through sheer dogged perseverance they survived and even prospered, at least relative to the spartan circumstances that they were to encounter there.

The practical consequences for Vladivostok, however, were the same. Its human biosphere had been reduced to a single genus and species, *Homo soveticus*. In that denuded state, the city was not destined to prosper.

✳ ✳ ✳

My days in Russia were winding down, too. Already, I pondered wist-fully the country's rough, intoxicating unreality — so different from the well-ordered and thoroughly homogenized society that awaited me back home. Ironically, it was something all my Russian friends who had managed to visit the United States commented on after they returned: the excessive regulation and regimentation of life in America. "All those traffic rules!" one of my wife's aquaintances complained. "I couldn't breathe!"

I was in Vladivostok for just a short while, to fill a summer staffing gap at the U.S. Consulate-General. Quality lodging was not the Lord of the East's strong suit. Off limits to foreigners for two generations, Vladivostok until 1992 had welcomed tourists of the very undemanding Soviet variety only. When the gates to the outside world were first flung open, the only remotely satisfactory place to stay was the Hotel Vladivostok, an ill-natured place better known for its insolent pimps and hookers than for its comfort or hospitality.

Instead, the Consulate put me up in the Vlad Motor Inn, the brain-child of a couple of Canadians who gambled they could make a living in the new Russia of fast *buksi* — dollars to those uninitiated in Russo-American slang. At over $200 a night, the Vlad Motor Inn had a more exclusive clientele than most Manitoba motels. It was located some dis-tance from Vladivostok's seedy downtown, among the city's poshest dachas and sanatoria. After some lively negotiations, the Canadians se-cured permission to assemble their prefabricated motel on a piece of ground next to the Pacific Fleet's rest home. In the annals of negotia-tions with the famously obdurate Russians, this maple leaf sleight of hand deserves at least an honorable mention.

The Vlad Motor Inn was like a cruise ship. Once one strode through its American-style double glass doors, Mother Russia was left behind on a sea of antiseptic comfort. The shimmering bathrooms hailed from Saskatchewan, the cocktail sauce from California. Nothing in the place originated in Russia, nor had even come into contact with anything recognizably Russian, excluding perhaps the chambermaids, who themselves had the gleaming porcelain quality of Nebraska soror-ity sisters. The cable TV provided two English-speaking channels and three Chinese, but not a single one from Russia. I had to rely on my shortwave radio to bring me news of that faraway place.

It was the weekend. I took my breakfast — grapefruit juice, two eggs, over medium, with bacon and toast — alongside the Alaska Airlines crew. They regaled me with stories of their twice-weekly adventures with Russian bureaucracy along the Anchorage/Vladivostok route. The Alaska Airlines flight — nicknamed "the bus" by its regular passengers — made refueling stops in Khabarovsk and Magadan, and almost always ended up leaving Russian airspace maddeningly late.

Not long before, the Alaska flight was forced to hold on the Khabarovsk tarmac for three hours while the airline's Russian-speaking, fly-along troubleshooter tried to find an official willing to sign for the remains of a deceased American being shipped back home. It was unusually hot, one of the pilots recounted, and the "package" was left outside in the sun for a long time. He let his voice trail off. "Well, you can imagine," he concluded, "how the old guy looked by the time we reached Seattle . . ."

The crew headed for the airport. I walked down the hill toward the Amur Bay, back ashore in the country known as Russia.

The Pacific Fleet Sanatorium had seen better days, although it was obvious from its chipped columns and dusty fountains that its builders had started out with the best of intentions. In 1945, during the waning days of wartime cooperation between the two countries, *Time* correspondent Richard Lauterbach passed by, and described the place as "a fancy pink birthday cake building with lots of statues and non-functional frou-frou." His Rolleiflex took in the palatial facade of the sanatorium, only without the shade trees that today line its entranceway.

In Lauterbach's photographs, sailors danced in the open air with high-heeled girls from Vladivostok, and even with each other. On the adjoining "Kilometer 19" beach, two-piece swimsuits were all the rage. Soldiers stood shirtless by the water, smoking, joking. There was an air of normalcy, even promise.

What had changed after almost fifty years? Not nearly enough, I reflected. There was still a spindly dock, an open-air café, and a volleyball court beside the beach. In the absence of cabanas, today's bathers continued to change behind the bushes. I, too, like Lauterbach, was approached by a couple to have their picture taken.

Yet the problem was the epic Russian one: namely, decay. Little or nothing had been done to keep up appearances since the war. The park benches were splintered and toppled over, and the amusement arcade where Lauterbach watched soldiers target-shoot had been abandoned to the elements. Clumps of weeds hid old saber-toothed cans and generations worth of shattered bottles.

The water looked fine, but it, too, had a somber story to tell. For years, the bay had been a dumping ground for spent nuclear fuel containers and other noxious waste generated by the Soviet Navy and the Primorskiy Krai's many defense industries. Fish stocks plummeted; those still taken by fishermen often displayed weird tumors and lesions. People, too, seemed to be falling ill more often. When the shackles were finally taken off the press during the *perestroika* period, the truth came out: the radiation levels in the bay were many times higher than normal. After Chernobyl, fewer and fewer people wanted to risk bathing at Kilometer 19.

At the far end of the beach, as I admired the view of the opposite shore, a man who had been shadowing me exposed himself. I decided I had seen enough of the beach and its denizens.

I took the *electrichka*, the suburban train, into town. Rather than mix with the hoi polloi, Russia's new money rode in chauffered, smoked-glass Mercedes. Meanwhile, the *narod* — the oft-trampled yet ever-patient Russian people — still carefully counted out their worn rubles to make the fifteen-cent fare.

The train snaked back and forth along the shore, past weed-choked lots larded with rubbish and rattledrum boat sheds tipped toward the shoreline. I stood at the end of one of the sweltering cars, shoulder to jostled shoulder with a tableau of nameless, faceless Russia. A beldam with a furry wart on the bridge of her nose clutched the handrail, nervously edging twin buckets of potatoes closer together between her feet. A factory worker mumbled to himself angrily as he dug through a shopping bag clanking with empty bottles. A pensive young man held a cheap briefcase and sweated, his shirt soaked with perspiration from his armpits to his belt. Two teenage girls in jeans and T-shirts chewed gum, gazing dreamily out the window.

The train clattered to a halt first at one station, then another. At one platform, I peered out the window with especially keen interest.

Here, in a narrow valley that debouched into the bay, once stood one of the most notorious Gulag installations of all: the Vtoraya Rechka transit camp. It was here that hundreds of thousands of "enemies of the people" disembarked from the Trans-Siberian railroad, and languished until they could be dispatched in slave ships across the Sea of Okhotsk to the dreaded Kolyma camps above Magadan.

When Vladivostok began to expand after World War II, the camp site was plowed up for a housing project. But reminders of the camp linger to this day. One or two of the original barracks were never torn down. Nearby, a careful observer can find traces of the stone quarry which the prisoners were forced to work. Evgenia Ginzberg, whose *Journey into the Whirlwind* is one of the more moving accounts of the camps ever written, recalls how she labored there, wracked with pellagra and scurvy, under a steaming July sun. The building that served as the camp's infirmary, where sick and dying inmates found precious little succor, also still stands.

Arguably the most brilliant poet Russia produced this century, Osip Mandelstam found himself at Barracks Number 2 of the Vtoraya Rechka transit camp in October 1938, already a broken man. In the spiritual blackness and filth that was the Great Terror, this was perhaps the period of deepest disconsolateness. The beast had roared furiously, and eaten prodigiously, and there was not a glimmer of hope in sight, not even for the children, and their children, and the untold generations to come. There was the dementia of Stalinism, and nothing else.

Unlike most of his Gulag fellows, at least Mandelstam was there for a reason, or what then passed for a reason. In a moment of characteristic literary bravado — he was otherwise a rather fragile man, physically and emotionally — Mandalstam composed a devastating poem about Stalin, and then recited it to a handful of his literary friends. He was arrested shortly thereafter; the secret police had already received an account of what they termed "a counter-revolutionary document without precedent." His wife, Nadezhda, expected he would be executed forthwith. Stalin's decision, however, was to "isolate but preserve" him, at least for the time being. It was the beginning of a painful, draining cycle of exile, illness, and depression that would only end here, on the frozen shores of the Amur Bay some four years later.

Not long before the poet passed away — from "heart failure," his NKVD keepers noted in the death certificate — a last letter from Mandelstam found its way to his brother. "I'm in poor health," he wrote, "completely exhausted, emaciated, unrecognizable. I'm not sure there's any sense in sending me food, clothes or money. You can try, all the same. I'm very cold . . ."

At Vtoraya Rechka, he was judged too frail to be sent north to Kolyma. He proved unsuited, too, for the camp cleanup tasks to which the least vigorous prisoners were usually assigned. He could not bring himself to eat the meager soup and bread ration that was all the sustenance to which the prisoners were entitled. As his widow Nadezhda was able to establish from former prisoners who encountered the poet while he was at Vtoraya Rechka, Mandelstam was afraid that his keepers might try to poison him, and in a sense, he was right: the camp authorities were all about venom and bile. A complete failure in terms of the Gulag, he was rewarded by the camp guards and their helpers with threats, curses, and — reportedly — even beatings.

Better than anyone else, Mandelstam understood how alien he was to the Soviet system. Reflecting on his outcast status, he once wrote:

> No matter how hard I work, even if I carried horses on my back or turned millstones, I would never become one of the working masses. The work I do, no matter what expression it takes, is considered mischief, something outside the law, a mere irrelevance. Such is my fate, and I agree to it. I sign with both hands.

The poet with the timid yet haughty expression faded rapidly. He had moments of lucidity, even reciting verse to his fellow inmates. One of them recalled Mandelstam declaiming rhymes by candlelight to a circle of hardened criminals, who in recompense shared their food with him. Increasingly, though, Mandelstam lost touch with the hellish world that surrounded him, wandering about the camp aimlessly in his torn leather jacket, each day closer and closer to death. By December he was in the camp infirmary, suffering from "dystrophy." The head doctor of the infirmary, himself an inmate, spoke to Mandelstam of their youth in Kiev — by sheer coincidence, they had been schoolmates — but the poet was only mometarily roused from his clouded state. He died on December 27, and his body lay frozen outside the dispensary for more than a week before anyone bothered to bury it.

Mandelstam's remains are thought to rest in a mass grave not far from the old camp perimeter. The shady road that leads to the site was renamed after him by the Vladivostok city council, but it is a spot that attracts few visitors. Mandelstam, a Jew who openly admired the West, has never been wholly embraced by Russians as one of theirs. He once complained, "Russian writers look at me with canine tenderness in their eyes, imploring me to drop dead."

Yet the impulse behind his art, as he himself once described it, was "nostalgia for world culture." In large measure, it is the same force that is today changing Russia. Forget the empty posturing among Russians and Westerners about the marvels of elections and market economic reform. Nor are the emphysemic calls for a return to the "values" of Leninism (whatever they may be) to be taken at face value, nor the overheated nationalist growling of punked-out brown shirts.

Like an amnesiac awakening groggily from a blunt-force trauma, Russia longs to understand what it once was and what it might have been — the first step toward restoring its true identity. The point of reference for a future Russia that one hears from Russians more than any other is not communism or democracy or fascism, or any other ideology. Instead, the word of choice is *tsivilizatsiya*, a condition believed to be sorely lacking in Russia and miraculously abundant in the West, which, curiously, is itself a benchmark that is both envied and loathed. "In civilized countries," a Russian will typically begin, meaning to set apart his or her particular notion of utopia from whatever obtains today in Russia. For Russians, what constitutes civilization remains the enigma. Where did we go wrong? How do we return — again, an archetypal expression in today's Russia — to *normalnaya zhizn*, normal life?

Every day on the streets of Vladivostok, on the streets of every city and town and village in Russia, people are going about their lives, trying to find in their own quotidian struggles an answer to that question.

The electric doors slapped open, and the train released its wistful cargo of humanity onto the platform of the Vladivostok station. The terminal, built in the high-flying days before World War I, was closed for renovation. Next door, in the passenger sea terminal, a brightly lit electronics store conducted a brisk business in Japanese VCRs and Taiwanese dishwashers. The clientele was young, relaxed, sophisticated — much like customers in an electronics store on any other continent. Across the way, a bustling snack bar served quite edible sandwiches at a reasonable price. That was one answer.

Outside, a furious hubbub surrounded the docking of a freighter, with people tossing tires off the deck onto the quay, lowering refrigerators wrapped in old mattresses, swinging motorcycles over the side at the end of ropes, a fantastic bazaar of greedy, grasping humanity, pushing, jostling, yelling, seizing what it could while it could. As if there were no tomorrow. That was another answer.

✳ ✳ ✳

My opinions on international finance are not to be trusted. The whole subject of banking, from deposit to withdrawal, is an utter mystery to me. It was with no small discomfort, then, that I found myself, not long after my arrival in Vladivostok, seated in a large auditorium trying to follow an event billed as "the first international banking conference in the history of the Russian Far East." The Chairman of the Russian Central Bank addressed the opening session, first declaring the dawn of a new age in Russian banking, then warning of the Russian financial system's impending collapse. His statements, I realized later, were not evidence of a confused mind. In fact, they neatly paraphrased the promise and peril of Russia's Wild West brand of capitalism.

Even to the untrained eye, it was easy to distinguish the Russian bankers from the foreign "observers," most of whom hailed from Japan and Europe. An overseas banker in Vladivostok, whatever his brief, figured by definition among the more adventurous of his or her breed. Yet the invited guests did not seek the spotlight. They wore quiet, dignified suits. Their gestures were, well, economical. Sadly, as the conference wore on, their enthusiasm for investing in Russia shifted from polite, if superficial, optimism to thinly disguised ennui.

In the rarefied world of international finance, little things can mean a lot. The fact that the conference organizers lacked, as one banker put it delicately, "a certain degree of professionalism" did not go unnoticed.

The simultaneous interpretation was unmistakably muddled, the long-winded speeches offered by the participants undeniably dull.

More importantly, the prospects for closing deals that a Western investor could actually sink his teeth into looked dimmer and dimmer as each droning figure stepped down from the rostrum. Yes, there were hundreds of private banks in Siberia and the Russian Far East where there had been none just a few years before. Their assets, too, were growing by leaps and bounds.

Yet what was really on offer? One provincial bank extolled its city's "social-recreational complex" — read swimming center — as a worthy candidate for a Western investment loan. Another group of investors sought billions of dollars to build a freshwater pipeline from Lake Baikal to the Pacific, the idea being to load Siberian drinking water onto tankers destined for the parched oil emirates of the Gulf. The real assets Russia had to offer, the virgin forests clamoring to be clear-cut, the fishing grounds aching to be denuded, the gold and diamond mountains crying out to be leveled, were not on auction here. That wealth would be shared with outsiders only grudgingly, and at a price, to be exacted through a maddening welter of specious taxes, duties, and outright bribes. Little by little, as the three days of plenary speeches wore on, the foreigners began to slip away, and by the closing ceremony, only the mindbogglingly disciplined Bank of Tokyo contingent had stayed anchored to its seats.

Broadly speaking, there were two types of Russian bankers at the conclave: the clever and the rustic. The clever were, on the whole, startlingly young. They spoke eerily colloquial English, and, occasionally, a smattering of Japanese or German. They slavishly aped the conventions of their world-weary foreign counterparts, down to their expensively tailored suits, gold wristwatches, cellphones, and sleek, perfumed companions.

In its bald-faced plagiarism, the new breed of Russian bankers displayed a dazzling precocity, a wisdom beyond its years. By talking the talk of big-time banking and walking the walk of international finance, the moneymongering Ivans and Sashas were embraced by Westerners on the lookout for Russian partners with whom they could "do business."

No one seemed to mind that these clever young men — only very infrequently were they women — ran operations that had little or nothing to do with banking as it is understood elsewhere. They knew how to lend money at exorbitant interest rates to desperate people, even though no one had introduced them formally to the term "loan shark." They were adept, already, at money-laundering, whether at the behest of organized crime groups or corrupt politicians. Tax evasion and creative accounting were other lines of work that they had mastered. With a Western naif beholden to them, El Dorado seemed close enough to touch. Letters of agreement would be signed, astronomical sums would fill their coffers, fortunes would be made, doubled, and redoubled.

They were also far too clever to bother with regular consumer banking services, to bog themselves down with savings accounts, small business loans, or the like. No, they had bigger fish to fry. Besides, fleecing the little guy was the province of the newfangled investment funds that grew up in the wake of the Yeltsin government's privatization campaign. The notorious MMM, for instance, ran an audacious pyramid scheme that defrauded hundreds of thousands of people before it collapsed in an uproar of nationwide proportions. MMM and investment funds like it gulled the masses with slick TV ads designed to bring out the greed in even the most humble babushka.

The other breed, the rustic, was a more laudable outgrowth of the Russian heartland. One example was the president of the "Bank of BAM," named for the Baikal-Amur Magistral, the cross-Siberian railroad that links a string of forgotten towns and sawmills over hundreds of miles of remote Siberian forest. A corpulent mound of painful sincerity dressed in a car dealer's pea-green sport jacket, he cut a distinctly unmod figure. When he proudly identified himself as the banker to BAM — synonomous in Russia with the worst of Communist-era planning — the audience did not even try to suppress its merriment. Each statistic he unfurled — five thousand depositors, branches in nine different towns along the rail line, over half a million dollars in assets, a favorable audit from a Swedish accounting firm — brought more chuckles.

Yet he did not flinch for a moment; he was unabashedly proud of his hick banking operation. I had a word with him afterward, to cheer him up, but I saw right away that he was unwounded. "Let them laugh," he said, "but my little bank will still be here when they are in jail or buried." I grew to appreciate his brand of Russian banker more than the

Gordon Gekko look-alikes: muddy Pakistani loafers more than Gucci, gold-capped incisors rather than the too-perfect smiles of more shrewdly manicured financiers.

The other group in evidence at the conference was Vladivostok's political elite. The Acting Mayor, who in homage to Gogol I will call Volochkin,[1] brushed past me on his way to the opening ceremony. I watched him work the crowd. He was handsome, in a wolfish sort of way, and he knew how to glad-hand and kibitz. His entourage, a mix of pale-complected lieutenants and menacing security goons, followed his every movement. At his most animated, his nostrils would flare expectantly — no doubt excited by the scent of money, the maker of political fortune on his continent now, just as it has been on ours for some time.

Why "acting" mayor? The roughshod ways of Vladivostok politics held the answer. The city's first municipal elections, hard on the heels of Yeltsin's rise to power, brought a crusading former submarine captain to the mayor's office. He had made his name with the public by denouncing the Soviet Navy for allowing sailors on nearby Russki Island to die of malnutrition one winter simply because no one had gotten around to sending the garrison any food supplies. Yet the man was an enigma, quirky in the extreme. Even his closest friends and associates described Mayor Shapochnik[2] as strange, perhaps mentally unstable.

His administration, staffed by idealists and intellectuals, got off to a rocky start. Shapochnik was blamed by his Vladivostok constituents for many of the dislocations of the post-Communist era: rising crime, idle plants, power blackouts, a transit strike launched by unpaid transit workers. Factories and enterprises were no longer obliged, as they had been under the Party, to send "volunteer" cleanup brigades out onto the streets. The city, never a model of urban cleanliness, grew filthier by the day. Shapochnik's calls for observing individual rights and promoting private enterprise, which had helped win him the mayorship, soon lost their luster as Vladivostok residents making do on Communist salaries felt the bite of free market prices.

Politically speaking, the mayor's blood was in the water. It did not take long for the sharks to find him, chief among them the new Governor of the Primorskiy Krai. An ambitious boss from a Soviet-era mining conglomerate, he was appointed to his job by Yeltsin. In

1 — *Volochitya* — to drag behind. 2 — *Shapochnik* — hatter.

short order, he put together an imposing, thoroughly predatory political machine. In the spirit of Gogol, I will name him Yevgeniy Rosomakin.[3]

The governor wanted Shapochnik out of the way. It had nothing to do with divergent political beliefs. Both figures supported reform, at least superficially. What was at stake, rather, was the exercise of power, the financial well-being of the governor's circle, his will to dominate everything he surveyed. Having someone in charge of Vladivostok who was not under his thumb was, to say the least, inconvenient. Rosomakin was an impatient, even impetuous man. He did not want to wait for the next election.

There were calls for the mayor's resignation from members of the city assembly loyal to the governor and from employee unions controlled by the governor. The governor's media allies — he called the shots at the local radio stations as well as at the largest-circulation paper in Vladivostok — launched a campaign to discredit Shapochnik's administration. Why, the radios blared, Shapochnik failed to meet the annual plan for harvesting potatoes! Shapochnik wants to put a tax on the sale of vodka! Shapochnik is a syphilitic!

When these efforts proved insufficient to provoke the crisis Governor Rosomakin longed for, he ordered more robust measures. One day, Shapochnik's car had its windows smashed. Then someone fired a shot at his apartment. Not long after, the mayor's teenage son was arrested on a trumped-up robbery charge. Family members, the governor understood, make good hostages.

Yet Shapochnik stood firm, even as his world began to collapse around him. He refused to go home, fearing that he might not be allowed back into City Hall. Instead, he set up house in his office, with his wife cooking meals for him in a nearby kitchenette.

Understandably, the mayor began to see conspiracies where perhaps there were none. For instance, he railed against Rosomakin's men for spreading toxic mercury along the corridors of City Hall. He told reporters that if he were to return to his apartment, the governor might blow it up. His heart condition worsened, and increasingly Shapochnik tried to run the city from a cot next door to his office. He refused to go to the hospital. There, he warned, his enemies, disguised as doctors, might finish him off.

3 — *Rosomakha* — wolverine.

Yet the governor had something else in mind for Shapochnik. With great solemnity, the regional prosecutor announced that Shapochnik had been accused of accepting bribes from an Afghan War veteran. The veteran, who was not identified, had immediately turned state's evidence. In fact, he was so accommodating to the authorities that he had even taken careful note of the serial numbers of the bills he supposedly had provided Shapochnik. In an extraordinarily fortuitous piece of detective work, the police discovered the very same bills hidden behind a safe in the mayor's office.

Not long after, the governor's police came for Shapochnik. In full riot gear, they charged into City Hall, forcibly expelling the mayor — who was dressed only in pajamas — from his office. Shapochnik's deputy also refused to give way to the governor's people. He was beaten and carried out of the building handcuffed. A few hundred of the mayor's supporters showed up later to protest, but were shooed away by the forces of order.

The following day, the governor appointed his "Acting" Mayor, Volochkin, who had finished a distant fourth in the municipal elections to Shapochnik. Yet there was hardly any sense of outrage among Vladivostok's residents. They expected little better from their political leaders. There had been a power struggle. The mayor lost. The governor won. Life goes on. Russian politics, in the eye of the average Russian, was as simple as that.

Not long after I arrived in Vladivostok, I paid a call on Vladimir Gilgenberg, the evicted vice-mayor. I took an immediate liking to him. Tall and gangly, he was a sloppily attired, chain-smoking intellectual, the type of Russian we foreigners warm to right away. He had the spare, soulful features of a weimaraner.

We connect to the Gilgenbergs because we think we see so much of ourselves in them. On the surface, at least, the Russian intelligentsia believe in the same things that we do: in the rights of man, in constitutions, in the nobility of the human spirit. But that is where the problem begins. In no other country are people more passionate about ideas, and less able to do anything constructive to realize them. The Russian intellectual's eyes never stray too far from the horizon, even as he risks falling headlong into the ditch just inches in front of him.

Gilgenberg was one of these Eurasian utopians. Russia should be governed by the rule of law; therefore he filed one suit after another to regain his rightful place running the city. Only an idealist — and a hopeless, quixotic one at that — could have put so much stock in seeking redress through the Primorskiy Krai courts, which were entirely beholden to the governor.

"I've just about recovered from the beating that the bastards gave me," Gilgenberg was saying, "so my plan is to go back and reclaim my office. They can't stop me, not legally. I'm still technically on the payroll, so they are really in a bind. Even if they do not let me take up as vice-mayor again, they are obligated by law to find me another job in the city administration. If they don't, I'll sue them."

Was this courage? Was it folly? Was it, deep down, titanic egoism? I wondered, but said nothing.

I asked him about Shapochnik, the former mayor. They had been through many tough battles together; they were, politically speaking, comrades-in-arms. Both he and Shapochnik had declared they would stand as candidates for governor, if the rumored gubernatorial election were to materialize in the fall. Why not join forces, I asked, in order to challenge the incumbent? Why not a coalition of all the democrats who were opposed to the governor?

"I'll tell you. Shapochnik is not really fit to hold office. He's gone a bit off, actually. Besides, he and I did not always see eye to eye. I have my own program, you know. Perhaps, if there's a second round of voting, I'd support Shapochnik." He paused, musing. "But would he support me? I'm not so sure . . ."

He dismissed out of hand the governor's other opponents (I have made up their names, too). "Why, Belov is completely corrupt, it's well known," he said of one. Chernov's prospects were even worse. "He has no voter support whatsoever," Gilgenberg insisted. "I polled twice as many votes during the last election. He's a joke, a buffoon." It was obvious; there would be no coalition.

Would there even be an election? The answer came within a few days. The governor had decided he needed more legitimacy. It was unseemly that city officials could be elected, and the regional legislators, but not the governor. Appointed by the Russian President, he served at Yeltsin's pleasure. In good times, it was a source of strength; in bad times, it might not be. A resounding electoral victory would strengthen his hand should Moscow grow impatient with him and seek to find someone else to fill his shoes. The governor, then, would have an election — but only on his own terms.

Every election, Governor Rosomakin had heard, required an electoral commission. He duly put one together, headed by a legal scholar. In remarkably short order, the commission drew up the voting regulations and set a date for the election. The campaign was to last all of six weeks; the governor was not a man to waste time. To be officially registered, aspiring gubernatorial candidates were to collect at least thirty-one thousand signatures — in three short weeks. The local media saluted, with an almost audible clicking of heels, the governor's democratic genius.

Gilgenberg's reaction, shared by the other opposition politicians, was typical. He filed suit. He argued, as did the others, that the election was unconstitutional, in that the Russian constitution did not have any provisions for electing governors. He also claimed that the high number of voter signatures required to register as a candidate violated Russian electoral law. Even the Communist candidate decried the governor's "coup" against "civilized democratic norms."

Gogol, who was such an acute observer of human nature, might have named the president of the electoral commission Professor Obmanov.[4] He was, in fact, the chairman of the University of Vladivostok's law faculty, a position he had occupied for approximately the same length of time Governor Rosomakin had been in power.

Like the governor, the professor was rather young. He enjoyed, he said, meeting with foreign visitors, particularly fellow jurists. I did not miss the nuance. He offered me a cigarette, nodding knowingly when I declined. "Yes, they say that in America now there are very tough regulations against smoking," he commented. "I would like to see the same here." As I digested this statement, I tried to ignore the cigarette smoke drifting up from the ashtray placed before him. It seemed he was well-traveled, if not exactly worldly. When the conversation allowed him to relate a vignette from his recent trip to Seoul, or from the conference he was invited to attend in Paris, he was positively voluble.

We were meeting in the electoral commission's offices, which were located, as it happened, a few floors below those of the governor, in the regional government headquarters overlooking the port. Professor Obmanov found nothing incongruous in this arrangement.

4 — *Obman* — deceit, fraud.

"Here we have the right facilities to keep in touch with the local election officials," he explained. "We have telephones, computers, even a fax machine."

I asked him about the opposition charges that the elections were being run so as to favor the governor.

"Nonsense," the Professor replied. "We are impartial. The elections will be conducted in the most democratic way possible. The people who are criticizing the commission are just publicity seekers or Communists who want to seize power again any way they can. They know they don't have enough popular support to win, so they accuse us of violating the constitution. But we're the real democrats."

I was intrigued by whom the Professor was referring to when he said "we." We election commissioners? Or we, the supporters of the governor? I did not have to ponder the question for long.

One by one, the Professor sought to refute the opposition's arguments. "Their charges are absurd," he began. "First, there is nothing in the constitution of the Russian Federation that prohibits governors from calling elections, even if they are appointed to office rather than elected. Second, the language on the percentage of voters required to sign each candidate's petition does not apply to local or regional elections." He shook his head disparagingly. "I'm not sure our opponents even know how to interpret a legal document properly. They don't even understand Russia's constitution!"

I asked him to comment on another objection offered up by the Professor's "opponents." It had not gone unnoticed, I pointed out, that the gubernatorial elections had been scheduled for a weekday, while a separate election for the regional legislature was to be conducted the following Sunday. Both elections required a fifty percent turnout to be considered valid. Suspicious minds, I explained, thought that the governor wanted to ensure himself a sufficient turnout — taking advantage of the fact that government offices and state-owned factories would send their employees to the polls from their workplaces — while reducing the chances for the legislative election results to be legally binding. Coming just a week after the gubernatorial exercise, and on a weekend, the chances of a large turnout for the second poll appeared remote. Without a valid result, the governor would be "forced" to carry out his duties without a state legislature for at least an additional six months, perhaps longer. The lack of a quorum, so to speak, would not have broken the governor's heart. The Primorskiy Krai legislature was where most of his political antagonists hung their hats.

"I've heard that all before," Professor Obmanov replied dismissively. "In point of fact, we urged a postponement of the parliamentary elections until next year. That was to avoid having a scandal. It would be a big embarrassment if too few voters showed up for the legislative elections. But the other parties insisted." He drew nearer to me, lowering his voice confidentially. "To tell you the truth," he added, "I'm not even sure we have enough money to go ahead with it. We may have to call the whole thing off."

Not long after, I spoke to Gilgenberg by phone. "I'll turn in as many signatures as I can put together, but there is no way that any of the candidates will reach that number honestly. The governor will get his signatures; his entourage will see to that. But who is he going to run against? He can't have an election without at least one opponent."

* * *

Finding lunch in Vladivostok was always a struggle, even though the Consulate was located in the very heart of the city. I was determined to find Vladivostok's hidden culinary treasures, were there any to find. Business was booming, and the stores were full of imported goods. Foreign visitors — bankers included — had money to burn, and would readily part with it for a decent meal. Here, in a city of over seven hundred thousand people, the new Russia had to have produced a least a few good lunch spots.

The Consulate's Russian employees did not have many suggestions for me. They made a practice of eating at their desks. It was partly a matter of economics; the Consulate's pay scale lagged well behind the prevailing rate of inflation. But when the subject of their hometown cuisine came up, most were deeply cynical. "There isn't a decent restaurant in the whole city," one clerk stated with Michelin-like authority. I left her to masticate her repast of sardines and pickled cucumbers. I was determined to prove her wrong.

I was able to eliminate a number of options almost immediately. Food baking under the sun at the city's kiosks — including sandwiches of dubious parentage and "pizzas" made up mostly of tomato paste and dough — I prudently declared hors de concours. I also eliminated Vladivostok's answer to McDonald's. An "American-style" fast food joint called Magic Burger was immensely popular with the city's teenagers, but its burgers and fries were, by any normal standard, utterly indigestible. It was a place with yellow plastic booths and no ventilation, as oppressively hot as it was grubby. It made the worst truck stop in Arkansas look like Maxim's.

The *Volna,* or Wave, the restaurant on the top floor of the marine terminal, had a breathtaking view of the port. However, with more than one hundred tables positioned around a dance floor, it resembled nothing so much as a small airplane hanger. It was designed for industrial-sized tourist groups rather than intimate tête-à-têtes.

The first time I ate there, I was treated to a very respectable crab salad, followed by a delicious borscht. I was one of three customers on a delightful, breezy summer day that made every flag and pennant in the harbor dance a rapturous jig. I thought I had found my culinary Shangri-la. Yet when I returned a few days later, the restaurant was deserted. "We don't have any food," explained one of the waitresses. "Try coming back next week. We are supposed to have a group of Japanese then." I took her advice, but I was to be disappointed. This time the restaurant was padlocked, the kitchen closed for its Soviet-style *sanitarniy den,* literally a "sanitation day." I wanted a decent meal, not a reminder of the peculiarities of Khrushchevian restauranteurism. The Wave, in sum, was not riding the crest of any post-Communist culinary revolution.

It should not have come as a surprise, I suppose, that one of Vladivostok's best-known landmarks was a North Korean restaurant. After all, the Korean border was not far away, and the Soviet Union was long one of North Korea's leading trading partners — to the extent, that is, that the North Korean regime engaged in anything as utterly bourgeois as international trade. In truth, the idea of a "North Korean cuisine" was an outright oxymoron, especially preposterous now in the light of the Communist bloc's collapse. Rumor had it that even staples like rice and bread were in short supply in Pyongyang, much less any gourmet delicacies that Kim Il Song, the great and beloved leader of the Democratic Peoples Republic of Korea, might have granted his subjects the favor of sampling.

Founded in the halcyon days of fraternal socialist relations with North Korea, the restaurant occupied the ground floor of an otherwise typical Soviet apartment slab. Its exterior was surprisingly attractive. Pagoda-like red tile arches jutted out over large picture windows and stone balconies. All the while praying I would not be drugged, kidnapped, and shipped in an oil drum to Pyongyang, I walked in.

The walls were bare but for a two-year-old calendar. Even at five paces, it was obvious the linen needed a thorough washing. While I stood dithering at the door, a waiter — Russian, not Korean — bumped into me without a word of apology.

I asked to see the menu. It was thrust into my hand impatiently, as if I had asked the less than impeccable *metrdotel* for a cash loan. Or was the man with the scarred forehead guarding the door responsible for seating guests? The menu was as dog-eared as an old prayer book, and decorated with the thumbprints of many past diners. I scanned the two pages for signs of a Korean dish. Bulgogi. Bibim bap. Kimchee, perhaps.

"Do you serve Korean food?" I asked the gentleman in the musty jacket and bemused expression.

"You want Chinese food? We have pork, good pork . . . "

Somehow, I was not reassured. "Nothing Korean, not even kimchee?" I inquired again.

"The Korean food is no good. No one likes it. We have good Russian meals. You want chicken Kiev? Pork cutlets? We have good pork." I looked over the man's shoulder and realized that there was not a single Asian — Korean or otherwise — in the restaurant. In fact, there was not one other patron, no one but the maitre d', the doorman, and the waiter with the brusque shoulder.

That left the Krishna Café, just a few blocks below the Consulate. In a city that not many years before would have thrown any bald young men dressed in long pastel robes into a mental institution, there was something startling about finding a vegetarian Hare Krishna restaurant on one of Vladivostok's main thoroughfares. Faster than an Orthodox priest could bang a tambourine, the forces of militant Hinduism had arrived on the post-Communist scene. It was still, seemingly, an awkward match. The café's decor was all gesticulating Shiva and beatific white elephants, but the plump Russian woman behind the counter was supremely un-ethereal in her blubberous sari.

I ate my curried rice and raisin bun in silent awe at the sheer im-probability of it. A recording of sitar music interspersed with rhythmic chanting blared above the clank of plates and pots in the kitchen. A fist-ful of incense sticks sent up scented blue contrails, pushing serpentine feelers about the café that probed every patron, every table, seeking out persons just intrigued enough by the Hare Krishna global meditation riff to sign on as whirling devotees.

The Krishna adepts behind the counter were mostly in their teens and twenties, yet the café's clientele was downright geriatric. The sect's convivial theological speculations about reincarnation had nothing to do with the popularity of the place. Rather, the Hare Krishna powers-that-be had concluded agreements with the Vladivostok authorities to offer senior citizens cut-rate meals. It was the reason that the cashier faced a steady procession of elderly diners, all thrusting coupons at her and quibbling over the number of *samosa* pies they were alloted.

"I can't stand the music, but the food is all right," explained the des-iccated man seated across the table from me. He hungrily dipped a strip of flat bread into the tailings of his yellow lentil soup. "A pensioner can barely afford to eat now," he commented. "Here I am, a veteran of the war. I fought the Nazis for three years before I was invalided. I was never a communist. But now I can barely buy a loaf of bread. Yeltsin and his band of criminals just want us to die off, and the sooner, the better."

That evening, the Hare Krishna people were to make an even more determined play for the affection of Vladivostok. I had seen posters around the city for a free outdoor rock concert, featuring an "American rock group." Intrigued, I walked down the hill to the Square of Revolutionary Fighters, Vladivostok's main plaza.

Another band of foreign interventionists had landed on Vladivostok's docks — in this case, a brigade of crusading blond Hindus. Dozens of glassy-eyed devotees stomped and swayed to what must have been the Mother Ganges of all Hare Krishna bands. The stage, erected across from the city's ridiculously melodramatic monument to its Bolshevik "libera-tors," was ringed by purple and saffron banners along with mountainous banks of speakers and lights. Rock musicians and singers clad in silk wraps lent a Bhagwan-meets-Woodstock aura to the event. Guitars wailed and synthesizers whined as the performers pounded out one insipid chant after another. The American lead vocalist, his shaved head glistening under the lights, worked the audience with imperishable lyrics like, "Hare, Hare, love is the universe. Hare Krishna Hare, the universe is love."

It was a fantastic, even supernatural effort. So much light, energy, music, flamboyant bliss, and yet the crowd outside of the whirling, gowned Hare Krishna devotees watched more out of curiosity and amusement than from metaphysical transport. The orange tents behind the stage were passing out dinners in styrofoam containers, and the passersby gingerly tried those too. The world had finally reopened to Vladivostok, yes, but it was a mixed blessing. Like the meals left behind after the concert was done and the audience had drifted away, there was much to stir, to taste, to discard.

✳ ✳ ✳

My new acquaintance was nervous, very nervous.

I had meant no harm when I called up the *Red Banner* newspaper's crime columnist to invite him to lunch. Having read in "Gleb Zheglov's Notebook" daily accounts of murders, kidnappings, arsons, bombings, and drug busts, I thought it would be interesting to meet a journalist who had his finger on the pulse of Vladivostok's notorious underworld.

The phone rang and rang. The woman who answered was in a hurry. "Zheglov, Gleb. Zheglov," she repeated. "There's no one here by that name."

"But he works for your newspaper," I insisted. "I read his column just this morning. He writes about crime."

"Just a minute," she said. She was gone from the phone for a long time, maybe five minutes.

When she came back, she had a slightly different answer. "There's no Zheglov, like I said. It's Georgi Kulakov who writes the column. Zheglov's just a pseudonym. Kulakov's a policeman."

She gave me Kulakov's number at the Primorskiy Krai militia's information office. The mere fact that the police had a public relations arm was already a departure from the tight-lipped Soviet era, when even misdemeanors were treated like state secrets.

To my surprise, Kulakov agreed to have lunch with me, an American diplomat — something else that would have been inconceivable in the old days. Meanwhile, I avidly followed his contributions to Vladivostok's newspapers. Some headlines were intriguing: "Border Regions Suffer the Most from Mafia," "More TV Viewers, Fewer Crimes." Others were simply lurid: "Kidnapping with Grenade Turns into Fiasco," or, under a full-page banner, "In Vladivostok, People Are Murdered Most Often by Kitchen Knives."

Post-Soviet Russia was drowning, it seemed, in a flash flood of criminality. It was not that crime had not existed under communism. After all, Lenin's paradise had in short order proved more criminal than even the Cosa Nostra. Millions were murdered by the Party under the pretext of building a just society. Tens of millions perished in wars and famines that the Communist state abetted or even encouraged. Against this backdrop, one supposes, murder, rape, and embezzlement were too pedestrian to even bear public mention. Hence the notion still held sway over the Russian mind that the Soviet Union, whatever its other failings, represented order and stability.

The Party faithful tried not to flaunt their wealth and privilege too openly before the workers they ostensibly served. This circumspection held up, generally speaking, until the late Brezhnev era, by which time many members had given up on the shopworn nostrums of Marxism-Leninism except when they were called upon to demonstrate their political loyalty in public. Both Gorbachev and Yeltsin built their political careers on the back of the resentment that corruption within the Party had wrought. In the beginning, the Party had attracted idealists; by its end, it was a magnet solely for opportunists.

In the new Russia, the wealthy and the well-off — a sizeable number of whom had once belonged to the Communist apparatus — made no bones now about their money or where it had come from. On the contrary, they paraded about robed in luxury, openly defying the anger over the inequities in modern Russian life that were welling up around them. Envy of profit and property, reinforced in the peasant and the proletarian by the dictums of the Communist period, had crashed head-long into the helter-skelter lifestyles of the Russian nouveau riche. No wonder that nostalgia for the once-reviled Soviet police state was so rampant.

None of this was to deny that crime had increased in the wake of Russia's democratization. The evidence was all around; all one had to do was read the papers. It had been a typical week in Vladivostok. A teenage boy was kidnapped by a Daghestani gang, which demanded $125,000 for his release. A businessman with ties to organized crime found a bomb under the seat of his Toyota Land Cruiser, which exploded as he tried to throw the device out of his window. An unarmed border guard was nearly beaten to death in broad daylight on a downtown street. A cabaret that had fallen behind in its protection payments burned down mysteriously in the wee hours. A suspected murderer was cornered on a residential street by police and captured only after a pitched gun battle. On a stroll through the city, one could almost hear the saloon doors swinging open and shut, the honky-tonk piano tinkling, the chorus girls kicking and giggling. For once the comparison to San Francisco was completely apt; Vladivostok was Russia's Barbary Coast.

The basement café where I met Kulakov was predictably dark and dingy. Most of the light in the place emanated from behind its well-stocked bar. I invited him to sit down with me at a gimpy table near the exit, and after edgily eyeing the other patrons, he agreed.

Kulakov was younger than I had expected, with the unvarnished earnestness born of a rural upbringing. Although he was bright, he declaimed rather more than he conversed. There was also something indefinably out of kilter with him. Was it a slight harelip, or a barely discernible crossing of the eyes? I could not tell, but trying to deduce the problem distracted me throughout the lunch.

Even in the dim light, I could see that Kulakov was perspiring heavily around the brow and under his nostrils. He was as pale as a sow's underarm. Perhaps he was having second thoughts about meeting me. Or perhaps it was just that his chicken bouillon was steamy, the basement stuffy.

He was, I discovered, a sergeant assigned to the Vladivostok police's public information office. He wrote separate columns for the city's newspapers, each under a different pseudonym. I did not bother to ask him about the journalistic ethics of writing for the press as a militiaman, especially incognito. I had learned long ago that whatever strides Russia was making in developing an independent media — and they were considerable, considering the legacy of Soviet censorship and propaganda — Russian journalism could hardly be characterized as either reliable or impartial.

Kulakov argued that whatever the vagaries of his role, his reporting had "social utility." He was making people aware of dangers to public safety, he explained, whether the source of concern was a serial rapist or the latest streetcorner currency-changing scam. He was helping to steer residents away from risky or illegal behavior by writing honestly about crime and its consequences — and without the once-obligatory overlay of Marxist rhetoric. This, I conceded, was a sharp break from the past.

Yet what had not changed was the public's traditionally wary view of the forces of law and order. Kulakov, lowering his voice, admitted that the average resident of Vladivostok felt little but disdain for the militia. It did not help when policemen themselves all too frequently turned out to be perpetrators, rather than opponents, of crime.

Otherwise, he was relentlessly upbeat. "There's been an eight per-cent drop in crime so far this year," Kulakov enthusiastically waxed on, "which demonstrates that the police are doing a better job. More than fifty percent of reported crimes are now being solved, an increase of ten percent in just twelve months."

I felt I had to interrupt. "Does anyone really put any stock in your sta-tistics?" I asked. The average city dweller probably found it impossible to believe that the crime rate had gone down. From the living room couch, the view was of a city on the brink of a law enforcement breakdown.

"Yes, yes, you're right," Kulakov replied impatiently. "But I can as-sure you, the data is accurate. We are making progress."

I nodded sympathetically. No one would ever believe the police ac-counting, especially now that the governor had begun to highlight the drop in crime as one of his foremost accomplishments. In the popular mind, the criminals, the politicians, and the police were all synonymous with something else that had taken on a larger-than-life significance in contemporary Russia: what Russians were labeling from one side of the country to the other as "the *Mafiya.*"

The word had manifold meanings. For every two Russians one might query, there were at least three definitions. In a society in which the law more often than not failed to restrain the powerful, it was al-most impossible to draw a clear line between genuine criminal activity and simple opportunism, particularly in light of the Soviet era's in-creasingly anachronistic laws and regulations. What was legal? What was illegal? The old Soviet rule of thumb that everything not explicitly permitted was prohibited could not cope with an economic system premised on the opposite idea. When were sharp business practices only that, and when did they cross the line into the realm of price-fixing, extortion, and fraud? No one had the answer. Yet the average Russian knew in his bones that a handful of his countrymen were getting rich off one or another dubious scheme, while he was left to ponder when — even if — he would receive his next paltry paycheck.

The worst of the mafiosi were thought to be the shifty, volatile thugs from the Caucasus who muscled a cut from everyone in sight, from the melon salesman to the multinational corporation. In Vladivostok, it was claimed that the Azerbaijani gangs predominated; in the nearby port of Nakhodka, the Chechens were said to rule the roost. At work in the popular mind was centuries worth of animosity toward Russia's dark-complexioned neighbors to the south, along with plenty of real-life unpleasantness fomented by the mountain people, who had a special talent for depositing on the city's streets bodies with neatly slit necks or elegantly machine-gunned backs.

If the presence of swarthy Caucausian gangsters were not bad enough, the Russians of the Primorskiy Krai had Asian interlopers to obsess over as well. Rumors were rife that Chinese and Korean gangs were now vying for the lucrative Vladivostok turf, even though no one could quite put a finger on which of the relative handful of Chinese migrant workers were actually playing, behind the scenes, the role of mafia kingpins. The few Chinese I had seen in the city were busy pouring concrete at a small construction site next to the Consulate, and they had none of the swagger and self-confidence that gang members — whatever their ethnic persuasion — normally evince.

The chief detective of Primorskiy Krai set me straight on this count. "There's not a shred of evidence of Chinese groups invading Vladivostok," he stated flatly. "I've seen some reports of a Korean gang, but I think it's made up mostly of our own Koreans — Russian citizens, I mean." He paused. "Still, we can't be too careful with the Chinese. There are one billion of them just across the border, and only a few million of us whites here. They're welcome to visit, but not to stay . . ."

I sat uneasily in his office. He and I were from different worlds. He was as bluff and unsentimental as I was loquacious. I cannot say why exactly, but I had the uncanny feeling as his crude features bored in on me that he knew more about me than I wanted him to know. He looked me over with a combination of wariness and disdain, as if we, too, like Turks and Armenians, were born to some sort of natural enmity.

In a bygone era, he might have beaten and strangled prisoners for a living. And it would not have had to be very long ago either, or very far away. As it was, he worked in one wing of the Bolshoi Dom, the Big House, which had seen many a prisoner stumble down its corridors to their doom. Over the years, it had served as the NKVD, then MGB, then KGB headquarters. Of late, there were new alphabet combinations beside its doors, fresh acronyms that may or may not represent a break with the traditions of the previous tenants.

"Yes, the other nationalities can be a problem," he was saying, "but we have plenty of our own *grupirovki,* too." He leaned toward me. "Besides, if the Chinese get out of hand, we'll deal with them the way we did with the Vietnamese. When their traders tried to take over the city's markets a few years ago, we had them deported. And that was the end of that."

The detective had a much bleaker view of Vladivostok's law and order situation than did my young friend Kulakov. The same statistics the governor was touting left him distinctly unimpressed. Since 1988, he pointed out, the crime rate had tripled. While the total number of reported crimes had leveled off, the qualitative peak, he argued, had yet to be reached. Local criminals were becoming ever more sophisticated — and ruthless. An increasing number of them demonstrated, in his words, "serious psychological problems." Meanwhile, his cops were less rather than more adept at solving crimes. His department was full of new recruits who lacked the experience and fiber of veteran cops. They were particularly ill-equipped to combat "economic crimes" such as bribery and theft of state property.

He ticked off some of the city's growing challenges: narcotics, prostitution, smuggling, extortion. These were the products, he went on, of unchecked political and economic reform. Everything had worsened since Yeltsin's rise to power. Youth clubs and school activities had been eliminated, and young people were now out of control. During the Soviet period, a gang-related murder was an extraordinary event, enough to declare a *cherezvychaynoe polozheniye* — a state of emergency. Now, events like it were everyday occurrences. While Vladivostok had

had a drug problem in the Soviet period (never publicly acknowledged, of course), addicts then were given treatment, and, one supposed, kept under strict observation. Now, users were roaming the streets, feeding the crime wave as they tried to support their habits. It was a problem, he added with heavy irony, with which an American should be particularly familiar.

"I'm confused," I said, quite honestly. "People mean so many different things when they talk about 'the *mafiya*.'" What does the word mean to you, a top police official?"

"A *mafiya* organization," he replied, "is one in which criminal elements work hand in hand with the political authorities." Then he realized he had been too bold. He had made a mistake by being too precise, and he was longing to attribute this particular observation to someone else. His hooded eyes narrowed into bunker slits. "It's just like in Govorukin's film, *The Great Criminal Revolution*," he added, more warily, "it's just the way he described it." Govorukin was a filmmaker turned parliamentarian, who had produced documentaries disparaging both the Commmunists as well as Yeltsin's self-styled "democrats."

It was an intriguing definition. My next question was obvious. "Do you have any *mafiya* groups, then, here in Vladivostok?"

The bunker's openings glowered, then nearly shut. "No," he replied coolly, "there are no *mafiya* groupings in the city."

✳ ✳ ✳

The Border Guard Museum — its official name is the Museum of Combat Glory of the Pacific Ocean Border Guard District — was just a block away from the Consulate. Rather than subjecting myself to another lunch of lentils and tabla drums at the Krishna Cafe, I decided to pay the museum a visit. I was surprised to find out that none of the other Americans at the Consulate had ever stepped foot inside. Once, a couple of American military attaches had been turned away at the door. No one had bothered to try again.

It was a typically ornate four-story building of the late Stalinist period: all boastful columns, balconies, and cornices. Fittingly enough, it was a shrine to a peculiar way of life, the life of the Union of Soviet Socialist Republics from the early to late twentieth century.

At the entrance, an outrush of unbearably stale air met me full in the face, hell-bent on escaping to the present-day outdoors. The door closed behind me with the peculiarly oppressive thud of a coffin lid closing, and the light went from sun-dappled to a dull canescence. I walked down a short marble entranceway, my feet treading the floor as lightly as mouse steps. I came face to face with a heavy red curtain. I pulled it open.

A woman seated at a small table frowned at me. Her face, gaunt yet restive, was garishly illuminated by the cobra head of a metal desk lamp. "Comrade," she began, "you must put on foot covers." I nodded. The floors had to be protected from the unplanned, unprincipled dirt of shoes.

She pointed me toward a wooden box that was full of canvas-bottomed foot covers. I selected two that I thought might fit. Then I sat down on a wooden bench and tied them awkwardly around my ankles.

The woman took a wooden ruler out of her drawer. She slowly and carefully lined up the ruler across a pad of tickets the color of bone. She tore off four tickets in one steady, practiced motion. "Fifty rubles," she announced, more as a weary statement of principle than from a longing for revenue. The amount was no longer real money; it represented just a few pennies.

There was something else absurd about it. "Why four tickets?" I asked.

The woman scowled and said nothing. I thought she had not understood me.

I repeated the question. "Why four tickets?"

She looked me in the eye and mumbled something to herself. Then she stated, without elaboration, "The museum has exhibits on four floors." That was Soviet logic, from a time when there were enough slaves to check tickets on each floor.

I asked her where to start. I had been trained in Russian museums to follow the route established by the administration, and not to deviate from it.

"Go up the stairs," she explained. "Then turn to the left." I took the tickets and walked past her gingerly. As I began to climb the steps, I heard her voice again behind me, reverberating with revanchist authority. "And, Comrade," she barked, "don't forget to turn off the lights behind you in each exhibit hall."

"Professions are chosen," went the old KGB recruiting slogan, "but poets and border guards are born." The cult of the border guard ran deep in a country where references to borders were more often than not preceded by the words "sacred" and "inviolable." The *pogranichniki* were chosen with considerable care; they were supposed to be unusually fit, alert, and ideologically tough-minded. By the mid-sixties, there were almost half a million of them serving from the Arctic Sea to the Chinese border, from the Baltic to the Pacific. They were romanticized in some of the most ridiculous Soviet agitprop films of all, whose directors had to struggle mightily to gloss over the overriding truth of border guard duty: awful weather, meager rations, and crushing boredom.

The image of the enemy was the glue that held the Soviet Union together. There were enemies for every occasion. Some were internal: wreckers, Trotskyites, rootless cosmopolitans. But the external enemy was a particularly potent force in keeping the Party's rule intact. Here, at the entrance to the Border Guard Museum's exhibit, was an early recruiting poster. "The borders of our republic," it read, "are being violated by spies, contrabandists, marauders. Those who want to join the Border Troops should contact the following address . . . "

The date was May 1918, just months after the Bolsheviks had gained power. The Border Guards were brought into being almost before the Soviet state — still struggling to maintain control in Moscow, much less Mongolia — had borders to defend. More to the point were some of the slogans of the Soviet era: "The frontier is guarded by all Soviet people" and "The frontier runs through people's hearts." The border had near-religious standing in the Soviet era, complete with its own saint's day, May 28 — Border Guard Day, marked by fireworks displays and the drunken revels of the guards themselves.

I was the only visitor in the entire museum. My canvas-covered feet shuffled dispiritedly across the wood floors. The early years of the Border Guards were captured in a dusty diorama of a guard post in the forest, dwarfed by a life-size taxidermic bear. Nearby were trophy weapons collected from the civil war interventionists: blunt-edged Japanese samurai swords, rusty American Springfield rifles.

The museum was silent except for the coughing of the woman on the ground floor. I turned off the light and climbed gingerly up the stairs to the next level. I brushed past the inane Leninalia above the door. Here the old catchphrases of Marxism-Leninism had not only not come down, but looked freshly buffed. On display were the sinister instruments of smuggling, rooted out by Border Guard vigilance. A doll, disassembled to reveal a cache of dollar bills. An abacus with a hidden compartment. The stuffed animal in this section was a German shepherd. According to a plaque beside his left paw, "Babiy" had arrested over one hundred "border violators" during a long and successful career. He looked a bit mangy, I thought. The dead dog stood stiffly, unnaturally at attention, tracking — through sawdust painted to resemble snow — scents that had gone cold decades before.

I dutifully switched off the light again, and walked up another flight. I had reached, on the top floor in the Border Guard chronology, the period of the Cold War. In 1952, one sign shrieked, the "American spy Golubev" was captured in flagrante delicto as he crept out of the water onto Soviet soil. His abject-looking mask, wetsuit, knife, and pistol were sprawled across the display — the enemy, for all to see, incarnate.

Only the mask and wetsuit were not American-made. In fact, they looked suspiciously like items I had seen on sale once in a Russian camping store. A U.S. Navy man I ran into later confirmed, "It wasn't even our gear . . . " There was other ostensible "spy equipment" on view, including a Rube Goldberg contraption that resembled a junkyard bicycle wheel with strings hanging off it, and, most bizarrely, a selection of waterlogged Japanese eight-track tapes.

I clambered back down the stairs to the ground floor and returned my footpads to the woman on duty.

"Do you see many visitors these days?" I asked.

"Oh, yes," replied the woman, her eyes glistening in the harsh light of the desk lamp. "We receive groups of schoolchildren," she explained, "excursions by soldiers and sailors, and other patriotic groups."

She saw me glance over her shoulder at the guest book. "You forgot to sign our register," she stated, a trifle scoldingly. As I had surmised, the recent entries were few in number, and there was not one reference to Lenin's shining example to be found. I wrote out my name in Russian and then added, under the column for place of residence, the letters "S.Sh.A.", the abbreviation for the United States of America.

The woman looked at what I had written, and then at me. "How did you like our museum?"

The thought crossed my mind: the Museum of the Big Lie. "It's extraordinary, almost unbelievable," I replied.

✳ ✳ ✳

I clambered out of bed early on my last Saturday morning in Russia. The rest of the vast Russian territory had grown sullen under autumn drizzle, but the songbird days of summer still lingered on in Vladivostok. Was the word landmass first invented to describe this country and its immeasurableness? The sky was a delicate baby blue, the breeze gentle as a fresh diaper. The breeze off the water caressed the shoreline as if this were a Mediterranean latitude, a south-of-the-border clime.

The fishing boat was waiting for us behind a low breakwater. Our hosts — one American, one Russian — introduced themselves. They were partners in a joint venture to build a U.S.-style supermarket on the outskirts of Vladivostok. One was a retired executive from the West Coast, who had come to the Russian Far East for a fresh challenge. The other was a former Soviet *apparatchik* who was dedicating himself now to capitalism with the same vigor that he once navigated the Soviet command economy.

The idea that an American food market could be transplanted to a Russia still ruled by graft, scarcity, and maladroit service was sufficiently heretical that the project had become a symbol of sorts. Politicians eager to promote more foreign investment in Russia touted it as the wave of the future. It would work, they promised. It would be the first of many. It was just a matter of time. I, too, believed. After all, the local authorities had agreed to lease the land. The groundbreaking had already taken place.

There were more than a dozen of us on board the boat, plus the three crew members. We backed away from the dock in a gurgitation of foam and exhaust and swung south, toward Russki Island. There was practically no swell; no one would need their sea legs on this excursion. We joined an informal flotilla of other pleasure boats and makeshift ferries, large and small, headed for the island's beaches and coves. Across the Amur Bay, the hills, freeing themselves from the morning sea mist, trailed off in the direction of the Korean border. I sat by the stern, watching Vladivostok's buildings melt into the mainland, the city growing lovelier with each kilometer we put between it and ourselves.

After an hour or so, our bare-chested Russian skipper eased off the boat's throttle and steered us into a small inlet along the west side of Russki Island. "Time to go fishing," he announced grandly. The crew pulled out our tackle — fishing line wrapped around wooden pegs — and began to bait the hooks. Meanwhile, the U.S. Consul-General sunned herself by the bow, curled up like a happy feline. As one by one we cast our lines into the water — which to my amazement was clear several fathoms down — the boat swung lazily around the axis of our anchor line, drifting in a wide circle about the tiny bay.

A rocky shore sheltered trees and thick shrubs down to the waterline. A deserted stone beach was littered with driftwood. After Vladivostok's dirt and odor, the inlet seemed miraculously undisturbed — with only one caveat. For just a moment, I did not even notice the single undeniably manmade feature. On the shore, hidden under a stand of low oak, was a concrete guardpost. Just large enough for a pair of sentries, it was a pint-sized pillbox designed to guard a beach that could never have accommodated more than about a dozen invaders. While it was no longer in use, it did not look as if it had been abandoned for terribly long.

Later, one of the crew members confirmed what I had suspected. Only two years before, all of Russki Island had been a closed military zone. It was one of those countless spots where the ever-vigilant border guards lay in wait, ready to pounce on interlopers. Yet about the only trespassers who ever set foot on Russki Island were swimmers, boaters, and fishermen from the city, intent on surreptitiously enjoying its scenic attributes.

Military zone or not, the fish were not biting. I, for one, did not mind. The water danced in the mounting sunlight with Dalmatian exuberance. We raised anchor and motored for another hour, reaching the southern end of the island a little before noon. There were fewer boats about, but those that we saw appeared to be headed toward the same spot. "I'm going to show you the best beach on the Amur Bay," our Russian host announced.

The captain had set us on a course that would have certainly gotten us in trouble with the authorities during the Soviet period. Off to starboard, a Russian naval station loomed. A missile cruiser and a couple of frigates were tied up at a pier. A handful of long, low buildings fronted a weedy clump of communication masts. Alongside were a cluster of large, round fuel tanks.

I had lived in the Soviet Union too long. Just by eyeing the facility and committing to memory the types of ships I saw, I somehow felt a pang of conscience, as if I really were a spy or saboteur. I looked about the rest of our boat, counting off one face after another, Russian and American. No one else was paying any attention at all. Was this a sign of the onset of "normal life?"

The beach was on a narrow spit of land just beyond the base. It was not the stuff of Caribbean travel brochures — above the high-tide line the beach was scruffy and strewn with litter — but for Russia, it was remarkable. Other boats, from kayaks to one well-worn landing craft, had found their way to the same spot.

The skipper powered the boat up to the beach as far as he dared. Then the passengers dropped over the side one by one into the calf-deep water. I had braced myself for a frigid splash into an inhospitable North Pacific. Instead, the ocean was astoundingly warm and welcoming.

The day's main event was to be a binational feast. Back behind the top of the beach, the boat's crew started up a roaring bonfire. The Russian partner's wife concocted the fish soup, tossing into the steaming water chunks of sea bass, carrot, and potato. The less inventive Americans had brought hot dogs and marshmallows. The latter were handled with intense curiosity by the Russians, who turned theirs over the fire more intently than three-year-olds. A bottle of vodka made the rounds of the campfire, at least among those unsqueamish enough to bring it to their lips after it had been swigged by so many new friends. The sun luxuriated on our pale backs. More and more, it was looking to me like *normalnaya zhizn*.

Americans are optimists, Russians confirmed pessimists. I spoke for a while to the American grocery executive's young assistant. He had a degree in Russian studies. He loved Russia. Yes, there were problems. But the supermarket would be built. "We'll have it up by the spring," he told me confidently. But I remembered the words of one journalist, who compared this moment in his country's history to a typical Russian building site. "It has churned-up soil," he intoned, "spilled concrete, bricks falling on innocent passersby, drunken foremen, curses and chaos. And theft, theft, theft." I was an American, and thus by nature an optimist. Yet I knew that the journalist was not wrong. The only question was whether he was only half-right.

The next day, a late-model Nissan with a bloodstained interior appeared outside the Consulate's doors. The windshield was spattered with blood and bits of flesh and bone. The owner lived in the apartment building next door. The night before, he had driven toward the airport with a friend. Along the way, they stopped to pick up a group of hitchhikers. As the car approached a militia checkpoint, one of the men in the back seat ordered the driver to turn back. When the driver hesitated, the man pulled out a pistol and shot the driver's friend. As it turned out, the victim was an off-duty militiaman. So was one of three men charged with the crime.

The day I left Vladivostok — and Russia — Governor Rosomakin's dacha burned to the ground. I wondered at the time whether it was some kind of omen. But the governor won his election that October — and to no one's surprise, rather handily. It turned out that the governor and a complete political unknown from the provinces were the only persons who managed to gather enough signatures to officially register as candidates. It came out later that the governor's lone opponent at the polls, the manager of a fishing concern, had also been a longtime associate of the governor's. It left little doubt as to the nature of Rosomakin's electoral victory.

The local legislators were not quite so lucky. As perhaps the governor had intended, their Sunday election date, following fast on the heels of his own, did not attract enough voters to be valid. The governor was to rule Primorskiy Krai, for a time, alone.

In Russia, past is prologue and too often epilogue as well. The weight of her history is too great, it often seems, to write new chapters with happy — even bittersweet — endings. Yet what accounts for all the things that are so rich and beautiful, sweet and unmournful, in the Russian experience? How does one explain the abiding spirituality of place, the lingering power of church and meadow and sky to inspire hope and provide solace? Even the dour, angry angels of Bolshevism could not finally destroy what they sought so hard to cripple: the longing for truth sheltered silently but hungrily in the inner orb of the

Russian eye. As long as there were still truth seekers, Russia might yet be saved.

Imagine Russia emerging from the embers. The dark and resplendent forest was burned right across by a savage fire, and left charred down into its very soil. The world wanted to call the first new growth a forest, but it was not. Yet leafy forests do return, sometimes more rapidly than we have any right to expect, sometimes richer and stronger than before. Unless there be other fires . . .

Be patient, be patient. I swam calmly, deliberately away from the beach as the afternoon shadows lengthened. The water was flat and radiant. A silvery school of minnows darted by me. I turned to the right, to face the gray frigates tied up across the way. Never had I imagined I would someday paddle about the vicinity of a Russian naval base, either with or without a wetsuit.

I could not tell then that the glorious American supermarket would never be opened, the partners splitting up exhausted and broke. Nor could I have known, as I floated on my back in the warm waters of the Sea of Japan, that Shapochnik, the slightly mad mayor, would win his court battle to be reinstated, and witness the humiliation of the governor.

Be patient, I thought, for the sake of Russia. It was Mandelstam who wrote, "In the breakers a boat is rustling; Like foliage . . ."

THE VIEW FROM THE EMBANKMENT

AFTERWORD

I AM BASKING IN THE SUN on a park bench high above the Volga at Nizhny Novgorod. Even the name of the city is a complex subject; in Russia, place names have proved more temporal than eternal. Today, Sverdlovsk is known once again as Yekaterinburg, Kuybyshev has given way to Samara. Yet some Russians still call Nizhny Novgorod — the country's third largest city — by its former name Gorky, which Stalin bestowed upon it to honor Maxim Gorky, Soviet literature's most exalted writer.

It was a perverse gift. For over half a century, Nizhny Novogorod went through life crowned by an adjective that did nothing to commend the city that bore it; *gorky* is the Russian word for "bitter." Borrowing his sharp-tongued father's nickname, a budding young writer named Aleksei Peshkov chose a nom de plume that captured the rebellious mood of the late Romanov dynasty. Yet the word "gorky" was never meant to be hung around the neck of an entire city — not for sixty years, not even for a day.

Like the other towns along the bluffs of the middle Volga, Nizhny Novgorod offers from its upper embankment a panorama encompassing city, river, and field. Ulyanovsk, once Simbirsk — the birthplace of Lenin, *nee* Vladimir Ilych Ulyanov — is another such place. Lenin and Gorky — born only two years apart — were a pair of bright, willful boys from the Volga region whose fates were to be intertwined in history as in life. Both were devoted to overthrowing the old order. Both loudly proclaimed their faith in the masses, all the while harboring doubts about the perspicacity of Russia's unwashed. Ironically, they were different in precisely the manner that obsessed the Bolsheviks the most; Lenin was the son of a hereditary noble (a highly inconvenient bit of geneology that was routinely denied by Soviet authorities), while Gorky was truly the salt of the earth.

Maxim Gorky was Nizhny Novgorod's favorite proletarian son. Orphaned, raised by an abusive grandfather who pushed him out of the house before he had even reached adolescence, Gorky might have ended up another dockside ne'er-do-well had it not been for his awesome willpower and thirst for knowledge. At twenty-one, his real-life experience living from hand to mouth in the company of the downtrodden surpassed that of all the parlor agitators in St. Petersburg and Moscow combined. Gorky understood in his bones what oppression and degradation meant; his revolutionary spirit was grounded in verity, not verisimilitude.

They were always uneasy coreligionists, he and Lenin. Starting at the turn of the century, Gorky the best-selling author helped underwrite the tiny Bolshevik Party; Lenin continually hounded Gorky to send more money. While Lenin's vision was relentlessly millenial, heedless of anything that smacked of bourgeois humanism, Gorky's great strength as a person — and, at times, as an artist — was his depth of insight into human character. In his moments of political and psychological lucidity — which grew less frequent as his life wore on — he saw through Lenin's calm, masterful, ideological pose to the megalomaniacal, almost hysterical, figure underneath. Within weeks of the Bolshevik Revolution, Gorky wrote these prophetic lines:

Lenin's supporters, imagining that they are Napoleons of socialism, are frenziedly finishing up the process of destroying
Russia, and the Russian people will pay for it with lakes of
blood . . . Lenin is a leader and a Russian nobleman; the psychological traits of that vanished social class are not foreign to
him, and that is why he believes himself authorized to use the
Russian people in a cruel experiment that is sure to fail.

Even then, before the Communists had been in power for a month,
Gorky knew the truth. Perhaps Catherine the Great best summed up
this Russian way of governing: "I shall be an autocrat: that's my trade.
And the good Lord will forgive me: that's his." Lenin may well have
been an atheist, but his willingness to sacrifice his countrymen in the
name of his political designs was just as unapologetic as hers.

The burden of standing up to the Bolsheviks soon took its toll on
Gorky. He was ostracized by Lenin and his associates, his "deviation-
ism" condemned in the harshest terms. His newspaper, *New Times*, was
shut down. Typical was Stalin's comment that "Gorky feels a fatal urge
to join the has-beens — well, it's up to him. . . . The Revolution neither
pities nor buries its dead." Eventually, Lenin urged Gorky to relocate
abroad — both to spare his consumptive lungs the rigors of the Russian
winter and to give the writer a chance to catch his breath politically. For
Lenin had sized up Gorky as shrewdly as Gorky had him. Lenin knew
that Gorky could not tolerate isolation from his old comrades for long.
He assured them: "Gorky will come back to us."

Gorky had indeed had enough. He decided that he would throw his
lot in with the new Soviet state, albeit on what he described as "an autonomous basis." He would continue to take issue with its excesses, but
mostly in private. It was the beginning of the end for a man who might
have served as his country's conscience in an era of terror and cruel dislocation.

At first he busied himself trying to save intellectuals and writers
who had run afoul of the Party. In this he had some success. Yet by the
late twenties, he was singing the praises of the Solovki camps, and
warning in *Pravda* that "if the enemy refuses to surrender he must be
destroyed." It was at Gorky's dining room table that Stalin first proclaimed his doctrine of "socialist realism": art and literature were to be

put at the service of the Party, "creative workers" were to see themselves as "engineers of the soul."

When on a cross-country tour Gorky triumphantly returned to Nizhny Novgorod ("the father of Soviet literature" came escorted by a party of secret service bodyguards), he was welcomed with genuine emotion by the populace. A few years later, the city was renamed. That Gorky in fact felt disdain for his birthplace was of no importance to Stalin. Nizhny Novgorod reminded the writer of his deprived childhood and of the old regime's indifference to the welfare of the poor and uneducated. However, for the "Boss" and his secret police chief Yagoda, the city's rechristening was a shrewd piece of flattery designed to bind Gorky ever closer to the Party. Besides, how sincere was Gorky when he expressed dismay at addressing an envelope for the first time with his own name in lieu of Nizhny Novgorod?

In point of fact, Gorky greatly preferred Sorrento — his place of residence abroad — to the piazzas of his gritty hometown. From Italy he could observe at a safe distance the thundering hooves of revolution and what was labeled then — without a trace of sarcasm — as "socialist construction." Every time that he wearied of the Bolsheviks, Gorky would find a way to slip out of the country, and give vent to his frustrations among the fawning exiles and household informers camped out in his villa. He was likely unaware — although by this time he was perhaps too sick or too compromised by the Soviet authorities himself to notice — that his mistress, his private secretary, and even his son Maxim were all in the employ of the Soviet secret police.

After his death in 1936, the Party meticulously tended to Gorky's memory, demonstrating the same scrupulous insistence on veracity that went into the hagiography of other Bolshevik icons. Gorky's hallowed name became more and more ossified, just as his works — his most cherished legacy — were read with less and less enthusiasm by his own countrymen. In contemporary Russia, he is as out of fashion as Melville, as irrelevant as Mencken.

✳ ✳ ✳

From the embankment, the multiple lives of Nizhny Novgorod unfold before me; the brick kremlin towers look down on the green roofs of the old trading houses along the river and the spare, obdurate constructions of the Soviet era. Beyond, the stuttering hydrofoils weave about the Volga like dragonflies, and the villages of the opposite bank — humble and heartwarming as chipped buttons and wornout shoes — yawn with indifference at it all.

It is now largely forgotten that before the revolution, Nizhny Novgorod was Russia's principal commercial center. According to one saying, St. Petersburg was Russia's head; Moscow, its heart; and Nizhny Novgorod, its pocketbook. As such, the city's fame went well beyond Russia's borders. It was the home of one of the largest bazaars in all of Europe, perhaps in all the nineteenth-century world: the Nizhny Novgorod Yarmarka. From mid-July until mid-September more than one hundred thousand merchants and vendors would fill the fairground, which was laid out along ten city blocks at the confluence of the Volga and Oka Rivers. The annual invasion typically doubled, even tripled the city's population. Thousands of ships unloaded their wares along its river wharves. Traders came from as far away as China and Arabia.

I have a book in my lap by a Presbyterian minister named Charles Augustus Stoddard entitled *Across Russia*. It is open to a chapter on the Yarmarka. "Shall we go to Nijni-Novgorod and its world-famous fair?" it begins, evidence that any enterprising American traveler in the last decade of the nineteenth century would have given the matter serious consideration. Stoddard's first impressions were not encouraging. "Rough and dusty streets, low and dingy houses with disagreeable looking shops," the author reported, "a variety of costumes indeed, but all so dirty that they were repulsive, nobody to meet us who could speak anything intelligible, and a shabby and disreputable atmosphere all about." These visitors were products of the Victorian era, so their social sensibilities were especially keen: "We regretted that the ladies had come at all, and were ashamed of the company in which we found ourselves wherever it was needful to eat a meal or enter any public place."

Yet, before long, their haughty reserve gave way to unconcealed fascination:

> It was interesting to stand on the bridge, in the midst of the long lines of drays and carts, laden with products of every kind, from chests of tea and Persian carpets to dried fish and salted

cucumbers, and watch the panorama. Far as the eye could reach down the Volga, it was alive with steamboats and barges with roofs over them; with tug boats and row boats; and in the sandy bed of the river, where the water had receded, were immense temporary lumber yards. . . . Along the wharves were immense piles of iron, and cotton bales, and tea chests, and thousands of laborers were loading and unloading the wares of different nations, the corn and salt, and wine and leather, and wool and silk, and dye-stuffs and metals, with crates of crockery and cases of manufactured goods.

The streets of the fairground were full not only of commodities and cargo: the pagentry extended to the human commerce as well. There were:

Persians and Armenians . . . with long blue and black robes girded by brilliant sashes, huge turbans or lofty Astrakhan caps upon their heads . . . Tartar workmen in rusty cotton jackets, with skull caps of the same material; monks and nuns begging from everybody; Europeans in gay, modern costumes — Germans, Austrians, and here and there an Englishman or American.

The fair, along with all of its vivacity and vagrancy, was unceremoniously done in by the Communists — it existed in name only in the decade before it was officially abolished in 1930. Today there is an effort to revive it, to bring the world, in some small measure, back to Nizhny Novgorod.

I am sitting on a park bench in front of the Yarmarka's old Main Building, one of the few that has survived. With me is Aleksandr Dektyar, an architect whose firm has a contract to rebuild part of the fairgrounds. Like my friend Troshin in Vorkuta, Dektyar is a dreamer, and he does not appear especially intimidated by the fact that the work of restoring the fair has come to a halt — "temporarily," he insists — for lack of money.

"The original fairgrounds were designed by some of the finest architects in Europe," he recalls. Indeed, the flavor of the event was resolutely international; there was room not only for the cupolas and belltowers of Russian architecture, but also for Mogul minarets and Chinese pavilions.

A serendipitous meeting place for all of Eurasian civilization, the fair worked on many planes at once: commercial, social, and cultural.

While the visiting Americans of a century ago were scandalized by the leggy burlesque in their hotel dining room and the nocturnal carousing of the fairground taverns — Alexandre Dumas labeled one part of the fair "the courtesans' district" in deference to the thousands of women on display there — Dektyar conjures up a more elegant side: "Shalyapin performed here frequently, as did other opera stars and orchestras."

There is a hunger among post-Soviet Nizhny Novgorodans to restore this aspect of their past, too. The annual Yarmarka ball has been revived. The Main Building's ceremonial hall was lovingly renovated, its chandeliers and the coats of arms of Russia's prerevolutionary *gubernias* returned to their original glory by a privatized armaments concern.

I ask Dektyar why this is, why "Nizhny" is so intent on opening itself up to the outside world and reliving its former glories. "It is because of the Gorky years," he explains. "This was a closed city, the biggest in the entire Soviet Union. We were locked up in a cupboard for more than a half century, so we know the damage that it can do." Thus the apparent paradox of Gorky's walled-off population electing Boris Nemtsov, the country's youngest and most energetic governor. Nemtsov, by training, is a physicist — a discipline more devoted to truth-seeking than most — and perhaps it is no coincidence that during his years in Nizhny Novgorod he set the standard for political and economic reform in the new Russia.

What does Dektyar, so enamored with Nizhny Novgorod's trading past, think of the post-Soviet merchant class — its name already besmirched by accusations of corruption, greed, and murder? "These people, they're a necessary evil," he replies. "For instance, some of my friends criticize their propensity to throw money senselessly at mediocre performers and wasteful charities. I hear people complain that the new rich don't know a thing about art, that they support the wrong people. But so what? It's better that they support something rather than nothing. And if they spend their money stupidly, to show off, their children may not — maybe they'll spend it the right way for the right reasons." He smiles, and adds: "Better nouveau riche than no one rich."

* * *

Still, one should not exaggerate Nizhny Novgorod's success. In many ways, this darling of the Western aid agencies remains a provincial town masquerading as a metropolis. It is as full of drunks as any backwoods village; I watched one of them puke miserably behind a rusty billboard as a scolding woman stood alongside. Nearby, the Kalinin Cultural Center for Sailors advertises a special regime for alcoholics; one session, claims the announcement, is therapy enough for life.

Hate, too, has anything but dissipated. The Communists still rally from time to time in the city center, albeit in diminishing numbers. An angry, bedraggled laborer in an army jacket and baggy pants tends a clothesline sagging under the weight of Lenin portraits and hand-lettered slogans. One sign reads: "Clinton — greatest enemy of the U.S.S.R." Another states baldly: "Yeltsin — tool of the American and the Jew." A platinum blonde in high heels argues with passersby, including a group of teenagers who are openly derisive. The dispute becomes heated; the man in fatigues takes down his Lenins and slinks off.

There are other forms of venom, too — some of them a throwback to an earlier time. A handbill posted in the city's Orthodox churches opens with a boldface headline "Warning! Protestants!" and then asks "Can a person commit treason against his faith, turn away from the Russian Church, from the body of Christ?" The answer is forthcoming: "A Russian who is not Orthodox is trash, a nonperson."

Alcoholism, prejudice, animosity: these are among the unhappy by-products of Russian history and Soviet life, of the grinding oppression over mind and body that was first the lot of the serf, then the fate of the factory worker. If, on the eve of World War I, Russia could be said to have hesitantly turned a corner toward reform, the seventy-five years of Communist rule that followed were a punishing detour away from the country's intended path. The damage wrought by Lenin and his successors was nowhere more in evidence than in the formerly closed cities and regions, where no one had ever bothered to gussy up the hollow eyes and sagging features of the dictatorship of the proletariat. Potemkin's methods were superfluous in places like twentieth-century Kamchatka and Tuva. The Soviet seraglio, full of discarded provinces grown haggard and morose from neglect, was bolted shut to outsiders.

What good could come of this gray harem, where the sultan's pleasure seemed to depend on a history torn from its foundations, a culture ravaged of its riches, an environment stripped of joy and beauty?

✳ ✳ ✳

Once again, in Nizhny Novgorod, I find myself in a post-Soviet suburb of atrophied apartment blocks and overgrown lots. Once again, I feel myself diminished, I mourn for an entire nation defiled. Only here, today, there is a difference.

The Sakharov Museum is located on the outskirts of the city, at the end of a tram line. It is set in a typically dreary neighborhood of fractured concrete, split glass, and dripping pipes, indistinguishable from so many places across the broken face of Russia. Likewise, one could only describe the museum in the humblest terms. On the ground floor of a twelve-story building, it is made up of two small apartments, furnished with the spindly divans and hutches that give many Russian homes an oddly institutional look.

The first apartment was occupied by Andrei Sakharov and Yelena Bonner during their six years of forced exile in Gorky; the second across the hall has been converted into an office and cloakroom. The walls are covered with photos of Sakharov and Bonner, including pictures from before and after their Gorky exile. On display also are copies of books and articles written by Sakharov; the draft of a telegram the academician sent to Andropov protesting a KGB break-in; and the phone that was installed by the authorities in order for Sakharov to receive Gorbachev's call announcing the physicist's release from exile. The kitchen linoleum, someone assures me, is the one on which Sakharov and Bonner walked. Is this the beginning of a Sakharov shrine? If so, it is a far more modest one than Gorky's childhood home across town, lovingly upgraded and remodeled to the point that Gorky would have been hard-pressed to recognize it.

Another irony: it was Sakharov, the world-famous dissident, who put the closed city of Gorky back on the map after decades in the shadows. His life's transit was, in many ways, the mirror image of Maxim Gorky's. As a young man, Sakharov was — from the perspective of the Communist Party — a paragon of virtue. He worked tirelessly at the secret Arzamas-16 installation to develop the Soviet hydrogen bomb. In recompense for his service to the Soviet state, Sakharov was made a Hero of Socialist Labor and awarded the Stalin Prize. In those years, the dictator's name had a different meaning for Sakharov. When Stalin died, he wrote to his wife: "I am under the influence of a great man's death. I am thinking of his humanity." He was, as he acknowledged in his memoirs, still under "the hypnotic power of mass ideology."

Little by little, however, Sakharov's outlook began to widen, then blossom. He began by questioning Khrushchev's policies on nuclear testing. Then he became acquainted with some of the early Soviet dissidents like Roy Medvedev, Pavel Litvinov and Larisa Bogoraz. Sakharov played an active role in one of the Soviet era's first environmental crusades — the effort to stop the construction of a giant factory on the shores of Lake Baikal. He owned a shortwave radio, and followed world events closely — especially the Soviet invasion of Czechoslovakia and the crushing of the "Prague Spring" reform effort. In this light, Sakharov's decision in 1968 to allow his essay "Reflections on Progress, Peaceful Coexistence, and Intellectual Freedom" to be published in the West came almost as an afterthought.

Yet it was an altogether momentous step, one that put Sakharov — an honored, pampered son of the Soviet nuclear establishment — on a collision course with the Communist Party and the Soviet government. He never turned his back on the truth again. His KGB file fills 520 volumes, an amount which a recent director of Russia's counterespionage service acknowledged might be a "Guinness world record." In Gorky, a guard sat outside Sakharov's door around the clock. He and Bonner were followed wherever they went in the city, and often filmed by hidden cameras. Twice, Sakharov's memoirs were stolen by KGB agents, once after he was drugged. He stubbornly kept writing. Right up to his last hours, when as a member of the Congress of People's Deputies he called upon Gorbachev and a hall full of hostile apparatchiks to accelerate the pace of perestroika, he spoke his mind. He said then, in 1989, that Gorbachev's policy of half-measures was doomed to failure, and — as in so many things — he was proved right. We still do not know exactly what kind of era was ushered in with the moral collapse of Communism in the late eighties, but it can be said that, more than any other single individual, Sakharov was its conscience, its muse.

There are many Russian proverbs, and this is another: "Truth does not burn in fire, nor drown in water." In every place I visited in Russia, memory had not given way to amnesia; rather, bald-faced lies had ceded their authority to a sometimes sad and somber reality. Falsehoods had proved no match, in the end, for the mighty labors of an architect in the tundra; an ethnographer in the Caucasus; a shaman in middle Asia; a tipsy museum guide in the taiga — and hundreds of thousands of unordinary people like them. The dislocations of Lenin's Soviet Union, Hitler's Germany, Pol Pot's Kampuchea are far from gone, but the miraculous truth about truth can give us hope, can spare us from despair. From the Nizhny embankment, that much is clear.

I am sitting at the tram stop outside of the Sakharov House Museum, waiting beside Masha Gavrilova for a ride back into town. Her wide light blue eyes are good, gentle, strong. She is distantly related to Yelena Bonner; as a teenage girl she recalls visits from Sakharov and Bonner to her family's apartment. She never visited their apartment; almost no one was allowed past the police cordon to see the two dissidents.

At the time, Masha worked at the Gorky Museum, a job which she does not remember fondly. She lectured schoolchildren on Gorky's revolutionary exploits, extolling his works, citing Lenin's praise of Soviet literature's self-styled "stormy petrel." She even ended up writing her doctoral dissertation on Gorky — specifically the portrayals of juvenile delinquents from his early works.

Now Masha works at the Sakharov Museum. She is mindful of the fact that many of Sakharov's old neighbors remain in situ — and not all of them are pleased by the presence of the museum. Some still think of Sakharov as a turncoat, or as a tool of foreign powers and the Armenian-Jew Bonner. The doctor who supervised the force-feeding of Sakharov at a local clinic is today its director. In a television interview a few years ago, he sought to justify his actions in the time-honored way. "We were only doing our duty, following orders," the doctor explained. "Besides, we looked after Sakharov even when the highers-up were denouncing him in the worst possible terms."

Not long before my visit, one of the two boys who had famously managed to evade the KGB and meet Sakharov while he was under virtual house arrest came back to the apartment for another look. The two had managed to speak to Sakharov for about fifteen minutes. The physicist offered them tea and cookies and was, by their account, very friendly. On their way out, the two were arrested and taken away. Their factory-worker parents were harassed by the authorities, and their school notified of their "hooliganistic" behavior. At the KGB's instigation, the parents called on Sakharov to complain about his behavior; they told him he should have turned the boys away.

Why had the boys risked it in the first place? Masha laughs as she relates what the boy turned man told her. "We had heard about the famous academician that no one was allowed to talk to," he explained. "Sakharov was kept under secret guard. They denounced him every day in the papers. So it was just too big a challenge to ignore."

The tram comes, we part, the doors open wide, and I see the possibilities of the human spirit anew.

> *What a strange, alluring, enthralling, wonderful world it is: the open road! And how wonderful that open road is itself: a sunny day, autumn leaves, cool air — wrap your traveling cloak more tightly round you, pull your cap over your ears, snuggle up more closely and more cosily in the corner!*
>
> GOGOL

SOURCE NOTES

Open Lands is not a scholarly work. It does, however, owe a great deal to the new generation of books on Russian history that have been published since Gorbachev's policy of *glasnost* began to bring down the barriers of secrecy in Soviet society. Russia during the Soviet period was a canvas darkened and muted by the sooty fires of the Communist experiment. Little by little, the restorers — historians, journalists, inspired amateurs — have wiped away the surface to reach the true colors below. The red patina has mostly washed away; gone are Marxism-Leninism, world revolution, the Five Year Plan. In fact, almost everything created by the salon that pantingly called itself "Sovietism" — on the assumption that it could boast of the same enduring achievement of, say, Impressionism — is no more.

True, some aspects of the Soviet experience were always easier to fathom than others. Soviet foreign policy, for instance, had the merit of being expressed — at times altogether too vividly — outside the U.S.S.R.'s borders. Thus it was subject to the more familiar dynamic of relations among nation-states. Inside the Soviet Union itself, however, the life of the average Russian citizen, the Communist Party, and the Soviet state, did not perforce share this characteristic. Out of fear, the man on the street obfuscated. Out of conviction, the Party member lied. Out of sheer habit, the imperishably byzantine state apparatus ground on in a world all its own. No wonder our best Cold War guesses about Soviet behavior read a bit speculatively these days. The line-up of leaders atop Lenin's mausoleum turned out to be very thin broth indeed.

The eternal minuet in Russian history between continuity and change continues unbroken to this day. However, the foundations of Russian historiography have been profoundly transformed. For instance, the access to state and Party archives enjoyed by the late General Volkogonov would have been as unimaginable under Tsarist rule as under the Soviet regime. His revelations, as well as those of other Russian writers like Radzinsky and Shentalinsky, put into sharp relief how much there was left to say about the Soviet period in the post-Soviet era. Likewise, Western historians such as Pipes and Conquest have done a great deal to expand our understanding of once-taboo topics like Lenin's attitude towards the use of terror, making use of a variety of sources never before available.

Yet the new understandings stretch far beyond the serial cataclysms unleashed by Lenin and Stalin. Today, there is a great deal less uncertainty, for instance, about why the Politburo decided to intervene in Czechoslovakia in 1968, or who among its members in 1985 favored turning to a relatively untested Gorbachev as General Secretary. One can now search out, without especial difficulty, the minutes of Politburo meetings and the (relatively) candid recollections of the participants and their immediate associates. Whole new spheres of inquiry have opened up to enterprising Western scholars; for instance, Forsyth's history of Siberia's indigenous peoples might not have been possible — or been at least anywhere near as compelling — had it been attempted in an earlier era. The host of local histories and individual memoirs I cite below would have remained, as the Russians say, "in the drawer."

My own modest efforts at historical discovery were necessarily eclectic and impressionistic. Just as I embarked on my trips around Russia with little anticipation of what I would find, I typically put my hands on source material as much out of happenstance as by design. The only real rhyme or reason in my "research" was the wayward course of itineraries through Russia's formerly closed areas. A fair amount of my information comes from random conversations in planes, trains, cars and buses — the past recounted, if you will, from the perspective of a third class coach. I hope the reader will bear with the inevitable limitations of this approach, and not mistake this book for what it does not pretend to be: namely, deliberate, exhaustive scholarship.

ARKHANGELSK AND SOLOVKI

The photo album edited by Dmitrenko contains a series of moody black and white photographs of the Solovetsky Monastery along with an essay about the island's history prior to the Bolshevik Revolution.

Solzhenitsyn writes in considerable detail about the Solovki camps, and to date *The Gulag Archipelago* remains the single most important source in English about the early days of the Gulag in the Solovetsky Islands. Tchernavin's 1930s account of the horrors of the Solovki camps was one of the first such works to see the light of day in the West; some reviewers at the time dismissed it as propaganda. Kennan's *The Decision to Intervene* describes in detail the political struggle between the Allies and the new Bolshevik regime in the waning months of World War I as well as Vologda's fleeting summer as a diplomatic capital. Goldhurst and Halliday both provide general accounts of the Allied intervention in North Russia in 1918-19, including the retreat from Shenkursk.

KABARDINO-BALKARIA

There is a growing body of literature recounting Stalin's repression of the North Caucasus peoples, the Balkars included. Alieva's three-volume work contains separate chapters describing the deportations of a wide range of Soviet nationalities, from the Karachay to the Koreans. It relies on essays, archival documents, memoirs, and poetry to convey to the reader the scale of suffering these minorities endured. In describing the NKVD massacres in Verkhnaya Balkariya, Azamatov and his collaborators make use of previously secret KGB documents along with the accounts of surviving eyewitnesses. Shabaev worked for four decades as an archivist in the Kabardino-Balkaria Ministry of the Interior, where he had access to official documents concerning the deportation and exile of the Balkars. My friend Musukayev has a long list of cultural and ethnographic works about Kabardino-Balkaria to his name, including those I cite in the bibliography. Kuliev's poetry is available in locally published Russian and Balkar bilingual editions, as well as in English-language poetry anthologies dating back to the Soviet period.

KAMCHATKA

The elder Kennan's account of his travels, *Tent Life in Siberia*, is a classic in American travel literature — witty, boisterous, and at times remarkably insightful. Bush's relation of the same expedition is far more stolid, but provides additional detail on life in Kamchatka. Travis's biography of George Kennan puts his Kamchatka adventures into the context of a very active and full life. Dobell visited Kluchi early in the nineteenth century and, like Kennan, witnessed a volcanic eruption. Bergman traveled across Kamchatka in the twenties, before the influx of Slavic immigrants (including kulaks deported from Western Russia and Ukraine) had overwhelmed the indigenous Koryaks and Itelmeni. The tragic fate of Stalin's children and relations is described by Volkogonov and Radzinsky in their biographies of the dictator, as well as by Kolesnik. The disparaging comments about Stalin's granddaughter Katia were made by Alliluyeva herself.

NIZHNY NOVGOROD

Sakharov and Bonner both wrote about their period of exile in Gorky. The Presbyterian minister Stoddard's travelogue describing the Russian Empire is one of a surprising number of such books authored by Americans prior to the twentieth century; it is most notable for its puritanical tone and undisguised anti-Semitism. A number of locally published works in Nizhny Novgorod capture the lost romance and vibrancy of the city's famous Yarmarka. Melnikov is a detailed and lavishly illustrated book; Filatov's purview is all of the city's pre-revolutionary architecture, including that of the Nizhny Novgorod fair.

TUVA

Most Soviet-era sources on Tuva are unsatisfactory, the products of the blatant sort of ideological paternalism the Party practiced in the Caucasus, Central Asia and among the "little peoples" of Siberia. Most of what is worthwhile reading about Tuva was penned by the handful of foreign travelers and specialists who have taken an interest in this romantic but far-off region. Carruthers has authoritative moments, even if his broad conclusions about the Uriankhai (as the Tuvans were known prior to the Soviet period) were altogether too dismissive. He has left us a particularly good account of the life of Tuvan reindeer herders, providing rather less insight into their steppe-dwelling cousins living south of the Sayan Mountains. Although I have heard criticism of the quality of the translation, the publication in 1992 of an annotated English language edition of Manchen-Helfin's *Journey to Tuva* is a boon for interested parties like myself who cannot read the book in its original German. Whatever passing errors Manchen-Helfin may have made in describing life in Tannu Tuva during its ever-so-brief period of independence, his is a surprisingly clear-eyed and prescient account of Soviet nationality policy — remarkable, in fact, considering it was written before the full flowering of Stalinism. Rupen made a worthwhile contribution to our understanding of the annexation of Tuva as part of Thomas Hammond's *Anatomy of Communist Takeovers* — this at a time when Tuva had been all but forgotten by the rest of the world. I am indebted to my friends Misha and Zoya Kozlov for bringing to my attention a series of articles and interviews from the Tuvan media concerning the Tannu Tuva Minister of Interior, Oyun Polat — one of the last surviving officials of that period. Kenin-Lopsan's book on Tuvan shamanism is as unconventionally organized as the man himself.

VELIKIY USTYUG

The true cognoscenti of old Russia — but precious few others — know about Ustyug. Even in Russian, there is a paucity of sources. Utechin's still useful pocket encyclopedia of Russia provided me with the first hint of Ustyug's charms — although the entry is only a paragraph or two long. Works by Teltevskii and Shilnikovskaya focus on the town's very considerable architectural heritage. I relied on Bobrick's fine overview of Siberian history to trace the impact of Ustyug-born explorers like Dezhnev and Khabarovsk on the Russian Empire's eastward expansion. The account of Sorokin's ordeal in Velikiy Ustyug is taken from his autobiography, *Leaves from a Russian Diary*.

VLADIVOSTOK

There is now a wealth of material about Osip Mandelstam in English, including Tracy's outstanding translation of *Stone* (the poet's best-known book of verse) and the GLAS journal's retrospective issue on Mandelstam and Bulgakov. Ginzburg's Gulag memoir is justifiably famous, and includes an account of the Vladivostok transit camp. Lauterbach's account of his trip from Vladivostok to Moscow in 1945 on the Trans-Siberian railway produced some interesting encounters with Russians in the final months of World War II. Markov's gritty little pocketbook is a walking guide to Vladivostok — full of interesting tidbits and anecdotes about the city. Finally, Stephan's survey of the history of the Russian Far East is outstanding.

VORKUTA

There are ample sources available on Vorkuta in the languages of the foreigners who were incarcerated there: especially German, Polish, and the three Baltic languages. As always insofar as the Gulag is concerned, Solzhenitsyn is an important point of reference, although the Memorial activists based in Vorkuta point out that he made a number of factual errors concerning Vorkutlag. I relied heavily on recently published Russian accounts of the Vorkuta camps, especially Kuznetsov's collection of Gulag memoirs and Voitalovskya's prison autobiography. Vasilyev's Vorkuta odyssey, which I recount at some length, is only one of a dozen or so first-person accounts included in *Pechalnaya Pristan*. The collection of prison songs and ballads edited by Dianov and others is, I am told, unique. Likewise, the dictionary of Soviet prison slang by Baldayev et al.

SELECTED
BIBLIOGRAPHY

GENERAL

Anschel, Eugene, ed. *The American Image of Russia, 1775-1917.* New
    York: Frederick Ungar Publishing, 1974.

Bobrick, Benson. *East of the Sun: The Epic Conquest and Tragic History
    of Siberia.* New York: Poseidon Press, 1992.

Conquest, Robert. *The Great Terror: A Reassessment.* New York:
    Oxford University Press, 1990.

Forsyth, James. *A History of the Peoples of Siberia: Russia's North Asian
    Colony, 1581-1990.* Cambridge: Cambridge University Press, 1994.

Gogol, Nikolai. *Dead Souls.* Baltimore: Penguin Books, 1975.

———. *The Inspector General.* New York: Bard Books, 1976.

Halperin, Charles J. *Russia and the Golden Horde.* Bloomington:
    Indiana University Press, 1987.

Laquer, Walter. *Black Hundred: The Rise of the Extreme Right in Russia.*
    New York: HarperCollins, 1993.

Lincoln, W. Bruce. *Red Victory: A History of the Russian Civil War.*
    New York: Touchstone, 1991.

———. *In War's Dark Shadow: The Russians Before the Great War.*
    New York: Dial Press, 1983.

Massie, Robert K. *Peter the Great: His Life and World.* New York:
    Ballantine Books, 1980.

Massie, Suzanne. *Land of the Firebird: The Beauty of Old Russia.* New
    York: Touchstone, 1982.

Medvedev, Roy. *Khrushchev.* New York: Anchor Books, 1984.

Pipes, Richard. *The Russian Revolution.* New York: Vintage Books, 1990.

———. *Russia Under the Bolshevik Regime.* New York: Alfred A.
    Knopf, 1993.

Radzinsky, Edvard. *Stalin.* New York: Doubleday, 1996.

Shentalinsky, Vitaly. *Arrested Voices: Resurrecting the Disappeared
    Writers of the Soviet Regime.* New York: Free Press, 1996.

Solzhenitsyn, Aleksandr I. *The Gulag Archipelago.* New York: Harper & Row, 1973.

———. *The Gulag Archipelago*, Vol. II. New York: Harper Perennial, 1992.

Stewart, John Massey. *The Nature of Russia.* London: Boxtree, 1992.

Tucker, Robert C. *Stalin as Revolutionary, 1879-1929: A Study in Personality.* New York: W.W. Norton & Co., 1973.

Utechin, S.V. *A Concise Encyclopedia of Russia.* New York: E.P. Dutton & Co., 1964.

Volkogonov, Dmitri. *Stalin: Triumph and Tragedy.* New York: Grove Weidenfeld, 1991.

———, *Lenin: A New Biography.* New York: Free Press, 1994.

———, *Trotsky: The Eternal Revolutionary.* New York: Free Press, 1996.

Zubok, Vladislav and Constantine Pleshakov. *Inside the Kremlin's Cold War: From Stalin to Khrushchev.* Cambridge: Harvard University Press, 1996.

ARKHANGELSK AND SOLOVKI

Bobrick, Benson. *Fearful Majesty: The Life and Reign of Ivan the Terrible.* New York: G.P. Putnam's Sons, 1987.

Cudahy, John (A Chronicler). *Archangel: The American War with Russia.* Chicago: A.C. McClurg & Co., 1924.

Dmitrenko, M.V., ed. *Solovetskiye Ostrova.* Leningrad: Izdatelstvo Iskusstvo, 1969.

Goldhurst, Richard. *The Midnight War: The American Intervention in Russia, 1918-20.* New York: McGraw-Hill Book Company, 1978.

Halliday, E.M. *The Ignorant Armies.* New York: Harper & Brothers Publishers, 1960.

Kennan, George F. *The Decision to Intervene.* New York: Atheneum, 1967.

Smith, Edward Ellis. *The Young Stalin: The Early Years of an Elusive Revolutionary.* New York: Farrar, Straus & Giroux, 1967.

Starr, S. Frederick. *Red and Hot: The Fate of Jazz in the Soviet Union, 1917-1980.* New York: Oxford University Press, 1983.

Tchernavin, Vladimir V. *I Speak for the Silent: Prisoners of the Soviets.* Boston: Hale, Cushman & Flint, 1935.

Ugryumov, A.A. *Narodnyi Kalendar.* Arkhangelsk: Severo-Zapadnoye Knizhnoye Izdatelstvo, 1993.

KABARDINO-BALKARIA

Alieva, Svetlana. *Tak Eto Bylo: Natsionalnye Repressii v SSSR 1919-1952.* Moscow: Insan, 1993.

Azamatov, Kyamil, et al. *Cherekskaya Tragediya.* Nalchik: Izdatelstvo Elbrus, 1994.

Blanch, Lesley. *The Sabres of Paradise.* New York: Carroll & Graf Publishers, 1984.

Kelly, Laurence. *Lermontov: Tragedy in the Caucasus.* New York: George Braziller, 1978.

Knight, Amy. *Beria: Stalin's First Lieutenant.* Princeton: Princeton University Press, 1993.

The Koran. Translated by N.J. Dawood. Baltimore: Penguin Books, 1966.

Kuliyev, Kaisyn. *Lirika.* Nalchik: Izdatelstvo Elbrus, 1987.

Lermontov, Mihail. *A Hero of Our Time.* Translated by Vladimir and Dmitri Nabokov. New York: Doubleday Anchor Books, 1958.

Miziev, I.M. and M.Ch. Dzhurubaev. "Istoriya i Dukhovnaya Kultura Karachaevo-Balkarskogo Naroda," in *Mingi Tau/Elbrus,* No. 1, January-February 1994.

Musukaev, Aleksandr I. *Ob Obychayakh i Zakonakh Gortsev.* Nalchik: Izdatelstvo "Elbrus", 1985.

———, *O Balkarii i Balkartsakh.* Nalchik: Izdatelstvo Elbrus, 1982.

———, *Traditsionnoe Gostepriimstvo Kabardintsev i Balkartsev.* Nalchik: Izdatelstvo Elbrus, 1990.

Ognev, Vladimir and Dorian Rottenberg, eds. *Fifty Soviet Poets.* Moscow: Progress Publishers, 1969.

Troyat, Henri. *Tolstoy.* Garden City, N.Y.: Doubleday & Co., 1967.

Shabaev, David V. *Pravda o Vyselenii Balkartsev.* Nalchik: Izdatelstvo Elbrus, 1994.

KAMCHATKA

Alliluyeva, Svetlana. *Twenty Letters to a Friend.* New York: Harper & Row Publishers, 1967.

Bergman, Sten. *Through Kamchatka by Dog-Sled and Skis.* New York: J.B. Lippincott, 1927.

Bush, Richard J. *Reindeer, Dogs and Snow-shoes.* New York: Harper and Brothers, 1871.

Dobell, Peter. *Travels in Kamchatka and Siberia.* London: Henry Colburn & Richard Bentley, 1830. Reprint, New York: Arno Press, 1970.

Fedotov, S.A. and Yu.P Masurenkov, eds. *Active Volcanoes of Kamchatka.* Moscow: Nauka Publishers, 1991.

Kennan, George. *Tent Life in Siberia.* New York: G.P. Putnam & Sons, 1870.

Kolesnik, Aleksandr. *Mify i Pravda o Semye Stalina.* Moscow: Tekhinvest, 1991.

Travis, Frederick F. *George Kennan and the American-Russian Relationship, 1865-1924.* Athens, Ohio: Ohio University Press, 1990.

NIZHNY NOVGOROD

Bonner, Elena. *Alone Together.* New York: Alfred A. Knopf, 1986.

Filatov, Nikolai Filippovich. *Nizhniy Novgorod: Arkhitektura XIV-Nachala XX v.* Nizhny Novgorod: Redaktsionno-izdatelskiy Tsentr Nizhegorodskie Novosti, 1994.

Melnikov, A.P. *Ocherki Bytovoi Istoriy Nizhegorodskoy Yarmarki 1817-1917.* Nizhny Novgorod: Izdatelstvo AO Nizhegorodskiy Kompyuterniy Tsentr Polzobateley, 1993.

Remnick, David. *Lenin's Tomb: The Last Days of the Soviet Empire.* New York: Random House, 1993; New York, Vintage Books, 1994.

Sakharov, Andrei. *Memoirs.* New York: Alfred A. Knopf, 1990.

———. *Moscow and Beyond: 1986-1989.* New York: Alfred A. Knopf, 1991.

Stoddard, Charles Augustus. *Across Russia: From the Baltic to the*

Danube. New York: Charles Scribner's Sons, 1892.

Troyat, Henri. *Gorky*. New York: Crown Publishers, 1989.

Vinogradova, T. P. *Nizhegorodskaya Intelligentsiya Vokrug N. A. Dobrolyubova*. Nizhny Novgorod: Volgo-Vyatskoye Knizhnoe Izdatelstvo, 1992.

TUVA

Aranchyn, Yu.L., ed. *Kultura Tuvintsev: Traditsiya i Sovremennost*. Kyzyl: Tuvinskii Nauchno-Issledovatelskii Institut Yazyka, Literatury i Istorii, 1989.

Anayban, Z.V. and G.F. Balakina. *Sovremennaya Tuva: Sotsiokulturnye i Etnicheskiye Protsessy*. Novosibirsk: Sibirskaya Izdatelskaya Firma RAN, 1995.

Basilov, Vladimir N., ed. *Nomads of Eurasia*. Seattle: University of Washington Press, 1989.

Carruthers, Douglas. *Unknown Mongolia: A Record of Travel and Exploration in North-West Mongolia and Dzungaria*. London: Hutchinson & Co., 1914.

Conquest, Robert. "Terrorists." *The New York Review of Books*, 6 March, 1997, 6–8.

Darcy, Samuel Adams. "Midwife to the Government of Tannu Tuva." *Friends of Tuva Newsletter #11*, Fall-Winter 1994.

Kenin-Lopsan, Mongush. *Magiya Tuvinskikh Shamanov*. Kyzyl: Izdatelstvo Novosti Tuvy, 1993.

Kolarz, Walter. *The Peoples of the Soviet Far East*. New York: Frederick A. Praeger, 1954.

Levin, M.G. and L.P. Potapov. *The Peoples of Siberia*. Chicago: University of Chicago Press, 1964.

Manchen-Helfen, Otto. *Journey to Tuva*. Translated and annotated by Alan Leighton. Los Angeles: Ethnographics Press, 1992.

Mannay-Ool, M. "Tragicheskii Period v Istorii Tuvy." *Tuvinskaya Pravda*, 23 January 1991, 2.

Peskov, Vasily. *Lost in the Taiga*. New York: Doubleday, 1994.

Polat, Oyun. "Ya Ne v Otvete za Toka." *Molodezh Tuvy*, 22 February 1991, 3.

Rupen, Robert A. "The Absorption of Tuva" in *Anatomy of Communist Takeovers*, edited by Thomas T. Hammond. New Haven: Yale University Press, 1977.

VELIKIY USTYUG

Shilnikovskaya, V.P. *Velikiy Ustyug: Razvitiye Arkhitektury Goroda do Serediny XIX v.* Moscow: Stroiizdat, 1987.
Sorokin, Pitirim A. *Russia and the United States.* New York: E. P. Dutton & Company, 1944
———, *Leaves From a Russian Diary.* Boston: The Beacon Press, 1950.
Teltevskii, P.A. *Velikii Ustyug: Arkhitektura i Iskusstvo XVII-XIX Vekov.* Moscow: Iskusstvo, 1977.

VLADIVOSTOK

Ginzburg, Eugenia S. *Journey Into the Whirlwind.* New York: Harcourt Brace & Company, 1975.
Lauterbach, Richard E. *Through Russia's Back Door.* New York: Harper & Brothers Publishers, 1947.
Mandelstam, Nadezhda. *Hope Against Hope: A Memoir.* New York: Atheneum, 1983.
Mandelstam, Osip. *Stone.* Translated by Robert Tracy. London: Collins Harvill, 1991.
———. *The Prose of Osip Mandelstam: The Noise of Time, Theodosia, The Egyptian Stamp.* Translated and edited by Clarence Brown. Princeton: Princeton University Press, 1965.
Markov, V. *Putevoditel po Vladivostoku.* Vladivostok: Dalnevostochnoye Knizhnoye Izdatelstvo, 1993.
Perova, Natasha, ed. GLAS # 5: *Two Literary Giants: Bulgakov, Mandelstam.* Moscow: GLAS Publishers, 1993.
Stephan, John J. *The Russian Far East: A History.* Stanford: Stanford University Press, 1994.
Struve, Nikita. *Osip Mandelshtam.* Tomsk: Izdatelstvo Vodoley, 1992.

VORKUTA

Baldayev, D.S., V.K. Belko, and I.M. Isupov. *Slovar Tyuremno-Lagerno-Blatnogo Zhargona*. Moscow: Kraya Moskvy, 1992.

Dianov, Yu.P., A.D. Muchnik, and T.N. Fabrikova, eds. *Pesni Nevoli*. Vorkuta: Reklamno-Izdatelskaya Firma FOKS, 1992

Khlebnyuk, O.V. *1937: Stalin, NKVD i Sovetskoye Obtshchestvo*. Moscow: Izdatelstvo Respublika, 1992.

Kuznetsov, I.L., ed. *Pechalnaya Pristan*. Syktyvkar: Komi Knizhnoye Izdatelstvo, 1991.

Tertz, Abram (Sinyavsky, Andrei). *Goodnight!* New York: Viking, 1989.

Voitalovskaya, A.L. *Po Sledam Sudby Moego Pokoleniya*. Syktyvkar: Komi Knizhnoye Izdatelstvo, 1991.

PHOTO CREDITS

Photos by Ivan Sigal, a freelance photographer who spent much of 1996 and 1997 traveling around Russia and the Caucasus.

INDEX

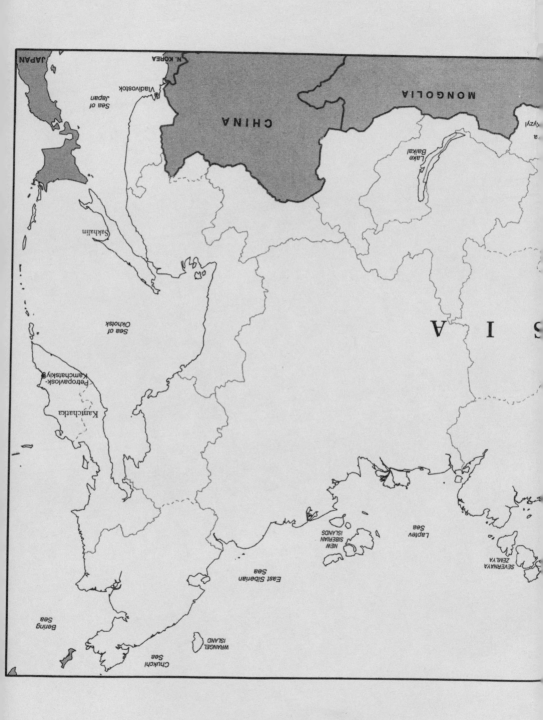

U.K.

North
Sea

Norwegian
Sea

NORWAY

DENMARK

SWEDEN

GERMANY

FINLAND

Murmansk

Barents
Sea

NOVAYA
ZEMLYA

Kara
Sea

Baltic Sea

Solovetskiy
Islands

Kaliningrad

ESTONIA

POLAND

LITHUANIA

LATVIA

St.
Petersburg

Arkhangelsk

Vorkuta

BELARUS

MOSCOW

Velikiy
Ustyug

MOLDOVA

UKRAINE

Nizhniy
Novgorod

R   U   S

Black
Sea

Kabardino-Balkaria
Nalchik

TURKEY

GEORGIA

K A Z A K H S T A N

Kras

ARMENIA

AZERBAIJAN

Caspian
Sea

Aral
Sea

IRAN

TURKMENISTAN

UZBEKISTAN

CHINA

0   500
kilometers

0   500
miles

2168 1-93 STATE (INR/GE)

Names and boundary representation are not necessarily authoritative